CRIME AND REPRESSION IN
THE AUVERGNE AND
THE GUYENNE
1720 — 1790

CRIME AND REPRESSION IN THE AUVERGNE AND THE GUYENNE 1720–1790

IAIN A. CAMERON

Senior Lecturer in History
University of Sydney

CAMBRIDGE UNIVERSITY PRESS

Cambridge
London   New York   New Rochelle
Melbourne   Sydney

Published by the Press Syndicate of the University of Cambridge
The Pitt Building, Trumpington Street, Cambridge CB2 1RP
32 East 57th Street, New York, NY 10022, USA
296 Beaconsfield Parade, Middle Park, Melbourne 3206, Australia

© Cambridge University Press 1981

First published 1981

Printed in Great Britain at the University Press, Cambridge

British Library Cataloguing in Publication Data
Cameron, Iain A
Crime and repression in the Auvergne and the
Guyenne, 1720–1790.
1. Law enforcement – France – Auvergne – History –
18th century
2. Law enforcement – France – Guyenne – History
– 18th century
I. Title
363.2'0944'59   HV8205.A9   80-841953
ISBN 0 521 23882 X

For my parents

Contents

Part II : Crime and disorder

Maps

Table

Preface

We live in violent times. The second half of the twentieth century has been marked by soaring crime statistics, by the troubles of urban ghettos and by bitter manifestations of social discontent in protest marches, student revolt, prison disturbances and terrorism. Not surprisingly, such an environment has produced a keen interest in crime and its repression among criminologists, penologists, sociologists, psychologists – and historians have not been left behind. Beggars, vagrants, debtors, thieves, bandits, prostitutes, smugglers, poachers, bread rioters, heretics, blasphemers and rebels of all kinds have become the *dramatis personae* of specialist studies. Discussion of the incidence of types of crime, moreover, could not have proceeded without further inquiry into the structure of the law itself – its prejudices and its relationship with an establishment concerned to use judicial procedures and punishments to preserve its control.

These have been particularly productive lines of development in the study of eighteenth-century France. Analysis of the intellectual framework of legal repression has combined with detailed local studies in Normandy, Flanders, Paris and Languedoc to produce some stimulating hypotheses – the argument, for example, that in the course of the eighteenth century the brutal 'assassin' was supplanted as the archetypal criminal by the conniving thief. This study seeks to contribute to these continuing debates with the crimes and disorders of two large and contrasting provinces – Guyenne, in south-west France, and the more backward Auvergne, in the mountainous centre. It attempts at the same time to fill a particularly striking gap left even by recent studies of ancien régime society and government – the problem of law enforcement and the policing of the French countryside. It is not a problem which can be ignored in a century which saw the first national police force and the European triumphs of Beccaria, who clearly warned his audience that the whole character of criminal justice depended on the size and efficiency of the police force.

The research undertaken in France for this study was made possible by generous financial assistance from the Scottish Education Department, from my parents, and from the Sir Alexander Cross Trust; I also wish to record my gratitude for a grant towards the preparation of the typescript from the Twenty Seven Foundation and the facilities for research provided by the University of Sydney. The whole enterprise would not have been started without the help and encouragement of Mr Stephen Johnson of the University of Glasgow, and would not have been finished without the friendship and gargantuan hospitality of the Pezi family in France, and the infinite patience, comfort and advice of Mr Charles Davidson in London and Sydney. I am particularly grateful to Dr Colin Lucas of Balliol College, Oxford, whose criticisms were responsible for major improvements in the text, but my warmest thanks go to Professor Olwen Hufton of the University of Reading. She suggested the research topic and both before and after the completion of the thesis which spawned this book, has been a tireless and inspiring guide and mentor.

Abbreviations

A. D. Dord.	Archives départementales de la Dordogne
A. D. Gir.	Archives départementales de la Gironde
A. D. P. de. D.	Archives départementales du Puy de Dôme
A. M. Bx.	Archives municipales de Bordeaux
A. M. Pér.	Archives municipales de Périgueux
A. de G.	Archives historiques de la Guerre
A. N.	Archives nationales

P. -v.	*Procès-verbal*
Inform.	*Information*
Interr.	*Interrogatoire*

Coinage

12 *deniers*	=	1 *sou*
4 *liards*	=	1 *sou*
20 *sous*	=	1 *livre*
3 *livres*	=	1 *demi-ecu/escu*
6 *livres*	=	1 *écu*
24 *livres*	=	1 *louis*
48 *livres*	=	1 *louis d'or*

L.	*livres*
s.	*sous*
d.	*deniers*

xiii

Glossary of French terms

á la clameur publique   spontaneous arrest by crowd or by police at crowd's demand
accomodement   formal agreement for aggressor to pay damages to victims of assault
Aides, Cour des   court dealing with taxation problems
ancienne(s) maréchaussée(s)   police companies before 1720 Reform
archer   lowest rank of policeman in *maréchaussée*; term replaced by *cavalier* in 1760
arrêt du conseil   decree of King's Council
assesseur   legal adviser of police officers
attroupement   illegal gathering of more than four people

bailliage   royal court (in northern half of France)
bande   more or less organised rural band of vagabonds or thieves
bourgeois vivant noblement   *bourgeois* living in the noble style, not working to hasten rise in the social scale
brigadier   police brigade commander
bris de ban   unauthorised return of convicted criminal sentenced to banishment from province or kingdom

cabaret   inn, drinking establishment
cahier   list of grievances presented to Estates General
Calas   Protestant merchant from Toulouse tortured and executed in 1762 for the murder of his son. With help from Voltaire he soon became a *cause celèbre* and was rehabilitated in 1765.
capitation   direct tax
cavalier   lowest rank of policeman
chauffeur   brigand who uncovered hidden loot by burning victims' feet
chevalier de St Louis   military decoration usually awarded after thirty years' service
chevauchée   cavalcade, combined operation by several brigades
commandant   deputy of provincial governor
commis   clerk, assistant
Connétablie   Paris court which tried both rebellions against *maréchaussée* and abuse of authority by *maréchaussée* throughout France
conseiller du roi   honorific title enjoyed by certain royal officials
consul   town councillor
corvée   forced labour on roads

dépôt (de mendicité)   workhouse for beggars

Eaux et Forêts   royal administration of waterways and forests
écuyer   lowest rank of nobility
élection   royal tax-collecting tribunal
enfant du corps   policeman whose father had also served in the force
étape   staging-post for troops on the move
exempt   highest rank of brigade commander
Extraordinaire des Guerres   special fund for military expenditure

Ferme   General Farm (salt tax collecting syndicate)

xiv

fermier   estate manager
fonds de mendicité   government fund which helped pay for repression of beggars
fusil   eighteenth-century varieties of shotgun

gabelle   salt tax
gabelou   the hated and despised collector of the salt tax
Garde des Sceaux   Keeper of the Seals
généralité   major unit of royal administration, equal in area to about three modern departments
gens sans aveu   poor who were unable to find someone trustworthy or respectable to vouch for them
gibier du prévôt   *maréchaussée's* traditional 'game' (i.e. vagrants, beggars, etc.)
greffier   clerk of court

hôpital général   hospital-cum-poorhouse

information   judicial investigation
intendance, intendant   office of intendant, man in charge of a *généralité*
Invalides   home for disabled soldiers

jacquerie   peasant uprising
jurat   town councillor (Bergerac and Bordeaux)

laboureur   landowning peasant (in north of France, the term had overtones of relative affluence)
lettre de cachet   arrest warrant signed by king, leading to detention at His Majesty's pleasure
lieutenance   area under supervision of police lieutenant
lieutenant-criminel   royal magistrate dispensing criminal justice
linceul   shroud, often used in Old French and *patois* sense of bed-linen

main-forte   police assistance to court bailiffs
Mandrin   legendary eighteenth-century smuggler
marchand   small-time merchant, shopkeeper or even peddler
maréchal des logis   higher rank of brigade commander
métairie   *métayer's* farm, often used to designate the barn
métayer   share-cropper, inevitably a poor peasant
milice, milicien   royal militia, and member of it
milice bourgeoise   local unpaid police force
monitoire   warning from pulpit to take knowledge of particular crime to authorities, or risk excommunication

négociant   better class of merchant

Parlement, Parlementaire   sovereign court (thirteen in eighteenth century France, including one in Bordeaux), and magistrate in it
patrouille bourgeoise   see *milice bourgeoise*
pays d'élection   areas of France subject to jurisdiction of *élection*
pays d'état   areas of France without *élection* but with provincial estates, and notoriously undertaxed
plainte   plaint at law
pognere   measure of grain (*c.* three bushels)
Ponts et Chaussées   royal institution dealing with repair and construction of bridges and roads
portefaix   street-porter, stevedore
Présidial   royal court, higher than *bailliage*; its permission was necessary for *prévôté* to proceed with a case

prévôt-général, prévôté   chief police-officer in a *généralité*, and his court of summary justice

procès-verbal (pl. *procès-verbaux*)   official report

procureur du roi, procureur fiscal   royal prosecutor, prosecutor in seigneurial or municipal court

rafle   police round-up

repris de justice   someone with criminal record

résidence   town where brigade of *maréchaussée* was established

sans aveu   see *gens sans aveu*

scieur de long   man who sawed planks, beams etc.

sellette   wooden stool on which prisoner had to sit for final interrogation

sénéchaussée   equivalent in southern France of *bailliage*, royal court

sergent   army sergeant or local court bailiff

setier   measure of grain (*c.* twelve bushels)

sindic   local resident appointed general administrator of village communities without mayor or council

sous-brigadier   lowest rank of brigade commander

sous-lieutenant   police lieutenant's deputy

subdélégué   local royal administrator, responsible to intendant

survivance   right of inheritance by legal heir

taille   major direct tax

Tribunal des Maréchaux   court settling points of dispute between nobles

vice-bailli, vice-sénéchal   police officer before 1720 Reform

vol-violence   'theft-violence', i.e. theory that theft replaced physical violence as major crime in early modern period

Introduction

A century and a half before England or any other European state, France had a nation-wide police force. The disquiet felt by modern British visitors to the French capital at the abrupt descents of the police into the Métro or the provocative bus-loads of policemen sitting endlessly at street corners, does not compare with the disgust felt by eighteenth-century Englishmen at the very notion of this institution, considered to be the executive arm of a foreign autocracy.

The Police of Foreigners is chiefly employed, and at an immense Expence, to enquire into and discover the common and indifferent Transactions of innocent Inhabitants and of harmless Travellers, which regard themselves only, and but faintly relate to the Peace of Society; this Policy may be useful in arbitrary Governments, but here it would be contemptible, therefore both useless and impracticable.[1]

French visitors to England, on the other hand, noted sardonically that 'the famous Turpin' was a national hero, that the English were constantly being robbed on their practically impassable highways, but preferred such a fate to being robbed by government ministers: 'if you ask the English the reason for these abuses, they will reply that they are unavoidable in a Land of Liberty such as theirs'.[2] Even a sympathetic observer of the French police structure like William Mildmay concluded that 'such an establishment is not to be imitated in our land of liberty, where the injured and oppressed are to seek for no other protection but that which the law ought only to afford, without flying for aid to a military power'.[3]

It was the military character of the French police which most troubled English writers. The national police force, the *maréchaussée*, had indeed originated in the thirteenth or fourteenth century as a court of military justice and an armed body of men used by the royal government to fight the depredations of troops making their way across country, or deserters who had to pillage to make a living, or vagabonds lately discharged from the army.[4]

1. John Fielding's Circular 'To the Acting Magistrates', 19 Oct., 1772 (S.P. 37/9), quoted in L. Radzinowicz, *History of English Criminal Law*, vol. 3 (London 1956) p.6.
2. J.-B. Le Blanc, *Lettres d'un François*, vol. 3, Lettre LXXIX (The Hague 1745), pp. 205–14.
3. W. Mildmay, *The police of France, or, an account of the laws and regulations established in that kingdom for the preservation of peace and the preventing of robberies* (London 1763), p. 41.
4. For the early history of the *maréchaussée*, see L. Larrieu, *Histoire de la Gendarmerie*, vol. 1 (Paris 1927).

M

Under the authority of the Marshals of France, officers called *prévôts* or *vice-sénéchaux*, among other titles, were appointed to provincial towns where they took responsibility for organising *ad hoc* collections of volunteers to contain and punish the rapacious soldiery. From the early sixteenth century, however, the post of *archer* was established under the command of the *prévôts* and put up for sale, and so regular companies of *maréchaussée* – 15 or 20, or 30 strong – came into being. From the sixteenth century until 1720 these *maréchaussées* had increasing contact with the population at large. They made periodic forays across the province of their jurisdiction to remind the people of their existence, but strayed from the beaten track and the fairs they liked to patrol only to descend on the scene of a crime they had heard about, to escort convoys of merchants and tax-collectors along dangerous stretches of road, or to pursue noblemen who had seized their neighbours' land, their peasants' cattle, or the daughters of the bourgeoisie.[5]

Throughout this period, the *maréchaussée* retained its military status but steadily accumulated powers of jurisdiction over civilians. As early as 1536 it was granted competence to try all highway robbers, whether military or civilian, whether they were vagabonds or had fixed abodes. Thereafter a whole series of Letters Patent, Declarations, Edicts and Ordinances, the most important of which was the Criminal Ordinance of 1670, transformed a rudimentary military court into an established tribunal with powers of life and death over a whole range of civilians. The *maréchaussée* was to retain most of its judicial powers until the Revolution. The police court – the *prévôté* – was given the power to deal with crimes thought to threaten public safety – premeditated assault, theft, if accompanied by breaking and entering or if committed on the public highway, and offences against the state such as counterfeiting or raising a private army. The Edict of 1731 officially limited the jurisdiction of the *maréchaussée* to commoners, but in practice it had always devoted most of its time to the poor – to the thieves and highway robbers as well as to the individuals on the fringe of the community whose very existence the Ordinances described as a public menace: vagabonds, beggars, or anyone previously convicted of an offence. By the time of the Revolution, there were Frenchmen as well as Englishmen to denounce the 'tyranny' of this military police and its 'booted justice'.

The judicial competence of the *prévôtal* court had a great, if not overwhelming, impact on the operations of the police force in the field. The *maréchaussée*'s efforts in the investigation of crime were restricted to *prévôtal* offences, but the police powers of arrest were wider than its judicial interests: the *maréchaussée* made arrests by executive authority of the government administrator, the intendant or his *subdélégué*; it acted as auxiliary to

5. M. Boudet (ed.), *Les Chevauchées des trois Lacarrière* (Riom 1900) – an invaluable but mutilated collection of the reports of the police officers (the *vice-baillis*) in the Haute-Auvergne (Cantal), from 1587 to 1658.

officials making arrests for other courts; and the *maréchaussée* could always arrest someone *in flagrante delicto* or even by public demand, 'à la clameur publique'. The control of vagabonds and beggars, subsequently dispatched to the *prévôtal* court, certainly took up a lot of the *maréchaussée*'s time, but with or without their presence, the police force still had to carry out its regular patrols, and while vagabonds and beggars constituted only an intermittent obsession, the general public was always there to be protected or controlled at fairs and markets throughout the year. In the latter years of the ancien régime, deserters took up more of the *maréchaussée*'s time than any other single species of offender; they were obviously a threat to public order and the security of the realm, but the *prévôtal* court was not responsible for their punishment: they were interrogated and sent back to their regiments.

Despite these qualifications, the legislators clearly intended the *maréchaussée*'s judicial competence to influence its police activity. One of the more subtle ways of doing this was to stipulate that the *prévôtal* court could not deal with a *prévôtal* crime (one of those defined as contrary to public security, such as highway robbery or vagrancy) if it had been committed in the town where the *prévôt* himself resided. This was designed to encourage the police to get out and about, to reinforce the essential character of the early police force as a small, mobile unit riding ceaselessly up and down the route of its patrol. By the seventeenth century, however, such a conception of police work was increasingly regarded as inadequate. When the extensive judicial competence of the *maréchaussée* was being codified in 1670, attention was drawn to the weakness and confusion of the police force which supported this imposing legal structure. The *maréchaussées* of France were a motley collection of companies, commanded by officers with a bewildering variety of titles, each with disparate and even overlapping areas of operation. The biggest force in the Auvergne area was the company of the *prévôt-général* of the Auvergne, based in Riom, but also operating in the area of the Basse-Auvergne were the company of the Combraille under the command of a *lieutenant de robe courte* in Montaigut, and a few miles to the north, the companies of the *prévosté* of Cusset and the *maréchaussée* of St Pourçain,[6] all quite autonomous and separate institutions from the company of the *vice-bailli* of the Haute-Auvergne. The *généralité* of Bordeaux in the late seventeenth century was an even greater hotchpotch of *prévostés* and *vice-sénéchaussées*: companies established in Montauban, 'Xaintonge', and Auch on the fringes, and in the area to be contained by its eighteenth-century frontiers, the *vice-sénéchaussées* of Libourne, Sarlat, Périgueux, of the Agenais and Condommois, of the Albret (established in Nérac) and of Guyenne and

6. 'Revue des compagnies du vice-bailli d'Aurillac, du prévôt-général d'Auvergne, de la Marche, de Combraille et de la généralité de Languedoy par l'intendant du trésorier de France, et le contrôleur commis à faire les montres de la maréchaussée', A.D. P. de D. C 6194.

the Bazadois (based in Bordeaux itself).[7] Apart from obvious difficulties of communication and cooperation between the separate companies, there was the problem familiar to the ancien régime of loss of control over office-holders who had bought their posts; seventeenth-century policemen were irregularly paid, and particularly, in the smaller *maréchaussées* where they were not directly accountable to a really senior officer or even a legal official, were unscrupulous in their methods of recouping their losses. Despite the denunciation of these problems in 1670, half a century was required to make the changes so obviously required as a complement to the judicial revision. It was worth the wait. The series of measures concerning the *maréchaussée* which were taken in March and April 1720[8] not only made radical improvements in the institution on which the government depended for the maintenance of law and order in the countryside, they also created the basis of a modern police force.

Of all the problems of the 'old' *maréchaussées,* the question of the multiplicity of companies was most satisfactorily dealt with. The problem was identified: 'The multiplication of these Companies, under officers with different titles, created disputes between them on the pretext of their autonomy',[9] and the rational solution implemented. All the old companies and titles were abolished. Every post – *prévôt-général, prévôt provincial, vice-bailli, vice-sénéchal, lieutenant de robe courte, exempt, archer* – was suppressed. The office-holders, of course, were to be reimbursed, and it is difficult to imagine any government before the Regency having the financial means to contemplate such expenditure. In place of the jostle of little *maréchaussées* a new company of *maréchaussée* was created in each *généralité.* Police boundaries were to coincide with the most meaningful unit of local government – virtually the only effective rationalisation of internal boundaries achieved by the ancien régime. It was a reform that was bound to strengthen the hand of the intendant in so crucial an area of public affairs. For the moment, the thirty-three companies remained formally separate bodies; this last survival of fractionalism was overcome by the Ordinance of 1778 which united the thirty-three companies into a single corps, made up of six divisions (still subdivided by *généralité*):

1st Division Isle de France, Paris, Voyages et Chasses du Roi, Soissonais, Picardie, Flandre, Haynault

2nd Division Champagne, Trois-Evêchés, Alsace, Lorraine, Franche-Comté

3rd Division Orleanais, Bourbonnois, Berry, Lyonnois, Bourgogne

---

7. *Revue* 1680 of the various companies of *maréchaussée,* A.D. Gir. C 3850.
8. (a) 9 Mar. 1720 Edit portant suppression des maréchaussées et établissement de nouvelles. (b) 16 Mar. 1720 Ordonnance concernant la subordination et discipline des *maréchaussées.* (c) 28 Mar. 1720 Déclaration portant règlement pour les nouvelles compagnies de maréchaussées. (d) 9 Apr. 1720 Déclaration concernant les nouvelles maréchaussées, avec l'état des officiers dans chaque Généralité. *Recueil chronologique des Ordonnances, Edits . . . etc. depuis 1715, jusqu'en 1756,* A. de G. X^F 1.
9. Preamble to Edict of 9 Mar. 1720.

4th Division	Touraine, Rouen, Caen, Alençon, Bretagne
5th Division	Poitou, Limousin, Aunis, Guyenne, Béarn
6th Division	Auvergne, Montauban, Dauphiné, Languedoc, Provence and Roussillon.

The sweeping reform left in existence the *prévôt-général* of the *Connétablie*, the *lieutenant de robe courte de Paris*, the *chevaliers de guet* in Paris and Lyon, the *prévôt des monnaies*, and the *prévôts à la suite des maréchaux*. In other words, the reform involved essentially the provincial *maréchaussées*.

Each *généralité* had a uniform company with the same hierarchical structure: the *prévôt-général* had under his command a small number (three to five) of deputies – lieutenants; each *lieutenance* was composed of a number of brigades made up of four *archers*, officially called *cavaliers* after 1760, and a brigade commander, who was a *sous-brigadier*, a *brigadier*, or an *exempt* according to his seniority. Each *prévôt-général* also had a *trompette* and the new *maréchaussée* was given a splendid new uniform – blue cloth with red lining and silver buttons. The brigades were scattered in permanent residence across the *généralité* – perhaps the most important principle of the 1720 Reform. The old *maréchaussée* before 1720 had often failed to make even the most desultory of promenades across the province to discourage disorder.[10] After 1720, the government could for the first time formulate the aim of developing a constant surveillance of the whole population. Each brigade was specifically directed to institute regular patrols, usually two *archers* at a time, over the entire extent of its district. Contact was made regularly with neighbouring brigades, so that the new system would establish permanent communication on all the main roads of the kingdom. It was a system which at least hinted at a new approach to the maintenance of law and order – the new brigades would keep a watchful eye on the whole population, get to know the area, in short 'be responsible for everything that happens in their district'.[11]

'Everything that happens' – already in 1720 we find the same overriding ambition which, as Foucault has pointed out, characterized the Paris police under Louis XVI: 'Police power must bear "over everything" . . . it is the dust of events, actions, behaviour, opinions – "everything that happens".'[12] As English observers in the eighteenth century realised, such sinister implications had always lurked behind the French understanding of 'police', a term only then being introduced into England from France. 'Police' in the eighteenth century did not have the precise meaning of a body of men devoted to the maintenance of public order and the detection and arrest of criminals. 'Police' involved rather the whole sweep of public administration, it meant

10. Preamble to Ordinance of 1716.
11. Ministerial circular to *prévôts-généraux*, Feb. 1721.
12. M. Foucault, quoting memorandum of Sartine written to answer Joseph II's questions on the police of the capital, *Discipline and punish: the birth of the prison* (London 1977), p. 213.

nothing less than 'managing and maintaining the life of the community'.[13] Delamare's famous *Treatise on Police* published between 1705 and 1738 listed eleven broad areas of police concern: religion; morals; health; food supplies; security and public tranquillity; highways and refuse (*voirie*); science and the liberal arts; commerce; manufactures and the mechanical arts; servants and labourers; and the poor. 'Police' in short, was a concept rather than an institution, and practically all the officials and corporate bodies in the state contributed to the policing of the community.

Delamare found this comprehensiveness of police work in the city states of ancient Greece and in Rome, while most of his contemporary examples concern the city of Paris. It was not surprising that in early modern society, the scope of such an all-embracing policy should make 'police' essentially an urban concept. At the beginning of the eighteenth century, it was the numerous policemen, the street lighting and paving and urban reconstruction of Paris which impressed foreigners; it was the provisioning of the grain markets of the towns which exercised the royal authorities; the 'lieutenants general of police' were urban appointments, at first in Paris (1677) and later in 1699, extended to the other major towns of the kingdom. What 1720 represented, therefore, was a declaration by the government that 'police' in its broadest sense should not be restricted to the big cities. With a national *maréchaussée* the small towns and countryside, and thus the vast majority of the population, should be offered far more of the benefits of 'police', so enthusiastically catalogued by Delamare, than they already enjoyed. But whereas the 'police' of the towns was assured by a host of institutions - the lieutenant general, the provost of merchants, the *Parlements*, the town councils, the city watch on foot and on horseback - in the countryside, the *maréchaussée* was practically alone.

Religion is proclaimed in the *Treatise* as the first and principal object of police work. The seventeenth century had seen some spectacular examples of the policing of the French provinces in this field, but by the eighteenth century this priority given to religion corresponded to reality even less in the countryside than in the towns. Police regulations were concerned with the minimal requirements of outward display - the public observance by butchers of Lent restrictions, the decorations for the passage of a religious procession, [14] and the rural *maréchaussée* did make itself responsible for the correct observance of religious festivals, stopping public amusements when it was time to go to church. They also contributed substantially to the policing of pilgrims wending their way across France towards Rome or Santiago de Compostella.

13. S. L. Kaplan, *Bread, politics and political economy in the reign of Louis XV* (The Hague 1976) p. 12.
14. M. Peronnet, 'La police et la religion', *Annales Historiques de la Révolution Française* (1970), pp. 375-97.

While the Paris police had an office for Jewish affairs, [15] the rural police limited their concern to the 'so-called Reformed Religion'. The *maréchaussée* investigated reports of Protestant church services, though no further action was taken; they interrogated English tourists on their contacts with French Protestant circles; most importantly, the reform of the *maréchaussée* allowed the *Parlements* to extend into the countryside their eighteenth-century campaign against the remnants of the Calvinist faith, and *cavaliers* of the *maréchaussée* were ordered to move into Protestant homes, and if necessary to carry the children to church for a Catholic baptism. The 'morals' of the rural community, on the other hand, were of no concern to the *maréchaussée*, sensibly leaving prostitution and allegations of sorcery and licentious living to the urban police or to the curé. The rural police did however keep a close eye on peddlers who organised games of chance on the marketplace, since policemen shared the assumption of the public that any stranger who made a living from gambling was certain to be a crook, and even more certain to provoke a disturbance.

Public health – the control of polluted air and water, the maintenance of hygiene in food production, the fight against plague and other infectious diseases - was naturally of far greater importance in the towns than in the country. The eighteenth-century *maréchaussée* did at least contribute to the control of cattle disease, when they established a *cordon sanitaire* around a disease-free province to prevent the movement of peasants, carts and livestock. Food supply, the provision of grain, was also of great concern to the *maréchaussée*, even if it did not operate at the same level of sophistication or with the same dictatorial powers as the lieutenant general of police in Paris.[16] The repressive task of the rural police was to patrol grain markets in small country towns, keep crowds under control and prosecute rebels, while they simultaneously played a more positive rôle getting supplies to market, hunting out surplus stocks which had been hoarded away, and supervising their ordered sale at reasonable prices.

It was in the area of 'security and public tranquillity' that eighteenth-century concepts of 'police' came closest to the modern definition of the word, and it was this area which remained by far the most important aspect of 'police' work in the eighteenth-century French countryside, far and away the most pressing concern of the *maréchaussée*. It was the security of the realm and the need to protect the tranquillity of the public which had given the *maréchaussée* powers to deal with such a wide range of crimes and offences,

15. M. Marion, *Dictionnaire des institutions de la France aux XVIIe et XVIIIe siècles* (Paris 1968) 'Police'.
16. S. L. Kaplan, 'Lean years, full years: the "community" granary system and the search for abundance in eighteenth-century Paris', *French Hist. Studies*, X, 2 (Fall 1977), 197–230.

and which denied the clientèle of the *prévôtal* court any right of appeal. It was the security of the realm which enabled provincial governors to use the *maréchaussée* to disarm civilians of shotguns, and which caused the *maréchaussée* to devote so much time to the militia – the calling together of young men, the drawing of lots, and the pursuit of those who had failed to attend. The continued surveillance of all main roads was meant to ensure that the traveller, the merchant and the peasant returning from market would feel as safe as on the well-lit streets of the capital. The rural police did not open private correspondence, but they did have their secret informers, if not a network of spies on the Paris scale. The Paris and provincial police forces both made special arrests by order of the king, or his representative the governor, often at the behest of the prisoner's family – and when the Paris police took their prisoners to the Bastille, the *maréchaussée* took them to 'houses of refuge', asylums and military forts. The institutions of censorship had no equivalent outside Paris and the *Parlementaire* towns, but on one occasion at least the Guyenne *maréchaussée* took time off from a grain disturbance to search for a 'libellous' pamphlet reputed to criticise the government.

The policing of the *voirie* was an overwhelmingly urban problem, embracing streets and roads, refuse disposal and town planning. The construction industry, street lighting and paving, fire and flood regulations, 'the embellishment and decor of towns', provided the most visible evidence of the superiority of French 'police' in the eighteenth century. The rural contribution was the network of main roads which were the technical achievement of the *Ponts et Chaussées*, and in which the *maréchaussée* played the vital rôle of supervising the *corvée*, the forced labour used to make the improvements. The countryside was notoriously free of police regulation in its manufacturing and commercial activities, and the only connection to be established between industry and the *maréchaussée* was the decision to locate a brigade in a town in the Auvergne reputedly plagued by strikes; there is no evidence however that the police were used there to intimidate workers. The *prévôtal* court was specifically barred from dealing with cases of theft by servants, as 'domestic' crime was a private matter foreign to an institution devoted to public security. No restrictions were in force, however, for the *maréchaussée*'s contribution to Delamare's final category of police activity: the control of the poor.

He was of course thinking of the very poor and the destitute. The destruction of mendicity and vagrancy would be of benefit to most of the other police departments: morals would improve, as begging and other forms of laziness only served to encourage vice; public health would improve when beggars and vagabonds no longer spread disease and infected the air; the public could sleep more safely at night when dangerous vagabonds had been confined to hospitals, workhouses and galleys; industry, commerce, agriculture, even the arts would benefit when so many idlers were forced to put their labour or their talents to use. In pursuit of these overwhelming advantages, urban and rural police forces alike devoted immense energy to the surveillance and control of the poor. They kept a close watch on inns and lodging-houses, checking the identity of their guests at any time of day or night; they harassed passing strangers with demands to see their passports or some other proof of good character and occupation. The most important weapon in the war against beggars and vagabonds was the order, periodically repeated, to arrest them, and the use of the *maréchaussée* to implement this legislation is a vivid illustration of the increasing resort to the police apparatus in handling social problems. The path of police reform runs parallel to the intensifying repression of the 'marginal' poor: the 1720 Reform of the *maréchaussée* made possible the first major attempt of the century to eliminate begging, in 1724; the 1764 legislation against vagabonds and subsequent moves against beggars were accompanied by structural improvements and increased numbers in the *maréchaussée*.

These developments were not simply part of the seemingly ageless process by which French governments sought to take more and more power into their hands. The greatest impetus to this policy of tightening control of the population came from the social and economic changes of the eighteenth century. In the last decades of the ancien régime increasing population, pressure of land, rising unemployment and better communications had all encouraged more and more people to beg and to take to the road and go off to look for work elsewhere, and so the police had to be strengthened to deal with a threat of unprecedented proportions. The industrial and commercial expansion of the towns was accompanied in many areas by profound changes in the countryside, with more and more communities being brought into contact with outside markets, and traditional relationships on the land threatened or undermined by efforts to increase productivity. In these conditions, vagrancy was not the only offence that was likely to flourish. 'The development of production, the increase of wealth, a higher juridical and moral value placed on property relations'[17] were bound to result in a rise of theft, which in turn provoked those with something to lose into demanding greater protection from the jealous poor, from the homeless vagabonds and the 'bands' of brigands they were assumed to form.

The cry for a stronger police force was given yet more voice by the eighteenth-century concern with legal reform. The Calas affair and the huge international success of Beccaria's treatise *On Crime and Punishment* testify to the intensity of public interest, an interest shared in the highest circles of government, in a subject which rewarded the *philosophes* with some of their rare practical achievements. Legal procedure and the penal system were perhaps aspects of government which could be tackled without endangering any

17. Foucault, *Discipline and punish*, p. 77.

major privilege; it was therefore safe to give vent to the genuine current of revulsion against the inquisitorial methods of investigation, and the brutality and degradation of the punishments. Safe, that is, when there was something to replace them, for the ancien régime system of law and order depended on discouraging offenders by the savagery rather than by the certainty of retribution. That the royal government did not abandon judicial torture until 1788 and left the cruel system of punishments intact until the Revolution, is a clear indication that the authorities had understood, perhaps more clearly than the *philosophes,* the immediate implications of Beccaria's demand for milder penalties to replace the traditional penalties of the harsh exemplary kind. The new Beccarian penal system had to rest on the foundation of a bigger and more efficient police force than was available to the royal government, for only such a force could ensure that sufficient numbers of criminals were caught to discourage the others.

And so the changing social conditions and the humanitarian writers of the eighteenth century together provided the practical and theoretical justification for a strong and effective police force. The government had only to provide the money. Obviously the money available determined whether or not the *maréchaussée* would be able to carry out the vast and ever-increasing range of duties assigned to it. The number of men available had important implications for the selection of towns where the *cavaliers* would be of most use, and for the way the police operated and thus for the incidence of police brutality and the choice of priorities amidst the tasks to be accomplished. The money available also determined the rate of pay, and it did not require a police trade union to realise that levels of pay would have an important influence on police efficiency and morale, particularly if the pay was so poor that there was a danger of indebtedness, 'moonlighting' or corruption. These were precisely the results of the level of financing established for the new *maréchaussée* in 1720, even if enough money was found to buy back the lower ranks of the old companies and replace them with appointed men. The increasing pressures for an improved police force made more money and more men available in the reforms of the 1760s and 1770s, but not until the Revolution was enough money found to create a force which even approximated to the institution required by the reforms of Beccaria. The ideal of certain punishment for all offenders, a dream shared by *philosophes,* government authorities, magistrates and property owners, was beyond the means of ancien régime government and society.

In order to compensate for this basic weakness of its police force, the government devoted considerable attention, particularly in the 1760s and 1770s, to the problems of the *maréchaussée*'s internal organisation. The 1720 reforms laid down perfunctory conditions of appointment – previous military experience and minimum physical requirements. The modifications introduced in the 1760s and in the Ordinance of 1778 make it clear that the

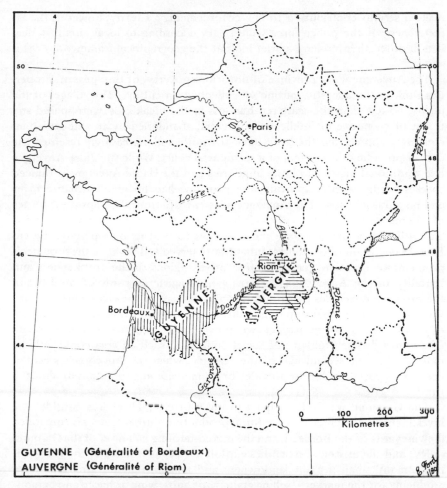

GUYENNE (Généralité of Bordeaux)
AUVERGNE (Généralité of Riom)

Map 1. The *généralités* of eighteenth-century France

authorities understood how a whole range of factors could affect police discipline and efficiency: the experience, and physical and intellectual capabilities of recruits; the prospects of promotion; the care taken of ill-health and old age; accommodation in barracks; the appointment of a policeman to his home district. The policemen of the ancien régime, in other words, deserve the same detailed attention which is beginning to be paid to the criminals they pursued. The brigades of *maréchaussée* must be followed in their daily rounds along the highways and byways of the provinces and an effort made to assess their impact on community life - a labour hitherto neglected by historians too ready to assume that the *maréchaussée* was too feeble an organisation to make a serious contribution to law enforcement.[18] Clearly, however, the effectiveness of the police force would vary according to local circumstance; it is in order, then, to have a brief look at the geographical framework of this study.[19]

The Auvergne was a province of notorious poverty, of tiny peasant properties sunk in the atavistic routine of collective agriculture. The villages of the plains, no less than the scattered hamlets in the bleak hills, were spared any threat of economic or intellectual progress, abandoned by an élite which increasingly appreciated the benefits of town life and increasingly resented the cost of providing the services of a seigneurial court. While the Basse-Auvergne had traditional paper and knife industries and the Haute-Auvergne produced cheeses hardly worth exporting, the province had no major urban centres and no rural industry. The Auvergne was cut off from the important routes of communication, particularly as it had only a tiny stretch of navigable river, and although it did not have the resources to feed its own people, the enforced emigration of its poorest inhabitants served less to solve the province's problems of isolation than to expose other regions to the drunkenness and brutality of the Auvergnats.[20] Poitrineau's magisterial study of rural life in the province concludes that the Auvergnat peasant of the eighteenth century was a primitive, normally apathetic through undernourishment but incapable of restraining his violent instincts when excited by alcohol or the atmosphere of a crowd.[21] The problems of social control in such an area could only be multiplied in the second half of the century, when the Auvergne's stagnant economy proved unable to provide for an increase in population of almost a third.

The Guyenne was both richer and more diverse. There was considerable investment by the élites in agricultural production – urban *notables* controlled the vineyards of the Bordelais and the mixed-farming *métairies* of the Garonne valley, and old aristocratic families exploited the vast forests of the Périgord. While many small peasant landowners and *métayers* in the province were producing for the market – selling grain, fruit, nuts, wine, tobacco and hemp – there were still peasants, particularly in the Périgord, who were trapped in the struggles of subsistence farming. Dominating the economic and social life of the province, however, was the city of Bordeaux, a boom-town at the height of its prosperity as a centre of trade with the colonies. Its phenomenal eighteenth-century success had a profound effect on the hinterland: the city's

18. For the slight bibliography on the police of the ancien régime, see Iain A. Cameron, 'The police of eighteenth-century France', *European Studies Review*, VII (1977), 71, an article which pays rather too exclusive attention to the more lurid shortcomings of the Auvergne and Guyenne companies of *maréchaussée*.
19. See bibliography on the two provinces, pp. 269–272.
20. O. H. Hufton, *The poor of eighteenth-century France* (Oxford 1974), p. 101.
21. A. Poitrineau, *La vie rurale en Basse-Auvergne au XVIIIe siècle (1726–1789)*, vol. 1 (Aurillac 1965), pp. 116, 619–20, 705.

population and its contacts overseas stimulated new industries and expanded markets for the agricultural produce of the Guyenne; the city's wealth and commercial bustle provided the surplus rural population with opportunities to be employed, to beg and to steal, as well as a haven for the sick and dying. Above all, Bordeaux and the intense river traffic which connected the city with the depths of the hinterland opened up the Guyenne to the outside world: 'Instead of closed communities [there were] rapid communications, multiple and permanent contacts ... even in small parishes where the "stranger" could no longer have been rare and exceptional.'[22]

The Guyenne of course was no more exempt than the Auvergne from the unfavourable economic conditions of the latter part of the century, and the prosperity of a colonial entrepot was particularly fragile. There could be no simple answer to the problems of law enforcement in such varied and unstable contexts, no uniformity in the impact of the 1720 *maréchaussée* or of the changes to the force fifty years later. Nor could there be any certainty as to the general public's reactions to these reforms in the different localities. Would the establishment of brigades in permanent residences and the maintenance of regular patrols accustom the people to cooperating with the police? Would the greater discipline which would hopefully result from the reforms of the 1760s and the 1770s encourage the people to regard the police with more respect? The answers would to a large extent depend on popular attitudes to a whole range of social institutions, from the militia and courts of justice to the village fête, as well as on the evolution of popular habits in violence and theft. Despite the ministerial optimism which made the new brigades of *maréchaussée* responsible for 'everything that happens in their districts', it will soon be clear that ancien régime France was a very long way indeed from the surfeit of policemen on the Boulevard St Germain.

22. C. Higounet (ed.) *Histoire de l'Aquitaine* (Toulouse 1971), p. 346.

PART 1

The means of repression

CHAPTER 1

A cheap police force

Accounts

'The accounts of the *maréchaussée* have always been very clear and very precise', an official noted in 1770.[1] In keeping with a national institution, each company of *maréchaussée* was paid by the central government. Even in the *pays d'état* money intended as payment for the police force was not controlled by the local estates, but conveyed to the central funds of the *maréchaussée*'s treasurers. With an efficiency remarkable for any government, let alone the ancien régime, revenue was calculated to match exactly the anticipated expenditure. Unfortunately the sum being so tidily collected and spent was for much of the eighteenth century less than two million *livres*,[2] a pittance when contrasted with the mountains of gold lavished on defence and

1. Anon. *Projet* on *prévôtal* finances – A. de G. X^F 1.
2. In 1721, the first full year of operation of the new institution, revenue and expenditure was 1,930,400l. 5d. The big increase in numbers of *cavaliers* in 1768/9 took the total to over three million, raised from the following sources:

20 généralités d'élection:	1,938,645 *livres*
pays conquis (including Lorraine)	481,917
pays d'état	273,531
Avignon	18,050
Gabelles du Dauphiné	2,700
Taillon	44,351
Extraordinaire des Guerres	20,000
Artillerie	5,000
Marine	10,000
Maréchaussée	2,000
Trésor Royal	399,328
Total	3,195,522 *livres*

(Accounts in A. de G. X^F 2.)

Within a *généralité* the money was raised, as for example in Auvergne in 1785, from:

1st *brevet* of the *taille*	127,393 *livres*
a supplementary 2nd *brevet* to pay fodder	14,915
a tax on towns with brigades to pay upkeep of barracks	7,237
Total	149,545 *livres*

(A.D. P. de D. C 6188.)

17

the army. The fight against 'internal enemies' was to be waged on the cheap.

Yet a very much better police service could have been purchased, in *généralités* like the Auvergne or the Guyenne, if the *pays d'élection* had not been obliged to subsidise the rest of France. In 1766, the Auvergne paid 127, 393L., yet the cost of the Auvergne company's pay came to only 54,200L.[3] The larger and more affluent Guyenne contributed 118,229L., though it received in return, in the form of wages, only 62,650L. This discrepancy did not go unnoticed or unchallenged at the time, particularly when it was made painfully obvious by the rejection of an Auvergnat request for an extra brigade – for Bort, for example, in 1762 – an addition which would have cost only 2,600L.[4] In 1778, the Auvergne was made to pay 15,000L. more for three brigades less, and the intendant could only lament 'the injustice of subsidising the *maréchaussée* in other *généralités*, when the Auvergne itself needed at least as many brigades as before the Reform'.[5]

No more than a token effort was made to bring the contribution of the privileged provinces more into line with effective expenditure when the financial arrangements were made for the great 1768/9 augmentation of the force. This had been long delayed 'by fear of an increase in expenditure which we would always like to spare our peoples',[6] so it was decided to spare the *taillables* – the largely peasant mass of the community who paid the *taille* and who had hitherto supported the cost of the *maréchaussée*; the new expenditure would fall on 'the richest class of our subjects, the class therefore which has most interest in the preservation of its possessions and the maintenance of its own security. The *capitation* was effectively raised by a tenth in the *pays d'élection* but its collection was uncertain in the *pays d'état* and the *maréchaussée*'s books were temporarily thrown into confusion. For the year 1771, the treasurer of the *maréchaussée* was 199,327L. 15s. short, and the total amount owed to the force came to 1,081,577L. – more than a third of the total annual expenditure on the *maréchaussée*, so the complaints of the policemen may be imagined. In 1773, the Périgueux police were not paid till June. The difficulties of this transition period were doubtless sorted out, for the next accounts which have survived, those of 1777 and 1778, showed that the books balanced at a total of 4,191,418L. 9s.9d.[7] How many men could be bought for this price?

Numbers

At no time in the eighteenth century was the government remotely able to hire enough policemen. Before 1720, the Basse-Auvergne enjoyed the pro-

---

3. A. de G. X^F 1.
4. Correspondence between Ballainvilliers and Turgot, A.D. P. de D. C 6187.
5. Intendant to du Deffan, 21 Nov. 1778, *ibid*. C 6190.
6. A. de G. X^F 2.   7. *Ibid*. X^F 9.

tection afforded by 12 officers or *exempts*, and 36 *archers*;[8] after the Reform 13 officers or brigade commanders, and 44 *archers*.[9] This increase of strength in the Basse-Auvergne – of limited absolute significance given the tiny numbers involved – was not extended to the Haute-Auvergne. Four officers or *exempts* and 25 *archers* were transformed into 6 brigade commanders, a lieutenant and 24 *archers*.[10] The province of the Auvergne thus had only 2 lieutenants and 2 *prévôtal* courts – in Riom and St Flour – whereas a smaller *généralité* like Soissons and the neighbouring *généralités* of Lyon and Limoges all had 3 of each. The confusion of *maréchaussées* in the Guyenne before 1720 had at least given the *généralité* 13 officers or *exempts* and 76 *archers* (24 in the Bordeaux – Libourne department; 21 in the Agenais and as many as 31 in the Périgord). The great Reform provided more posts of responsibility – 4 officers, and 19 brigade commanders – consonant with the spreading of responsibility involved in the scattering of isolated brigades. The 3 lieutenants and *prévôtal* courts were easily situated in the chief towns of the three 'departments' – Bordeaux, Périgueux, and Agen. But there were still only 76 *archers*, redistributed to the benefit of the Bordelais, which increased its tally to 36, while the Périgord slumped to find itself on a par with the Agenais at 20 *archers*.[11] The restructuring of the *maréchaussée* had left the surveillance of France as a whole to 565 brigades, a total force of less than 3,000 men. Fifty years later there were still only 576 brigades, still only 2,839 ordinary policemen. It did not need a Letrosne to point out that the brigades of *maréchaussée* were not numerous enough 'to patrol the countryside continuously and be everywhere they are required'.[12]

When Choiseul set about making long-overdue changes in the force in the late 1760s, the intendants collectively demanded an increase of at least 365 new brigades. The Minister had been prepared to offer 191 and compromised on 200. Discussion of the proposed increases made it clear why reform had been so long delayed. In his demand for twenty-seven new brigades, necessitated by the mountainous terrain and the ferocious inhabitants 'habitually fighting amongst themselves and uniting against the *cavaliers* of the *Maréchaussée*', the intendant of the Auvergne made it plain that the province could not afford to pay for increased police protection; he suggested the desperate expedient of creating foot brigades, 'made up of invalid soldiers on their pensions'.[13] The idea was not taken up and the emotional appeal was rewarded by seven new brigades. The Guyenne, on the other hand, was given

8. *Revue de la compagnie du prévôt-général*, 1719, A.D. P. de D. C 6194.
9. *Etat du personnel*, 1719–21, *ibid.* C 6173.
10. *Contrôles de maréchaussée*, A. de G. Y[b] 858.
11. *Ibid.* and *Revue* in A.D. Gir. C 3850.
12. J. F. Letrosne, *Mémoire sur les vagabonds et sur les mendiants* (Soissons 1764), p. 59.
13. *Etat des brigades demandées*, A. de G. X[F] 1.

eleven brigades, only one short of the twelve requested on the simple grounds that more were needed for such a 'vast' province. These increases were even more meagre than they had appeared. As until the reform all brigades included a *brigadier* and 4 *cavaliers,* the intendant of the Auvergne was surprised to gain only 28 men, rather than the 35 he had expected. The new force of 113 men was to be spread more thinly, in eleven brigades of 5 men, ten of 4, and six of 3. Similarly in the Guyenne, the thirty brigades represented only 120 men; the number of 5-men brigades was reduced to eight along with fourteen of 4, and eight of 3.[14]

Ten years later numbers were actually reduced, by six brigades in both the Auvergne and the Guyenne, so that those which remained would have enough to live on. This desperate admission of the financial plight of the institution was received everywhere with consternation; the intendant of the Auvergne suffered 'much pain', and returned to the need for an increase in such a desolate and violent province; the intendant of Bordeaux, who had sought an increase of one third and received a decrease of a sixth, foresaw that the service would suffer greatly from the increased distances between brigades, which would make it difficult to keep up the regular contact between them.[15] While *prévôts-généraux,* intendants, and *commandants* agonised over which brigades to disband, and which *cavaliers* to sack or retire, the government considered 'representations from its Provinces' expressing a desire to make a greater contribution to the financing of the institution. Once the cuts had been made, it was decided to halve the reduction, and the Guyenne and the Auvergne found they had three brigades to restore.[16] The composition of the brigades was altered yet again to a uniform 4 (*brigadier* and 3 *cavaliers*), with the Auvergne company having a total of 100 men, and 112 in the Guyenne.

The government continued to receive informed criticism that there were still too few men: 'Such a small force of around four thousand men scattered over an immense kingdom is supposed to be able to contain 26 million people. Such a thing is impossible, and public security will never be assured until the force is enlarged.'[17] The money was not, however, found to augment the force until November 1789, when each *généralité* in panic signed on an extra 20 policemen, [18] giving a final ancien régime total of 96 *cavaliers* and 26 brigade commanders in the Auvergne, compared with 103 *cavaliers* and 29 *brigadiers* in the Guyenne. [19]

14. *Etat des brigades, Ibid.* X^F 4.
15. Correspondence from intendants to Montbarey A.D. P. de D. C 6190 and A. de G. X^F 4.
16. Ordinance of 3 Oct. 1778, A. de G. Y^A 58.
17. Dejean, *Observations sur la maréchaussée* (n.d.) composed some time after 1778, *ibid.* X^F 4.
18. *Contrôles de maréchaussée, ibid.* Y^b 754.
19. *Etat de la maréchaussée,* 1 Jan. 1790 – see appendix I.

Pay

There had seemed to be a clear understanding before 1720 of what needed to be done. The Preamble to the Reform Edict identified the meagreness of wages and the failure to pay them regularly as crucial faults of the old *maréchaussées*. And, apart from the confusion of the late 1760s and early 1770s, the reformers had ensured that payment would be exact. Until 1769, the companies of *maréchaussée* were paid at the *prévôt-général*'s review every three months. Each brigade commander and *cavalier* signed an individual receipt. Although this system was reckoned to guarantee regular and exact payment, an Ordinance of 27 December 1769 was issued to simplify matters by substituting the review of the War Commissioners every four months. These reviews would have to make detailed mention of absences, changes in residence, and unfilled places; lieutenants would have to give receipts, and if necessary, other measures would be taken to verify that correct payment had been made. The Ordinance recommended that advances be made every two months, but inspectors were still commenting in 1772 and 1773 that although the lieutenants were paying the men what they were due, 'payment is deferred too long as they are paid only every four months . . . they should be given an advance at least every two months, so that the *cavalier* has the means to make ends meet'. [20] Nothing was done until 1778, when it was decided to make payments on the new salary scale in monthly instalments.

The basic rates of pay covered by the annual accounts had remained unchanged from the Reform of 1720 until 1769. In fact the senior officers – *prévôts* and lieutenants – got virtually no rise before the Revolution. The eighteen *prévôts*, including those of the Auvergne and the Guyenne who had bought their posts for 40,000L. received an annual 4,000L. . 1,200L. for their judicial functions, and 2,800L. for their pay as military officers. The eleven *prévôts* of smaller *généralités* who had bought their posts for 30,000L., got 3,000L. a year, and lieutenants who had paid 15,000L. got 1,500L. The strictly legal appointments as *assesseur* and *procureur du roi* in the *prévôtal* court were worth only 300L. as it was reckoned that the men who would fill these posts would do so on a part-time basis; *greffiers* got slightly more, 350L. By 1778, the *prévôts* and lieutenants had had a small increase in their military pay. The *prévôt* was paid 3,568L. and the lieutenant 1,700L. 10s. The legal officers however had sunk to 267L., and the clerk to 311L. 10s.[21]

The three ranks of brigade commander had been established respectively in 1720 at 700L. (*exempt*) 600L. (*brigadier*) and 550L. (*sous-brigadier*), and the *cavalier* at 500L. On just over 27s. a day, therefore, the *cavaliers* should not have been faced with the constant threat of penury – they did earn more than most of their artisan neighbours, who rarely got more than 18s. a day.

20. *Ibid.* Y^b 791 and 798.
21. *Ibid.* X^F 9.

It did not however leave much in reserve, after the *cavalier* had fed and clothed himself, his family and his horse, and complaints were frequently made in years of economic distress that policemen were unable to afford bread. The rate of pay was not increased until 1769, when the whole system was restructured to cope with the inflation of half a century. The cash payment made to individual *cavaliers* was reduced to 270L. a year, 324L. for a *sous-brigadier*, 360L. for a *brigadier*, and 450L. for an *exempt*. This was a daily rate of 15s., 18s., 20s., and 25s., respectively, raised in 1778 to 20s. a day for *cavaliers*, and 25s. for *brigadiers*. This money would cover personal subsistence only, for the loss was to be more than compensated for by the payment of additional single items. The new pay scale in 1769 amounted in practice to an increase of 20-22 per cent, and the 1778 award was a further rise of 12-15 per cent.

Forty *livres* a year was allocated for the *cavalier*'s clothing (with corresponding amounts for the higher ranks), and 20L. towards the upkeep of the horse. This was in addition to the horse's fodder, which would be paid as a variable annual amount based on an estimate made in the brigade's residence for a ration of fifteen pounds of hay, five of straw and eight of oats. Government accountants suggested this would cost an average of 250L. a year, but in the time of high food prices and difficult economic circumstances of the early 1770s the Auvergnat *cavaliers* were given only 210L.; the complaints of the *prévôt-général* were supported by the inspectors, who argued that 230L. would be the minimum in some areas, 250L. in others. Steps were effectively taken by 1778 to bring the rate more into line with local prices, and the amount paid out varied from 222L. per horse to 324L. in the Auvergne, and from 255L. to 462L. in the Guyenne. [22]

The 1769 reforms also cleared up an area of financial confusion of great importance to the *cavalier* - subsidised housing. Between 1770 and 1769 *cavaliers* who were fortunate enough to have their own homes could live in them; others were subsidised either by the intendant or by the inhabitants of the locality. They could be lodged in barracks or individual houses, and the sums contributed for this purpose to an Auvergnat brigade could vary from 24L. a year (in St Flour) to 120L. (in Langeac). [23] The system of barracks was made universal and compulsory in 1769, thus relieving the *cavaliers* totally of the cost of housing.

As part of the restructured pay scale introduced in 1769, the lower ranks of the *maréchaussée* were allocated 30L. per year to be paid into a fund for buying new horses, the *masse de remonte*. This was the most unsatisfactory aspect of the new pay arrangements, perhaps because it was only the first

22. *Ibid.* X^F 4 and X^F 9.
23. *Etat* of 'Impositions pour les casernes de maréchaussée', A.D. P. de D. C 2893.

attempt to deal with what had always been the *cavaliers'* greatest financial problem. As the Auvergne *prévôt* du Deffan noted, the obligation to buy their own horses on entering the force led *cavaliers* immediately into debt, and they were 'destitute after that for the rest of their lives'.[24] The 1769 measures did nothing to tackle this problem. They were concerned only with the cost of the *cavalier's* second horse and even this was done imperfectly. The new fund covered only the exact amount the *cavalier* had paid in, therefore if he needed a new horse at a price of say 380L. after three years, he would get help to the tune of only 90L. The Treasury would advance the rest, and be paid back by the automatic retention of part of the *cavalier's* wage, at a rate of 2s. 6d. a day. It was obviously extremely serious that a sixth of an already modest wage be deducted, but matters got even worse if the new horse needed replacing before payment had been completed, which was quite likely to happen since the original 380L. could take up to six years to reimburse. Payment for the second new horse could either begin at the end of the first six years, or concurrently, in which case the *cavalier's* pay was decreased by a third, a catastrophic 5s. a day.

By an Ordinance of 13 December 1774, a new scheme was worked out which would institute a kind of no-claims bonus system. The annual surplus from the fund, after payment of claims, would be divided among those who had not lost their horses. The first dividend was made by a once-and-for-all payment of 113,740L. from the surplus left over from the previous four years, a hand-out designed to satisfy the claims of those *cavaliers* and *brigadiers* who had been making contributions and getting no return.

From 1 May 1775, no more advances would be made for replacing horses – they would be covered by the fund, a sum equal to 1200L. for a *lieutenance* of 40 men. If at least half the total was left after payments had been made, it could be distributed among non-claimants (in equal parts except for *exempts* who were reckoned to contribute a fifth more than the others, and were to be reimbursed in proportion). A replacement horse at 300L. meant ten years' exclusion from the bonus and it was hoped that non-claimants would benefit by 30L. a year. But still nothing had been done to help new *cavaliers*, who still had to provide their own horses, and who therefore continued to get themselves into debt.

The Ordinances, of course, always quoted the policemen's basic pay in terms of the gross figures, before tax. *Cavaliers* and *brigadiers* were exempt from the *capitation*, though the *exempt* and senior officers were not.[25] All ranks were liable to pay the *taille*, and the force was reminded in 1740 that

24. Du Deffan to Choiseul, 9 Oct. 1770, A. de G. X[F] 4.
25. The *exempt* 9L., the lieutenant 15L., and the *prévôt-général* 30L.: Ord. of 17 Dec. 1771, A. de G. X[F] 1.

their privileges were limited to exemption from 'the *collecte* [assessing individual *taille* contributions for the parish and ensuring their collection] , the lodging of soldiers, *tutelle* [guardianship of a minor] , *curatelle* [representation of a minor for legal purposes] , and other public charges'.[26] The members of the *maréchaussée* however also had the privilege of being assessed ('taxés d'office') by the intendant personally. It was a right which the *prévôt-général* was occasionally called upon to defend, particularly for the benefit of the few *cavaliers* or *brigadiers* who owned a little land and found themselves included on the roll drawn up by local collectors. The *prévôt* of the Auvergne had to intervene in 1782 to protect the brigades of St Flour and Chaudesaigues who were 'included in the community assessment roll . . . although they are lodged in the barracks, have no private business in the town and have no taxable possessions or land'[27] Taxation 'd'office' was a privilege which saved the Brioude brigade the 3L. 12s. they had been told to pay between them, and reduced the tax assessment of Brugier, a *cavalier* in Chaudesaigues, and his wife, who owned a house and a piece of land which they let for 80L. a year, from 17L. to 3L.[28] The most common assessment was the nominal 10s., and this was raised to one *livre* if the *cavalier* had a part-time secondary job and higher if he possessed some property. Pagès, the *brigadier* in Murat, paid 1L. 10s. for the house he owned in St Flour; the Langeac *brigadier* Cristal 8L., which also covered his wife's *pâtisserie* in St Flour; the St Flour *cavalier* Crotte paid 10L. for himself and his mother-in-law, and applied for a reduction when the roof of his house was carried away by the wind. The Aurillac brigade made unusually substantial contributions to the exchequer: the *brigadier* Lasalle had the highest assessment of any in the company – 18L. – to take account of his leather business. The *cavalier* Christophe d'Ecry married a widow, and acquired a house which put them in the 2L. bracket; Cheylus and his wife had a shop which earned them tax dues of up to 9L.; and Patey and his wife had the good fortune to appear on the roll as 'the heirs of Canon la Veissière', liable for 11 or 12L.[29] There were a few *cavaliers* with a bit of land, there was a *brigadier* in Coutras who owned an estate, and a *cavalier* in Agen who owned the barracks which accommodated his brigade and which brought him an income of 500L. a year.[30]

Such good fortune was rare in the ranks of the *maréchaussée*, and it was fortunate for *cavaliers* that their basic pay was not their only legitimate source of income. Many of the duties performed by the *maréchaussée* were

26. *Arrêt du Conseil,* 4 June 1740. A.D. P. de D. C 6184.
27. Du Deffan to intendant, 1752, A.D. P. de D. C 6190.
28. *Etat* 1765, *ibid.* C 4218; *Plumitifs des cottes d'office,* 1733, *ibid.* C 2924.
29. *Plumitifs des cottes d'office, ibid.* C 2932ff.
30. De la Crompe, *gentil-homme, – mémoire* by *prévôt-général,* 10 Apr. 1763, A.D. Gir. C 2179; letter from *prévôt* to intendant, 16 June 1786, *ibid.* C 4035.

not reckoned to be part of its routine job, and were paid separately as 'extraordinary' service. This concept of overtime was supplemented by commission – the reward for the capture of a criminal or the arrest of a beggar. The *raison d'être* for these payments was not just to encourage the *cavaliers'* zeal, it was also to compensate them for activities which often involved considerable expense: escorting prisoners, beggars or deserters far from home; militia operations and the pursuit of thieves; acting as auxiliaries to court officials; escorting tax receipts to such a distance that the *cavalier* had to spend the night away. For all these activities *cavaliers* could claim expenses, usually at a rate of 3L. a day. Militia operations were worth either 3L. or 1½L., depending on the distances involved; supervising the forced labour (*corvée*) on the roads was rewarded at 2L. a day, the same rate for chasing those who had failed to turn up. If garrison on reluctant Protestants was worth only 20s., military duties brought a most interesting 4L. a day. Further stimulus to the zeal of the *maréchaussée* was provided by occasional rewards for faithful service which did not qualify for regulation payment: patrols which had calmed down public disquiet even without the capture of brigands, the successful exclusion from the *généralité* of animals banned by disease regulations, an *ex-gratia* payment to replace a horse which had fallen in a grain riot. These however were the exceptions. The rule was that the *cavaliers* were given nothing for an unsuccessful pursuit, or for any task from killing a sick horse to protecting surveyors against public hostility which could be regarded as a contribution to the maintenance of good order. Claims for expenses were also ruthlessly reduced even when the right conditions were met if the controller-general felt that too many *cavaliers* had been used, or that too much time had been taken, or even if the operation had taken place in summer.

There were four main funds from which the *maréchaussée* could claim payment for 'extraordinary service' – the royal Domaine, the *Extraordinaire des Guerres*, the *fonds de mendicité*, and the fund constituted from the confiscated property of fugitive Protestants. Trouble and delay often resulted from the *cavaliers'* failure to apply correctly to the different funds, and lists sent to the controller-general frequently had items crossed out for that reason. Even if correct formalities were observed, *cavaliers* could expect difficulties with every fund in actually extracting payment, and since most of the operations involved had cost considerable time and effort, the subsequent difficulties in obtaining due recompense must have had a discouraging effect on the conduct of service. The Belvès brigade, for example, protested eloquently in 1779 that they had made several journeys to Bergerac in 1778 to suppress grain riots, and arrested no less than twenty-three thieves at the Montpazier fair; claims for expenses and rewards, however, had been left unanswered 'and we have been anxiously waiting for a long time for the repayment of considerable sums of money',[31] The *maréchaussée* of the Guyenne in 1764, was still claiming payment of over 2,000L. for anti-Protestant operations carried out in 1756.[32]

The Guyenne brigades did receive over 6,000L. from the Protestant fund, manna denied to the Auvergne company. Beggars, fortunately, were more widely distributed than Protestants, and after 1769, 3L. was paid for each beggar subsequently sentenced to the *dépôt* or to the galleys. Payment from the mendicity fund was supposed to be made quarterly, but the Auvergne Lieutenant de la Ribbehaute complained in June 1769 that his brigades had received nothing since 1768 and that this oversight was undermining the effect of the encouragement he gave them to carry out zealously the king's instructions on mendicity.[33] The major problem about this form of remuneration, however, was that a few brigades in the major centres of population were able to augment their pay packets far more substantially than more isolated *cavaliers*. The distant brigades had less work to do because they had less people to arrest, but this advantage was lost in time spent transferring their prisoners to court. The brigade in Riom, therefore, could make 126L. in the first half of 1768, while all the brigades of the Haute-Auvergne between them made a total, in 1768 and 1769, of 42L. In hard times, when beggars proliferated and prices were high, the extra *livres* to be made from the mendicity fund, if they were not too long delayed, could have been significant in helping the *cavaliers* to make ends meet, but it was in such years that the difference in the amounts paid to the brigades was most striking. For their contribution in 1740/1 to the grain supply, for arrests, investigations and escorting of prisoners to the *prévôtal* court,[34] for closing inns which were giving refuge to vagrants, the three 'judicial' brigades of Riom, St Flour and Clermont were paid 1220L., 883L. 5s. and 831L. 5s. respectively, compared with the 40L., 36L., and 33L. paid by the Domaine to the *cavaliers* in Tauves, Brioude and Chaudesaigues.[35] And if the Haute-Auvergne suffered in comparison with the Basse-Auvergne, the contrast with the Guyenne was greater still, for while 550 beggars were arrested in the Auvergne between the Declaration of 1764 and 1773, the Bordeaux company arrested 4,313.[36]

The Guyenne *cavaliers* were also able to supplement their income with the capture of deserters far more easily than in the Auvergne, and despite the enormous variation of sums paid for a deserter,[37] at the very lowest

---

31. *Ibid.* C 4638.
32. *Ibid.* C 2179.
33. Ribbehaute to intendant, 1 June 1769, A.D. P. de D. C 1110.
34. There was a 'conjunctural' upsurge in condemnations to the galleys – see Poitrineau, *La vie rurale*, vol. 2, graph 79.
35. A.D. P. de D. C 1588.
36. C. Paultre, *La répression de la mendicité sous l'ancien régime* (Paris 1906), p. 603.
37. One letter from the *prévôt* indicates 30L. was the usual sum (1755, A.D. Gir. C 4368); Larrieu, *Histoire de la Gendarmerie*, vol. 2, p. 255, quotes a figure of 50L.

estimation he was worth ten times as much as a beggar. This was of no small importance when as many as seventy-three deserters could pass through the Bordeaux *prévôtal* prison in a year,[38] but the administrative records of the Guyenne *maréchaussée* contain numerous replies from the *Extraordinaire des Guerres* that it had no money to meet its claims.

Given its financial problems, it is not surprising that the government encouraged the concept of getting individuals to pay for the cost of their own arrest, or encouraging the family to defray the cost of escorting one of its disturbed or troublesome members. When it was a question of imprisoning a local hooligan by order of the intendant, the government's cost-saving appears to have led to a curious sort of class distinction operating in favour of the destitute. The order went out to arrest a blasphemous drunkard specifically because he had the means to pay the *maréchaussée* for his arrest.[39] Expectations of private payment were frequently not realised, but even if the Domaine stepped in, delays were such that the *cavaliers* had to resort to borrowing, at such ruinous rates of interest that the *prévôt* expected them to be forced out of the *maréchaussée*.

It is impossible to say how often this happened - the registers of the members of the force, the *contrôles de maréchaussée* - give no explanation for voluntary resignations, but it was rare for the situation to reach the dramatic proportions of the 1730 crisis in the Auvergne, when lack of payment for militia operations brought the brigade in Riom to the verge of strike action. When they protested that they would participate in no further operations of the same sort until paid, the intendant Trudaine threatened instant dismissal, but the *prévôt* defended his men, and argued that their action only served to draw attention to the considerable debts they had built up as a result of extraordinary operations in the previous few years.[40]

When all obstacles had been overcome, and money for *service extraordinaire* was forthcoming, *cavaliers* still faced the problem of budgeting their expenditure, when revenue came in lump sums at irregular intervals. The Bordeaux *prévôt*, M. Barret de Ferrand, confessed to being 'tormented' by the *cavaliers* creating difficulties for themselves by failing to organise their finances better.[41] When they got their pay, they would celebrate at the

from the Ord. of 1775; A. Corvisier, *L'armée française*, vol. 2, (Paris 1964), p. 718, cites payments of 100L. in the years 1718–27. In 1775 the brigade in Castres was paid 400L. for 2 deserters (11 Sept. 1775, A.D. Gir. 11 B 12). *Cavaliers* also received half the fine of 200L. (until 1736, thereafter 400L.) paid by those convicted of exchanging civilian clothes for a deserter's uniform.

38. *Registre d'écrou*, A.D. Gir. 11 B 1.
39. Intendant to Giat *subdélégué*, 1756, A.D. P. de D. C 1540.
40. Correspondence between Trudaine, Urion (Riom *subdélégué*) and Dauphin, Dec. 1730 – *Ibid.* C 6177.
41. A.D. Gir. C 4635.

cabaret or waste the money in some other unspecified but unseemly way. In this way, *cavaliers* in Bordeaux had been unable to cope with inflation, had incurred debts, and in time, the *prévôt* had been forced to dismiss *cavaliers* who could not carry on the job.

To remedy the situation, he decided to open a 'boete commune', a kitty into which the *cavaliers* in Bordeaux would put a fixed proportion of the payment on each 'profitable day' of 'extraordinary service', until a sum was collected sufficient to pay for the annual purchase of grain and fodder. The principal beneficiary of the system was the *cavalier*'s horse: its feeding was a 'privileged debt', the only item for which the *cavalier*'s pay could be retained. The statutes of the fund were signed by the two Bordeaux brigades on 1 April 1750, and in its first year of functioning, it produced a sum of 1,030L., enough to buy hay and oats for the whole year.

No other brigades were so organised, and even in Bordeaux, such arrangements appeared to the *prévôt-général* as mere palliatives. There was a more basic problem than the government's slowness in paying its bills or paying them in amounts which the *cavaliers* found difficult to handle. As Barret de Ferrand pointed out, the rate paid for many of the duties included in 'extraordinary service' was totally insufficient. On 3L. a day, *cavaliers* could not afford the long journeys involved when their basic pay was 24s. and a few *deniers* a day – 'which is not nearly enough to feed themselves and their horses in their town of residence, let alone when they have to make long journeys out of their district'.[42]

Exactly the same point, enforced by graphic illustration of the implications, was made ten years later in July 1769 by the *brigadier* in Mauriac. He estimated the *cavalier*'s net pay, after payment of fodder, at 16s. a day; on this kind of money, 'extraordinary service' could only be undertaken on borrowed money. Yet these expenses 'are only refunded very late and never in full', especially since inflation, affecting every kind of commodity, had over the years made nonsense of 3L. a day when a *cavalier* could easily spend 4L. or 5L. He was forced to 'dip into his own money', or – as in the case of two *cavaliers* in his brigade – pile up debts. The *brigadier* stated as a categorical fact that a single trip to escort the tax-receipts coach kept the *cavalier* away from home for three days, and cost half a month's pay.[43] Extra payments for overtime and arrest, in short, were far from solving the financial problems of the *maréchaussée*, indeed, they could even exacerbate the difficulties of a body of men plagued by the problems of poverty.

The implications of poverty

Distress was particularly acute for the *maréchaussée*, as it was for the popula-

42. *Ibid.* C 2178 (1759).
43. A.D. P. de D. C 6187.

tion at large, in the years of economic crisis: 'We know that the whole *maréchaussée* is destitute [de Vic wrote in 1771], but the Guyenne company suffers more than any other from the excessive cost of fodder of all kinds, the price of food, and more expensive accommodation than anywhere else'.[44]

'This time of *cherté* [high food prices] in the Auvergne prompted du Deffan to intervene on behalf of his 'unfortunate *cavaliers*' suffering 'the most dire poverty'. Many of the Auvergne *cavaliers* were married with children, and faced with the 1770 grain prices, too poor to afford bread. 'What can you ask of a man dying of hunger ?'[45]

It was at such times that the perennial problems of the chronically under-paid policemen of the eighteenth century caught up with them; the strain of paying off debts incurred by having to borrow money against overdue payment for 'extraordinary' service really showed and it became impossible to keep up the repayments due on the debt incurred to join the force in the first place. The institution, however, did not put up forever with men who were 'encumbered with debts', or 'encumbered with debts and children', or worst of all, 'encumbered with debts, family and age'.[46] It was in 1770 that St Aubin, *exempt* in Pont-du-Château, found he had to leave the force, having nothing to live on after paying the interest on the loan he had con-tracted to enter the force and in 1773, a year of grain revolts, that Morel, *brigadier* in Lesparre, found that it was 'quite beyond him to continue in the service'.[47]

The majority of *cavaliers* and *brigadiers* survived the crisis, and stuggled on as best they could. The continual need to count every penny could have serious repercussions on the way the policemen performed their duties. To save money the Mauriac *brigadier* took to combining the tax-receipts opera-tions with the escort of prisoners. Because of their irons and the fatigue en-gendered by a long wait in jail, the prisoners were usually unable to walk; transport was provided only for women, since carts were being refused even for claims backed up by a medical certificate and his *cavaliers* were forced to carry the prisoners on the backs of their own horses. What would have hap-pened, he asked rhetorically, if the coach had been attacked while the *cavaliers* were encumbered by prisoners? 'It is difficult to do two duties at once'.[48]

The Mauriac brigade was one of those most criticised in the eighteenth

44. Inspection 1771, A. de G. Yb 789.
45. Du Deffan to Choiseul, 15 Nov. 1770, *ibid.*
46. E.g. Chambon, *cavalier* Marmande; Gambault, *cavalier* Lesparre; Terme, *cavalier* Nontron; Bataille, *cavalier* St André de Cubzac; and Mayne, *cavalier* Bordeaux, dismissed 'for indebtedness' (Revue par Tourny, Dec. 1751 A.D. Gir. 11 B 2). Testard, *cavalier* Sauveterre; Henry, *cavalier* Brioude; Regnies, *cavalier* Lesparre; des François, *cavalier* Mauriac; Perrier, *cavalier* Chaudesaigues; and Jacquerel, *cavalier* in Ste Foy, all resigned when they could no longer cope.
47. Inspections in series Yb, A. de G.
48. Mauriac *brigadier* to intendant, 1769, A.D. P. de D. C 6187.

century. It was only fair for the *brigadier* to point out that 'the *cavalier* of whom more is demanded than is possible loses heart and necessarily does his service badly'. The only *cavalier* who was so financially independent that he did not need the job had been asking permission to retire for two years, and the *brigadier* had always blocked it, for the simple reason that he could not afford to lose him. Not only did the vast majority of *cavaliers* need their job in the *maréchaussée*, many of them also needed another job. Practically everyone under the ancien régime had more than one source of income, but it was the privilege of the poor to hold down two jobs. The Edict of 1720 itself had expressly set out to obviate the need for *cavaliers* to do a part-time job which would distract them from their principal occupation; the financial provisions of the Reform, however, were such that they would starve without their various professions, 'which distract the *cavaliers* from, and disgust them with, their duties in the *Maréchaussée*'.[49] There is no evidence that *cavaliers* in the Guyenne had secondary jobs, but a secret inquiry carried out by the Auvergne intendant in 1760 revealed that more than half the force worked part-time at an alternative job, while those who remained full-time policemen, like the members of the Issoire brigade, were all 'far from well-off', plagued by difficulty in making ends meet.[50]

The favourite occupation among these *cavaliers* noted for their drinking habits was running an inn. It was a good choice for in the years before barracks existed, it provided accommodation, could be run by wives and children when the *cavaliers* were on duty, and kept the policemen in touch with local gossip. *Cavaliers* in St Flour, Brioude, Tauves, Mauriac, Clermont and Chaudesaigues all ran *cabarets*; three of the four *cavaliers* in Montaigut were innkeepers, earning some 'very handy' extra money, so handy, the *subdélégué* complained, that they preferred working for their own profit to chasing after deserters. Gondar, *cavalier* in Mauriac, led the other innkeepers of the town in their refusal to close on Sundays during divine service. When a new, less accommodating, official arrived in 1742, he was insulted by Gondar, and told that the *cabarets* had enjoyed 'complete freedom' for over thirty years. The other dissidents yielded before the force of the new authority, and for a time the *cavalier*'s *cabaret* was the only place in town to get a drink on Sunday, but reprimands from the intendant eventually forced the policeman to respect the Sunday observance regulations.[51]

In the small town of Brioude, on the borders of Le Velay, the *maréchaussée* had a virtual monopoly of the entertainment industry; half the brigade ran

49. T. de la Morandière, *Police sur les mendians, les vagabonds [etc]* ... (Paris 1764), pp. 223–4.
50. Correspondence between intendant and his *subdélégués*, Aug./Sept. 1760 – A.D. P. de D. C 6186.
51. Correspondence between Granier, the intendant, Fontfreyde, and the abbé de Mauriac, Apr./May 1744. *Ibid.* C 1531.

cabarets, the other half billiard saloons, and the brigade also provided the town's official tobacco-dispenser. Official posts were suitable for members of the police force; a Mauriac *cavalier* was the town's postmaster, in Chaudesaigues, Brugier sold the official salt and tobacco, Botte and Vaissier both ran tobacco shops in Clermont. The brigades stationed in the commercial capital of the province were very commercially-minded: Vaissier sold vegetables and cheese as well as tobacco, and five of his colleagues were small shopkeepers, with three grocers, one *cavalier* specialising in ironmongery, and a *sous-brigadier* who sold lace. Shopkeepers from the Auvergne company elsewhere in the province ranged from the *sous-brigadier* in Murat, Anjolet, who traded in grain, to Gondar in Mauriac, who in discouragement had given up his inn to take over a business as a cloth merchant. The *subdélégué* lingered for a moment on the image of this policeman going round the fairs and markets in the neighbourhood, not to look dignified and intimidate trouble-makers, but to set up his stall and spread out his wares. A small business was clearly a good proposition for the hard up *cavalier* - it needed no training or skills, and minimum capital resources. Like the inn, it provided employment for the family when the *cavalier* was inconveniently required to do police work. It was often in fact the wife who brought the shop or business with her dowry. Beauregard, the *cavalier* in Montaigut, worked in the *cabaret* owned by his wife, Grandporet worked in St Flour for his wife who rented a general store with an annual turnover of 200L. In Chaudesaigues, Rougier's wife had brought him a house in the town and a piece of land worth 80L. a year, and Patey made an equally sensible marriage to acquire a piece of land, at the very gates of Aurillac, big enough to feed four cows. If however the policeman's wife did not bring riches, or serve behind the counter alongside her husband, she would have to get herself a job alongside the wives of all the other labouring poor of the ancien régime. Most of the Auvergne company wives worked in the textile industry - Mme Lavigne in Clermont made clothes for servants, Mme d'Herment, wife of the Montaigut *brigadier* was a dress-maker, Mme Bibi spun wool and made it into cloth. Other wives earned their keep as hairdressers, or laundry-women.

For most of the eighteenth century the authorities turned a blind eye to the policeman's off-duty employment, provided a certain amount of discretion was exercised. The intendant intervened in Mauriac not because Gondar ran an inn, or dispensed drink at illegal hours, but because he staged a public brawl with a government official. It was a rather different situation in the case of Queriau, who tried to combine the eminently responsible job as *exempt* in Clermont with a position as inspector for the *Ponts et Chaussées* which constantly kept him away from Clermont, 'wherever the road works took him'. Complaints reached D'Angervilliers himself that the *exempt* 'does none of his duties and spends his time attending to matters which have nothing to do with the job he's supposed to do', and Queriau was obliged to leave the

Ponts et Chaussées.[52] It was only the financial rearrangements of Choiseul in 1768/9 which gave the government the courage to 'order the *cavaliers* to refrain from all commercial activity and forbade them to carry on any trade or profession'. With the gradual confinement of *cavaliers* to barracks after 1770, it was increasingly easy to supervise their activities, and the devotion of time and energy to part-time jobs seems to have been effectively curtailed. The *cavalier* Villerand, whose father had got away with running an inn in Clermont, was ordered in 1779 to get rid of his inn in Veyre.[53]

A part-time job was one major source of revenue for the hard-pressed *cavalier*. The other was graft and corruption. When a *cavalier* had to load himself with debt to enter the force, and face 'indigence for the rest of his days. . . beware dishonesty and villainy'.[54] Struggling to make ends meet from day to day, *cavaliers* were under great temptation to cut corners and make a few illicit *livres*, a temptation intensified by the knowledge shared by all policemen that their position made detection extremely difficult. Yet evidence can be found and like the evidence of part-time jobs, almost all of it from the Auvergne, from the province where the *cavaliers* made comparatively little from commission for arrests, where there were fewer opportunities for carrying out remunerative military jobs like disarmament or the escort of deserters.

Corruption began when *cavaliers* made arbitrary use of their power at the expense of the public, when the Chaudesaigues brigade, for example, confiscated a peasant's furniture by way of payment for an auxiliary operation to retrieve a debt of 87L. After the local judge had ordered the furniture to be handed back, the *brigadier* Cristal returned and helped himself to the furniture again.[55] Such an operation would have been unnecessary if payment from the Domaine for 'extraordinary service' had been confidently expected. A more sinister use of police power was demonstrated by Courdon, the Brioude *brigadier*, when he arrested the merchant Alouis by authority of a fake *lettre de cachet* forged by his friend Boyer de la Branche; the subtle touch was to warn Alouis two days in advance of his impending incarceration, while waiting comfortably at the *cabaret* with Boyer, 'in collusion with this man who was only seeking to intimidate Alouis into making a settlement with him in a lawsuit they have together'.[56]

Most of the 'irregularities' committed by the eighteenth-century *maréchaussée* were for petty financial gain. The *cavalier* Villedary was reduced to pilfering hay and firewood from his colleagues in the Périgueux

---

52. Correspondence between d'Angervilliers and intendant, July 1729, *ibid.* C 6176.
53. A. de G. Y^b 805.
54. de Vic's *Mémoire sur le peu d'inconvénients dans l'ordonnance du 28 Avril, 1778, ibid.* X^F 4.
55. *Plainte* by Brugeal, *laboureur* at Liontades (n.d. – 1750) A.D. P. de D. C 7686.
56. Intendant to Breteuil, 3 Oct. 1724, *ibid.* C 6174, and A. de G. Y^b 858.

brigade,[57] but extortion from the public was more common. The standard rate was 6L. per *cavalier* - 6L. for letting an armed robber go on his way, 6L. 'on the pretext that he had settled a dispute about the exchange of a cow between the *laboureur* Cazes and another individual'; when St Privé de Richebourg let a man go free after he had been arrested in a hue and cry, he had the unusual panache to ask for 27L.[58] St Privé was allowed to resign, but his successor as *exempt* in Courpière made a less elegant exit from the force when he was sacked for the more serious offence of arresting a merchant on a frivolous pretext and releasing him on payment of 48L.[59] It was rare to find such malice aforethought - the corruption of the *maréchaussée* was better exemplified by a reluctance to let opportunities go by. When the Aurillac brigade found a cowhide brought into town despite the regulations enforced by an outbreak of cattle disease, the Aurillac *exempt* and the St Mamet *brigadier* sold the skin themselves and kept the 20L.[60]

Suspicion of being corrupt was one of the occupational hazards of the eighteenth-century police force. Even when a *brigadier* enjoyed the reputation of an honest man, his *subdélégué* felt it necessary to add that he had been unable to discover whether or not the *brigadier* had his price.[61] Libellous rumours about a brigade tended to proliferate whenever it let a prisoner escape or failed to capture a wanted man, and the intendant and *subdélégués* were just as inclined to be suspicious as the public.[62] When the Langeac brigade failed to capture a local man who had returned to the area after escaping from Riom prison, who refused to pay taxes and threatened anyone who approached, the intendant complained that the whole area knew two days in advance of any impending descent on his house; the *cavaliers*, he had heard, were being paid to be indiscreet.[63] It was also the Langeac brigade which was denounced as untrustworthy by the St Flour *lieutenant-criminel* when it was a question of arresting the notorious Georges Langlade, an innkeeper accused by his wife of murdering the guests.[64] It was the same brigade's 'infidelity' which was assumed by the intendant to be responsible for the continued freedom of three men involved in a grazing dispute.[65] It

57. Inquiry by lieutenant at Périgueux barracks, 19 June 1773, A.D. Dord. B 647.
58. Montaigut *subdélégué* to intendant, 30 June and 5 Aug. 1734, A.D. P. de D. C 6182; *Evocation sur le bailliage de Vic-en-Carladès à la Connétablie*, 1 Mar. 1777, A.N. Z[IC] 388; *subdélégué* in Thiers to intendant, 1731, A.D. P. de D. C 1522.
59. *Contrôles de maréchaussée*, A. de G. Y[b] 859.
60. Correspondence, 1724, A.D. P. de D. C 6174.
61. Contribution of Duprey, *subdélégué* in Ambert, to the intendant's secret *Enquête*, Dec. 1732. *Ibid.* C 6177.
62. The intendant found it difficult to believe that a prisoner (accused of sedition) had escaped from the custody of the Besse *exempt* and *cavaliers* by climbing over a wall 'wearing leg irons' - intendant to Besse *subdélégué*, 1762, *ibid.* C 1621.
63. Intendant to *brigadier*, 1732, *ibid.* C 1523.
64. Rochebrune to intendant, 21 Aug. 1743. *ibid.* C 1531.
65. Intendant to Langeac *subdélégué*, 8 Jan. 1763, *ibid.* C 1545.

was hardly surprising that an escaped convict with a relative in the Langeac brigade was never caught, or that the three men who had committed a burglary near Ambert avoided arrest when it was rumoured that the *brigadier's* own daughter was implicated in the theft.[66] Accusations of dereliction of duty could hardly fail to circulate when the Mauriac brigade failed to capture their colleague Royer, who had shot someone dead in the street at the fair, and then had time to move out of town with his wife, his children and all his furniture.[67]

While the Auvergne company had a number of tainted individuals or brigades, the *maréchaussée* of the Guyenne, as we shall see, was popularly assumed to be riddled with corruption in only one field – disarmament. Only two *cavaliers*, however, were actually caught and punished for extorting fines from innocent, unarmed victims, and the only other hard evidence of disarmament corruption was produced in the trial of the first Bordeaux *prévôt-général*, de Robéric – eight certificates from the administration of the Agen *Hôpital* indicating that the hospital had received none of the money from the fines it was supposed to have been given for the relief of the poor; in the same trial the Bordeaux *brigadier* Lebrun was convicted of keeping two-thirds of the disarmament fines he had collected.

Between 1720 and 1790 the only court competent to try *cavaliers* of the *maréchaussée* for corruption – the *Tribunal de la Connétablie et Maréchaussée de France à la table de marbre à Paris* – convicted a total of 19 *cavaliers*, 10 brigade commanders and one *prévôt-général* from the companies of both provinces; the intendant and *prévôt-général* of the Auvergne were also satisfied that two brigades – Aurillac and Chaudesaigues – had been guilty of corrupt practices, though no prosecution seems to have resulted. Unproven accusations were laid against a further 2 *cavaliers*, 3 *brigadiers* and five brigades, while in the Robéric trial, the *Connétablie* rather surprisingly acquitted the Agen lieutenant, one *exempt*, a *brigadier* and a *cavalier*. The bald figures of proven police corruption tend as always to confirm the complacency of those who argue that there will always be a few rotten apples in the barrel, but the wonder is not that evidence of police corruption is slight, but that the evidence exists at all. Even if we accept that the Guyenne company was comparatively lacking in the petty corruption inspired by poverty, it must be said that it was not without its organised rackets, inspired by greed.

There is evidence that the *maréchaussée* served as a recruiting agent for the army, whether the conscript was willing or not. The *cavaliers* of the Guyenne did not have the misfortune of two *cavaliers* from Champagne who forcibly enrolled the *fermier* of a magistrate in the Paris *Parlement*,[68] but a

66. Madur to intendant, 1752, *ibid.* C 1537.
67. Fontfreyde to intendant, 18 May 1744, *ibid.* C 1531.
68. Corvisier, *L'armée française*, vol. 1 p. 188.

plan devised by the Mussidan brigade to find a young man for the captain of the La Fere regiment went just as disastrously wrong. The policemen managed to pour drink into the metal-caster Chanier, pronounce him a newly engaged soldier, and lock him into a cell. His violent resistance, however, attracted public attention, and a troop of Chanier's workmates from the Planteau iron foundries stormed the prison and released the 'recruit'.[69]

In these marginal activities the *cavaliers* and *brigadiers* of the *maréchaussée* could scrape together a little extra money, but they would never make their fortune. Corruption on a grand scale required the power and opportunities of rank. The first *prévôt-général* of the *généralité* of Bordeaux after the 1720 Reform, the Sr de Robéric, was not exposed till 1735, after more than a decade of 'extortion, peculation and abuse of authority'. Between January 1723 and November 1730, he arrested on his own authority, without cause or complaint, 69 individuals who were entered on the prison register as deserters, or thieves, or vagabonds, or simply imprisoned. They were held in prison for a few weeks or a few months, left ignored in the cells with no charges brought against them and no investigation held until they were released without a word of explanation or apology, under no judicial authority. It is not known how many of them paid to be released, it is unlikely that their illegal detention was satisfaction enough for Robéric. One of his victims, Jean Nougueret, who was himself *brigadier* of the *maréchaussée* in Bordeaux, was incarcerated in May and June 1729 and let out when he signed a receipt for the wages he had not received for the first quarter of 1728. There were obvious motives of financial benefit involved in the *prévôt*'s arbitrary release of eight prisoners who had been legally arrested on official warrant. P. Savarlaud, accused of a murder which the *prévôtal* court had been declared incompetent to try, paid 300L. for his freedom and two men who had murdered a certain Rabion on Ash Wednesday 1724 paid 500L. for inquiries to be dropped. Civil suits were much more lucrative for law officers than criminal prosecutions by the Crown: Robéric therefore 'forced' the laundryman François Brisson to make himself a civil party in the case against Loubard and Lestoursiarque, who had stolen cloth left out to dry in a meadow; Brisson had also been obliged to provide the *prévôt*, his clerk and his *archers* with food and drink. In a similar vein he had extorted 400L. from the Sr Midau, curé of the parish of Gournal, 'to draw up a report of the damage done in a burglary'.

The really lucrative gambits required accomplices, and the 125 *louis d'or* stolen from the Sr Verdier stuck to a variety of fingers after they fell into the hands of the *maréchaussée*: the Lipostey *cavalier* who caught the thief in Preignac made one *louis* when he altered the report from 125 to 124; his

---

69. The brigade commander was suspended for six years, a *cavalier* for nine, and a second *cavalier* banished for six years, A.N. Z^{IC} 357, 358, 361 and 434.

brigadier expropriated ten *louis*; the *prévôt* and his secretary, who posed as an official clerk of the *prévôtal* court 'demanded that the Sr Verdier's widow and children "lend" them sixty *louis d'or'*. Other stolen goods recovered by the *maréchaussée* - silver *louis*, gilt snuff boxes, walking sticks - all found their way into the *prévôt's* possession together with a percentage of the profit from the sale of prisoners' belongings, auctioned off 'without legal formalities' to contribute towards the repayment of debts or the cost of their stay in prison.

When Robéric's greed no longer permitted him to wait for opportunities to present themselves, he sent *archers* out on 'private' visits, 'to extort with violence various sums of money'. The *archers* certainly received every encouragement to keep the money they collected in fines for arms offences. The Bordeaux *brigadier* Lebrun also used violence to extort from Brisson the 90L. for which Robéric had given him a writ of execution and a further 30L. for his own operations; P. Lafon, *sous-brigadier* in Langon, arrested, imprisoned and released J. Guillemin on payment of 45L.

If a handful of *brigadiers* and *cavaliers* were Robéric's accomplices, many more were his victims. The *prévôt-général* robbed his men of extraordinary amounts from their pay, most of it, apparently, 'on the pretext of buying uniforms for his company': his judges ordered him to repay a total of 13,623L. to 16 *cavaliers*, 4 *brigadiers* (in Coutras, Blaye, Agen and Villeréal) and the *exempt* in Nérac. This sum, together with the 3,100L. to be repaid to civilians, and 300L. to the *hôpital de Bordeaux* was to be raised from the sale of his post as *prévôt-général*. The government also was defrauded in an imaginative scheme Robéric devised to earn a few hundred more *livres*. He invented phantom *cavaliers*, whose pay of course he kept to himself, to fill vacant posts in Blaye. There was the annual problem of the review, by the commissioner of the *maréchaussée*, which the *prévôt* solved by sending real *cavaliers* from Coutras and Ste Foy to impersonate their imaginary colleagues, and hope they would not be recognised. When François Sellier, appointed *cavalier* in Sauveterre, failed to turn up to start work, Robéric continued to have him paid, and employed the wife of Ricard, the Ste Foy *cavalier*, to sign receipts on Sellier's behalf.

It is not surprising that such a combination of activities permitted Robéric 'to live well'; and what was not spent on gracious living was used to buy a cavalry company for his son. For all these offences Robéric was duly sentenced, in his absence, to nine years in the galleys. The judgement was posted up in Bordeaux, and ordered to be read to 'every company of *maréchaussée* in the kingdom'.[70]

The Robéric trial of the 1730s was clearly an exceptional case - extortion

70. *Conclusions du procureur* 2 May 1735 and *Sentence de la Connétablie* 3 May 1735, the only remaining evidence, *ibid.* Z^{IC} 334.

on such a scale and with such organisation would not be found again in either the Auvergne or the Guyenne. Petty corruption was not so easy to get rid of without improving pay scales or tightening discipline. We have seen that the pay structure for *cavaliers* and *brigadiers* was in fact improved in the 1760s and 1770s – a factor which must have played a big rôle in the decline of corruption. Of the dozen trials for corruption to come before the *Connétablie* between 1720 and 1790 involving policemen from both provinces, eleven took place before 1760, and these eleven included the most serious cases. The reputation of the *maréchaussée* improved in consequence. Apart from the special case of Guyenne disarmament, local officials reported strong rumours and unproven accusations of corruption ten times in the eighteenth century – on seven occasions before 1760, and three in the early sixties. Such an improvement in the behaviour and standing of the *maréchaussée* was not just a matter of money, however; the decline of part-time jobs and corruption were only two signs of the success of a series of measures designed to tighten the discipline of the force.

CHAPTER 2

Police recruitment and discipline

The officers

The Reform of 1720 created an institution divided within itself. On one side of an unbridgeable gap were the men appointed to the lower ranks who could be dismissed at will. On the other side were the officers, who retained the right to buy their posts and leave them to their heirs.[1] These 'cowardly intruders scarcely amenable to discipline', it was claimed, the result of police work remaining a venal occupation, would bring about 'the bastardization of a force which should be vigorous, proud and terrifying to Rogues'.[2] The government could see the problem, and imposed an important proviso to the right of *survivance*. When the Riom Lieutenant du Jouannel was retired in 1742, the Minister of War refused to confirm the appointment as successor of his son, on the grounds that he had had no previous military experience. The nominee of the intendant and *prévôt-général*, the Sr Cellier, one of the army's accountants for ten years and treasurer of the *maréchaussée* itself for a further thirteen, was rejected for the same reasons and du Jouannet was told to find a buyer within a period of six months. After a year had elapsed the Minister asked Rossignol, the intendant, to look for a suitable candidate, for 'in the sales made by private contract, there are always arrangements which are harmful to the service and which eliminate the best candidates'.[3] If the intendant found someone poor but suitable, the government itself was prepared to pay the 15,000L., which was compatible with the letter but hardly the spirit of venality. In this case the government was able to save its money, for du Jouannel staggered on for another six years, giving up in 1749 at the age of 78, after forty-five years of service, and so crippled by gout that he was quite unable to mount his horse. He had however provided time for his son-in-law to acquire six years' experience in the Piedmont Cavalry regiment (one and a half as cadet, four and a half as ensign); Gannat de la Ribbehaute, who now became lieutenant and subsequently became *prévôt-général* combined this military qualification with a legal background – his father was *procureur du roi* in the Riom *élection* court – and with an enviable financial status. As his sister was to be packed off to a convent, the new

1. *Prévôts-généraux* bought their office for 40,000L. (30,000 in a few 'minor' provinces, not including the Auvergne or the Guyenne), lieutenants for 15,000.
2. Morandière, *Police sur les mendians*, pp. 35-6.
3. Letter from d'Argenson to intendant (1743) A.D. P. de D. C 6184.

lieutenant and his brother were to inherit over 20,000L. and 'expectations which are said in Pont-du-Château to be rather considerable', while his wife was to inherit the bulk of du Jouannel's estate. 'Apparently he has everything it takes'.[4]

The right of *survivance* was formally abolished by Choiseul's Edict of 25 February 1768, and the implications of the progressive undermining of venality finally realised ten years later. The Ordinance of 1778 established the principle that vacant posts as *prévôt-général* and lieutenant would no longer be sold, even if only for life, but would be filled by promotion from the lower ranks. Having solved one problem the reform created new problems. Designed to encourage healthy competition, it was found that 'this rivalry is more concerned with intrigues of protection than with personal merit', that there was a regrettable lack of lieutenants worthy of promotion,[5] but the reform permitted Revoux de Ronchamp, an *exempt* of the *maréchaussée* in St Jean d'Angely to become lieutenant in Montaigu (Poitou) and subsequently *prévôt-général* of the Guyenne.[6]

The six years Ribbehaute spent in the army made him a comparative newcomer among the hardened soldiers who became *prévôts-généraux* in the eighteenth century. César Dauphin had spent more than twelve years in cavalry regiments, while du Deffan, who succeeded Augustin in 1764 brought thirty-six years' experience in the Royal Dragoons.[7] In the Guyenne Barret de Ferrand could claim eleven years' distinguished service in the Conty and La Reine infantry regiments having participated in the siege of Philipsbourg, the siege of Prague, and the Bohemia campaign.[8] Thirty years later his successor, Barret de la Tour, took over after no less than twenty-eight years in the regular army – ten years as ensign and lieutenant in the Nicolas Dragoons, eighteen as captain in the Dessalles Cavalry.[9] But if the formal requirements for potential *prévôts* were less than exacting – four years' military service increased to twelve in 1769[10] – it was felt that the reputation of the force required a leader who could command the respect of 'the *élite* [*gens en place*] . . . all the nobles with seigneurial courts and châteaux'.[11] In a century when social distinction depended on birth, 'and, unfortunately, money . . . . it is essential that as well as a sharp mind, honour of every kind, and physical fitness, a *prévôt-général* has birth, and enough of a fortune to be able to live in society, more or less on equal terms with everyone'.[12]

---

4. Letter from intendant and Urion (*subdélégué* in Riom) to d'Argenson, 1749, *ibid.*
5. de Vic's *Mémoire*, A. de G. X^F 4.
6. *Réception* as lieutenant, Mar. 1770, A.N. Z^{IC} 374.
7. A. de G. Y^b 787.
8. *Ibid.* Y^b 859.
9. *Ibid.* Y^b 789.
10. Ordinance of 1769. The twelve years had to include five as captain.
11. de Vic's *Mémoire, ibid.* X^F 4.
12. *Ibid.*

The eighteenth-century *prévôts-généraux* had almost identically respectable if not brilliant backgrounds. They all came from the dignified ranks of the local magistrature, which, in conjunction with their own military experience, was regarded as good preparation for the dual rôle they would be called upon to play as leader of the *maréchaussée* and judge of the *prévôtal* court. Ribbehaute's father, as we have seen, was *procureur du roi* in the *élection* court, and left his son 'very comfortably off'.[13] His predecessor, Panay du Deffan, was the son of Claude Panay du Deffan, seigneur du Deffan, *Conseiller du Roi, procureur du roi* in a Riom court; his superiors were satisfied that he enjoyed all the consideration 'conferred by birth, distinguished service and a constant application to his duties'.[14] The Dauphins were members of a bourgeois family which originated in Tauves and had, like the Panays, invested in office and seigneurial estates. César, the son of the first president of the *élection* court in Clermont, and seigneur of Charlannes and Serettes, married Catherine Villot de Boisluisant, daughter of the 'Commissioner of Reviews of the *maréchaussée* of the Auvergne'; two of their sons went into the church, one into the army, and the fourth, born in 1720, was Augustin. The family clearly had a certain wealth (even if at the expense of two ecclesiastical vocations), for Augustin was able to acquire the *seigneuries* of Leyval, Traslaigues and Villossanges, and the title of 'baron de Montel de Gelat'.[15]

Among the *prévôts* of the Guyenne, also *seigneurs, chevaliers de St Louis* and *écuyers*, the longest-serving and most active, Barret de Ferrand, stands out, 'an officer of distinction, in every regard, rich, keeping up a very honourable household'.[16] Such qualities however did not mean that he was universally respected by every member of the local *élite*. Like the *prévôts-généraux* of the Auvergne, and his own successor, Barret de Ferrand was a local man. The antipathy of the Auvergne *prévôts* to control by the *intendance* was well known, but Barret de Ferrand was seen to be a *Bordelais* serving the interests of a national institution, and thus exposing himself to the opprobrium of his compatriots. Much of the bitterness in the feud between the *maréchaussée* and the *Jurats* came from the charge that Barret was 'a bad fellow-citizen, a man who encroaches every day on the rights and privileges of his native city [*patrie*]'.[17]

The *prévôt*'s deputy, the lieutenant, also required an impeccable military background - four years' service, increased in 1768 to eight. Even the Auvergne Lieutenant du Jouannel, for years crippled by gout, had been a

13. Letter from Urion to intendant, 1749, A.D. P. de D. C 6184.
14. Inspection of 6th Division, 1779, A. de G. X^F 4. He was a descendant of Panay du Deffan, *prévôt-général* in 1685.
15. A. Tardieu, *Histoire de la ville de Clermont-Ferrand*, vol. 2 (Moulins 1870-2), pp. 220-2.
16. Inspection by de Vic, 1771, A. de G. Y^b 789.
17. Letter from Barret de Ferrand to intendant, 11 Mar. 1755, A.D. Gir. C 2189.

dragoon and a musketeer in the days of his youth. While the regulations prescribed up to eight years in the army, most lieutenants had been there for
longer. Dastier had been soldier, sub-lieutenant, and ensign, for almost eighteen years; Soleau took up his duties as lieutenant in St Flour after twenty-
five years' service and four campaigns; de Sauveaud became lieutenant in
Agen after sixteen army years; Gigounoux de Verdon came to Périgueux
after twenty-one years in the Fumel Cavalry and the Vermandois Infantry.[18]

Like the *prévôts-généraux*, the lieutenants bought their posts until 1778,
and as with the superior rank, the authorities moved timidly towards promotion by merit. At first it was worthies like d'Escayrac de la Grave, who assumed
the *lieutenance* in Bordeaux after only four years as brigade commander in
Villeréal and Sarlat. Democratic tendencies became more marked as the
appointment committees grew more accustomed to the 1778 Ordinance, and
by 1785 it was possible for an André Richard (the son of a Parisian building
contractor and the godson of a carpenter) to struggle his way to the Clermont
lieutenance after eleven years in the *Gendarmerie* and twenty one years in
the *maréchaussée* as *sous-brigadier, brigadier, exempt,* and *sous-lieutenant.*
The later years of the century did see a break in the monopoly of the landed
bourgeoisie and petty nobility – after Pierre de la Roche de Brisson, St Flour
had as lieutenant the son of a Dijon merchant, then Soleau, who was the son
of a 'bourgeois of Châlons'.[19] The Périgord lieutenants in the 1780s however, were de Bellevaux, de Bergeret (son of a Lieutenant des Chasses du
Prince de Conty), and Jean Armand de Gigounoux de Verdon, the scion of
a family ennobled in 1730 for military services.[20] Perhaps there would have
been more enthusiasm for the 'career open to talents' had the promoted subordinates proved to be more talented. Desaignes, the *sous lieutenant* who became lieutenant in Bordeaux a year after the Ordinance, had to be sacked in
1783. The merchant's son, Bouquet, was a disaster; after he had died on the
job, it was found that 'everything is neglected' and the new lieutenant had to
rebuild discipline from scratch. Richard was invariably described in the annual
inspection as 'very exact in his service' as lieutenant, which in officialese
meant that he displayed a greater degree of conscientiousness than flair.[21]

The men

The 1720 Reform made one radical change in the condition of the lower ranks –
venality was abolished. Otherwise not much thought was given to the sort of
person who would make up the great bulk of the institution. Anyone who had

18. *Contrôles de maréchaussée*, A. de G. Y^b 753, 858.
19. *Ibid.* Y^b 859, and *Réceptions*, A.N. Z^{IC} 383, 405.
20. St Saud, *Magistrats des sénéchaussées, présidiaux et Elections.* (Bergerac 1931),
   p. 193.
21. *Contrôles*, A. de G. Y^b, passim.

served in the army for four years without disgracing himself was eligible to apply. Appointments to the rank of *cavalier* were regarded as so uncontroversial a matter that they were left to the discretion of the *prévôt-général*. Later in the century, however, the institution became more particular. After 1760, *cavaliers* had to be five feet four inches in height, and literate 'as far as possible', and by 1769 the army qualification had stiffened to eight years, with preference given to those 'who had done two terms of service'. For brigade commanders, a minimum of twelve years' service was prescribed, another move towards increasing stringency designed to improve the quality of the service, and to 'have these posts considered as reward or retirement for officers and soldiers'.[22] While the concept of the *maréchaussée* as a 'retirement' from the rigours of military life proper may help to explain why so many *cavaliers* of the *maréchaussée* were allowed to stagger on in the force till they dropped, or till they were carried off, white-haired and arthritic, to the *Invalides*, it is possible that not all applicants regarded service in the police as a reward. The only *brigadier* to leave behind an analysis of his motives for joining the *maréchaussée* after thirteen years in the Infantry and campaigns against the Austrians, had been transferred to the Auvergne militia regiment, 'to make room no doubt for *protégés* of the minister', with nothing to do in peacetime and with rumours rife that the militia was to be disbanded. 'Afraid of being at a loose end', he asked for a job in the *maréchaussée*.[23]

Entry qualifications were toughened so drastically by the 1778 Ordinance that the *prévôt* in the Guyenne, de Ronchamp, commented with ironic understatement that 'the *maréchaussée* does not recruit the same way as other troops'.[24] The Ordinance insisted that in future all *cavaliers* would have served for no less than sixteen years in a cavalry regiment, and as before provided 300L. to pay for the horse, saddle, and all the other equipment necessary for service in the *maréchaussée*. After repeated representations from *prévôts-généraux*, the Minister yielded ground only to the extent of considering soldiers from infantry regiments. This minor concession did not prevent the loss of good potential candidates, as it was the financial qualifications which had the most restricting effect; there were not many soldiers who could cope with the expense of buying a horse, boots, a saddle, and suede breeches. Ronchamp was rightly indignant at the suggestion that he personally could be blamed for empty places in his brigades: 'I do not have the gift of manufacturing men of the height . . . and with the financial faculties required by the ordinance'.[25] The inspectors of the *maréchaussée*, however, directed

22. 'Réponses aux observations de MM les Maréchaux de France sur le projet de la nouvelle ordonnance concernant les maréchaussées' (Ordinance of 1769), art. 2, *ibid*. X^F 2.
23. Letter from de Gironde, *brigadier* in Ambert, to intendant, 17 Sept. 1779, A.D. P. de D. C 6189.
24. Letter from Revoux de Ronchamp to intendant, 27 Sept. 1787, A.D. Gir. C 4636.
25. *Ibid*.

their fire at the sixteen-year clause. If a soldier of sixteen-years' standing had any capabilities whatever, they argued, he could expect to be promoted, and have no desire to enter the *maréchaussée* as a humble *cavalier*. On the other hand old soldiers with no hope of advancement had normally stayed in the army because of a complete lack of initiative or resources, a taste for debauchery, or a fear of work; 'What has he gained by sixteen years in the services ?' they asked, 'Almost always numerous venereal diseases, consequently a worn-out, sick body useless for the service of the *maréchaussée*, a taste for drunkenness, in short a character worthy of a guardhouse where all the talk is of violence and plunder'.[26] Virtually all the *cavaliers* recruited after 1778 had served for sixteen years.

The rule had been included in the Ordinance not with the interests of the *maréchaussée* in mind, but in the hope of encouraging soldiers to sign up again for the regular army on the expiry of their first engagement. The *maréchaussée* had an annual intake of about fifty *cavaliers*, hardly a significant enough loss for the French army to justify such a drastic restriction of the *maréchaussée*'s choice of recruits. Whatever small benefit the clause brought to the army, it did no good to the police force, for 'those who have private means do not sign up again, yet these are the very men the *maréchaussée* wants'. The search for *cavaliers* with means sprang not only from the fond hope that the men would be able to compensate for the perennial financial deficiencies of the institution, but also from an assumption that the penniless soldier would be uneducated and illiterate, unable to perform the modicum of paper-work expected of him, his service suffering from all the restrictions imposed by illiteracy. After sixteen military years, 'poor and worn out, no longer can he resort to marriage', and the worse his poverty, the more easily he would be tempted by corruption. The ideal policeman therefore, like the ideal officer, was 'comfortably off'; with money came education, health and the respect of the community.

Before 1778, soldiers of the army had had no difficulty meeting the service requirements of the police force. Most *cavaliers* in fact had done far more military service than was required. When the requirement was four years, the average military experience in the Auvergne company was nine and a half years; when the requirement was eight years, the average was over twelve.[27] The increasing stringency of regulations therefore was more apparent than real, and the 1778 insistence on sixteen years was not so drastic a change as it appeared on paper – it simply followed a century-old trend.

The trend towards increasing length of military service was accompanied by the gradual elimination from the force of those with no military experience at all. The latter were comparatively common in the very early decades of

26. de Vic's *Mémoire*, A. de G. X^F 4.
27. *Contrôles de maréchaussée, ibid.* Y^b 858, and inspections of 1771, 1772, *ibid.* Y^b 753 and 754.

the century, though none was permitted after 1736. Many of those with 'no previous military service' were men who had served in the pre-1720 *maréchaussée*, the personnel of which passed *en masse* into the new organisation, concentrated, naturally, in the towns where the old companies had been based. Exemption from previous service requirements was also granted in the early part of the century to the young men charmingly referred to as *enfants du corps* – the 20, 18 or even 17-year old youths accepted into the *maréchaussée* if their fathers had served in the force before them. They could be found in the Auvergne – indeed Duplessis, the *brigadier* in Ambert had both his teenage sons in his own brigade – but they were much more common in the Guyenne. So many family groups emerge from the registers of the *maréchaussée* that it may have seemed to contemporaries as if the lower ranks of the Guyenne police force had acquired some of the characteristics of the other closed professions of the ancien régime. They enjoyed privileges denied to others – *enfants du corps*, for example, were the only members of the *maréchaussée* for whom the service requirements were waived after the initial years, right up till the 1770s. *Enfants du corps* were also privileged in the field of promotion: one in every 2 *enfants* was promoted to the rank of brigade commander compared with only one in every 13 of those who did not have a father in the Guyenne company, and an even rarer one in every 17 in the Auvergne.[28]

There were even dynasties of policemen. The first Reveilhac to appear on the eighteenth-century registers had been in the Périgueux company since 1713; when he retired in 1731, he was succeeded by his son Etienne who spent the rest of his long working life in Périgueux as *cavalier* till 1754, *sous-brigadier* and *exempt* till 1777; the third generation, Etienne's son Gabriel Reveilhac, worked as *cavalier* from 1772 till his death in 1785. The Chevauchau (or Chevochos) de Champagnac family covered virtually every corner of the Guyenne. Léonard Chevochos de Champagnac, in 1720 a *cavalier* in Sarlat, became *sous-brigadier* in Créon (1721) and *brigadier* in Périgueux (1724) where he remained for thirty years. Meanwhile his son Bertrand joined the Périgueux brigade in 1732, but moved the same year to Mussidan, and yet again to Lesparre as *sous-brigadier*, at the age of 22. By 1734 he was *brigadier* in Lipostey, and in 1737 *brigadier* in Villeréal, and in 1746, back in the Périgord as *brigadier* in Nontron where he died three years later. He was succeeded by his son, a *cavalier* since 1744 in Lesparre, Villeréal and Nontron itself, where he became *sous-brigadier* on his father's death. Three years later however the *sous-brigadier*, Bertrand junior, was sacked for 'negligence and contempt of service' to be succeeded as brigade commander, after a two-year interval, by his grandfather Léonard, who was prepared to

28. In the Guyenne, 54 *cavaliers* promoted to rank of brigade commander from total of 681; in the Auvergne, 20 from a total of 340.

leave Périgueux for what was undoubtedly a quieter life as *brigadier* in Nontron in the final years of his service. The family was not quite finished with the *maréchaussée*, however, for when a new *cavalier* was needed in 1757, none other than Bertrand Chevauchau was given the job, the disgraced *sous-brigadier* with the police force in his blood, who returned to serve uneventfully as *cavalier* until his retirement to the *Invalides* twenty years later.[29] Other families took less time to infiltrate the force. Roudet de las Gourgues and Elie Greilh, *cavaliers* in Sarlat and Mussidan, and Paignon, the Périgueux *brigadier*, all gave 2 sons to the *maréchaussée*, in the Greilh case both confusingly called Jean. Mestrand, the *cavalier* in Coutras, and Landry, the *exempt* in Sarlat, each had 3 sons who all joined the *maréchaussée*. Other family groups include at least four pairs of brothers whose fathers had followed a different career, but the most common relationship – twenty-two cases – was the straightforward father and son. It says something for the corporate spirit of the ancien régime that the sons of so many ordinary *cavaliers* were prepared to face the same life of monotonous highway patrols, popular hostility, and financial hardship, even with the privileges of *enfants du corps*. The *esprit de corps* was reinforced by the pattern of friendship and intermarriage. Grasset, *cavalier* in Mussidan, married Elizabeth Cherchouly, sister of two *cavaliers* in the Brantôme brigade; when he remarried, two of his witnesses were *cavalier* Signolles, and the *brigadier* Dubois.[30]

For *cavaliers* who wanted promotion, the Guyenne was the province to choose, for it was a company with a far more democratic career structure than in the Auvergne. In the south-west *généralité* more than half of all brigade commanders had previously served in the ranks as humble *cavaliers*, whereas in the Auvergne the corresponding proportion was less than a quarter.[31] This impressive disparity was the result of the shortage of Auvergnat candidates suitable for promotion. Although the desirability of appointing brigade commanders from among the *cavaliers* was not formally recognised till the Ordinance of 1778, it had long been the authorities' desire to make such promotions, 'to stimulate competition',[32] but it was difficult to make progress with the quality available.

When Culerier, the *exempt* in Chaudesaigues, died in 1732, 4 candidates

29. Tracing the Chevauchau de Champagnac through the gaps, inaccuracies and contradictions of central and local *rôles de maréchaussée* involves reference to A. de G. Y^b 753, 789, 796, 804, 858, 859; A.D. Dord. B 558 (a *procès-verbal* by Léonard Chevochos, 22 Feb. 1758) and A.D. Dord. 5 E 306/7 – burial in parish church of St Sauveur de Nontron, 10 Oct. 1789, of Bertrand Chevauchau, sieur de Champagnac, 39 . . . fils de Léonard de Chevauchau, brigadier [à] Périgueux, et Dlle Marie Chambert.
30. A.D. Dord 5E 545, – parish Thiviers, 29 July 1783. Three months before the wedding, Grasset was godfather to Signolles' daughter Margaret, *ibid.* 29 Apr. 1783.
31. In the Guyenne, 54 *brigadiers* from a total of 96; in the Auvergne, 20 out of 91.
32. Letter from d'Argenson to intendant of Auvergne, 4 Apr. 1743, A.D. P. de D. C 6184.

were proposed and rejected before a decision could be made. The rank of *exempt* was normally a reward for efficient *brigadiers*, such as Duplessis, *brigadier* in Ambert, 'an excellent fellow much to the taste of the *prévôt*', but discounted as unwilling to move house.[33] Intervention by the Sr Fouves de la Coudre in favour of an external candidate, Delpeuch du Chambon – foundered on reports which reached the intendant that Delpeuch was 'a drunkard', and possessed an estate near Chaudesaigues, which would take up his time, 'and give him opportunity to abuse his authority'. *Cavaliers* were included in the running, as Dauphin wanted to downgrade the post and keep the *exempt*'s supplement for Duplessis, but the *prévôt*'s own *protégé*, Pagès, was 'a very bad sort' who drank, smuggled, slept with numerous women, and had abandoned his wife and children who begged in the street: such a candidate was not considered suitable. The Minister eventually appointed the *cavalier* Féfelin as the new *brigadier*, but Féfelin had to turn down the job on the grounds of his illiteracy.[34] The job was finally given to the *cavalier* Poisson, presumably literate, 'of a good family', in fact *écuyer*, and at the age of 41 'well behaved but indolent'.[35]

The attempt was often made to smooth the path of potential *brigadiers* with intrigue and influence. Even the inspectors of the *maréchaussée* blamed the inefficiency of the Sarlat brigade on Faurie, the *brigadier* appointed 'by protection . . . unknown to his *prévôt-général* who has never considered him worthy of promotion'.[36] There were unsuccessful appeals to the Auvergne intendant by M. de Diène in favour of an impoverished gentleman de Tierceville, who also interested Mme de Roussille and had to his credit twenty-five years' service: 'this man of rank has several wounds'.[37] M. de St Aubin, whose previous career of twenty-eight years in the dragoons was no more distinguished, appeared to be blessed with no more than 'a pleasant face and an advantageous height', but succeeded for he was 'the *protégé* of M. l'intendant'.[38] It was not a lucky choice – St Aubin left the force within two years and does not make a single appearance in the surviving registers of the *maréchaussée*.

It was difficult, however, to fill responsible posts in the Auvergne company at least as long as illiteracy remained so general among the *cavaliers*. They usually managed no more than the most shaky and laborious of signa-

---

33. Duplessis became *exempt* the following year, without having to move.
34. Intendant to d'Argenson, 4 Mar. 1733 A.D. P. de D. C 6177. Féfelin remained a *cavalier* in Murat until his death in 1751.
35. Intendant to d'Angervilliers, 4 Mar. 1733. *Ibid.*
36. Inspection 1777, A. de G. Yb 804 and 859. Throughout his career in five residences (Ste Foy, Lesparre, Bergerac, Brantôme and Sarlat) 'he is always more occupied by his own affairs than by his official duties'. For the good of the service he was dispatched to the *Invalides* in 1781.
37. Correspondence 1756, A.D. P. de D. C 6185.
38. Correspondence 1769, *ibid.* C 6189.

tures. *Brigadiers* of course were obliged not only to read and write but also to put words into sentences and draw up reports. Spelling and grammar often left a lot to be desired: 'je ne pas manquer au sitot dexpedie de point a point . . . led. Cavallier a ne pas torde suivant quil a estoit accuse'.[39] This letter from Fontfreyde may not in fact have been written by Fontfreyde, for the *subdélégué* had reported that the *exempt* 'does not know how to write a single report or letter and makes use of Royer, one of the *cavaliers*, for the purpose';[40] the *exempt* in Aurillac, it was alleged, wrote reports at the dictation of his friend the abbé Montsalvy, 'for du Theliol is not capable of drawing up the least document'.[41]

The problem of literacy in the *maréchaussée* was not considered seriously before the Ordinance of 1778, and the review of 1779 was the first to test the *cavaliers* from this point of view. Such a change in priorities came hard and reluctantly to the Auvergne, for the inspectors forgot to raise the question with half the company. Of the remainder, 29 *cavaliers* could not write, compared with only 15 who could.[42] The situation in the Guyenne, however, was quite different. The question of literacy was taken so seriously that only 14 individuals were not vetted, most of whom were *brigadiers* who could safely be assumed to know how to read and write. No less than eight subtly graded categories of academic achievement were established. At the bottom were those who could neither read nor write - only one[43] - and 6 *cavaliers* who could only sign their names. Three *cavaliers* fell into each of the carefully differentiated categories 'reads a little', 'reads a little and writes', and 'reads, and writes a little', but the basic criterion, 'can read and write', had a very creditable 33. Particularly impressive, however, were the 14 men who could not only 'read and write' but also 'verbaliser' (draw up a report), and the 24 men, including 11 ordinary *cavaliers*, who could 'bien verbaliser'. It was natural that educational achievements should be higher among *brigadiers* - as the Auvergne intendant commented, 'just a little bit more breeding and education are required for these sorts of jobs'.[44] The remark

---

39. Letter from Fontfreyde, *exempt* in Mauriac to intendant 18 May 1744, defending Royer, accused of murder. *Ibid.* C 1531.
40. Report, 1731, from Mauriac *subdélégué* to intendant in intendant's secret *enquête*, *ibid.* C 6177.
41. Aurillac *subdélégué* to intendant, 1731. *ibid.* C 1617.
42. 'Can write' and 'Cannot write' were the only alternatives. None of the *cavaliers* in Riom, official capital and judicial centre of the *généralité*, could write, A. de G. Y^b 805.
43. J. Despujols, 55, *cavalier* in Libourne 1769-80s. There were still illiterate *cavaliers* at the time of the Revolution, and when the Dept. of Seine-et-Oise suggested that the formation of the *Gendarmerie Nationale* provided an opportunity to get rid of them, the Assembly decided otherwise: *Dépouillement des Tableaux des brigades existantes en chaque département et de celles demandées en augmentation*, 1791, p. 14. A. de G. X^F 9.
44. Trudaine to d'Angervilliers, A.D. P. de D. C 6182.

was inspired by the exception to the rule – Gaignon, *brigadier* though the son of a peasant from La Roche Mirefleur, and clearly a man the intendant would have preferred ·to remain in the ranks. For the great majority of policemen who were not *enfants du corps* were men who had risen, or at least transferred, from the lowest ranks of the army, the sons of peasants, or urban artisans from the town, like Mage, *cavalier* in Périgueux, son of a pewterer in La Roche-Chalais and married to the daughter of a shoemaker.[45] This indication of the social status of *cavaliers* is confirmed by the company they kept: at the baptism of the son of Jean Ribeyrol, *cavalier* in Mussidan, the godfather was a locksmith.[46] When the Thiviers *cavalier* Baralier got married, only one of the witnesses was literate.[47]

The brigade commanders, on the other hand, included many of the policemen with bourgeois or noble backgrounds. Dubois de Wolek, 'bourgeois de Paris', joined the force as an *exempt*; de la Crompe, 'born a noble', joined the *maréchaussée* as *brigadier* in Lipostey and was soon promoted to *exempt*; his younger brother, after only a year as *cavalier*, quickly rose through the ranks to become *sous-lieutenant* in Libourne. Most of the brigade commanders who joined the force without going through the ranks had names like Chevreuil de Valence, Fonteney de Fontette, or de St Georges. The registers of the *maréchaussée* dwell respectfully on the few policemen from the Second Estate – Vernejoul, *écuyer*, *cavalier* in Bordeaux for two years before promotion to Créon; or de St Privé de Richebourg, the noble *brigadier* in Courpière. Honest annotations make clear what kind of circumstances had reduced the offspring of respectable families to such a humble occupation. De la Garrigue, 'born a noble', was in such financial straits that as a *cavalier* in Maurs in the 1770s and 80s he was in constant need of 'gratification'. The Sr de la Bretesche, *exempt* in Ambert and Riom, had begun his career in the *maréchaussée* 'after having lost part of his inheritance in the bank notes crash [the John Law scandal of 1720]'.[48] François des François also 'born a noble', a *cavalier* in Maurs, was not only 'very poor' but also 'unintelligent', the same combination of qualities which drove into the *maréchaussée* Deschaux de Romefort, a 'man of standing' from the 'bourgeoisye'.[49] Ribeyre, though 'the son of a good bourgeois' distinguished by a 'sense of honour', was a *cavalier* in Besse: 'only the disturbance in his financial affairs obliged him to take this position'.[50]

It was also possible for *cavaliers* of humble birth and with no relatives in the force to make at least the first step to a career and reach the grade of

45. A.M. Pér. GG 24, parish of La Cité.
46. A.D. Dord. 5E 294/2. parish St Georges de Mussidan, 17 Mar. 1785.
47. *Ibid.* 5E 560/2 parish of Vaunac, 11 July 1771.
48. La Bretesche to intendant, 1752, A.D. P. de D. C 6192.
49. A. de G. Y^b 804, 805.
50. *Enquête*, A.D. P. de D. C 6177.

brigadier or *sous-brigadier*. The 1778 Ordinance recommended a testing period of at least five years; *cavaliers* normally had longer to wait in the Guyenne, in fact, about double that time, with the delay lengthening as the century wore on, as more literate *cavaliers* appeared providing more competition. In the Auvergne there was usually less time to wait. Most of the *cavaliers* promoted to the command of a brigade had been *brigadiers* or *sergents* in the army; the rank of *maréchal des logis* was regarded as a sign of merit and responsibility, and could reduce the period in the lowest ranks to a few months. The brigade commanders appointed straight from the army had all shown their command potential in a galaxy of promoted army posts - sergeants, sub-lieutenants, lieutenants, royal guards and ensigns. The senior officers were always on the look-out for *cavaliers* with command potential, and such a recommendation - 'capable of commanding a brigade', or 'fit for promotion' - in the annual inspection was always a passport to greater things. Paignon, the *cavalier* in Bergerac 'keen and liking his job, good at discovering evil-doers . . . continually out on the roads and streets of the residence' became *brigadier* in Bordeaux three years later; the Périgueux *cavalier*, Dubois, 'good at carrying out a delicate operation and still keeping his honour intact' was clearly 'made for promotion'.

Before the drive to improve standards made for tougher entry qualifications, it could have been said that it was easier to get into the *maréchaussée* than it was to get out. In the first thirty or forty years of the revamped institution practically the only way to leave the force was to be sacked or to die. All the *cavaliers* who served in Clermont died while still on active service. By the 1770s however, it had become more common to be awarded a place in the *Hôtel des Invalides*, for *cavaliers* and brigade commanders officially designated 'in no state to continue in the service' or simply 'infirm'. There was however a perpetual shortage of places and those recommended for the *Invalides* by the inspectors often had to wait months or even years; the brigades therefore still had to find room for *cavaliers* too old or infirm to carry out their duties. 'They tire their comrades' du Deffan complained, 'and service to King and public suffers'. No room could be found in the *Invalides* for Greilh, aged 67, and so overweight he had to be helped on to his horse, or for Cantegrist, 'so worn out' after forty-five years' service; even Vigouroux, a 70-year-old *cavalier* in Agen had to soldier on for a couple of years after he had been found 'absolutely past it'.[51]

As an alternative to an institutional old age, the Ordinance of 1778 offered a retirement pension.[52] With the full pension awarded automatically after thirty years' service it became possible for policemen to retire in their

51. A. de G. Y^b 792.
52. Art Ier. tit.14: *prévôts*, 1200L.; *Lt* 600L.; *sous-Lt* 400L.; *maréchal des logis*, 250L.; *brigadier* 168L. and *cavaliers* 126L. per annum. *Retraites, ibid.* X^F 9.

fifties, rather than struggling on grimly till a place fell vacant in the *Invalides*. The new provisions prevented the recurrence of a situation like the one in Casteljaloux where one of the three *cavaliers* in 1771 was 67 and another 70. The age structure of the force was fundamentally altered over the century, for the elimination of the most geriatric was balanced by the elimination of *enfants du corps* and other youngsters with no military experience, and although there continued to be large numbers of relatively young men who stayed in the force for a short time and moved on, more *cavaliers* were tempted to struggle on and serve out their thirty years. These changes compensated for each other, and the average age of the eighteenth-century policemen remained constant at about 44.

Illness or injury, however, could overcome a policeman of any age. More than half the men forced to retire through ill-health had not even reached 44. When the Aurillac *cavalier* La Papy was asked to retire 'he had not left his room for eight months because of his infirmities'.[53] *Cavaliers* and *brigadiers* at various stages of 'putting on weight' were numerous; they were dismissed when their size or deformity interfered too seriously with their work. Rheumatism was an affliction so common as to be banal; there were bad cases of 'violently painful sciatica and rheumatism' and *cavaliers* who were 'stiff in the limbs' or even struck by 'paralysis'. It was surprisingly unusual for *cavaliers* to be detected suffering from venereal disease – the only case to be recorded was Boutet, a *cavalier* in Lipostey of all places. *Cavaliers* were on occasion sacked for being found to 'have epileptic fits', or to have 'gone mad'.[54] With the aid of eighteenth-century medicine, the most simple accident was enough to incapacitate a *cavalier* for life. Imberdy, a *cavalier* in Pont-du-Château, simply broke a leg falling from his horse but had to be consigned to the *Invalides*. Barrier, *brigadier* in La Tête de Buch had had an operation for stones and the wound opened up every time he mounted his horse. Eyesight was particularly important for a policeman, and vulnerable. Soubaret, a Montaigut *cavalier*, lost an eye from a rifle shot while giving *main-forte*, but was able to carry on in the force; there was a one-eyed *cavalier* in the Lipostey brigade, while Cosse, *cavalier* in Sarlat, La Bastide in Villeréal and Millet in Blaye were all going slowly blind. Most of them got into the *Invalides*, and the inspectors made a special effort for Fouquet, *cavalier* in La Tête de Buch, whose growing loss of sight was blamed on the residence 'in the moors by the sea side'. The eighteenth-century *maréchaussée* ran the gamut of human misery – from vulgar aches and pains to blindness, deafness, hernia, impotence, and incontinence; from *cavaliers* with chests attacked by 'violent illnesses' which left them gasping for breath or spitting

53. *Ibid.* YA 805.
54. The Castillonnès *cavalier* was eventually sent to the *Invalides* 'as the alienation of mind could increase, there being examples in his family'. *Revue* 1780 A.D. Gir. 11 B 2.

up blood, to a *brigadier* suffering from 'a colic which very often makes him incapable of doing his duties'.[55]

The annual inspections make clear, however, that the most common cause by far of temporary or permanent incapacity was drink. Drinking frequently led to dismissal from the force, once the *cavalier* was 'an incorrigible drunkard'. There was often a connection between drunkenness and the other scourge of the *maréchaussée*, indebtedness. Origal was one of those to compound his chances of dismissal by drowning his sorrows while 'he owes money everywhere and lives in the most dreadful poverty with a wife and seven children'. Alcoholism often entailed a whole succession of problems, and when combined with poverty, brought the *cavaliers* down to distressing levels of degradation. Coste, *cavalier* in St Flour was 'sunk in debts, a drunkard, insubordinate and dissolute'; Daunis 'drunk, dissolute, lazy and dirty'.

The evidence of drunkenness in the police force from internal sources does at least help to corroborate the expected complaints from the general public, in particular from the *subdélégués*. Addiction to alcohol was one of the major complaints which emerged from the secret inquiry the intendant of the Auvergne launched in December 1732 into the general character and conduct of the company.[56] The *subdélégués* were discerning enough to distinguish the fact from the embroidered rumours and accusations which circulated. The Besse *subdélégué* dismissed the rumours spread by 'a few people' that Boyer and Vincent were 'drunkards' as quite without foundation, 'for in a dispute the two had some time ago I noticed nothing'. In Montaigut, on the other hand, the general public appeared to accept the local brigade's drinking habits, for the only complaints concerned the *cavaliers'* failure to pay their bills; whereas the *subdélégué* himself found that the *brigadier* 'drinks too much wine', the *cavalier* Boucher 'is equally fond of drinking', the *cavalier* Taillandier was 'no less partial to wine', and the *cavalier* Josses 'given over to wine'. The Langeac *subdélégué* was so critical of his *brigadier*, 'drinking wine . . . with no authority over his cavaliers', that he asked the intendant to burn his letter. In Murat the *brigadier's* drinking – and the *subdélégué* admitted he drank too much – 'does not distract him from his duty', as he restricted his indulgence to his leisure time, and stayed at home, his wife running a *cabaret* 'to support his family'. Even such a tolerant *subdélégué* however had to record that wine made the *cavalier* Barthoneuf violent and aggressive, particularly towards his colleagues, and he had on numerous occasions been put in prison to sober up.

Nightly carousals at the *cabaret* tended to discourage any nocturnal operation – the *sous-brigadier* in Montaigut 'operates reluctantly at night';[57] and

55. Inspections, A. de G. Y^b *passim*.
56. Circular to all his *subdélégués*, 10 Dec. 1732, and replies Dec. 1732, Jan. 1733, A.D. P. de D. C 6177.
57. Letter from *subdélégué/Lt criminel* to intendant, 26 Dec. 1759 *ibid*. C 1552.

when the Aurillac brigade had to guard a prisoner overnight, they arrived at the prison so drunk they could hardly stand up and 'had a few more flagons of wine brought, and spent the night drinking and sleeping'.[58] It was perhaps more serious for the efficiency of the police that *cavaliers* acquired the habit of having a drink at the fairs and fêtes they were supposed to police. Drink was certainly a factor which helps to explain the *maréchaussée*'s failure to keep cool in difficult situations. In the case of the Vissac rebellion, for example, when Andrieu rode his horse through the dancing, firing into the air 'with a kind of fury', it was established that he had failed to preserve the sang-froid expected of him, in short 'that he had been drinking'.[59] At the fête in Valcivières, the riot was started by two *cavaliers* from Ambert 'intoxicated by wine', fighting two *laboureurs* and inflicting serious injuries with their sabres.[60]

In their over-indulgence in the pleasures of this world, eighteenth-century policemen did not of course restrict themselves to wine. A number of *cavaliers* were reprimanded, or sacked, for unspecified 'debauchery', or 'frequent debauchery' and even 'continual debauchery'. To lead to destitution, their debauchery, which probably included drink, must have been on a Bacchanalian scale, for the *cavalier* Pagès – 'who spent his days in the cabaret and his nights with women' – was not only retained by the *maréchaussée* but promoted to the command of the Murat brigade.[61] The Guyenne company was just as inconsistent: Dubreuilh, a *cavalier* in La Roche-Chalais was sacked for being 'something of a libertine' though in other respects a good *cavalier*, while Antoine de Beauquesne, who filled the considerably more responsible post as *exempt* in Nérac, was simply told that he needed to 'correct his taste for gambling and other pleasures'.[62] Anonymous allegations about the *cavaliers'* conduct were made from time to time – one received by the *subdélégué* in Issoire told of a girl 'who dresses up as a layman to get into the prison and carry on her wicked trade with *cavaliers*'.[63] As a rural police force, the *maréchaussée* certainly had limited opportunities to exploit the world of prostitution. There were *cavaliers* resident in Bordeaux, of course, but they were not caught *in flagrante delicto*. One solitary piece of evidence comes from the corrupt atmosphere which prevailed during the period of office of the notorious Sr de Robéric. Two *cavaliers* were convicted of enjoying the favours of a 'very dissolute prostitute' in exchange for revealing the names of criminals whose arrest had been ordered by the Secretary of State.[64]

58. *Subdélégué* of Aurillac to intendant, 1731, *ibid.* C 1617.
59. Observations by Langeac *subdélégué*, 1755, *ibid.* C 7299.
60. Correspondence between d'Angervilliers, intendant and *subdélégué*, August 1733. *ibid.* C 6181.
61. See above p. 46 and A. de G. Y^b 859.
62. Both in *Revue* of 1772, A. de G. Y^b 796.
63. Letter to intendant, 1731, A.D. P. de D. C 1522.
64. Intendant to d'Armenonville, 14 June 1726. A.D. Gir C 2188.

The level of public complaint and the serious consequences – both for individual policemen and for the service of the *maréchaussée* – which would result from these pastimes, all contributed to the authorities' desire to improve discipline within the force. The reforms of the 1760s and 1770s were justified by the hope that the best way to achieve this was to emphasise the military character of the institution.

The *maréchaussée*'s military personality had of course never been entirely forgotten, despite the intimate contact with the civilian population brought about by its police duties and judicial competence. The 1720 Edict had reiterated the force's subordination to the Marshals of France, its official status as part of the *'Gendarmerie'*. Both men and officers were subject to the military rule book: *cavaliers*, for example, who absented themselves without leave were to be treated as deserters;[65] those who survived into old age were admitted to the *Invalides* in common with regular soldiers, cavaliers and dragoons, in third class accommodation. Assessment of length of service for the award of pensions, or honours like the *Croix de St Louis*, was made by simply adding years of service in the *maréchaussée* to years of service in the regular army.

The first major shot in the campaign to improve discipline was fired, as we have seen, by the decision to lengthen the period of preliminary military service required of all ranks. This was supplemented in 1778 by changes in the structure of the force which reduced the autonomy of the brigades and emphasised the hierarchical chain of command so characteristic of the army. Since 1720 there had been too big a gap between the higher ranks – officers and gentlemen who continued to buy their posts – and the brigade commanders and the men, for whom venality was henceforth abolished. At the top end of the scale, there was little differentiation between the *prévôts* and the lieutenants, who were expected to run their own show in their own departments. Until the Ordinance of 1778 specifically spelt out the lieutenant's subordination to the *prévôt*, conflicts of personality frequently arose. The more important problem of the potential lack of communication between lieutenant and brigades was exacerbated by the 1720 system of scattering brigades across the countryside. Whatever the disadvantages of the old system, it had at least had the advantage of keeping officers and men in close contact. After 1720, supervision of the brigades' activities was the responsibility of the lieutenant, but the great majority of brigades saw very little of him, for with all his duties as an officer of the *prévôtal* court, he could not afford the time and expense of constant or even regular tours of inspection. The Ordinance of 1778 attempted to remedy the situation in two ways: firstly by improving the status of individual brigade commanders, filling the post with better paid, more responsible men through the use of the higher

65. Ordinance of 17 Mar. 1720, art. 11.

grades – *brigadier, exempt*, plus the additional one of *maréchal des logis*; secondly by creating the post of *sous-lieutenant* to relieve the lieutenant of routine supervisory duties, and to ginger even the most isolated brigades into more efficient service.[66]

The efficacy of this closer supervision had already been promoted by Choiseul when in 1770 he made barrack accommodation compulsory for all brigades of *maréchaussée*. This reform was seen as so important that de Montyon, the Auvergne intendant at the time, took the greatest pains to overcome the recalcitrance and suspicion of local municipal dignitaries, visiting parishes which his predecessors had not seen for thirty or forty years to find suitable buildings. A new building was constructed in Clermont, and in both Langeac and Riom, the barracks was established in one of the finest mansions of the town.[67]

In the Guyenne, however, it is clear that some of the advantages of the reform were vitiated by the inadequacies of the accommodation provided. Rents were higher, and many municipalities unwilling or unable to provide anything but the first ramshackle construction that came to hand. In Bordeaux itself, the 'privileges' of the town forbade the establishment of a police barracks, and so the *cavaliers* were lodged separately and allowed only to have a common stable.[68] In Castillonnès the brigade was crammed into half of the building, as the rest was crumbling to ruin, while in Nérac, the floor was periodically flooded by heavy rain.[69] The Langon *cavaliers* would have had good quarters, 'if there had been a well and latrines'. When the Bergerac brigade got their own place after their initial stay in the Hôtel de Ville, it turned out to be a hovel, with no courtyard, no well, the *brigadier* and *cavaliers* squashed into two small rooms, and a stable described as 'very unhealthy'. The Brantôme *cavaliers* stored the horses' fodder in an attic above their rooms, accessible through a trap door, a system which exposed the fodder to damp, and the men to fire risk. In the 1780s, the brigade watched the barracks steadily collapse about their ears – 'the walls are cracked, and the floors, windows and shutters rotten'. The *cavaliers* in Villeneuve d'Agenais crawled exhausted home from the policing of their 178 parishes to an underground hovel; the fact that the barracks was four feet below ground level 'has a great effect on the health of the brigade, especially of the commander, who lives in the unhealthiest part'. There were so many holes in the roof of the Blaye residence that the grain, fodder and furniture got wet in every shower of rain. 'The ruined fodder has undermined the horses' health, the water and draughts ruined the men's health'; the absence of a well obliged the *cavaliers*

66. Thus a *sous-lieutenant* was established in Bergerac in the Périgord, and Brioude in the Auvergne.
67. De Montyon to Choiseul, 1 Oct. 1770, A.D. P. de D. C 6203.
68. A. de G. Y^b 789.
69. *Etat des brigades*, A.D. Gir. C 4636.

to use the common well in the street (the main road to Paris), so that after a day riding across the countryside, they had to trudge several hundred yards loaded with buckets to collect water for all their needs: 'the water they are obliged to drink is polluted by dust and water from gutters and very often the children of the neighbourhood throw rubbish into it which doesn't fail to affect the *cavaliers*' health'.

The incarceration of policemen in barracks clearly had the effect of restricting their informal contacts with the community. The same process was further advanced by the posting of fewer and fewer *cavaliers* or *brigadiers* to the residence nearest their home parish. The incompleteness of the *contrôles de maréchaussée* do not make for categorical conclusions, but of the *cavaliers* whose birthplace is known, 32 were appointed to their home town in the Auvergne in the 1720s and 30s, only 8 in the 1770s and 80s. Guyenne *cavaliers* born in another province increased from 36 in the two early decades to 57 in the last two decades.

These changes were no doubt designed to restrict the unhealthy degree of intimacy which encouraged corruption and collusion and the combination of these measures with the greater militarisation of the force produced a more responsible and disciplined *maréchaussée*. The evidence can be found not only in the decline of the petty corruption which found its way to the court of the *Connétablie*, but also in the fact that police officers had to resort less and less frequently to the most severe disciplinary measure - expulsion from the ranks. The *maréchaussée*'s registers reveal that a total of 68 *cavaliers* from both companies - an average of 17 per decade - were dismissed between 1720 and 1760 for one form or other of 'knavery', incapacity or insubordination, compared to a total of 10 - only about 9 per decade - in the last thirty years of the ancien régime.

Not all of the changes, however, were unmixed blessings. There had been advantages in appointing recruits to their home district. *Cavaliers* who were local men, or who stayed in one brigade for a long time, were able to get to know their district. They got to hear about the activities of undesirable local residents, and to acquire a basic knowledge of the lie of the land, the highways and byways, the simple facts of geography which rescued them from an over-reliance on guides. Nor, as we shall now see, were the sort of changes being brought about in methods of operation likely to increase the sense of security felt by a population thus deprived of informal contact with the militarised police. It was by no means evident that a more disciplined police force would be a more efficient police force.

CHAPTER 3

The *maréchaussée* at work

Prévôts-généraux

It is difficult to see any relevance whatsoever in the years of military experience demanded of these men, for after their appointment they became
executive pen pushers, slaves to their paper-work. Operations in the field
were carried out, organised, and directed by their lieutenants. The *prévôts*
devoted their lives to administration, which meant in practice correspondence
on matters of finance – compiling claims for expenses on behalf of their
cavaliers, justifying them to higher authority, complaining when the money
was not forthcoming:

I must inform you that not one of my *cavaliers* has been paid for the days spent supervising road works. . . My company is on the point of collapse and in no state to do any
duties other than its routine patrols . . . particularly as it has been used for many years
to carry out special assignments for which it has not received the smallest gratuity.[1]

The *prévôt* of the Auvergne was equally obliged to devote his energies to
increasing the effectiveness of the force by trying to make it financially
viable, and like Barret de Ferrand, du Deffan resorted to emotional appeals
on behalf of 'those unfortunate *cavaliers* . . . who are in no state with their
pay to be able to afford these extraordinary expenses' and 'these unfortunate
cavaliers most of whom get into debt buying a horse . . . and who are wretched
thereafter for the rest of their lives'. Du Deffan had no illusions about the
nature of his rôle as *prévôt-général*: 'I am forced by the duties of my office
to make you these representations and paint for you the picture of my
company's poverty'.[2]

The *prévôt-général*, of course, did not spend all his time making charity
appeals. He maintained overall responsibility for the discipline and performance of his company, and while he left the details of day-to-day operations in the hands of the lieutenants, he could intervene to order the brigades
to devote their time and attention to a particular issue if special circumstances
demanded a change in priorities. When the Massiac brigade was ambushed
while escorting the tax collection to St Flour, and one of the *cavaliers* was
killed, du Deffan got his brigades to drop everything else, and 'make a

---

1. Letters from Barret de Ferrand to Silhouette, controller-general, 1759, A.D. Gir.
   C 2178.
2. Letter from du Deffan to Choiseul, 15 Nov. 1770, A. de G. X^F 4.

thorough search' for the killers. On the other hand, a particular activity could be dropped for a while, as when du Deffan took it upon himself to suspend all arrests of beggars after the 1770 harvest failure.[3]

On a rare occasion when the *prévôt-général* did attend to the precise details of an operation, it was because César Dauphin's integrity had been called into question. Rumour had it that the continued liberty of the Sieur Dubois de St Julien, eighteen years after a warrant for his arrest had been issued, was due to family connection with the *prévôt*. Four brigades were dispatched in two detachments. Tauves and the second Clermont brigade by day, the other Clermont brigade and Besse at 2 a.m., and they confirmed that St Julien had long since gone to live on his estate in the woods near the Limousin border, so that further moves were obviously pointless.[4] The intendant Trudaine denied ever having doubted Dauphin's integrity: 'I know that this sort of suspicion should not fall on a man like you', and to confirm the reputation of M. Dauphin, an appeal arrived the same month from the Limousin intendant asking for help in locating an almost unique eighteenth-century specimen of robber baron, de Chaleix and his cohort of gentlemen: 'I have heard it said that you have in the Auvergne a *prévôt-général* well able to follow your instructions on such occasions and others even more difficult'.[5]

Lieutenants

Despite the prestige of the *prévôt-général*'s title and his correspondence with government ministers, the linchpin of the *maréchaussée* was the lieutenant. He needed the imagination and breadth of conception to determine the character of law enforcement operations in an area the size of a modern department. He had much more contact with operations in the field than the *prévôt-général* and he carried also the greatest burden of the *prévôtal* court, the interrogation and sentencing of beggars, the long trudge through criminal investigations and trials. The creation of the post of *sous-lieutenant* in 1778 was in part a belated recognition of his excessive workload.

The workload, of course, to some extent depended on the individual lieutenant. The volume of *prévôtal* cases dealt with by various lieutenants differs considerably. Exemplary in this regard is the Périgueux Lieutenant Gigounoux de Verdon. The sheer volume of documentation which dates from his term of office between March 1763 and February 1784, the thoroughness of his investigations, the numbers of vagabonds and thieves who paraded before the lieutenant and his judicial officers, testify to the effort he made to bring law and order to the province.[6] Such was the 'multiplicity of cases continually

3. *Ibid.*
4. Correspondence between Dauphin and intendant, May 1732, A.D. P. de D. C 6177.
5. Intendant of Limoges to Trudaine, 9 May 1732, *ibid.* C 1523.
6. See below, chapter 4.

under investigation at the said court' that the Périgueux *prévôté* had to hire an extra clerk.[7] The lieutenant's enthusiasm for work even drove him to ask for competence to deal with offences which did not fall within *prévôtal* jurisdiction.[8] Above all, the reputation he built up in the province meant that people came to him to denounce a crime, and pay tribute to his reputation as a zealous scourge of evil-doers. He toured the province continuously, inspecting his brigades and receiving reports of crimes and criminals from Nontron to Domme.

The greatest single responsibility of the lieutenant outside the courtroom was not his attention to the details of daily patrols, but the organisation of 'special' operations to meet a particularly difficult situation. The contribution of the lieutenants of the *maréchaussée* to public order must be judged by the criteria they used to establish what constituted a dangerous situation and the efficiency with which the means to deal with it were put into effect.

The 'special circumstances' requiring the lieutenant's intervention were of four main types: alarm and despondency in a given area after a series of successful thefts; reports of a 'band' of brigands; a big public event, such as a major fair, where trouble could be expected as a matter of routine; and a threatened or real grain riot. All of these situations were dealt with in the same basic way – the grouping together of the scattered brigades to make a show of force – though the difference in circumstances in each case produced variations on the theme. It was again Gigounoux de Verdon who played the theme with greatest versatility – he was the most active and the most lauded of eighteenth-century lieutenants, and the range of his techniques provides a good illustration of what could and could not be accomplished by an eighteenth-century police officer.

The first sort of crisis situation arose in the Bergeracois in the winter of 1776, when within the space of two months, six burglaries were reported closely followed by two murders, including one in the market square of Bergerac itself. The police were told these were all the work of the notorious 'Anjou' and his band of accomplices; the only information the lieutenant had about Anjou was that he was known to travel under a range of disguises – as a blind man, as a monk, or as a woman.[9]

Verdon's first response was to adopt the same technique as his prey, so that two centuries before the antics of the New York police, the *cavaliers* of the *maréchaussée* were combing the Périgord in disguise. It was a technique however which could be employed only sparingly, as he had so few *cavaliers*

7. *Procès-verbal* by Dubois, *greffier*, and *prestation de serment* of M. Gaillard, the new *greffier*. 29 May 1769, A.D. Dord. B 608.
8. Letter from Bertin to Verdon, 7 May 1767, diplomatically indicating that the Declaration of 1731 made such a suggestion unthinkable, but reminding the lieutenant he could deal with 'ordinary cases' in their early stages, and then pass them on to other courts. *Ibid.* B 585.
9. Letter from Verdon to intendant, 6 Feb. 1777, A.D. Gir. C 2181.

at his disposal, they could easily be recognised, and were needed in uniform for other purposes. The lieutenant therefore relied on spies to do his basic detective work – the anonymous *mouches* [spies, informers] who crop up in all his reports. The *cavaliers* meanwhile made highly publicised patrols – through the countryside by day, through the streets of the town at night – for the purpose of being seen, to give the impression that something was being done, to allay public anxiety, to reassure *Périgourdins* that they could sleep soundly in their beds at night, protected by the *maréchaussée*. His reaction to a robbery in St Alvère two years later was precisely the same: 'I have sent several of my spies into the neighbourhood to find out who committed the crime; the *cavaliers* make frequent patrols to restore public tranquillity in the area'.[10] It was an intelligent exercise in public relations, depending on illusion, and on the moral authority of 'booted justice'. And if these methods did not work, Verdon let it be known that he was prepared to pay 'a small reward' for information.

The use of these relatively sophisticated manoeuvres, however, did not prevent the *maréchaussée* resorting to the *rafle*, its time-honoured, crude and usually ineffective device of piling up as many suspects as possible in the hope that at least one of them might provide some kind of lead. The ever-present vagrants would be hauled in to face the lieutenant, establish their antecedents and their alibis, and deny their association with the villain of the moment. Rumours that Anjou occasionally donned clerical disguise had the inevitable effect of directing police attention to the dubious characters who formed the ragged fringes of ecclesiastical society. Not just the obvious frauds like Brother Pomier, 'Frère de la Charité', *repris de justice* and former soldier who claimed to have met Anjou in a barn near Clérac and to have formed a brief association with him for the purpose of begging; but also the genuine ecclesiastical down-and-outs like Théophile or André Verdier, two of the wandering clerical poor who were, in these two cases, the victims of the abolition of the Jesuit order four years before.[11]

The clerical line of approach to Anjou proved unrewarding, but the Anjou band was reputed to be operating from the Forêt de Lanquais, just to the south of the Dordogne valley between Bergerac and Ste Foy, and the Ste Foy *cavaliers*, conscious of the lieutenant breathing down their necks, rushed to capture every unknown vagabond whose presence was reported. Anjou himself was finally caught six months later not by the *cavaliers*, but 'by means of my spies and the confidential agents whom I had sent to various places in the countryside'.[12] Anjou could not be implicated in any of the crimes which had led to his pursuit, but at least the public would sleep easier in their beds.

10. Letter from Verdon to intendant 7 Apr. 1779, *ibid*. C 2186.
11. *Interr.* (Mar. 1777), nat. St Estienne de Condé, 45, *sans profession*, A.D. Gir. C 2182.
12. Verdon to intendant, 22 June 1777 – *ibid*.

The calling together of brigades for an impressive foray across the province was not of course a new idea. It was in fact the system of the Lacarrières in the sixteenth and seventeenth centuries which the reforms of 1720 had intended to make obsolete. It was revived as early as the 1730s, by Dastier, lieutenant in the Haute-Auvergne, in the *grande chevauchée* of all the brigades of the Haute-Auvergne organised in March 1733 against an incursion of smugglers. The winter was still on the mountains when for nine days they galloped across the province – across the Cézallier to the north of Allanche, west as far as Cheylade and Bort.[13] Though no one was caught except the innkeepers and other accomplices known to have dealings with smugglers or give them shelter, *gabelous* 'disguised as smugglers' confirmed that the *maréchaussée's* activity 'had spread such terror in the whole country that the houses everywhere were closed to smugglers and the tocsin was rung when they appeared'.[14]

In 1733, the *maréchaussée* of the Auvergne were called in when the smugglers murdered a *gabelou*; in 1778 bandits appeared in the Sarladais, 'forced' the local population to buy their tobacco, and murdered three agents of the *Ferme* in Martel.[15] For Verdon it was an opportunity to employ his own particular version of Dastier's technique. He did not use all the brigades of the Périgord – Dastier's operation had come to an end when the intendant became worried by the fact that most of the province had been left to its own devices – but got 16 *cavaliers* together and split them into two detachments. One went south to Montignac and Sarlat, the others, under the *sous-lieutenant* Terme, along the main road towards Brive, while the lieutenant remained in Terrasson, on hand for reports coming in from his spies. His informants' reports, in fact, came to determine the course of events, as Verdon's strategy evolved into a simple matter of reacting with a show of strength wherever the spies thought bandits were to be found.[16] As they assured the lieutenant that 'suspicious-looking people' were arriving in the province from the Limousin for the fair at Beauregard, one of the two detachments was despatched for Beauregard at three in the morning. The other continued to patrol the Montignac area, with half the *cavaliers* in disguise. News of this development, a spy reported, had caused panic to two bandits who 'tried to sell their tobacco to those who wanted it for a song'. It was difficult to see these two smugglers as the Mandrins of the Périgord, but more serious news came of a band of 'ninety' brigands in the Souillac area, just across the

13. *P.-v.* by Dastier, *ibid.* C 1628 – cf. M. Juillard, 'Le brigandage et la contrebande en Haute-Auvergne au XVIIIe siècle', *Revue de la Haute-Auvergne*, (1937), 33–5.
14. Letter from intendant to *Fermiers généraux*, 1734, A.D. P. de D. C 6182.
15. *P.-v.* by Verdon 16 June – 1 July 1778, A.D. Gir. C 2186.
16. The lieutenant's report does not spell out in detail what his spies had to say, except for an agent in Terrasson who reported that 'many suspicious people appear every day in the place', a jeweller, for example, with several names and no merchandise. *P.-v.* 19 June, 7 p.m., *ibid.*

border in Quercy, and being led toward the Périgord by Troupel, a redoubtable escaped convict who had often been sentenced to be hanged. A *cavalier* in disguise was sent into enemy territory with another 'confidential agent'. His report, and word from spies scattered through the area, led the lieutenant in a fruitless pursuit all the way down the Dordogne, past Domme (where the smugglers were known to have passed because of a theft of corn), as far as St Cyprien. The chase was not abandoned till the lieutenant and his troop reached Lalinde, and the spies finally admitted that they had lost track of the smugglers. Dastier had arrested innkeepers whose participation in smuggling helped to make it such a thriving industry. Verdon caught no one with any smuggling connections.

It must be said that Verdon never enjoyed the luxury of a report pre-warning the police of the exact time of the burglary of a château by a gang of thieves. Only once were the *maréchaussée* in such a happy situation, and as the report mentioned the château de Duras, it was the responsibility of the Libourne lieutenant, Fauchey de la Combe. Despite the participation of several brigades of *cavaliers*, the operation was bungled, the thieves escaped from the trap which had been set, and the police itself lost a *cavalier*, shot dead by a local peasant who mistook him for a prowling thief.[17]

Verdon's reputation was undoubtedly helped by his avoidance of such fiascos, but also by the impression of efficiency he managed to convey by his reports, which were always laced with ambition and optimism: 'Despite the care I take day and night to have exact and thorough searches made in all the suspect places in these parts so as to have all the vagabonds and thieves arrested, I have not yet managed to clear the country of them entirely'.[18] Reports from the Agen Lieutenant de Sauveaud were similar in content to those coming from Périgueux but unprotected by the same ring of confidence. What intendant could trust in the efficiency of a lieutenant who wrote 'supposing that I manage to discover the criminals' hiding place' or who began a report by admitting that the operations therein described 'have not been as successful as I had hoped' ?[19] Gigounoux de Verdon always took action on the strength of secret reports, mysterious sources of information, and only once hinted at public concern, when *after* the capture of Anjou he noted that business activities had been disturbed by the brigand's activities (but would now presumably return to normal). Sauveaud began his reports intimating clearly that he had lost control of the situation. Part of his district, an area straddling the main Bordeaux–Toulouse road, was a prey to 'assemblies' of armed brigands, nocturnal disorders, and highway robberies, and he had had to be informed of the situation by his subordinate, Le Maître de

17. Documents relating to the case in A.D. Gir. 11B 9 (1772).
18. Letter from Verdon to intendant 17 Jan. 1779, *ibid*. C 2186. This self-conscious introduction was followed by news of a burglary in St Martin de Gardonne.
19. Letter from de Sauveaud to intendant, 28 Jan. 1779, *ibid*. C 2186.

Chancelée, *sous-lieutenant* in Marmande. Worse still, the maréchaussée had acted by public demand ['sur clameur publique']. Alternatively he would make it clear that the operation in question was part of a short-lived effort of the kind which always followed the publication of new legislation, in Sauveaud's case the Ordinance of 1778, *titre* III, article 25, which gave the lieutenants formal instructions to assemble brigades if necessary for public order;[20] Verdon on the other hand stressed the importance of his personal initiative, and never sought to give the impression that he was doing no more than what was expected of him by the regulations.

Sauveaud seems above all to have been more concerned with results than with public relations. He no sooner got his brigade together to deal with 'a dozen armed brigands' in the Gonteaud area between Tonneins and Marmande, than he disbanded them, for two suspects had been arrested, and this would have given the alert to their 'colleagues'. Verdon would certainly have continued to march his men up and march them down again in the hope of giving the populace the illusion of police protection, and with little thought to the apparent inconsistency in his preferred police techniques, for the patrols designed to reassure the public were bound to scare any real criminals he wanted into lying low. This must have been obvious from the reports of his spies, perpetually unable to pin down the villains who were their *raison d'être*. The concern to reassure the populace may well have been the right priority given the reasonable assumption that there *were* no dangerous criminals or large organised fearsome 'bands' masterminding the theft of every apron and sheet that went missing in the Périgord.

Having captured the two local residents who were his gang leaders, the Agen lieutenant prepared his next move carefully. He himself stayed on in Gonteaud in disguise for four or five days, gathering information from all over the area. He struck at 3 a.m. on 21 January (1779) with a three-pronged attack involving three brigades of *maréchaussée*, supplemented by 18 men of the Gonteaud *milice bourgeoise*, another 18 from Tonneins, and 24 from Fauillet. It was not perhaps a good idea to employ so many local people for an operation depending on secrecy and surprise – for two days the three detachments searched all the places of refuge the brigands were supposed to use, and found only 2 women 'belonging to the accused'. Sauveaud's success rate, however, was just as good as Verdon's, particularly when 3 more suspects – 2 of whom were branded V – were captured before the end of the month, this time with the aid of the *patrouille bourgeoise* from the town of Clérac. This success encouraged the modest lieutenant to hope that 'by ac-

20. The article ordered the lieutenants of the *maréchaussée* to 'go everywhere not only to record crimes and offences . . . but also to assemble the number of brigades they think they will need to put a stop to disorder and re-establish tranquillity, reporting immediately to the Commandant of the province, to the intendant and to the *prévôt-général*' – as worded by Lt de Sauveaud, *P.-v.* 13 Jan. 1779, *ibid.*

quiring information little by little I will deliver this district from the scourge upon it'. He was not prepared to do it, however, by the increasingly fashionable resorting to large-scale *chevauchées*. As his biggest problem of lawlessness was confined to one area, he solved it by a return to the principles of 1720, by creating a temporary brigade in Tonneins with *cavaliers* borrowed from other brigades, and himself in residence till it had time to get well established.[21]

It was good sense, however, to gather several brigades together when trouble could be expected – as at the November fair in Bergerac. With horse dealers, merchants, peddlers, pickpockets, vagabonds and beggars arriving from all over south-west France, the local brigade clearly needed assistance, even if it did leave the rest of the province temporarily defenceless. The *cavaliers* would parade up and down the streets, and do the rounds of *cabarets* and lodging-houses at midnight with unwonted officiousness. The Lieutenant liked to be present at these occasions, even if it was all fairly routine, and did not require of him the same degree of imagination which might be necessary in a grain disturbance.

There was a standard procedure for police reaction to the outbreak of a riot: 'act with caution if there is a large *attroupement*', but if only a few people were involved, 'threaten strongly to imprison them and brush them aside'. In other words, compromise, yield, when the opposition was strong; stand firm, take the offensive, when the opposition was weak. This was the usual technique in the *maréchaussée*'s eighteenth-century operations, and it was successfully applied by Gigounoux de Verdon when faced in 1773 by widespread grain disturbances in Bergerac and surrounding countryside.[22]

The year 1779 was a difficult one throughout the Guyenne.[23] The crisis had been brewing since the succession of frozen winters and summer hailstorms in the late 1760s, and the generally calamitous year of 1770. Thousands were reduced to begging in the Agenais; there were riots in Bordeaux. Hungry peasants poured into Marmande, and order was restored by the régiment de Médoc. In the Entre-Deux-Mers the Créon brigade had to face an armed mob of 6,000; the *brigadier* had all the available bread distributed at a derisory price. Verdon knew what to expect, therefore, when Biron warned that 'the town of Bergerac is threatened with disturbance by a revolt and a sedition similar to those which several other places in the province have already suffered'.[24]

It was a veritable council of war in Bergerac – the *jurats*, the *subdélégué*,

21. Letter from Sauveaud to intendant, 28 Jan. 1779, *ibid.*
22. Rumours of approaching trouble first reached Verdon at 9 p.m. on 21 May 1773, in a letter from M. de Biron, a Bordeaux *subdélégué;* it kept him occupied till 13 July. *P.-v.* A.D. Dord. B 648.
23. P. Caraman, 'La disette des grains et les émeutes populaires en 1773', *Revue Historique de Bordeaux*, III (1910), 297–319.
24. *P.-v.* 19 May, A.D. Dord. B 648.

the magistrates of the *sénéchaussée* – which called in the *maréchaussée* on 18 May after a series of threatening letters and rumours that the town would be put to fire and sword if wheat was not sold at three *livres* the *pognere*. On receipt of the summons, the lieutenant sent messengers through the night to Sarlat, Montignac, Belvès, Mussidan, even as far north as Brantôme and Thiviers; it was to be a sizeable police detachment which would descend on Bergerac.[25] In Bergerac itself, the *jurats* consulted with the 32 officers of the bourgeois militia, the clergy, and other 'principal inhabitants', who were asked for their cooperation in order to 'stifle this fire'; not relying solely on the moral persuasion of the *notables*, the authorities ordered the entire body of the bourgeois militia, over 300 men, to turn out for the next grain market, on the 22nd. After the arrival of the 22 *cavaliers* of the *maréchaussée*, a neat demarcation of responsibility was established. The militia manned five permanent guard-houses – three near the warehouses of the town's biggest grain merchants, a fourth at the corn market, and a fifth in the Place Malbec. The *maréchaussée* complemented these fixed posts with mobile patrols through the streets, keeping an eye open for any *attroupement*, disarming the people of iron bars, daggers, scythes, hatchets, billhooks and firearms.

This show of force did not prevent people gaining the first victory when after a morning of haggling at the grain market, the *consuls* came down from the 5L. and a few *sous* they wanted to charge for a *pognere* to the 3L. which, the populace alleged, had been the price fixed by the king in Bordeaux. The police lieutenant had become increasingly involved in the bargaining, if only because cries were heard of 'Boure, boure' [patois for 'strike']. According to his own account Verdon shouted back 'Patience, I will give you justice', to be rewarded with popular confidence: 'Let M. de Verdon see to it, he'll bring these thieves of grain merchants to their senses'. Threats to hang these merchants redoubled on all sides, and in the midst of the anger, the lieutenant enacted a touching scene. A pregnant woman took his hand in hers, and with tears in her eyes, said 'M. de Verdon, help me, help me, for me, my husband, my three little children will starve to death if you don't get us corn. I'll stab myself before your very eyes'. He offered to lend her money, but was still unwilling to agree to a price of 3L. for the grain merchants would be ruined, and so would let the people starve. A strange dialogue developed between a police lieutenant who was torn between the demands of law and order, the protection of constituted authority, the rights of the grain merchants, and a humane desire to relieve the starving population and the people of Bergerac who with one voice ('everyone shouted', 'the populace replied') demanded

25. Verdon's *procès-verbal*, written from day-to-day like a diary, is the fullest account of the episode, though much of it overlaps with the version of the Bergerac municipal authorities published in G. Charrier (ed.), *Les Jurades de la ville de Bergerac*, vol. 12 (Bergerac 1900), pp. 382–97. The relevant entry is headed 8 May 1773, a misprint for 18, as the text makes clear.

grain at three *livres*, and threatened to 'couteler' [local word for stab]. It was a tense confrontation, and the collective nerve of the authorities, 'forced to give way to violence', was the first to crack.

Later the same day, with the judicious use of a little more violence, the people won another round when they laid siege to the grain store of the Sr Gimet, who had himself barely escaped their clutches for the loss of his wig. When the lieutenant arrived on the scene, 'the whole populace cried out "God bless you, you're just in time. I hope you'll give us justice"'. In this act, the chorus threatened to pillage, burn and murder, while Verdon harangued them on his concepts of social justice: 'in this world, everyone has to have his own, the rich as well as the poor', and although Gimet had robbed the poor, 'according to the laws, it is unjust to rob a thief'. The verbal persuasion was cynically accompanied by a crude attempt to buy off one of the ring-leaders – one of the most angry women was taken aside and offered as much as she wanted for free. She turned down the deal, and the authorities agreed to sell off cheaply Gimet's entire stock. Their weakness was only underlined later in the afternoon when the crowd stopped a boat loaded with grain coming up the Dordogne. By the time the *maréchaussée* arrived, the grain had been distributed, and all was peace and quiet.

The authorities had one more day of real anxiety, Sunday, 23 May, for on hearing of the town's success in acquiring cheap grain, peasants moved in, and a crowd of 2,000 gathered in front of the Hôtel de Ville, less numerous than the day before but more dangerous since it was entirely composed of men from the countryside armed with sticks. Still conscious of its weakness, the municipality agreed to sell off most of the grain which remained in the town, that of the Sr Lespinasse, for virtually the same prices as the day before – wheat for 3L. 10s. the *pognere*, rye for 2L. and maize for 1L. 10s. The maréchaussée only took the offensive when the crowd dwindled to a size which could be confronted with some hope of success; when a small crowd tried to break in to the store of the grain merchant Bertier on Sunday afternoon, the lieutenant led a mounted charge of *cavaliers*, flashing his sabre, shouting to his men that all prisoners would be hanged. For the first time, the forces of law and order were left in possession of the battlefield, and only three *cavaliers* were injured, compared with forty of the enemy. It was a turning point, for as the peasants left that evening, they vowed to return and put the town to fire and sword. The townspeople were naturally led to reflect that they had not starved, and that so far they had all fared rather better in the town than in the country. Urban community spirit grew with the realisation that urban privilege would have to be defended.

On the 24th, the *maréchaussée* switched their patrols from the streets of Bergerac to the roads leading to Monbazillac. The town council instructed all shopkeepers to sell no powder, lead, or bullets to peasants; no innkeeper was to lodge a peasant or serve him with any kind of food or drink. All

'notable inhabitants' were instructed to report to the Hôtel de Ville, guards
were posted on the bridges across the Dordogne to search all peasants and
confiscate their sticks. The bourgeois militia even asked Verdon to take over
the command, in the best interests of coordinating the defence of the town.
The authorities could now control the situation in Bergerac precisely because of the danger from the countryside. The *jurats* noted a new disposition
on the part of their fellow citizens to cooperate, and the *consuls* encouraged
this attitude by deciding to distribute the little grain that was left to residents
of Bergerac, and to 'send back those who lived in the country'. Lieutenant
Verdon sent for the remaining *cavaliers* in Périgueux, Sarlat, Mussidan,
Montignac and Belvès, and used the *cavaliers* he already had to patrol outside
Bergerac, in the suburbs and across the plain of the Dordogne and up the hill
to Monbazillac, with orders to 'go through the very pockets of peasant men
and women, who were rumoured to be carrying inflammable material to burn
down the town'. When the lieutenant was interrupted at lunch by a peasant
from Mouleydier asking him to open the granaries in these rural parishes,
Verdon, who had not scrupled to haggle over the price of grain in Bergerac,
replied that grain supply and price fixing were none of the *maréchaussée*'s
business, and had the peasant expelled from Bergerac with the warning that
he deserved to be hanged.

To make the lesson quite clear, the lieutenant put an end to an
attroupement of Bergeracois in the Place Malbec after lunch, and further
strengthened his position by a ruthless exploitation of the fear which peasant
savagery could still arouse in the town. It was a remarkable piece of demagogy.
News had just come, he told the crowd, that peasants were massing in the
countryside near Lalinde, preparing to march on Bergerac, where no doubt
they would rob, murder, burn and pillage 'the poor as well as the rich'. For
the rest of their lives, the Bergeracois would bear the shame of having caused
the tragic deaths of their mothers and fathers, wives and children, 'since these
peasants had no reasoning faculty'. However if they helped the lieutenant,
instead of causing him trouble, he would forget the past; together they would
repulse the rural 'scum'. Lieutenant Verdon would protect the townspeople from arson and pillage, and he was sure there would be grain for
them, having just sent a *cavalier* to intercede with the intendant. To cap
Verdon's triumph an apprentice shoemaker, an ex-grenadier, cried out:
'Long live M. de Verdon! Leave it to him, I know him, I saw him in the war.
I know he doesn't give a f . . . for taking risks, let's believe him, let's follow
him, and he won't abandon us. We don't give a f . . . for this scum from the
country who'd carry off our food and burn down our houses'. These sentiments were received with general acclaim.

The new alliance between the *maréchaussée* and the populace was sealed
a few hours later when some grain appeared which the merchants and the
authorities were prepared to sell at 4L. 10s. A few troublemakers in the crowd

wanted it for 4L., till Verdon returned to the Place Malbec 'and in a raucous voice asked who were the ones who were making fun of me'. The crowd shouted back that it was only a few 'f. . . knaves' who would be promptly thrown in the Dordogne. To keep the confidence of the crowd the lieutenant left no Machiavellian stone unturned, and had two 'strangers' arrested, one peasant from the Quercy and another from the Limousin. He threatened to hang them as vagabonds if no one in Bergerac would vouch for them. One man spoke up, having known them when he was a stevedore in Bordeaux, 'and asked me for a reprieve, which I had every intention of granting', Verdon commented, 'in order to win their confidence'. The day ended peacefully, the joint patrols of the *maréchaussée* and bourgeois militia having confiscated 6,509 clubs.

On the morning of the 25th, news came that six or seven hundred sacks of corn destined for Bergerac were held up on the quayside at Mouleydier and Couze, a few miles downstream. The peasants in the area were themselves hungry, but the authorities were concerned only about the welfare of the town, and the trust between the police and the townspeople was such that the detachment sent to escort the grain to Bergerac was composed of 12 'principal inhabitants' of the town, 64 artisans, and only 4 *cavaliers*. The mission was successfully accomplished, apart from a few sacks which the people of Mouleydier managed to hold on to for themselves. In Bergerac itself on the 25th, there were only a few murmurs of discontent, mostly in the suburb of La Magdeleine. Ever resourceful, Verdon dealt with the situation by distracting the people's minds from their stomachs. He got the *maréchaussée* to put on a show 'to entertain the populace' with fife and drums, and laurel branches on their hats. The performance ended with the *cavaliers* singing in chorus 'We bring you corn'. At this climax, 'everyone began to shout "Long live M. de Verdon, long live M. de Verdon".'

On the 26th, the people of Bergerac were treated to the extraordinary spectacle of the lieutenant of the *maréchaussée* making his patrols round the town accompanied by hired musicians on horseback playing 'rigadoons, reveilles and rondos'. The police unfortunately could not provide dance music for the whole canton, and so to quieten rural discontent, the lieutenant sent messengers to spread the word that if grain was still stored in the province, he would have the granaries opened and the grain distributed to the people. 'I made use of this pretext to entertain the populace until I had munitions. . . and troops'.

The 27th brought new alarms from the countryside, reports of peasant unrest from the Lieutenant's spies in the villages: 'They would get themselves cut to pieces or hanged', the peasants were saying, 'and were no more averse to being killed than to starving. In that way, they would really have the bourgeois and the nobles, who would be forced to work their land for themselves'. In Bergerac itself the *maréchaussée* did not hesitate to imprison a butcher's boy for uttering 'words likely to incite sedition', a minor offence compared to the rioting and pillaging of the previous few days, and a sure sign that the *maréchaussée* were in control again. The lieutenant's concern now was the countryside, and his concern was redoubled when he heard that a peasant was buying flints, 'since in Bergerac the people are not accustomed to smoking'. He was so concerned by a report that fourteen parishes were to join up to come pillaging and looting that he overruled an order from the *prévôt-général* himself that one of the brigades in Bergerac transfer to Ste Foy.

Reports from the countryside were even more alarming on the 28th. Verdon was woken at 3 a.m. by the news that peasants on the south bank were planning to invade Bergerac later in the day, and if the bridge was closed, they would raze La Magdeleine to the ground, throw the debris in the river and sow grain where the houses had stood. The women, the lieutenant learned, were planning to skin Gimet alive, and put pieces of his skin on their rosaries; a peasant who had bought a pound of meat in Bergerac had gone home to the other side of the river, and told the neighbourhood that it was a piece of Gimet. It was still useful to keep the townspeople in their place, and so a woman said to have gone from village to village stirring up trouble, was arrested and dragged through the streets of Bergerac bound hand and foot. The forces of authority no longer needed to amuse; it sufficed to intimidate. At the pig market that day, the lieutenant made his obligatory speech, but made no tear-jerking appeal – he simply warned the crowd 'in vulgar dialect' that anyone who formed an *attroupement*, women included, would be hanged. The army had arrived in Bergerac on the 28th, a small detachment from the régiment de Vexin, closely followed in the early hours of the 29th by the complete cavalry companies of the régiment de Condé. The grain market on the 29th passed off with no incident more noteworthy than another spectacular arrest, a woman dragged off to prison 'with all the honours of warfare'.

It was now all over bar the trial of the small band of men and women arrested during the week's disturbances.[26] On the streets of Bergerac, however, and down the country lanes all round the town, the *maréchaussée* continued to patrol for another month and a half. Wherever the peasants continued to 'murmur' *cavaliers* appeared 'to calm and flatter these people by giving them hope'. Units of the regular army continued to come and go – the Vexin and Condé companies were replaced by the Dauphin regiment of dragoons, the bulk of which left in June, but four companies were left on indefinite garrison. At last the bourgeois militia was able to go home after being on permanent call since 22 May; 'ignoring the exemptions conferred by nobility, military service, or position (the magistrature, for example), they all tried to outdo each other in the help which depended on them'.

26. They were in fact released 'provisionally' without trial, after the initial interrogation.

Any remaining fears for law and order were dispelled on 31 May when the grain which the intendant had procured for the town and sent upriver from Bordeaux arrived in Bergerac – 1,400 bushels of wheat and rye.

The postscript to the tale was written two years later, when the lieutenant was informed by letter from his *sous-brigadier* in Bergerac that according to the *Premier Consul*, Gimet the grain merchant had been warned by a servant that she had heard that the following Saturday, 'there would be a fiercer revolt than in 1773'.[27] Gigounoux de Verdon liked to think he had his ear close to the ground and took this fourth-hand information seriously. The *sous-brigadier* from Belvès, a *cavalier* from Thiviers, and three *cavaliers* from Mussidan were ordered to Bergerac; Verdon himself left Périgueux with three *cavaliers* on a tour of the Bergeracois – La Monzie, Mondidier, St Caprèze and Lalinde – before arriving in Bergerac itself in time for the grain market on 10 May 1775. With his usual thoroughness, he sounded out opinion from his habitually nebulous *confidantes*: 'one of my spies', 'a trustworthy person', 'a bourgeois', 'a person of distinction', all of whom had heard someone on the marketplace declaiming against the price of grain and proposing that the women form an *attroupement* against the grain merchants. None of the lieutenant's sources of information was able to reveal the identity of the rebels, or who was spreading the rumours. There was no shortage of corn, and the market passed off quietly.

Apart from Dastier's operation against smugglers in the 1730s, itself a deviation from the routine tasks of the *maréchaussée*, the gathering together of brigades for a *'chevauchée'* was very much a phenomenon of the 1760s and 1770s. In other words the contribution of the lieutenant to police operations went in the same direction as the contemporaneous structural reforms within the force: the fact that *cavaliers* were sent off to chase brigands or grain rebels at the other end of the province inevitably meant less contact between the community and the local brigade on its regular 'beat'. The sophisticated manoeuvres of the lieutenants had been extremely useful in a short-term situation, but they do not detract from the essential rôle of the brigades in the maintenance of law and order in every parish, every day of the year.

The brigades: location and patrols

The numerical weakness of the *maréchaussée* made it imperative that economical use be made of the policemen the institution could afford to employ. It was a matter of particular importance to station the small and scattered brigades where they would be most effective, but there was room for considerable disagreement on the priorities which had to be established for the best utilisation of scarce resources. The stated preference of Le Blanc,

27. *P.-v.* 4 June 1775 A.D. Dord. B 668.

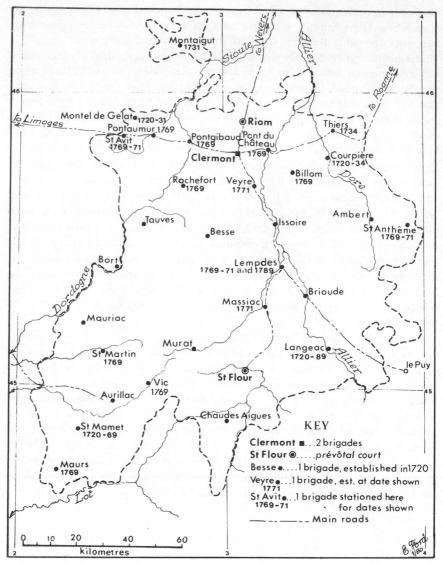

Map 2. The *maréchaussée* of the Auvergne in the eighteenth century

the creator of the new *maréchaussée*, for a concentration of brigades in areas
where the mountainous terrain made life particularly dangerous,[28] should
have benefited the Auvergne where the inhabitants were so 'hard and brutal'

28. Letter from Le Blanc to Boucher, intendant, 18 Sept. 1719, A.D. P. de D. C 6173.

that 'it would be both unwise and dangerous for a brigade to intervene in order to put a stop to their ferocity'; one-third of all the crimes tried by the *Parlement* of Paris were committed by Auvergnats, driven by 'the necessities of subsistence' to 'contempt for danger and the habit of crime'.[29] But there was no concentration of police strength in the Auvergne. Nor was the criterion taken seriously within the Auvergne. While brigades down on the plain of the Limagne were no more than three-hours ride from each other, up in the hills La Chaise-Dieu was left to its fate, surrounded by hostile forests full of thieves, apparently, who descended on the town at night to break into shops and carry off livestock.[30]

As far as the disgruntled inhabitants of this 'poor abandoned country' could see, the chief priority for the establishment of a brigade of *maréchaussée* was seigneurial intervention. The abbé seigneur of La Chaise-Dieu, the Cardinal de Rohan, was clearly above pulling strings for one of his remote *seigneuries*. In fact other requests were made for brigades and turned down, even when Mme la Marquise de Broglie intervened on behalf of St Amant. The area had no shortage of thieves or 'rapscallions', the intendant agreed, but it was not on the main road, 'where it is essential to obtain security'.[31] Priority was given not to the areas of greatest lawlessness, but to towns on the main road, the road used by troops, the road 'where public coaches and messengers pass'.[32] 'I applied myself to protecting the main roads by preference', de Montyon confirmed,[33] and the town of Maurs was granted a brigade not because of the swarm of 'rapscallions', who were common in every Auvergnat locality, but because it was on the main road from the south to Aurillac, an 'overnight resting-place for troops'.[34] The 1769 reform established new brigades on all the important routes across the province: Billom and St Anthème on the road to Lyon; St Avit and Pontgibaud on the road to Limoges; St Martin and Rochefort on the road to Aurillac; Vic, half way between Aurillac and St Flour; Pont-du-Château, the strategic crossing of the Allier on all roads east from Clermont; and Lempdes, the junction of the roads to the capital from Le Puy and from the Haute-Auvergne.[35] The *prévôt-général* was happy with the government's priorities as the improvement in road communications brought about by *corvée* would add to police problems in the area, he felt, by increasing the number of strangers passing through.[36]

The main roads of course were essentially the lines of communication be-

29. Letters from de Montyon to Choiseul 23 Jan. 1768, and 10 Feb. 1768, *ibid.* C 6188.
30. Petition from inhabitants of La Chaise-Dieu to intendant, 1778, *ibid.* C 6190.
31. Correspondence between the Marquise de Broglie and the intendant, 1768, *ibid.* C 6188.
32. Letter from Le Blanc to intendant, 16 Sept. 1719, *ibid.* C 6173.
33. Letter from intendant to *prévôt-général*, 1768, *ibid.* C 6188.
34. *Etat des emplacements des nouvelles brigades,* 1768, *ibid.*
35. Letters from Choiseul to intendant 9 July 1768 and 17 Dec. 1769, *ibid.*
36. Letter from Dauphin to intendant 1768, *ibid.*

tween major towns, the large centres of population, the sites of important fairs and markets, and all the principal towns of the province had their brigade of *maréchaussée*. Riom and Clermont had three between them despite their close proximity. The only exception in the company founded in 1720 was Thiers, which was passed over in favour of Courpière. The anomaly was corrected after a well-argued submission from Trudaine, who overwhelmed the minister with a barrage of every conceivable criterion: Courpière was an insignificant little town of less than 3,000 inhabitants, Thiers was one of the most populous in the province with over 18,000; Courpière saw little traffic as it was on no main road, Thiers was on the direct road from Clermont to Lyon; and from a convincing new angle, he argued that the *maréchaussée* in Thiers would be useful to contain the mutinous workers at the paper factory, who threatened to ruin the enterprise by going on strike just when they were most needed.[37] The transference of a brigade from Montel-de-Gelat to Montaigut in 1731 was solely on the grounds that the latter town was larger, on a road used by troops and served by a regular postal service; in every other respect Montel-de-Gelat was the rational choice for a residence of *maréchaussée*: it was a centre of the smuggling industry, and much more centrally placed to cover the north-east corner of the *généralité*, and police the numerous fairs and markets at Herment, Giat and Pontaumur.

Before 1731 the Montaigut area had been happily served by the brigade in Pionsat, which belonged to the Moulins company, but such inter-*généralité* cooperation was undertaken with the greatest reluctance. The one area which cried out for, and was denied, a brigade was around Bort, where geography made nonsense of administrative boundaries. The town of Bort was in the Limousin, but only existed as the commercial centre of the Auvergnat cantons of Champs, Tauves, Latour and Condat, and the *subdélégué* was responsible to the intendant of the Auvergne. It was the intendant of the Limousin, Turgot, who raised the problem of law and order in the area after receiving complaints about the frequent disorders caused by the antipathy between Auvergnats and Limousins. The lack of a brigade of *maréchaussée*, which the Limousin was reluctant to provide as it would be of most use to the Auvergne while the Auvergne was unwilling to deploy its scant resources on foreign soil, gave full rein to the local 'ferocity': 'what makes violence of every kind and even murder so much more frequent is that they are almost certain of impunity'.[38]

As the treatment of Montel-de-Gelat had shown the policing of fairs and markets took second place to the protection of travellers on the main roads. When Choiseul established criteria for the 1768/9 increase, main roads had

37. Letter from Trudaine to d'Angervilliers, 15 Sept. 1734, *ibid.* C 6182.
38. Letter from Turgot to Ballainvilliers, 8 Jan. 1762, *ibid.* C 6187. The Limoges company eventually established a residence in Bort which undertook patrols in the Auvergne cantons.

a triple significance: for the capture of deserters, the safety of travellers, and the transport of the tax receipts. Only when this criterion had been met could attention be given to the other justifications for a brigade's existence, such as keeping the peace on market day or providing assistance for local court officials.[39] Through the complicated manoeuvres of suppressions, restorations and establishments in the 1770s and 1780s, however, a new criterion began to emerge - a tendency to encourage concentration of strength. As early as 1771, the 1769 map of brigade residences was redrawn: St Avit and St Anthême, both on main roads at opposite ends of the province, but both almost on the boundary of the *généralité* (with the Limousin and the Forez) lost their brigades to towns equally strategically placed but much more central - Veyre, the first town of any size on the main road south from Clermont, and Massiac, at the junction of the roads to Clermont from St Flour and Aurillac. The purpose of this development was to station *cavaliers* in locations which would facilitate the assembling of brigades in cases of emergency.[40] This change in the reasoning behind the choice of *résidences* foreshadowed and facilitated a basic shift in the whole pattern of police operations in the last decades of the ancien régime, as the hopes engendered by the 1720 dispersal of brigades looked increasingly frayed, and the search for strength in numbers, continuously frustrated by the government's refusal to make more appointments, was driven back to bringing brigades together.

It was a trend which was also becoming apparent in the Guyenne. Even in 1720 there had been a concentration of resources in the central department of the Bordelais, given nine brigades compared with the five left in the Agenais and the Périgord. But at this stage there was still a desire to 'cover' the entire province with the police blanket, and brigades were scattered to all corners of the *généralité*, from Nontron in the far north, to Biscarrosse on the far south coast, or Lesparre at the very tip of the Médoc peninsula. The ambition of covering the edges left some awkward gaps in the middle - there was, for example, no brigade in Libourne, on a strategic point at the confluence of the Isle and the Dordogne, and astride the main road from Bordeaux to Périgueux and Limoges; there was no brigade in Bergerac, one of the principal towns of the Périgord, and no brigade in Villeneuve, the second town of the Agenais, and in its geographical centre.

All the increases and adjustments after 1720 tended to make for concentration rather than dispersal. By 1733 the Biscarrosse brigade had moved to become the second brigade in Bordeaux itself. Libourne and Villeneuve got their brigades in 1769, Bergerac a year later. Also in 1770 the Nontron brigade was brought south to Thiviers, on the main Périgueux-Limoges road,

---

39. Letter from Choiseul to de Montyon, 26 Dec. 1767, *ibid*. C 6188.
40. Letter from de Montyon to Choiseul, 1768, *ibid*. 'In general I have taken care to adjust the distances between brigades as far as the situation permitted in the interests of assembling several brigades'.

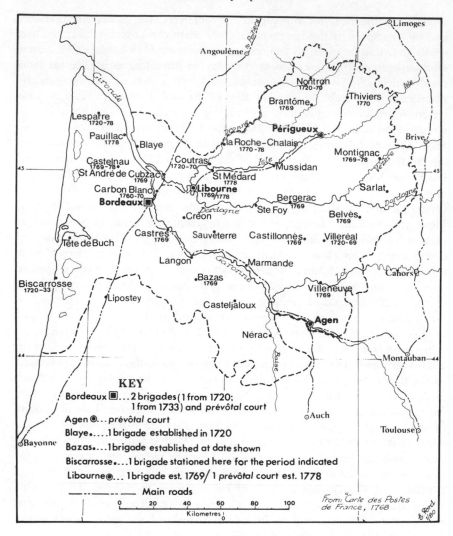

Map 3. The *maréchaussée* of the Guyenne in the eighteenth century

while in 1778 the Lesparre brigade was brought down to Pauillac – 'a very suspect place' where the *maréchaussée* could also keep watch on the Gironde in wartime. The 1769 increases were concentrated in the Bordeaux area, and when new brigades in Castelnau, Bazas, Castres, Libourne and St André de Cubzac were added to the existing ones in Langon, Créon, Sauveterre and Blaye, the circle of surveillance over every possible approach to the city was complete. In the decade after the climactic struggles with the *jurats*, these changes were perhaps a tacit recognition of their case, that the real strength of the *maréchaussée* should be located 'on the approaches to the town', an argument the *maréchaussée* recognised even more fully by transferring (even if temporarily) one of the Bordeaux brigades to Carbonblanc, a bottleneck on the principal avenue to Bordeaux. The establishment in 1778 of a *lieutenance* and a *prévôtal* court in Libourne, despite the rival claims of Sarlat, was just another contribution to the concentration of strength in the immediate hinterland of Bordeaux.

The protection of road communication was, as in the Auvergne, a constant priority when allocated brigades. It was the only possible rationale behind the retention, throughout the century, of a brigade in Lipostey, a virtually non-existent village in the Landes on the road from Bordeaux to Bayonne. The defence of the main road from Bordeaux to Périgueux was the only excuse for the transfer of the brigade in La Roche-Chalais to St Médard; in St Médard the brigade was better able to protect the transfer of tax receipts, but the *cavaliers* had to put up with disgraceful accommodation, a lack of all the necessary amenities and go to Coutras to buy their provisions or have their horses shod.[41]

St Médard did seem to have a better claim to the *maréchaussée*'s protection than La Tête de Buch, a fishing village on the Arcachon basin. It was squeezed between the sea and the Landes, still in the eighteenth century a desolation of moor and marshland populated by a few itinerant shepherds, and the brigade had to look after only thirteen parishes, which managed to organise an annual tally of thirteen markets and thirteen local fêtes.[42] By the time room had been made for such eccentric establishments, and for highway patrols, and for the ring of steel round the city of Bordeaux, it was too late to try to standardise the districts individual brigades had to supervise. The numerical disadvantage suffered by the two inland *lieutenances*, which grew comparatively worse as the century progressed, left the Périgourdin and Agenais brigades with enormous areas of responsibility. Unlike most of the brigades of the Bordelais which jostled shoulder to shoulder on the outskirts of the city, the brigades in Périgueux and Agen were employed by their duties at the *prévôtal* court as well as providing assistance to the other royal courts and the routine escorts and patrols on the main roads - Périgueux on the Limoges-Bordeaux route, Agen on the even busier highway between Bordeaux and Toulouse - yet the Périgueux brigade was responsible for the enforcement of law and order in 122 parishes, which mounted 160 fairs, 250 markets and 122 fêtes. The Agen *cavaliers* had an even more immense district encompassing 168 parishes, with 250 fairs, 291 markets and 230 fêtes.[43] In 1778 the brigade in Montignac was dispensed with and its work-

41. 1778 Reform, Guyenne - A. de G. X^F 4; and *Tableau des brigades* drawn up for Boutin, intendant in the 1780s, A.D. Gir. C 4636.
42. *Tableau des brigades* drawn up for Bordeaux intendant in 1780s, A.D. Gir. C 4636.
43. *Ibid.*

load was added to the burdens of Périgueux, and to a brigade in Sarlat already 'overworked' by its court duties and its hundred parishes. The most the *prévôt* could bring himself to admit was that the brigade in Belvès with 88 parishes, was 'one of the least tired'; only one brigade in the Périgord, Thiviers, had less than 80. Brantôme, 'ceaselessly occupied by the escort of tax receipts to Angoulême', which took up to four days a week, had to find time to attend 182 fairs – 'the most tumultuous in the province' – and no less than 311 markets. In the Agenais only one brigade, Castillonnès, had less than 100 parishes. The Nérac brigade, 'tired out by the requisitions of the *procureur du roi* in Condom and other legal officials', who were inconveniently based twenty-one kilometres away, was responsible for the surveillance of 198 parishes, and in the course of a single year, for keeping order at 225 fêtes, 262 fairs, and 332 markets.

These were the enormous areas which the *cavaliers* were required to keep under permanent surveillance 'in the most essential part of their services'[44] – the regular patrols round the district. The *cavaliers* were supposed to do fifteen patrols a month, taking them two to three leagues from their residence and spending five to six hours on horseback. To make sure that they did in fact progress round the district, they had to get the curés or other *notables* (usually *sindics* or seigneurial agents) to sign a certificate that the *cavaliers* had passed through the parish and properly carried out their duties. It was an unsatisfactory method of control from more than one point of view. *Cavaliers* often had difficulty finding someone on hand to sign their certificates, particularly when they were occupied patrolling the public highway; for one month the Brioude brigade sent in only four certificates, three of which had been signed by butchers, though the *subdélégué* knew 'that they have spent twenty-five days patrolling the countryside'; in the same month the *cavaliers* of the Tauves brigade had spent many days 'carrying out secret orders of the court', and were unable to cover their activities with the usual paper-work.[45] It was the most primitive kind of paper-work – a few lines scrawled on the first piece of paper which came to hand, and most of them have been lost, a good many, no doubt, by the *cavaliers* themselves. Practically none have survived from the period after the *maréchaussée*'s emancipation in 1734 from *subdélégué* surveillance of its day-to-day patrols. Without such surveillance the *cavaliers* had no difficulty manipulating the system if they did not simply ignore it. The Murat brigade had a stock of signed certificates to which the date could be added as required.[46] 'The Auvergne brigades

44. D'Angervilliers to Trudaine 12 Feb. 1733, in *Mémoire sur les maréchaussées*, A.D. P. de D. C 6192. The *maréchaussée*'s printed 'Journal de service' also stressed that the 'patrols in the parishes and on the highways are the first duty and the daily duty of this Troop'. (*Ibid*. C 6254.)
45. *Etat des courses* Apr. 1733, *ibid*. C 6219.
46. Correspondence between Murat *brigadier* and intendant, Aug. 1733, *ibid*. C 6221.

practically never left their residences although every month the commanders sent certificates for the rounds they were supposed to have done'.[47] Not that the *maréchaussée* always made extravagant claims. In May 1733, only seven brigades of the Auvergne company claimed to have made any patrols at all: St Mamet had done its regulation fifteen, Chaudesaigues almost managed, at twelve, but the Besse brigade had gone out on nine days of the month, Courpière and Aurillac on seven, St Flour on six, and Riom only one.[48] There was certainly no 'typical' month – the supposedly regular patrols of the *maréchaussée* were totally erratic. While the brigade of St Mamet did no patrols at all in July 1753, in August the *cavaliers* were on the road twenty-eight days out of thirty-one.

All the brigades had, officially at least, some kind of routine – for the Courpière brigade Monday meant the patrol to Billom; Wednesday, Cunlhat, and Domaize on the way home; Thursday, Thiers; Saturday, Lezoux. The Besse brigade spent every Monday and Thursday in the home town to be on hand at market. Fairs and fêtes imposed their own annual pattern. Many of these festive occasions avoided the worst months of winter: the Besse brigade, for example, had to attend seven fairs at Compains every year, between 25 May and 14 September.[49] Smugglers too preferred to move about in relatively clement conditions – the *cavaliers* of the Haute-Auvergne who were brought together for Dastier's operation in the early spring of 1733 were still taking time off routine patrols against smugglers who straggled through into August and September.[50] Even if no smugglers appeared on the scene the summer patrols were regularly disrupted by militia and *corvée* operations.

Even without seasonal distortions, the service provided by the *maréchaussée* in outlying parishes was effectively reduced by the habit of counting days spent at the market in the residence itself as the patrols forming part of their obligatory total of fifteen. The Besse brigade got away with performing a third of its service at home in this way. There was clearly not enough time left to cover the whole district, and the choice of route taken by the patrols naturally tended to reflect the same criteria that had been in operation at the establishment of the residence – keeping order at fairs, and patrolling main roads, particularly when they passed through dark and sinister woods.[51]

The *cavaliers* treading their weary way along the roads of France – this was the archetypal image of eighteenth-century policemen. If the *cavaliers* were not made nervous by the oppressive atmosphere and gloomy reputation of Périgourdin forests, the roads presented other difficulties to contend with. Outside the sparse network of principal highways linking the chief centres

47. Letter from d'Angervilliers to Trudaine, 12 Feb. 1733, *ibid*. C 6192.
48. *Etat des courses* May 1733, *ibid*. C 6219.
49. *Ibid*.
50. *Etat des courses*, Ambert, St Mamet, Murat, *ibid*. C 6221.
51. *Ibid*. C 6219.

of the kingdom, the condition of the road surface delayed or prevented patrols, and added considerably to the effort required of the police. To maintain any kind of surveillance over the province of Guyenne, for example, the *cavaliers* could not confine themselves to the track of reasonable surface which led from Paris through Bordeaux to Toulouse. The Agen brigade had the benefit of this road, but elsewhere in the Agenais, the tracks were 'broken up by ravines, washed away by waterfalls, interrupted by streams'; the streams had to be forded as there was a lack of bridges and all communications were interrupted by heavy rain.[52] In the Périgord, the sections of track which did exist only served to draw attention to the technical incompetence of their engineers, for as the Napoleonic *Annuaires statistiques de la Dordogne* pointed out, the roads did not attempt to negotiate hills with carefully managed curves, they heaved the traveller, or the *cavalier* of the *maréchaussée*, in a straight line to the summit.

Cavaliers in the Auvergne undoubtedly had a worse time, despite improvements brought about by eighteenth-century *corvée*. When Le Grand d'Aussy arrived for his tour round the province in 1787, he noted that 'the stranger who knew it only from the map of postal services would imagine it an uninhabited desert'.[53] There were two highways [*grandes routes*] – Clermont to Lyon, and the north–south route from Moulins to Clermont, and on to Brioude and Le Puy – supplemented by twelve 'interior roads' [*chemins intérieurs*], even the modern sections of which had, as in the Guyenne, such steep climbs and descents that in many places they were impassable. It was not until the last two or three years of the ancien régime that the administration of the *Ponts et Chaussées* gave up the struggle to maintain these roads. In the Haute-Auvergne it was decided to abandon the steep descent into Aurillac from the heights of the mountain to the north, and in 1787 work began on the 'detour' still in use through Lascanaux.[54] The lack of consideration for geography caused extraordinary difficulties of communication in the Basse-Auvergne, where the traveller was led across the frozen summits of the Margeride hills, and plunged abruptly down to the crossing of the Allier at Lavoute-Chilhac, and up again. The river which divides the province was 'an impetuous torrent liable to sudden floods, as the river often changes course' – but the three bridges and thirty-six ferries across it took no account of the bed of the river, they were thrown across wherever the straight line from point A to point B demanded it.[55]

52. *Cahier* of the Agenais nobility, in A. de Mondenard, *Les Cahiers de l'Agenais* (Villeneuve-sur-Lot 1889), p. 317.
53. Le Grand d'Aussy, *Voyage fait en 1787 et 1788, dans la cidevant Haute et Basse Auvergne*, 3 vols. (Paris, Imprimerie des Sciences et Arts, Ans II and III), vol. 3, p. 226.
54. F. Imberdis, 'Les routes de la Haute-Auvergne au 18e siècle', *Revue de la Haute-Auvergne* (1933), 24–5.
55. F. Imberdis, 'Bacs et ponts sur le cours auvergnat de l'Allier au XVIIIe siècle', *Revue de Géographie alpine* (1929), 611–36.

Commerce and communications in the whole of central France were periodically thrown into confusion by the sudden floods of the Allier, and throughout the Auvergne, the onset of spring brought melting snow, flooded streams, mud and delay.[56] Winter brought its own problems – the roads of the Haute-Auvergne were often blocked for weeks by the drifts of snow piled up by violent winds. The route north from Aurillac up the west side of the province to Mauriac was particularly vulnerable as it had to cut across the five valleys and ridges which lie from east to west. In the winter of 1786-7, *cavaliers* of the Haute-Auvergne came across a peasant who had frozen to death on the road; a deserter they were escorting to Clermont lost two fingers through frost bite, and the *cavaliers* themselves, though they went on foot to keep warm, 'were so frozen that they had difficulty reaching the next village'.[57]

The condition of the roads in the Mauriac district must certainly be taken into account when assessing the apparent failure of the *maréchaussée*, or any other authority, to bring a semblance of law and order to the area. The *brigadier* himself argued that it was impossible to negotiate the rock-strewn tracks up the hillsides in the dark, and so the brigade did not set off in pursuit of a murderer till 6 a.m., seven hours after the *subdélégué* had passed on a secret report from the judge in Trizac informing the *brigadier* where the villain could be found.[58]

Military, civil and municipal duties

Given the military character of the *maréchaussée*, its subjection to the Marshals of France, it was inevitable that the brigades would be used by the military hierarchy, at least in the Guyenne which in the eighteenth century still had a governor who was invariably a Marshal. The governor and his aides – the *commandant en chef* and the *lieutenant-général* – all had the right to call on the services of the *maréchaussée*, and in the eighteenth century were quite prepared to use it as a branch of the regular army if wartime conditions demanded it. *Cavaliers* of the *maréchaussée* were found useful running the military postal service which carried dispatches between the commanding officers and headquarters on the Atlantic coast during the Seven Years War. With an English invasion expected daily, and Richelieu on duty in the Saintonge, there had to be regular and dependable lines of communication between the governor and the fortress of Blaye.[59] The closest contact between the military and the *maréchaussée*, however, developed in the protracted efforts to disarm the civilian population.

This had become a major government objective immediately after the

56. *Mémoire*, (n.d.) A.D. P. de D. C 4638 and Poitrineau, *La vie rurale*, vol. 1, p. 685.
57. Story recounted to Le Grand d'Aussy by the *cavalier* who accompanied him in the Haute-Auvergne, *Voyage fait en 1787 et 1788*, vol. 2, p. 174.
58. Fontfreyde to intendant, Dec. 1761, A.D. P. de D. C 1536.
59. *Etat* of expenses 1760, A.D. Gir. C 2179.

death of Louis XIV, when in 1716 the Regent ordered a general disarmament to reduce the number of weapons which had fallen into civilian hands during the War of the Spanish Succession.[60] Like other piously optimistic legislation of the ancien régime, the Ordinance had to be repeated as early as 1719, under the name of the Marshal Berwick. It was the creation the following year of a national police force exercising some kind of permanent surveillance over the whole country that made possible a policy of general civilian disarmament. Such a policy sprang from a triple necessity. The demands of a peaceful, civilised society could not admit the law of the jungle, where each man trusted to himself to protect his own. Disarmed, the subject would be much less able to rebel against the authority of the government. And the disarming of all subjects except nobles and seigneurs would put a stop to popular encroachment on the privilege of hunting. Disarmament, in short, is only one indication we shall find of the class bias inherent in the rôle of the *maréchaussée* and of the identification of interest between the central government and the seigneurs.

There could be no doubt about the scale of the task to be undertaken. The *maréchaussée* was told to confiscate all kinds of equipment used in hunting – knives, nets, traps, even dogs – but for purposes of general security as well as for the suppression of poaching, most of the police efforts were directed against weapons: *fusils* (a term used to cover any kind of gun), pistols (both pocket and saddle), swords and sabres. The most dangerous were clearly the firearms, and the supply would not easily dry up so long as the regular army suffered a desertion haemorrhage of 20-25 per cent every year.[61] Any gun confiscated by the police could easily be replaced by soldiers anxious to dispose of a highly marketable but uncomfortably conspicuous commodity. Soldiers who left the army by more legal channels brought their weapons with them, and the corrupt guards of the king's arsenals all contributed to the supply of what was practically a free market in guns, pistols and swords.[62]

That the general edicts from Versailles ordering the confiscation of all these weapons did not remain a completely dead letter depended entirely on the zeal and enthusiasm of the local military command. The Auvergne sadly missed a provincial governor in this regard, while disarmament in the Guyenne was almost entirely a question of the governorship of the Marshal Duc de Richelieu from his appointment in 1758 till his loss of interest and influence on the death of Louis XV in 1774. Almost all the *maréchaussée*'s registers speak of weapons confiscated 'by order of the Marshal de Richelieu', but despite his use of the royal police force, it is probable that Richelieu himself was motivated more by the desire to protect the interests of the nobility

60. Ordinance of 14 July 1716, Corvisier, *L'armée française*, vol. 1, p. 69.
61. *Ibid.* vol. 2, p. 736.
62. *Ibid.* vol. 1, p. 68.

than to enhance the despotism of the central government. He complained that 'the tyranny of the cardinal de Richelieu [his great-uncle], the irascible character of Mazarin, the pride of Louis XIV, had abolished all free administration in the interior of our provinces',[63] while the population of the Guyenne was firmly reminded that the only people with an absolute right to bear arms of any kind were nobles.[64]

Despite his contempt for the Cardinal's tyranny, however, the Marshal was a worthy successor to a great-uncle who had done so much to destroy the military independence of the towns. The seventeenth-century Cardinal had razed to the ground fortifications and siege walls, like those of Bergerac, and established massive army garrisons in towns like Bordeaux to remind the populace of their loyalty to the central government. It only remained for the eighteenth-century Marshal to destroy the privilege, claimed by bourgeois throughout south-west France, of bearing arms. A deputation from the Périgueux municipality failed to persuade the governor that such a privilege was justified,[65] and repeated 'Ordinances of general disarmament' issued by the Marshal or his staff stipulated that all weapons in the towns of the Guyenne were to be deposited at the town hall, and transferred to a military garrison, like the Château du Ha or the Château La Force, for safe-keeping. After the 'general disarmament' of Bergerac in June 1767, the *subdélégue* organised the removal of the best weapons to the Château Laroque, leaving behind 221 rifles, 129 pistols, and 85 swords and hunting knives in poor condition.[66] This operation completed the 'rigorous disarmament' of the town started in 1758, and arms were sorely missed by the anxious citizens of Bergerac in 1773, as they waited from day to day for the onslaught from the hungry countryside.[67] In 1789, the panic-stricken municipality described Bergerac as a town 'open, defenceless and dismantled, assailed from all sides by more than twenty thousand armed men'.[68]

The Marshal de Richelieu was no more prepared to make exceptions for claimants – usually merchants, lawyers or royal officials – who pointed out that their fathers had been granted arms permits by his more accommodating predecessors. The very existence of special permits proved that there was no legal basis to their claim, and exceptions could only be considered when the general rule had been established. This was clearly not the case when Richelieu arrived in Bordeaux – 'it is essential to begin with the greatest possible severity in the application of the law'.[69] Seigneurs were to be allowed a

---

63. Maréchal de Richelieu, *Mémoires*, vol. 5 (Paris 1792), p. 171.
64. Richelieu's 'Ruling on Disarmament' – the *Règlement fait par Mgr le Maréchal duc de Richelieu sur le désarmement*, A.M. Pér FF 187.
65. *Règlement*, article on 'Les privilèges de la ville de Périgueux'.
66. Charrier (ed.), *Jurades de Bergerac*, vol. 12, pp. 340–2.
67. *Ibid*. p. 396 and below, ch. 7.
68. *Ibid*. p. 346: letter from municipality to Comte de Fumel, 22 Apr. 1789.
69. *Règlement*, article on 'gens vivant noblement'.

shotgun only on their estate, but the governor recognised that the nobility were 'extremely poor' and depended on their hunting rights to eat, and so granted arms permits to gamekeepers on condition that he was kept informed of their names. Wolves were still the scourge of many parts of the Guyenne in the eighteenth century, and provided prior permission was obtained, Richelieu allowed the distribution of guns for organised hunts. Wild animals, however, were not the only security problem faced by isolated country-houses, and the governor was prepared to grant an exceptional permit to an exceptional individual like M. Allieu, Master of Surgery, member of the Royal Academy of Surgeons, bourgeois of Bordeaux, resident in the parish of Baurech. Run-of-the-mill surgeons could not expect such indulgence, and no less than 88 of them, with 16 of their apprentices, had to hand over their weapons. Exceptions *were* made for those royal officials who were likely to be exposed to the violence of a vengeful population – the *collecteur* or the *sindic* responsible for the collection of the *taille*, for example, was allowed to protect himself with a gun during his year of office, just as court bailiffs were given the right to arm themselves during the exercise of their official functions.[70]

The Disarmament Ordinance issued by Richelieu's *commandant-en-chef*, de Beauvau, in 1766 suggested that a more liberal policy would be followed as it encouraged bailiffs, magistrates and lawyers to carry swords, pistols and hunting-knives for self-protection at all times outside the towns where they lived, and permitted travelling merchants, *laboureurs* and 'principal artisans' to arm themselves, but this recommendation made less impression on the *cavaliers* of the *maréchaussée* than the stricter injunctions of Richelieu himself; between 1758 and 1774, 21 bailiffs were deprived of weapons not being used for official business, while 24 notaries, 32 barristers, 6 local judges, 6 royal *procureurs* and numerous government officials in tobacco distribution, the postal service or manufacturing all fell foul of the disarming zeal shown for sixteen years by the governor and the *maréchaussée*. No allowance was made for the occupational hazards of carters, carriers and coachmen, and only once did the Marshal recognise the dangers faced by merchants when he issued a permit to carry pistols to two brothers, merchants in Ste Foy, who were to do the rounds of the province to collect outstanding debts. This indulgence was lost in the welter of the 252 merchants [107 *négociants* and 145 *marchands*] who were relieved of a hotch-potch of *fusils*, swords, pistols and knives. These commercial travellers constituted one of the *maréchaussée*'s most faithful category of customers and every branch of commerce shared in the common mistrust of police protection. They had come from all corners of France, from other European countries and from America before encountering the zeal of the Guyenne

70. Registers, A.D. Gir. C 3728.

maréchaussée. Artisans – principal or otherwise – were dealt with just as ruthlessly, whether they were lace-makers, blacksmiths or candlestick makers, or purveyors of any commodity from carpets to lemonade or wigs. With more than 600 disarmed peasants, and 200 disarmed vine-growers, it is clear that the possession of a weapon was too deep-seated in French society to be confined to the rich or the peripatetic. But while peasants and artisans caught with shotguns insisted the weapons were essential to guard the house at night, they did not need to add that guns were also useful by day, for poaching.

The *maréchaussée*'s onslaught on illicit weapons was largely interpreted by the majority of the population as an attempt to cut off a major supply of food. Three-quarters of all disarmament operations involved shotguns which could be used for hunting. The hatred of pre-Revolutionary peasants for seigneurial game monopolies has often been described, but in this age haunted by permanent fears of dearth, all sections of the community kept a weapon for a cheap provision of meat. Innkeepers, notoriously freethinking and disrespectful of Sunday drinking laws, could hardly be expected meekly to obey regulations which prevented them adding a cheap but meaty dish to the menu, or offering themselves the comfortable reassurance that they had at their disposal some means of defence against unruly customers, unwanted guests, and bawdy soldiers. Many servants and *commis* were also caught hunting, which seems, in fact, to have been one of their routine tasks. The respectable classes were usually disarmed of pistols, swords or knives, as they sent their servants out to hunt with a *fusil*.[71] Ecclesiastics were particularly partial to game – the disarmed servants included the valets of thirteen curés, two priors, the *Pères de la Mercy* in Bordeaux and the servant of the *Dames de la Visitation* in Agen. Poaching was an opportunity for the young to contribute to the family economy, and over 150 young men and boys (*'fils de'*) were disarmed by the police. Both the sons and the poaching adults came from every branch of commercial and industrial activity and every level of the rural hierarchy from *métayers* to estate managers. Only the destitute could not afford a weapon,[72] and although women could thieve and smuggle, and were by no means helpless in a brawl or a rebellion, they do not appear to have poached, and for their battles used weapons which the police could not confiscate – lime, sand and stones, or at close range, nails, teeth and feet.

The possession of a weapon was more than the means to procure a free meal or to ward off thieves. In an age when the wearing of a sword was the most undisputed and most obvious sign of social distinction, bearing

71. 58 innkeepers; 26 *commis*; 45 servants, 3 cooks, 132 valets.
72. Between 1758 and 1774, the Guyenne company disarmed no beggars or vagabonds, only one representative of the most menial or rural workers, the ditch-digger, and four of his urban counterparts, the *portefaix*.

arms was an important element in social pretension. It must therefore have been a profound humiliation for *gens vivant noblement*, for bourgeois and for urban government officials to be fined and disarmed on the highway by a *cavalier* of the *maréchaussée*.[73] For less dignified members of the community – students, the young, the *commis* sent out by their employers to do the leg work in the street – a weapon could provide a dash of bravado if worn with sufficient ostentation. For large numbers in the rural and urban communities, the possession of a weapon, even kept hidden under the bed, meant the protection of self, home and family, with all that represented in terms of independence and self-respect. For others still, for sailors or entertainers of all kinds, the carrying of a weapon was a sign of virility indispensable to the profession. It was therefore inevitable that a police duty so inimical to the *mores* of the whole population between the privileged élite and the destitute fringe should provoke intense resentment. As we shall see in chapter 7, disarmament inspired more rebellions against the *maréchaussée* than any other social grievance. Even if the public reaction did not always go so far as open revolt, disarmament could only proceed in an atmosphere of hostile suspicion. Charges of graft and corruption were more rife in this field of police activity than any other. Since disarmament was the ancien régime's equivalent of a parking offence *cavaliers* had the right to convict and collect a fine of ten *livres* on the spot, and confiscate the weapon, on their own authority.[74] Even in the case of a false and malicious denunciation, it was easy to extort money from the alleged offender. The Bordeaux *cavalier* Dussaux was caught out in this racket and imprisoned in December 1759 – clearly not for long as we find him disarming others in March 1760. *Cavaliers* could easily be tempted into demanding more than the 10L. which they were entitled to collect – Delpont, another Bordeaux *cavalier*, took 24L. from a tailor he caught with a *fusil*.[75]

In theory, the *cavaliers* were allowed to keep half of each ten *livres* fine; from time to time, to encourage their zeal, they were granted the whole amount.[76] In practice, the sum they took home varied considerably, as a certain portion was allotted on the *cavalier*'s own initiative to informers, to those charged with investigating the truth of an allegation that a particular individual was concealing a *fusil*, and to the clerks who wrote out the *cavaliers*' reports and kept their accounts. To the *maréchaussée*'s credit, there were many occasions when the full 10L. was not exacted from an

73. The *Règlement* specifically excluded *bourgeois vivant noblement* from consideration from arms permits: 156 bourgeois were disarmed, and as well as the officials and magistrates we have seen, the *jurats* of St Macaire, Antaignac and Castelnau. The mayor of Castillonnès was disarmed at the fair in his own town.
74. Fifty *livres* if the disarmament met with resistance.
75. Register, Oct. 1760, A.D. Gir. C 3728.
76. 'Lettre circulaire aux brigades' from the *prévôt-général*, 5 May 1766, *ibid.* and *Circulaire sur le désarmement*, from the *prévôt-général*, 11 Sept. 1773, *ibid.* C 3729.

offender 'on account of his poverty', 'because of his indigence'. If the offenders could afford to scrape up part of the fine, 9L. would be accepted, or 6 or 4. Others paid in promises.

The ordinary *cavalier* was in a position to exercise his initiative, and while this permitted a commendable flexibility, there were obvious disadvantages. It was easy to charge the police with partiality in the administration of the law, and the authorities were flooded by complaints that more peasants were armed than ever before, and that the *maréchaussée* was to blame for this 'perpetual infringement of both arms and hunting regulations'. The constables and brigade commanders were accused of pretending to obey the orders, by confiscating only old and useless weapons; or by forgetting the weapon altogether and collecting only the fine, 'the object, it is said, of their greed'.[77] The policeman's relatives and friends were naturally assumed to be the prime beneficiaries of this 'inattention'. The *cavaliers* had constantly under their gaze the example of people who like themselves had a constant struggle to feed themselves and their families, and who eased that struggle by poaching. It would be surprising if the *cavaliers* themselves, conveniently armed with *fusils* on their lonely patrols across the countryside, did not occasionally fill their saddle bags with the odd rabbit or game bird. Their superiors however were only troubled by complaints in cases of extreme indiscretion, when the *maître* of the Bordeaux *Eaux et Forêts*, for example, complained to the Minister of War that the *archers* of the Bordeaux brigade were not only hunting partridges in the vineyards and pine forests near the city whenever they felt like a roast partridge, but organising hunting parties with noblemen and professional hunters and dogs. The investigation which the *Eaux et Forêts* had begun into these activities was deliberately dropped after the intendant argued forcibly that to proceed against the *maréchaussée* would have all sorts of dangerous consequences, particularly regrettable when such a 'slight misdemeanour' was concerned. The police naturally made enemies, 'and local judges are not the men who wish them the least harm'; if the case started by the *Eaux et Forêts* were allowed to proceed, *archers* would be accused of poaching every time they entered a field or a vineyard. The hunting policemen therefore were not prosecuted; the *maître* of the *Eaux et Forêts* was rebuked for his 'petulance'.[78]

The small, inefficient and suspect organisation of the 1750s was hardly the instrument Richelieu required for the disarmament of the civilian population. To mitigate the evils of the *maréchaussée*'s 'precipitation' and 'malversations', the governor decided to adopt a slow, bureaucratic approach. Action would be taken by the police on orders from the governor or the commandant wherever it had been learned, and confirmed, that arms were

77. 1773 *Circulaire sur le désarmement*, *ibid.*
78. Correspondence between Martin, *maître particulier aux Eaux et Forêts*, the minister Baudry, and the Bordeaux intendant, 1730, *ibid.* C 3632.

to be found. In other words, Richelieu was attempting to supplement the police by encouraging the complicity of the population. The public was invited to inform.

There was no shortage of denunciation from the privileged classes: Du Breuil, the marquis de Hautefort, Ferret de Montflanquin, de St Cricq, Mme la Comtesse du Périgord, the duc de Fumel. The governor also had the support of the judicial establishment, from local judges whose status was similar to that of many of the offenders to the most elevated *Parlementaire* magistrates. The *présidents* Lalanne and Pichard reappear regularly in the 'informer' column, in company with their colleagues Jauge and de Gascq, usually to denounce poachers on their estates. The *Parlementaires*, like other seigneurs, did not object to using the state to protect their seigneurial interests. The First Estate likewise made use of the secular arm – occasionally at a humble level, a *vicaire* or curé who objected to an individual coming to mass in hunting gear, or the curé who denounced a wool-carder for firing on his poultry – but the weight of ecclesiastical numbers on this side of the barricade lay with the higher clergy, the monks and prioresses and archbishops with seigneurial rights to defend. A motley collection of royal and municipal officials, army officials and municipal policemen lent their support to the disarmament movement, but the only 'blue-collar' informers were the unidentified neighbours who denounced a father and son to the Langon brigade for possession of a *fusil* and two pistols, and a solitary weaver in Créon who proved the undoing of a local cooper. Richelieu and the police got no meaningful cooperation from the mass of the populace. In these circumstances it is perhaps remarkable that in a decade and a half, the civilian population was deprived of at least four and a half thousand weapons.

It is of course impossible to know how many weapons were held in the province at any time: it is equally impossible to estimate how many weapons were confiscated by the *maréchaussée*. The registers which were kept after a fashion between 1758 and 1774 suggest that about 4,280 disarmaments were carried out, some of them involving several weapons; the main components of this stock were about 3,250 *fusils*, 340 hunting knives, 230 pistols and 260 swords. These figures are certain to be very conservative as the registers contain evidence of another 3,094 'disarmaments' ordered by the Marshal or his staff, many of which the *maréchaussée* must have carried out even if it did not keep up with its paperwork. In May 1766, the Villeréal *brigadier*, Daunis, justified an appeal for financial assistance to feed his ten children by 'the quantity of disarmament fines collected by my assiduous work in which I have used up my own children's inheritance'.[79] Yet only three disarmaments by this brigade are officially recorded for the whole of 1766 and five for 1765.

79. Letter from Daunis to *prévôt-général*, 22 May 1766, *ibid*. C 3728.

Given the methods by which the police operated, it is not surprising that about two-thirds of all disarmament operations were performed as a result of a specific order from a superior officer, Richelieu himself or less frequently the *prévôt-général* or the *commandant*. Disarming *in flagrante delicto* was common only in the two garrison towns of Bordeaux and Blaye and in Langon, strategically situated in the Garonne valley. Despite the importance of game to the armed population, there was no increase in confiscations during the hunting seasons. The annual totals however show the initial impact of the arrival of Richelieu (and to a much lesser extent the reminder of the priority given to disarmament issues by the *commandant* de Beauvau in 1766). Many of the weapons were provided by deserters and by the militia forces armed to defend frontiers and coasts in wartime, and we find the availability of weapons for confiscation rose to a peak in 1763 (652 disarmaments), with the climax of the Seven Years War. Peace came in conjunction with the flagging interest the *maréchaussée* always displayed after initial enthusiasm (79 disarmaments in 1769). The renewal of 1771 (233) was no doubt the result of the 1769/70 reorganisation of the police force, which entailed the creation of new brigades, but the reinvigoration was temporary, and by 1773 all the brigades of the Guyenne, their intention firmly concentrated on grain disturbance and mendicity, managed to confiscate only seventy-three weapons.

After April 1774, no one bothered to enter disarmaments on the register. Corvisier, however, pays tribute to the *maréchaussée* and its seigneurial allies for having brought about the 'disappearance' of illicit weapons from the hands of the people, while admitting at the same time that the weapons resurfaced during the Revolution.[80] The people of the Guyenne were not in fact prepared to wait so long to make use of the weapons so carefully preserved from the clutches of the police. In December 1784, as the brigades of the Agenais made their way home from a review, past snowy fields and trees bare of foliage, they heard shots 'on all sides'.[81]

The Guyenne brigades had at least helped to make the province a rather safer place than the Auvergne. There was no doubt that the Auvergne missed the forceful inspiration of a governor. Although without the coasts and large garrisons of the Guyenne, there were certainly far fewer illicit weapons to worry about. The president of the Aurillac royal court, the *Présidial*, complained about the multiplication of weapons in the Haute-Auvergne, illustrating the dangers of the ready availability of weapons by the number of fatal shootings and even patricide which had occurred in the province. His fears were confirmed when a boy in Aurillac 'walked singing past a mill', knocked

80. Corvisier, *L'armée française*, vol. 1, pp. 70 and 73.
81. *Procès-verbaux*, 20 Dec. 1784 by Marmande, Nérac and Casteljaloux brigades, A.N. Z^IC 461.

his rifle against the shutter, and shot dead the woman who happened to be looking out the window. The intendant, however, made no more than a complacent and lackadaisical response. The few peasants who had rifles, he argued, kept them for protection against wolves, and this representative of central government authority was prepared to leave the whole question to seigneurs, who would, he presumed, be anxious and able to protect their hunting rights.[82] It was nevertheless the practice, quite unthinkable in the Guyenne, to give travellers permission to carry firearms, 'for self-defence', just as it would have been unthinkable in the Guyenne for an *exempt* of the *maréchaussée* to 'warn' three poachers that if they did not stop hunting, he would be forced to disarm them.[83] The *Conseil supérieur* in Clermont-Ferrand noted in 1772 that 'artisans, bourgeois and peasants' were poaching with complete impunity, and directing their weapons against anyone who might get in their way.[84]

With its military discipline and military activities, there was no gainsaying the military character of a force created 'to wage perpetual war against internal enemies [les ennemis du dedans]',[85] against the people referred to in royal ordinances on the *maréchaussée* as 'the internal enemies of the state'. But although it was, as Maurepas neatly put it, a military body 'in its discipline, uniform, and bearing', it was a civilian force 'in its functions'.[86] Even where specifically military duties were concerned – the arrest, for example, of deserters, and the calling-up of the militia – the police had contact with the War Ministry through the intendant or his *subdélégués*. Louis XVI's *Garde des Sceaux* exerted all his influence against the *maréchaussée* becoming such a militarised institution that it would lack the 'prudence' of magistrates or civil administrators: 'This force must be controlled by administrators accustomed to the sight of people's misfortunes and to being moved by them'.[87]

For the *cavaliers*, constrained as they were by military discipline, the ever-present directing force did not come from the Marshals of France, or even from the Minister of War, but from the intendant, and his *subdélégué*.

Every time the *prévôt* proposed men for promotion, the Minister did not appoint them till he had sought the opinion of the intendant. When it was a question of clothing the *maréchaussée*, the Minister asked the intendant what was the state of uniforms and equipment. The same thing for the replacement of horses. If the *prévôt* needs a period of leave, he writes to the Minister who refers it back to the intendant.[88]

---

82. Correspondence between M. Bochault and intendant, 1763. A.D. P. de D. C 1728.
83. Letter from M. Sadourny to intendant, 1763, *ibid*.
84. *Arrest du Conseil Supérieur*, *ibid*.
85. De la Morandière, p. 225. The Englishman Mildmay described the *maréchaussée* as being 'in perpetual war not against a foreign enemy but against such of the native subjects as disturb the peace and violate the laws of their country, and who, as such, must be deemed common enemies to all societies' – Mildmay, *The police of France*, p. 31.
86. L. Lèques, *Histoire de la Gendarmerie* (Paris 1874), p. 81.
87. *Ibid*.
88. *Mémoire*, A.D. P. de D. C 6192.

The records of the Auvergne intendant at least provide ample evidence to justify such a Tocquevillean interpretation, from the bald enumeration of duties accomplished by all the brigades of the province headed 'Operations by order of the intendant', to the intendant's personal interventions to reprimand negligent policemen. The *subdélégué* in Brioude personally directed operations by the local brigade to capture criminals.[89] The Lempdes brigade was sent out by the *subdélégué* to recapture a worker from the Royal Glass Factory in Apremont whose 'escape' had unsettled the other workers; the St Flour *subdélégué* sent *cavaliers* out into the snow to find a load of Spanish wool.[90] The *maréchaussée* was regularly and systematically used by the intendant to contain outbreaks of cattle disease, establishing *cordons sanitaires* along the Limousin or Forez borders, supervising guard posts, confiscating carts which tried to break through.[91]

The intendant relied on the *maréchaussée* to ensure that *corvée* duties were carried out. The *maréchaussée* could be used to garrison a parish from which all the men had decamped;[92] more frequently the *cavaliers* arrested individual fugitives on orders from the intendant. The normal procedure, when a list of absentees had been drawn up by the engineer, was to choose the most obstreperous and the most comfortably off, as 'good for prison', and get the *maréchaussée* to arrest them.[93] Guyenne *cavaliers* also spent time at the intendant's behest as a 'garrison' on those who had considerable tax arrears. Two *cavaliers* from Périgueux, for example, sat for fifty-one days in 1760 in the *salon* of M. de l'Escardie, *lieutenant général* of the *sénéchaussée* of Périgueux to encourage him to pay his tax dues for 1759 – almost two months when they could have been patrolling the roads and protecting the lives and property of all *Périgourdins*.[94]

Despite the existence of the *Ferme*'s private army, the *maréchaussée* was often directed by the intendant to contribute to the fight against smuggling. At least until the 1730s, each brigade of *maréchaussée* in the Auvergne was provided with a copy of a register compiled by the intendant of the Dauphiné containing the names and descriptions of smugglers likely to cross into the

89. E.g. a letter from intendant to Brioude *exempt*, 1756, concerns the arrest of three murderers, *ibid.* C 1540.
90. Correspondence between *subdélégués* and factory managers, 1754, *ibid.* C 1528.
91. Letters from *subdélégué* in Thiers, 21 Apr. 1748, and Lezoux paid tribute to the *maréchaussée*'s effectiveness – *ibid.* C 1528. Cf. correspondence on Limousin outbreak, C 333, mentioned in Poitrineau, *La vie rurale*, vol. 1, p. 686; L. Vialatte, *Rossignol, intendant de la généralité de Riom* (Aurillac 1924), p. 159.
92. Letter from Bertin, intendant in Lyon, to Auvergne intendant 3 May 1756, A.D. P. de D. C 6185. Cf. payment of *cavaliers* in Guyenne 'pour établissement de garrison chez les redevables de la Corvée', *Etat*, 1759, A.D. Gir. C 2178.
93. It was of course the prisoners who would pay the *cavaliers*' expenses of 3L. a day. Correspondence between MM. Borleau and St Seyne, 1762, A.D. P. de D. C 6187.
94. *Etat* 1760, A.D. Gir. C 2179. The intendants in Lyon and Clermont at this time apparently did not use the *maréchaussée* for this purpose. Letter from Bertin to Auvergne intendant, 3 May 1756, A.D. P. de D. C 6185.

central provinces. The incursions of smuggler bands in the 1730s severely interrupted the *maréchaussée*'s normal work: the prosecution of *prévôtal*
cases in St Flour was held up and the draw for the militia could not take
place. This disruption took place because the intendant and the lieutenant
of the *maréchaussée* had ordered all the brigades of *maréchaussée* in the
Haute-Auvergne to mount an expedition against the smugglers who had
murdered a *gabelou*.[95]

This particular operation, led as we have seen by Lieutenant Dastier, involved the brigades in expensive forced marches from the beginning of
February to the middle of March, and the *Ferme* was so mean about repaying
expenses or offering rewards – a mere 200L. was to be shared between the
whole company – that the intendant himself foresaw that in any future
involvement of the *maréchaussée* against smugglers the *cavaliers* would only
serve under coercion. The *maréchaussée* was officially encouraged to cooperate with the *Ferme* in an Ordinance of 1736 which enjoined all the
king's troops to lend *main-forte* to the *gabelous* in return for the reward
of a proportion of the captured salt and equipment, while the *arrêt du
conseil* of 6 June 1738 ordered the *maréchaussée* to arrest smugglers and
confiscate their merchandise. In practice, however, the *maréchaussée*'s
contribution to the repression of smuggling was extremely limited after
the 1730s. It was not only a question of the *cavaliers*' reluctance, the authorities themselves realised that this particular diversion of the police from
their regular duties had grave disadvantages: 'By sending them against
smugglers, who usually form bands of a considerable size, we would expose
cavaliers pointlessly to their vengeance; it would also be dangerous to gather
several brigades together for an operation against smugglers, for that would
leave the province to the mercy of thieves who would not fail to profit
from the opportunity'.[96] Smugglers, therefore, were to be left to the *Ferme*.
Only the murder of three *gabelous* and the particular zeal of Lieutenant
Gigounoux de Verdon involved the *maréchaussée* in any subsequent operation against smugglers.

There could however be no let up in the intendant's use of the *maréchaussée*
to keep order by arresting troublemakers – the 'terror of the parish', the
'disturber of the peace' who could be thrown into prison at the drop of a hat
by the intendant. Such powers, of course, did not escape Tocqueville's attention: 'We see from the correspondence between *subdélégués* and the intendant
that the intendant would order them to have the "nuisances" arrested, not to
put them on trial but to hold them in prison'.[97]

To illustrate the incidence of administrative powers of detention, Tocqueville quotes the case of a landowner who requests the arrest of an inconvenient neighbour: 'The intendant of Paris begs his colleague of Rouen to

95. Letters from Trudaine to *Fermiers généraux*, 1734, *ibid.* C 6182.
96. Controller-general Séchelles to all intendants, A.D. P. de D. C 6183.
97. A. de Tocqueville, *L'Ancien Régime et la Revolution* (Paris 1856), p. 447.

render this service to this proprietor who is his friend'. The unpleasant implications of such an example are not confirmed by the use of the *maréchaussée* by the intendant and *subdélégués* of the Auvergne.

The people the administration wished to detain were 'a nuisance' not just because they inconvenienced a neighbour, but because they inspired fear, insecurity, or outrage among a wide section of the community. Jacques Chenebras went around armed with a pistol and a *fusil*, and was denounced by his curé for armed robbery as well as for repeated brawls and 'debauchery'; the *subdélégué* added his weight to the allegations, but the intendant merely warned Chenebras to mend his ways. A stonemason in Langeac who to the scandal of the town 'ruined' a young girl, and made violent threats against anyone who criticised his behaviour was only arrested, while 'sleeping with his girlfriend in a barn', when he failed to turn up for the militia. Pichot, recommended for three months in prison by the Murat *subdélégué*, had taken a scythe to his neighbour; Besson was notorious for attacking someone everyday – one of his victims would have lost a foot had the blow from the axe not been parried by his clog. Ribeyrolles, the butcher of Rochefort, had not taken the sacraments for ten years, and when he did go to church, he loudly imitated anyone in the congregation who coughed or spat; his parents accused him of beating them; his first wife's 13 year-old daughter had been thrown on to the street and the town *consuls* bore painful testimony to the maltreatment they had received when he refused to pay his taxes. Apart from singing and banging doors at night, 'he had usurped an orphan's garden . . . and a large part of the commons'.[98] When the intendant did order the *maréchaussée* to make this sort of arrest, he did not act on a personal whim, but merely responded either to a considerable weight of evidence or to unusually insistent popular demand. He did not take any action at all when curés suggested that the *maréchaussée* could catch offending couples in the very act of *libertinage*.[99]

While he exaggerates the triviality of the cause of arrest, Tocqueville also fails to underline the triviality of the subsequent punishment. A shepherd, for instance, was imprisoned for only a month after twice molesting a seven-year-old girl; though the *subdélégué* complained that shepherds and cowherds preferred children 'all too often', the intendant decided that a month in jail was a useful deterrent 'to restrain these sorts of people who have no other feelings than those of man in his natural state'.[100] Tocqueville however does not seem to have been unfair when he drew attention to the unfortunate individual imprisoned by the intendant for a fortnight after insulting the *maréchaussée* itself.[101] The son of the Montaigut prison *concierge* was imprisoned for a week on the charge laid by Taillandier, *cavalier*, of 'invective

98. Correspondence from *subdélégués*, A.D. P. de D. C 1521, 1527–9, 1538.
99. Curé of Ambert to intendant, 16 Feb. 1759, *ibid.* C 1543.
100. Correspondence between intendant and *subdélégué* of Brioude, 1759, *ibid.* C 1543.
101. Tocqueville, *L'Ancien Régime*, p. 447.

against our whole corps and myself', and throwing stones at the *cavalier*. Such behaviour hardly encouraged respect for the force, and the intendant recommended that the prisoner be 'so confined that his imprisonment is a real punishment'.[102]

Insulting any royal official had overtones of *lèse-majesté*, and a *cavalier* of the *maréchaussée* was himself imprisoned for a week for being rude to a *subdélégué*.[103] Any prolonged disharmony between the two usually dependent bodies like the *maréchaussée* and the officials of the *intendance* was a matter of grave governmental concern. The quarrel between the *subdélégué* and the *brigadier* in Besse led to the intervention of the *prévôt-général*, the intendant, and the Minister of War. The *subdélégué*, M. Besseyre, had, according to Dauphin, the *prévôt-général*, prevented the *brigadier* arresting a drunk at the local fair and called the brigade commander a 'tramp' in the midst of the fracas. 'If the brigades are treated in this way by those who are supposed to command them', how could a brigade command the respect of the four thousand peasants who attended the fair?[104] The intendant Trudaine was less concerned by the brawl itself, which he blamed on the *brigadier*'s drunkenness, than by the brigade's persistent insubordination. For three months the *cavaliers* had not passed on to the *subdélégué* the routine patrol certificates. The *brigadier* Gaignon, Trudaine alleged, had refused to arrest militia absentees. The personal conflict, in fact, had reduced militia operations to a shambles, and Trudaine was determined that Gaignon should at least be forced to apologise; otherwise 'my *subdélégués* would be exposed every day to such scenes and could make no use whatsoever of the *maréchaussée*'.

The intimate relationship between *maréchaussée* and *intendance* was bound to lead to friction, and militia operations were particularly fertile in conflict. *Brigadiers* constantly felt that they were being exploited: 'Two days and a night with snow and ice up to our horses' bellies', moaned the Ambert *exempt*, only to have the fruit of the chase released by Madur, the *subdélégué*, on the frivolous pretext that the fugitive, a 17 year-old boy, was not tall enough.[105] Much of the bitterness in the exchanges came from the permanent financial worries of the *maréchaussée* – the release of the fugitive meant that the brigade would not be paid for all its effort.

These disputes were indicative of a general pattern of *prévôtal* resistance to administrative tutelage. César Dauphin's vigorous campaign against interference from the intendant won the first victory, when he received ministerial approval for his direction to brigade commanders not to furnish the

---

102. From the voluminous correspondence in 1732 between the intendant and the Montaigut *subdélégué*, A.D. P. de D. C 1523.
103. A *cavalier* in the Limousin town of Bort, which had a *subdélégué* working for the Auvergne intendant. Letter from M d'Aine to intendant, 18 Nov. 1777, *ibid.* C 6189.
104. Accumulation of correspondence on the affair in *ibid.* C 6182.
105. Undated letter from de la Bretesche, *exempt* to *intendant*, *ibid.* C 6184.

subdélégués with detailed reports of their activities. The officers of the *maréchaussée*, Trudaine subsequently complained, 'spurred on above all by the *prévôt*, believe themselves relieved of a subordination which they found very uncomfortable and are announcing their triumph'; as a result, he concluded, the *subdélégués* were deprived of knowledge of the functioning of the brigades, and so would no longer be able to direct their work.[106]

The *maréchaussée*'s triumph was more apparent than real. Certainly the *subdélégués* would no longer be responsible for the detailed itinerary of every patrol. The *prévôt-général* himself now had the responsibility for the carrying out of such routine tasks laid clearly at his door. The intendant still kept overall control, and the *prévôt* had to draw up a monthly report covering all the brigades' activities. As d'Angervilliers concluded in his letter to Trudaine, 'You are at all times in complete control of indicating to *prévôts* the places where you think they ought to send the brigades'.[107]

The skirmishing took up again twenty-five years later, with a different *prévôt-général*, César's son and successor Augustin, under a new intendant, Ballainvilliers. Against a background of widespread dissatisfaction, amounting in the Auvergne to alarm, with the work of the *maréchaussée*, an ordinance on discipline in the force was issued by Choiseul. He took the trouble to stress the importance of the *maréchaussée*'s routine duties – searching out criminals, keeping order on the roads – thus criticising, if only by implication, the diversion of the force to special duties, most of which were assigned by the intendant. Dauphin himself pushed these implications to the limit, and reprimanded a brigade which had obeyed an order from the intendant to arrest some 'rebels' who had beaten up a tax-collector, and ordered his brigade commanders, particularly the *exempt* in Clermont, not to take any more orders from Ballainvilliers.[108]

This was clearly a more serious challenge than César's fight to keep the daily patrol free of subdelegation control. Ballainvilliers himself naturally predicted the direst consequences – law and order would break down, bands of smugglers would take over the countryside, and prevent the collection of the *taille*. Ballainvilliers did not intend to pay such an indirect compliment to the *maréchaussée*'s effectiveness in normal times, so much as draw attention to the limitations of the area in which the *prévôt-général* could act autonomously and on his own initiative (an important question to consider since the *prévôt* was refusing to act on the intendant's initiative), and reminded the controller-general that *prévôts* could order someone's arrest only when he was accused of a specifically *prévôtal* offence – vagrancy, highway robbery and so on.[109] Despite the variety of ways in which the *maréchaussée* was used

106. Letter from Trudaine to d'Angervilliers 6 Aug. 1734, *ibid*. C 6182.
107. Letter from d'Angervilliers to Trudaine, 9 Aug. 1734, *ibid*.
108. Letter from Ballainvilliers to St Florentin, 22 July 1760, *ibid*. C 6180.
109. Letter from Ballainvilliers to controller-general, 6 Aug. 1760, *ibid*. C 6186.

as a tool of government policy, the *prévôt* himself could not have any concept of 'Police' in its eighteenth-century sense of the general framework of
public order. The central government this time backed the intendant – the
Chancellor Lamoignon regarded the *maréchaussée*'s case as a pretext for
laziness,[110] and the War Minister lost no time in curtly informing Dauphin
that the 'singular pretension' which he shared with a number of *prévôts*
seemed to stem from a false interpretation of the Ordinance. 'I must warn
you that the king's intention is that all orders given to the *maréchaussée* by
intendants must be carried out at once without question.'[111]

In the Auvergne, the *maréchaussée* had to live with the fact that the
intendant enjoyed a position of unchallenged authority. The existence in
Bordeaux however of powers with the political weight to challenge the
supremacy of the intendant tended to encourage an attitude of independence
in the *maréchaussée*. Governors and *commandants* could be called in to redress the balance so obviously lacking in Riom, and on occasion, the *prévôt-
général* was able to play off one power against another. When a decision had
to be made on the siting of a new *lieutenance* and *prévôtal* court, the *prévôt-
général*, who enlisted the governor's support for Libourne, was able to reverse
the intendant's choice of Sarlat, despite the intendant's friendship with the
Garde des Sceaux in whose department such judicial decisions had to be
made.[112]

The subservience of the *maréchaussée* to the *Parlements* was much more
nominal than its obedience to the directives of governor or intendant. There
was no judicial contact, as there were no appeals from the *prévôtal* court,
which was furthermore incompetent to deal with *prévôtal* crimes committed
in a town where a *Parlement* was established.[113] *Parlementaires* had their own
employees and the urban police at their disposal for the auxiliary duties required by every court, and were content to leave the policing of the peasants
to institutions equipped to deal with such people. In the cause of religious
intolerance, however, the *Parlementaires* were prepared to step down into the
arena, and send *cavaliers* into the houses of Protestants who had refused to
baptise their children in the Catholic faith.[114] The *Parlement*'s right to call on
the services of the *maréchaussée* was confirmed by the Ordinance of 1778,
which directed the force to obey orders from *Premiers Présidents* and

110. Letter from Lamoignon to Ballainvilliers 29 Feb. 1760, *ibid.*
111. Letter from Belle-Isle to Dauphin 2 Aug. 1760, *ibid.*
112. The intendant could see no grounds for such a bizarre establishment, other than the
     fact that the new lieutenant had a property near Libourne, Esmangart to Le Noir,
     20 Mar. 1773, *ibid.* C 3460.
113. Art. 16, Declaration of 1731.
114. Four *cavaliers* of the Nérac brigade were involved in Dec. 1764, staying with a
     family from five to thirteen days. Most parents submitted when the *cavaliers*
     received orders to carry the children to church themselves. *Etat de journées*, 1764,
     A.D. Gir. C 2179.

procureurs généraux, while the *Parlementaires* were given the duty of informing the Chancellor or Secretary for War of reprehensible conduct on the part
of the *prévôt-général*.

The Nérac brigade had taken action against 'the so-called reformed religion',
by *order* of the *procureur général* of the Bordeaux *Parlement*, and 'by requi-
sition of the *procureur du roi* of the *Présidial* court in Nérac'. Only the
Parlement could command; lower courts had to request the *maréchaussée*'s
assistance. In fact it was a mere difference of form – *cavaliers* and officers
were 'obliged to execute writs, warrants and court orders when so requested
by our Judges'.[115] There was however an important proviso to the assistance
provided by the *maréchaussée*: ushers of the court had to be present. The
purpose of the *cavaliers'* presence was to assure the execution of a judgment
by protecting the bailiffs, not to assume the rôle and status of court ushers.
There was always the suspicion that lending a hand [*main-forte*] was some-
how beneath the dignity of a military force – the Inspector of the Auvergne
company was particularly critical of local magistrates for exploiting the
cavaliers 'for duties which are degrading for the *Maréchaussée*', such as wasting
excessive amounts of time escorting prisoners from the gaol to the court-
house.[116] In the absence of a senior officer in Riom, it was the responsibility
of the *exempt* to consider such requests; Bourdige was particularly sensitive
about the form in which the request was made, and when a magistrate at the
Présidial did not ask nicely enough, he was told to 'f . . . off' and the magistrates were kept waiting for three hours.[117] The protection of bailiffs was in
fact the *maréchaussée*'s only contribution to criminal investigations or judicial
processes outwith the confines of the *prévôtal* court. The royal police force
was even forbidden to accept orders from the royal 'police judges' – the
Clermont commissioners [*commissaires*], for example, who regarded themselves as 'veritable examining magistrates' on a par with the *commissaires* in
the Châtelet, [criminal court in Paris], or the various 'lieutenants of police'.
In the Guyenne, as we shall see, these officials could make use of urban police
forces, but the poverty-stricken Auvergne could not afford such a luxury.
Clermont itself had no watch, and this was indeed the principal reason for the
creation of a second brigade of *maréchaussée* in the town.[118] The Clermont
exempt Lebey was however vigorously supported by his chief when he refused
to obey 'orders', from the *commissaires*. Apart from the *commissaires'* status
as judges who could only 'request', the *maréchaussée* was, du Deffan argued,

115. F. Serpillon, *Code criminel, ou commentaire sur l'ordonnance de 1670*, vol. 1
    (Lyon 1767), p. 278.
116. Inspection 1772. A. de G. Y[b] 791.
117. Correspondence on the issue between d'Aguesseau, Duchey (*Lt. criminel* in the
    Riom *présidial*), Urion (*assesseur de maréchaussée*), and the intendant, 1737, A.D.
    P. de D. C 6183.
118. *Mémoire* (n.d.) by Clermont *commissaires de police*, during tenure of *prévôt-
    général* du Deffan, *ibid*. B 00384.

a force created to police the countryside and not the backstreets of Clermont. The same battle was fought in Montaigut and Thiers, which could not afford bailiffs to carry out the decisions of the 'police judges'; despite the 'anarchy' which reigned there, the *maréchaussée* was given official support in its refusal to provide a substitute – 'the *maréchaussée* is not subordinate to ordinary judges, nor to police officials, besides which the *maréchaussée* was not established for the benefit of towns'.[119]

The concern shown by the officers to protect the institution's good name was not necessarily shared by the men. *Cavaliers*, it seems, were only too willing to accede to requests for *main-forte*; some even made it their principal occupation, if it paid them to do so. Assistance to court bailiffs brought in expenses, which was more than could be expected from routine patrols. The *prévôt-général* of the Auvergne undertood to eradicate the abuse, to prevent his company falling into 'complete degradation', but given the economic difficulties of the *cavaliers*, even the clearest stipulations in the Ordinances would not eradicate the problem. Many officers did not give a proper lead as they did not fully comprehend the precise, limited, rôle of the *maréchaussée* in this field, or were happy to see their men earn a little extra money. Under the *prévôt*'s watchful eye, *cavaliers* in Clermont at least learned to decline requests for *main-forte* from any local magistrate even if the *exempt* did not happen to be around.[120]

The *maréchaussée* of the Auvergne was, then, in the happy position when it could never do enough. The institution had been created as a rural police force, designed to fit around and complement whatever urban police forces could be found. In the Auvergne, there were none, and this lack was keenly felt as a heavy extra burden on the *cavaliers* of the *maréchaussée*, who despite their reluctance to be diverted from their natural duties, were often obliged to do so, by requests for *main-forte*, by tasks imposed by the intendant and his staff who had no one else to turn to, by force of circumstance every time fairs and markets were held in the capital of the province. No assistance could be expected from the Auvergne bourgeois militia, formed in 1694 ostensibly to patrol the streets at night, in fact to squeeze some money out of those prepared to buy posts as 'colonels', 'majors', 'capitaines'. In the Auvergne this

119. Letters from d'Angervilliers to intendant 13 Mar. 1738, *ibid.* C 6183 and from de Paulmy to intendant, 1758, after complaints by Sieurs Rudel, Henry and Rochias, *juges de police, ibid.* C 6185. The *cahiers* revealed a certain annoyance that the *maréchaussée* had been so punctilious on this matter. 'May the *cavaliers* of the *maréchaussée* obey the commands of judges in all courts, even if given verbally'; and would that the officers of the *maréchaussée* lose their infuriating habit of declining responsibility at crucial moments by falling back on their 'military status' and demanding written requests in moments of emergency: 'while they prepare, the crime is consummated', *cahiers* of Mortagne, St Pierre le Moutier, and Neauphle-le-Château, in A. Desjardins, *Les cahiers des Etats Généraux en 1789, et la législation criminelle* (Paris 1883), pp. 364–5.

120. *Mémoire* of the *juges de police*, A.D. P. de D. B 00384.

was never a relevant institution – as early as 1695 the new 'capitaine-major' of the St Flour *milice* protested against his nomination, which he blamed on the 'intrigues' of Isaac Bigot, 'who had been appointed first and who managed to get out of it'.[121]

In the Guyenne, the bourgeois militia preserved at least a token existence in the larger towns, although the major companies in the Périgord at least – in Périgueux, Bergerac, and Sarlat – led an existence which was primarily one of 'vain and antiquated parade'.[122] Périgueux could muster for ceremonial occasions five companies of 'artisans', forty men apiece, and a mounted guard of 200 men.[123] The records of the municipality of Bergerac are replete with grand and ostentatious occasions when the bourgeois militia could grace the streets. In the procession to the service held for the repose of the Dauphin's soul, the consuls were preceded by 16 *sergents de quartier* and 120 *fusiliers* carrying their halberds adorned with black crêpe.

A serious effort was made to revive the institution throughout the province shortly after the appointment of Richelieu as governor. His 'Ordinance concerning the Bourgeois Patrols' of July 1761[124] ordered each town and bourg in his province to form a militia of a size proportionate to the size of the town. It would be divided into companies of forty men under the command of a captain, a lieutenant, two sergeants, and four corporals, to be appointed by the town council from among the 'principal inhabitants'. These companies would be responsible for a nightly patrol of four or five men to keep order from 10 p.m. till dawn, to make sure the *cabarets* shut on time, to arrest vagabonds and 'evil-doers' and hand them over to the authorities. The patrols would be armed with municipal rifles, clearly marked 'patrol rifles'. The governor also wished to ensure the tranquillity of the countryside, and for this purpose permitted the collector of the *taille* in every parish to have a depot of six rifles which could be used to arm groups of vigilante peasants prepared to take action against vagabonds, evil-doers, mad dogs and wolves. This was the only concession made by Richelieu in his campaign for general disarmament.

It may be that the Ordinance was not entirely ignored, as there are instances of bourgeois militia, at least in the 1770s, being sufficiently reliable to be called upon by the *maréchaussée* itself for support in major operations. The Bergerac militia was particularly useful to Verdon in the grain disturbances of 1773 and 1775, and his Agenais counterpart, as we have seen, made use of local companies. But not even Richelieu could revive the moribund bourgeois militia of Bordeaux itself. In theory, the militia represented 'the commune

121. *Ibid.* C 6171.
122. *Les Milices communales et les Gardes bourgeoises dans le Périgord avant la Révolution* – pamphlet by Lt G. de Cardenal, of the 50e Régiment d'Infanterie, A.M. Per. AA 79.
123. *Ibid.* p. 8.
124. The copy used to inform the parish of St Saud (Périgord) is kept in A.D. Dord. IV E 113.

itself armed for its own defence', by keeping watch at night from guard posts, by patrolling the river banks, visiting inns and lodging houses, and examining suspect merchandise. Every male resident under 60 was eligible except for nobles and doctors, the lame and the incurably sick, but in practice most militia-men paid substitutes, often described as 'the scum of the people', drunk or so exhausted by their daytime job that all they could do was sleep. The only benefit of the system was the redistribution of a few *sous* to the very poor, but it did not make for effective police work.[125] This was not of immediate concern to the *maréchaussée* for the national police force was not responsible for the policing of Bordeaux.

It was not just a question of the limited rôle reserved for the *maréchaussée* in *Parlementaire* towns; an even more formidable deterrent to *prévôtal* activity in the city was the municipality's defence of its ancient rights and privileges. Since before the English occupation of Aquitaine, the *jurats* argued, the city of Bordeaux had organised its own police - not only the patriotic militia, but a paid professional body, the watch [*guet*].[126] This was certainly an institution enjoying a much greater concentration of force than the *maréchaussée*, which never had more than nine or ten men in any town. In the mid-eighteenth century, the Bordeaux watch had 40 men on foot and 30 on horseback, and by the Revolution, the total had risen to over 200. It was a body responsible for every branch of public safety: street patrols, the arrest of criminals, the observance of municipal regulations on opening hours, public hygiene, gambling, mendicity, the wine trade, and even bathing in the river.

For most of the century, it seems that the watch did not have the authority which its numbers, professional status and breadth of competence entitled it to enjoy. Pay was so poor (10s. a day for an *archer*) that numerous ordinances had to be issued against police corruption; police work in the city was often abandoned in favour of more remunerative overtime jobs helping court officials in the suburbs; the officers allowed patrols to be abandoned and the guard-house was left deserted.[127] In the latter part of the century, however, increases in numbers and pay helped to remedy the worst of these abuses. Such an improvement might account for the hesitant retreat of violence from the streets of the town which has been detected towards the end of the ancien régime.[128] The effectiveness of the force was no doubt improved also by the creation of twelve police commissioners after 1759, who were paid

125. A.M. Bx EE 7, 12.
126. *Ibid.* Series FF, and *Inventaire des Registres de la Jurade* vol. 12. For the arguments of the *jurats* on their local 'privileges', and their dispute with the *maréchaussée*, see A.D. Gir. C 2188 and 2189.
127. Preamble to Ordinance of 31 Dec. 1757, A.M. Bx FF 82a; and Representations of *Substitut du procureur sindic*, 9 Feb. 1743, *ibid.*
128. M. Laveau, 'La criminalité à Bordeaux au XVIIIe siècle', Univ. de Montpellier, Recueil de mémoires et travaux. Société d'histoire du droit, 1970, fasc.VIII, *Droit pénal et société méridionale sous l'Ancien Régime*, 85-144.

600L. a year to inspect markets and shops in their respective areas, keep a register of all strangers, patrol lodging houses (especially during the fair) and carry out the investigations which formed the basis of the prosecutions conducted by the municipal procurator.

The *maréchaussée* did not attempt to compete with the watch or challenge the responsibility of the *jurats* for the policing of the city. They did of course have to be present in the city for certain clearly defined duties: escorting *prévôtal* prisoners, supervising the execution of *prévôtal* judgments, passing in review before the intendant, and carrying out the king's orders, a catch-all clause generally interpreted to refer to *lettres de cachet*, and orders from the Minister of War or from the *Tribunal des Maréchaux*. The former meant that *cavaliers* were continually occupied checking places of birth and stated addresses, descriptions and enrolments, summoning soldiers whose leave was up to rejoin their regiments, searching out and arresting deserters, and posting up sentences. For the *Tribunal*, *cavaliers* were concerned with the *Point d'Honneur* [a tribunal settling disputes of honour between noblemen], and with debts; they arrested debtors or were garrisoned on them; they were assigned to escort nobles around the town to protect them from assaulting or being assaulted.[129] But the *prévot-général* agreed with the *jurats* that the service of the *maréchaussée* was more essential in the countryside than in the town, and suggested that the two police forces should cooperate in the fight against crime and disorder. There was ample scope for such cooperation, if only an exchange of information on criminals who did not find the city boundary insurmountable. On one occasion the *archers* of Bordeaux were used to replace absent *cavaliers* for the escort of galley-slaves to Rochefort. Yet this simple episode is the only case to be found of the cooperation between local and national, between the urban and rural police forces, which was so desirable and so feasible. The advantages to be gained by a warm relationship between the two forces were lost by the strength of ancien régime territorial imperative.

Neither side was free from blame, and the mutual suspicion and hostility was evident at all levels of the hierarchy. The urban policemen always referred to their counterparts in the *maréchaussée* as 'the hangman's valets', and the *cavaliers* returned the compliment with 'town valets' [*valets de ville*]. The *subdélégué* recorded an exchange of insults in the street, culminating in a shot which narrowly missed a *cavalier*. The watch, however, operated under the command of the *jurats*, who took the lead in the conflict with the *maréchaussée*.

Nervously anxious to prevent any encroachment on urban privilege, they argued that the *maréchaussée* had no business in the city at all. Both before and after the 1720 reforms, the *jurats* protested against the *maréchaussée*'s

129. Intendant to d'Argenson, 14 Aug. 1752, A.D. Gir. C 2188.

appearance in uniform in the city. In 1726, the municipality clapped a *cavalier* of the *maréchaussée* in prison, and kept him in irons for his alleged mistreatment of a woman he had arrested by order of the intendant; the *jurats* were not competent to press such charges and had to pay 360L. damages. It was however in the early 1750s that the tensions between the rival authorities broke out in a series of petty confrontations, denunciations and harassment. In the unedifying squabbles of 1752/3, the *maréchaussée* made 'provocative' appearances in and around the town hall, and were banned from attending the theatre within its precincts. The *jurats* initiated long investigations into recent *prévôtal* operations in an effort to prove abuse of authority and embarrass the *cavaliers* by subsequent prosecution. There were even municipal protests in 1755 when a night patrol of the *maréchaussée* in the suburbs caught some shopkeepers and an army deserter stealing grapes, even although they were transferred within twenty-four hours of arrest, as citizens of Bordeaux, to the town hall. The *prévôt-général* concluded that such public denunciations of regular police activity could do nothing but discredit the service of the *maréchaussée* and undermine the morale and efficiency of the force. Thereafter the mutual vilification relented. The suspicions, however, remained, to flare up again in the 1780s in a fierce demarcation dispute, when to the outrage of the *prévôt-général*, *archers* of the watch were sent out to arrest a murderer in La Tête de Buch (a rational deployment of resources as the *maréchaussée* itself had allowed the La Tête brigade to be run down to a single *cavalier*).

For the *maréchaussée*, the Bordeaux problem represented its claim to the right 'to do anything, go anywhere by virtue of the orders of the king, of his ministers and our superiors'. So long as the royal authorities respected the city's privileges and the *maréchaussée* kept within the agreed limits of its duties within the city, this was not unreasonable. It was perhaps more ambitious of the *prévôt* to claim that the *maréchaussée* should have the right to be present wherever and whenever the public could assemble − it implied a *prévôtal* responsibility for public order which in Bordeaux it did not possess.

The *jurats*, however, while they fretted under the *maréchaussée*'s 'continual presence', may ultimately have been concerned less with its potential interest in the city's judicial procedures or crowd control than with its rôle as the administrative agent of the intendant. Apart from a few deputies and secretaries, the intendant, symbol of centralised government power and the destruction of local rights, had only the *maréchaussée*. At the height of the dispute between the municipality and the *maréchaussée* in 1753, the *prévôt-général* was convinced that the quarrel was not in fact between the *jurats* and the *maréchaussée* but between the *jurats* and the intendant. The intendant himself always came to the *maréchaussée*'s defence, and indeed wrote to d'Argenson: 'With the constant need I have of the *maréchaussée*, I find that I have too much interest in the matter not to seek to forewarn you against the allegations'.[130] The only time the *jurats* carried harassment of the *maréchaussée* to the point of imprisonment was the arrest of Riassol in 1726 for abuse of authority while carrying out an order from the intendant. The intendant after all was a more worthy foe for the *jurats* of Bordeaux than the *maréchaussée*. The *maréchaussée* had neither the legal powers nor the manpower to threaten the municipality's control of urban 'police'.

The arrest of vagabonds and beggars

If carrying out tasks at the behest of governor or intendant could be regarded as a distraction from the *maréchaussée's* regular duties, the same could not be said for its pursuit of beggars and vagabonds, the traditional *prévôtal* clientèle since long before 1720. No more typical example of the efficacy of the eighteenth-century police can be sought than the operations of the *maréchaussée* in this sphere, and nothing is more obvious than the episodic character of the repression of mendicity and vagabondage, the 'brief and violent spasms of repression',[131] the 'passing storm' from which beggars and vagabonds had momentarily to take shelter. For they knew as well as anyone that 'whatever the *maréchaussée's* zeal to begin with [dans les premiers mouvements], all activity is liable to slow down with time'.[132]

The 'first movements' of the *cavaliers* were clearly not inspired by the weather or economic circumstance driving the *gibier du prévôt* out on to the roads. On the contrary, in times of economic distress, the *maréchaussée* concerned itself with beggars only with reluctance. In 1770 misery in the Auvergne had reached such proportions that the *prévôt-général*, as we have seen, suspended the arrest of beggars altogether: 'I would have to arrest in one day in the brigade residences alone more than four thousand people of both sexes and every age'.[133] In the Périgord, *cavaliers* arrested only twenty-seven beggars in the three years from 1770 to 1772, the result of a policy decision and certainly not of any improvement in the critical economic situation, for in 1770, there was a new crisis throughout France, 'but especially in the Périgord . . . In May 1770, the tax-receiver in Périgueux wrote that the measure of grain which had been worth 4 *livres* 10 *sous* the previous September was selling for 8 *livres* 10 *sous*, the highest price in living memory', while 1771 and 1772 were no less 'calamitous'.[134] It was inevitable that the *maréchaussée* of the Périgord take the same decision as the *prévôt-général* of the Auvergne – to suspend the arrest of beggars in the face of the enormity of the problem,

130. 14 Aug. 1752, *ibid.*
131. Poitrineau, *La vie rurale*, vol. 1, p. 579.
132. Letrosne, *Mémoire sur les vagabonds*, pp. 29 and 45.
133. Du Deffan to Choiseul, 15 Nov. 1770, A. de G. X^F 4.
134. M. Marion, 'Les classes rurales dans la Guyenne au XVIIIe siècle', *Revue de la Société des études historiques* (1902), 470–1.

the over-crowding of *dépôts* and hospitals, the impossibility of regarding begging as an offence in such circumstances.

It required in fact a direct command from their superiors for the *cavaliers* to be stirred into life. Government Edicts, Declarations and Ordinances were the rocks thrown with violent but short-lived effect into the *maréchaussée*'s tranquil pool. After the Declaration of 18 July 1724, for example, the intendant of the Auvergne instructed his brigades to devote at least three days a week to the capture of beggars, in both the town and the country.[135] The ripples began to subside after a couple of years, dying away quickest in the small country towns where the brigades suffered even less supervision and interference than in the big centres like Clermont.[136] By 1732, a faint attempt by Trudaine to revive the declaration led to the arrest of four beggars: a 'Moor' in Montaigut; a cripple in the same town; a fellow in Riom who spoke and sang in a strange language, accompanying himself with handclaps and 'extraordinary gestures'; and a girl who recounted extraordinary adventures and called herself the daughter of the marquis de Pompadour.[137] Another declaration, issued on 20 October 1750, and accompanied by instructions to officers and *archers* to redouble their vigilance, had no more lasting results than in 1724.[138]

The Declaration of 3 August 1764 caused bigger and more lasting waves. No other piece of legislation made such an impact on the *cavaliers*' consciousness, and as the new law turned the *maréchaussée* against 'vagrants, vagabonds and *gens sans aveu*',[139] rather than against 'beggars', its immediate effects were felt by vagabonds.

Before 1764, vagabonds had not had much to fear from the *maréchaussée*. The punishment for vagabondage was banishment, but few vagabonds were

135. Circular to all brigades, A.D. P. de D. C 1046.
136. The percentage of beggars confined to the hospital, after arrest, as opposed to those who had presented themselves voluntarily, remained at a higher rate, for longer, in Clermont than in Issoire; as in Lyon, 'the repression of begging was more rigorous in the important towns than in the small towns and villages'. See J.-P. Gutton, *L'Etat et la mendicité dans la première moitié du XVIIIe siècle: Auvergne, Beaujolais, Forez, Lyonnais* (Lyon 1973), pp. 101–4. Gutton's 'rapid study' of the correspondence between the *intendance* and the *maréchaussée* up to the 1730s (P. de D. C 6172–84) confirmed that the repression of mendicity hardly figures among the important concerns of the Auvergne *maréchaussée*, at a time when large-scale operations could be mounted against smugglers. Cf. Paultre, *La répression de la mendicité*, p. 347, on the application of the 1724 Declaration in the Auvergne, and Joseph Coiffier, *L'assistance publique dans la généralité de Riom* (Clermont-Ferrand 1905), *passim*.
137. Correspondence between *subdélégués* and intendant, A.D. P. de D. C 1523.
138. Coiffier, *L'assistance publique*, pp. 111–12.
139. See Olwen Hufton's discussion of the terminology of poverty in 'Begging, vagrancy, vagabondage and the law: an aspect of the problem of poverty in eighteenth-century France'. *European Studies Review*, II (1972) 97–123.

exposed to such a feeble threat as the *cavaliers* were so desultory in their im-
plementation of orders to arrest them. In 1730, the Mussidan brigade became
suspicious of Jean Rivière when he admitted to being a native of Tulle, and
was 'very embarrassed in his replies', as well he might be with his pockets
full of a dead mole, a church candle, and 'a fine pewter plate, folded in two,
the better to disguise the theft and make it fit more easily into his pocket.'[140]
A peddler of pins, who had been wandering the Périgord, the Limousin, and
the Bordelais for years was arrested in 1728 to establish 'that he had no connection with thieves the police were looking for'.[141] One vagabond who appeared to have been arrested on the Mussidan brigade's initiative, was asked
with incredulity by the lieutenant how he had managed to get himself
arrested:

Replied that while asking for alms at the curé's house [in St Médard], having found an
open door, he saw an old pair of shoes and was about to try them on when the curé
rushed up and hit him twice, seized him and cried 'stop thief!' The local peasants gathered,
seized him, and handed him over to the brigade of *maréchaussée* which was passing at the
time.[142]

To be arrested as a vagabond in the Périgord was such a rare event
before 1764 – with one vagabond arrested on average every five years – that
it seems to have required the most unusual carelessness or ill-fortune. Etienne
Chateaureyneau, an old soldier 'very badly dressed', had the misfortune to
ask everyone in a Périgueux inn at lunchtime if they wanted to buy his horse,
including the up-and-coming *cavalier* of the *maréchaussée*, Etienne Reveilhac;
in the resulting on-the-spot interrogation, 'Chateaureyneau's confusion and
lack of confidence gave us the impression that the horse was stolen.'[143]
While the chances of meeting a *cavalier* in an inn were not too remote,
Jean Julien, a vagabond 'with no home or profession', decided to stake out
the house of M. de la Tour (near Brantôme) at the very time M. de la Tour
was receiving a visit from his relative Chevochos, the *brigadier* of the Villeréal
maréchaussée, and came through the gate at 9 p.m., at the precise moment
Chevochos came out on to the verandah to empty a bucket of water. It
was a clear night, the vagabond was spotted in the moonlight, and the
brigadier's cries for help roused the servants who pursued and captured Jean
in the fields nearby.[144]

Things were never quite the same again after 1764. The reports of the
years immediately after its publication testify clearly to a preoccupation
with the terms of the new law. Patrols were mounted and any suspicious
character was taken in for questioning, by virtue of the Declaration of 3

140. *P.-v.* 15 May 1730. He intended to boil and eat the mole, A.D. Dord. B 372.
141. *Interr.* of Armand Saleuilh, 12 Nov. 1728, and letter from Canaye to Lt de la Dersse,
    6 Dec. 1728, *ibid.* B 363.
142. *Interr.* 15 Aug. 1731, *ibid.* B 392.
143. *P.-v.* 17 Sept. 1740, *ibid.* B 421.
144. *P.-v.* 20 Feb. 1739, *ibid.* B 437.

August 1764. The Declaration was invoked forty-four times between its first appearance, on 18 September 1765, and the time it had faded from memory, after 23 February 1772. The fervour which immediately succeeded the Declaration would naturally die down, but *cavaliers* would no longer be able to forget for years on end that they were responsible for the repression of *vagabondage*. Inspired by 'the complaints We constantly receive about the disorders committed by Vagabonds and *Gens sans aveu*, the number of whom appears to multiply daily', the crackdown was directed against all those 'who have carried on no profession or trade for six months and who having no estate or means of subsistence cannot be vouched for by trustworthy persons'.[145] The repression of vagabonds under the ancien régime, therefore, became a question of documentation, and the rôle of the policemen was to find those individuals among the wandering poor who did not have the necessary passports, the certificates, the character references. Before the *cavaliers* could verify papers, however, there was the preliminary and crucial selection to be made of who to ask to produce passports and certificates, as the *maréchaussée* did not have the time, the energy, or the nerve to invite everyone they met to identify themselves and establish their good character.

As the Preamble to the Declaration of 1764 ascribed the prevalence of *vagabondage* to laziness, and as anyone without a job or source of income for six months was likely to be short of funds, the obvious suspect to be told to produce papers was the beggar. Even before 1764, the rare prisoner registered as a vagabond who was not also accused of theft had been accused of begging – Pierre, for example, 'who does not know any other name, nor his place of birth, nor his age', a beggar who had never known his father or mother, and who described himself as 'an idler who'd never got used to work. . . who had never stopped in one place more than three weeks'.[146] After 1764 there was no shortage of beggars around the streets of the *maréchaussée*'s *résidence*, nor of official encouragement to arrest them, so the repression of *vagabondage* was merged with the repression of mendicity.

They could never become synonymous, however, for it was obvious to the *cavaliers* that if a vagabond lived by theft, as his public image insisted, he would not need to beg. The *cavaliers* knew too that many beggars were local people on hard times, so rather than 'beggars', the crucial criterion for a suspected vagabond was 'unknown'. Countless reports of the police brigades justify their stopping and questioning of a passer-by on no more detailed a charge than 'arrested as a suspect stranger'. It is a useful reminder of the smallness of the ancien régime world that a handful of overworked policemen felt they ought to know by sight everyone in their districts, but it was no more than a logical extension of the principle behind the very existence

145. Preamble and Article II of Declaration of 3 Aug. 1764, *ibid*. B 683.
146. *Interr.* 1 Sept. 1744, *ibid*. B 459.

of passports, that even in the 1760s and 1770s a closed and static community was still the norm. The *maréchaussée* did not concern itself with respectable-looking merchants or travellers; three British travellers – a Bristol merchant, an Oxford student of rhetoric, and an Anglican archdeacon – were 'arrested' and interrogated in Périgueux, but the suspected 'vagabonds' were questioned in their inn and not dragged down to the police station; they were asked about their religious contacts in France, not to show that they had means of support.[147] For a real vagabond, therefore, the important criterion was his appearance, and the *prévôtal* prisons were filled with 'badly dressed' strangers. Francois Lavigne was arrested as a 'suspect stranger. . .dressed in an old coat and jacket all patched up and sewn together';[148] the Bergerac *cavalier* Greilh, hurrying from the Monclard fair to the market in Cleren, stopped to arrest a man 'dressed like a tramp'.[149] Judged by the informal standards of the eighteenth-century poor, their rags must have been tattered indeed. The impression made by a passing stranger naturally had a strongly subjective element, and the *cavaliers* of the *maréchaussée* did not hesitate to recognise this factor when drawing up their reports. The Périgueux *cavaliers* Dubois and Villedary arrested the Breton locksmith Julien René Souffron 'because he looked of bad repute';[150] the Mussidan *cavaliers* Greilh and Plaudet were on their way home from the Monpon fair when they met and arrested 'two unknown men who looked suspect because they were very badly dressed and had a nasty countenance [*une villaine fisionomie*]'.[151]

Adopting the precepts of their lieutenants, the *cavaliers* did not go out of their way to find vagabonds until there was an alarming outbreak of thefts. In normal circumstances the police preferred to deal with the vagabonds who frequented the same fairs and markets and main roads as the *cavaliers* – presumably not the more dangerous species of brigand – as well as the occasional individual they came across by chance in the course of their duties. Barns and *métairies* were left undisturbed except in a hue and cry after thieves, but the *cavaliers* were prepared to keep a check on taverns and *cabarets*. The first police report 'in conformity with the Marshal's orders and because of the Ordinance of 4 March 1764' was concerned with the arrest of a 'stranger' in a tavern in Nontron.[152] Jean Peyrinet, a peddler of ironmongery from Terrasson, described to his wife how the police operated:

My dear wife, I write you these few words to let you know the state of my health which is excellent thanks to God and at the same time to tell you about what happened to me in Sainte-Foy the 20th of September in an inn where I was on business. The *cavaliers* of the *maréchaussée*, who pursue vagabonds, came into the inn, took me with them, asked

147. *Interr.* 28 Sept. 1768 of Fisher, Wear and Edwards, *ibid*. B 598.
148. *P.-v.* 21 Oct. 1769, *ibid*. B 609.
149. *P.-v.* 12 June 1771, *ibid*. B 628.
150. *P.-v.* 21 Apr. 1772, *ibid*. B 638.
151. *P.-v.* 1 May 1767, *ibid*. B 585.
152. *P.-v.* 7 June 1766: P. Dachier, 31, former street-porter, *ibid*. B 574.

if I had a passport or certificate. I said no, and immediately they took me to prison with the others. After that they took us to Périgueux. It is really disgraceful for me to be arrested without doing harm to anyone, but I can tell you that everyone without a passport is arrested on the spot.[153]

If the police did not head for the *cabaret* of their own accord, they could always be directed there by local residents suspicious of strange customers, but such encouragement was not usually necessary. When Gigounoux de Verdon was told by the consuls of Villefranche en Périgord 'that a number of strangers were roaming through the town and its vicinity, robbing and assaulting passers-by', the lieutenant's first request was to be shown the 'inns and taverns where the strangers lodge'.[154] On Christmas night 1765, the four Périgueux *cavaliers* were all out on patrol, and in an inn in the suburbs 'met a man, a woman and little child sleeping in a bed'; this Christmas story ended with the family in Périgueux prison.[155]

Perhaps the most dangerous move for any vagabond to make was to panic at the approach of a *cavalier* and try to flee in the opposite direction. It is not surprising that many vagabonds did react this way after 1764, when they had heard about the round-ups being organised by the *maréchaussée*, and learned the new and more dreadful punishment which awaited them. Reveilhac was leading a search for a notorious thief with *cavaliers* from three brigades, when he felt obliged to stop to question 'two people we saw dashing off the main road'.[156] The *maréchaussée* was not so successful if the vagabond had a few minutes' warning of their approach. When the Nontron brigade investigated reports 'that a man and a woman were sleeping in the woods and at night destroying fish in the rivers and ponds', the husband escaped into a dark bush-encumbered wood, leaving his wife and their two-month old child.[157] The woman, after all, risked three years' board and lodging in an *hôpital général*, the man would face the galleys.

The 1764 Declaration had made a dramatic difference to the repression of vagabonds, but it was easy to predict the impermanent character of the policemen's awareness of the problem. There were seven references to the Declaration in 1765; the following year awareness reached its peak with fourteen references, and thereafter steadily declined: eight in 1767, six in 1768, five in 1769. The same problem could be expected with the repression of mendicity, to which the *cavaliers* were directed not by the Declaration which did not mention beggars, but by a series of supplementary instructions – an *arrêt du conseil* of 21 October 1767, ministerial instructions on 1 August and 20 November 1768, and again on 19 February 1770. After 1768, the whole process of confining beggars was streamlined. Lieutenants of the

153. Dated 5 Oct. 1766, Périgueux prison, *ibid.* B 574.
154. *P.-v.* 26 Apr. 1772. B 638.
155. *P.-v.* 25 Dec. 1765: arrest of J. Lavergne, 33, beggar (Limousin), and his wife Marie, 31, *ibid.* B 576.
156. *P.-v.* 8 June 1772, *ibid.* B 638.
157. *P.-v.* 7 Sept. 1767, *ibid.* B 587.

maréchaussée only had to ask them a few basic questions and sign an 'ordinance', while the zeal of the *cavaliers* themselves was stimulated by a reward of three *livres* for each capture.

It had not only been the inadequacies of the police force, however, which had caused the failure of the 1724 and 1750 Declarations. The inadequate hospital facilities, and even more the inadequacies of the staff; the general refusal to regard begging as an offence to be 'repressed' which coloured and formed the *cavaliers'* inability to regard begging as something worthy of their serious attention; the unwillingness of hospitals to accept beggars from 'outside' villages and towns; the non-cooperation of administrators of local hospitals 'who submitted reluctantly to the priorities imposed upon them by the intendants'.[158] All of these factors had to be borne in mind if the *cavaliers* were not to be encouraged by the impossibility of applying the law to sink back into their usual apathy. This time they were at least forewarned of difficulties ahead, and told to prevent prisons and *dépôts* becoming 'clogged up'. As the winter of 1769 drew on, and it became increasingly obvious that begging 'will again become a necessary vice for a great number of the poor' the lieutenants were told to keep all brigade commanders informed of the places available for beggars on a day-to-day basis.[159]

It was by 1769 that the *maréchaussée's* attention was firmly concentrated on mendicity, and in that year 155 beggars were arrested in the Périgord. The *procès-verbaux* of that year make it clear that Choiseul's instructions had been forcefully reconveyed by the *prévôt-général* to all levels of the hierarchy. And it was as a result of orders from the minister de Monteynard, and from the *prévôt-général*, that the repression took up again in 1773. The vagaries of the economic situation cannot be entirely excluded from the operations of the police: the huge upsurge of arrests in 1773 - 299 - reflected the crisis conditions of that year, with rioting throughout the province from the Entre-Deux-Mers to Bergerac, and two cavalry regiments called in to supplement police efforts to contain a 'frenzied populace'.[160] But the arrest figures also reflect the deliberate decision to repress: when basic questions of law and order were at stake, the police could not afford to adopt an easygoing sympathetic approach. This attitude was retained through 1774 (248 arrests) and 1775 - 286 arrests in a year when the lieutenant of the *maréchaussée* was alarmed by reports of an impending revival of the 1773 riots in Bergerac. Gigounoux de Verdon mounted an operation to intimidate the Bergeracois in June 1775, and it was in June of that year that the graph of arrests of beggars reached its peak. In September, the *cavalier* Formiger, on patrol under the watchful eye of the Lieutenant, arrested 28 children who had been begging in Montpazier all their lives.[161]

158. Gutton, *L'Etat et la mendicité*, pp. 97–8, 104–33, 221–3.
159. *Mémoire*, n.d., A.D. P. de D. C 1113.
160. Marion, *Les classes rurales*, p. 472; and Caraman, 'La disette des grains', pp. 297–319.
161. A.D. Dord. B 648–9.

Cavaliers felt the pressure not only of their immediate superiors and the more distant interventions from Versailles, but also of local *notables* who had been caught up in the enthusiasm of the moment. It was a meeting with 'several notable ladies' in Gardonne that encouraged Gagneret, *cavalier* in Ste Foy, to investigate a house frequented by 'all kinds of tramps, beggars and so on'.[162] The Thiviers brigade made 28 arrests after receiving complaints from the curés and 'principal residents' of a number of parishes in its district – Nanteuil, St Saud, Coulaure, St Paul, St Clement, Sarrazat, St Jean de Cole.[163] The following year the same brigade hatched a plot with the curé of Coulaure to capture the crowd of beggars assembled in his courtyard. He wanted the *maréchaussée* to seize the old, and the bigger children, leaving the mothers and young children – 'it's the curé's job to help them within the family'.[164] At the first attempt the crowd of 200 beggars got wind of the *cavaliers'* arrival, and dispersed; three days later, the brigade managed to capture eighteen beggars. The local population could even intervene to ask the *maréchaussée* to keep particularly troublesome beggars in the *dépôt*; the peasants and carpenters of St André de Labauze impressed upon Verdon that the release of Jean Nouvel, an illegitimate 15-year-old orphan, 'would lead to the desolation of the whole district', and would only encourage his *'adjoint'*, the 11-year-old Pierre Paris, 'to get up to his little tricks again'.[165]

The curé La Feuillade had realised that even in the spasmodic intervals of pell-mell arrests, there was room for priorities, that even with their unrefined techniques the *cavaliers* of the *maréchaussée* could at least try to be discriminating. The government itself told the brigades that for practical purposes they could ignore beggars less than half a league from their home[166] – a radius that was sensibly increased to two leagues by the *procureur du roi* in the *maréchaussée*.[167] Any beggar who had a permanent home, a piece of land or a job to support him, or even if he just promised to work and could 'get himself vouched for by trustworthy persons' had nothing to fear from the *maréchaussée*. *Cavaliers* therefore were instructed to direct their efforts in two principal directions: on one hand, they should take into custody as many 'deserving' victims of genuine poverty as there were places available in the *dépôts* – the old, the sick, the imbecile, the infirm, and the very young. On the other hand they should seek out and arrest the five 'dangerous' categories of beggars – those who feigned illnesses or infirmities; those who

162. *P.-v.* 23 Jan. 1774, *ibid.* B 658.
163. *P.-v.* of 8, 11, 13, 15, 16 and 18 Dec. 1774, *ibid.*
164. La Feuillade to Chambaudry, 16 Mar. 1775, *ibid.* B 668.
165. *P.-v.* 10 May 1769, *ibid.* B 610.
166. Controller-general to *MM. les intendants*, (1767/68) BN Fonds français 8129, fol. 147.
167. Chirol to Aurillac brigade 2 May 1768, A.D. P. de D. C 1096.

begged with insolence or menaces; beggars who formed '*attroupements*' of more than four (excluding children); those who were armed, and those who were also deserters.[168]

It was in the nature of things that there should be more 'deserving' than 'dangerous' beggars, and that the *cavaliers* should prefer to handle the weak and infirm. The dichotomy seems to have been clearly fixed in their minds, perhaps even excessively as children, who took up so much of their time in the years of febrile activity, were rather optimistically placed in the deserving category. In the Périgord they were never accused of one of the 'dangerous' expedients adopted by adult males, the deception of the public by the play-acting of non-existent handicaps and injuries. This presumably reflects a quirk in the system of repression rather than a degree of honesty which was conspicuously lacking in the children of other provinces. Judging by the documents which have survived, the children who begged in the streets and roads of the Périgord were arrested only in the special circumstances of the wholesale round-up, when detailed analysis of each beggar's *modus operandi* went by the board. It would in any case have been pointless for the *cavalier* to waste time and ink proving that a child or woman had aggravated the offence by pretending to be crippled; whereas counterfeiting infirmity meant a difference of two years in the galleys for a man, the woman or child would still be sent to the *dépôt*.

It should also be noted that despite complaints from the public, the police did not regard charges of *libertinage* as a factor which aggravated the accusation of mendicity. A girl who had left her mother and dressed as a boy in order to sleep in inns with a *brigadier* of the General Farm was sent to the *dépôt*,[169] but she was only 15 and the *maréchaussée* could hardly have done otherwise. Girls arrested for begging and vagrancy certainly had morality sermons to listen to in court, as they were the ones who had got pregnant in the hay of some anonymous barn. But *cavaliers* persistently took no notice of allegations of immoral living unless the woman was also charged with 'insolent' begging or, preferably, theft; and the lieutenant's subsequent interrogation was always more interested in the woman's economic circumstances or criminal associations than in the procreation of her illegitimate children. The *maréchaussée* could even act on occasion as a welfare organisation coming to the aid of girls, if no longer maidens, in distress. Marie Lapeyre, a 17-year-old sewing-maid from Angoulême, was 'delighted' to follow the *brigadier* Guy when he found her in a *cabaret* in Périgueux 'weeping and lamenting' her fate. She had met a sergeant from the Régiment de Cambresis who persuaded her to come with the regiment to Périgueux after promising, of course, to marry her. 'She prefers young men to old', the Angoulême *lieutenant de maréchaussée*

168. *Instructions concernant le service des maréchaussées*, vol. 2, p. 222. A. de G. X^F 6.
169. 22–3 April 1784, A.D. Dord. B 831.

reported, 'but joking apart', she had been a blameless servant and was sent back to her old employer in Angoulême.[170]

If the *maréchaussée* refused to regard loose women as a public danger, it was very much their duty to distinguish the dangerous fakes from the deserving cripples. The easiest form of affliction to simulate was an inability to speak; for the beggar however it had the disadvantage of failing to provide obvious symptoms of disability which might attract the attention and sympathy of passers-by. Jacques Berger had to get his brother Pierre and cousin Louis to spread the word that he had been a slave in Turkey and had his tongue cut out: the court was not amused by his play-acting, and sent him to the galleys for five years.[171] Arrests in 1770 and 1771 of dumb beggars able to speak confirm the general pattern which emerges from the much more numerous cases of beggars claiming to have a deformity of one limb or another: it was a charge never made by the *maréchaussée* during the spasmodic and indiscriminate round-ups which interspersed the repression of mendicity. In these years, the *cavaliers* did not have the time or energy to investigate the authenticity of epileptic fits or the degree of blindness afflicting the beggars they picked up.

In more relaxed times *cavaliers* would stop suspicious-looking cripples and force them to remove bandages and clothes. Etienne Maurain, who appeared to be missing a left arm was stripped on the main road through the centre of Ste Foy[172]; Antoine Dumas, who claimed to have 'cancer' in the arm, and would risk death from loss of blood if it was uncovered, had his bandages ruthlessly removed at the fair in Berssat de Beauregard.[173] The occasions when *cavaliers* tore off the bandage to reveal a genuine suppurating wound are not recorded. The most that can be found is moments of doubt, when the uncovered arm looked convincingly unhealthy, but which recovered in prison from self-inflicted disfigurement twenty-four hours after arrest.[174] When the *cavaliers* looked under ragged bandages and found that 'certain herbs' or 'certain drugs' had been applied, they were none too clear about the chemistry of the process, and knew no more technical details than their prisoners were willing or able to tell them. The number of fake cripples the *maréchaussée* was able to unearth was small compared to the number of real crippled or sick or deranged beggars, and even when they did identify a beggar with a healthy arm in a sling, he might prove to be riddled with venereal disease, covered with small-pox pimples and ulcers, or his deception would be forgotten alongside more serious accusations of theft.[175]

Nevertheless the *maréchaussée* did treat counterfeiting infirmity as a more

170. *P.-v. de capture*, and *interr*. 21 Oct. 1783, and letter from Angoulême lieutenant to Gigounoux de Verdon 27 Nov. 1783, *ibid*. B 756.
171. *Interr*. 16 Aug. 1770, Sentence 23 Jan. 1771, *ibid*. B 619.
172. *P.-v*. 7 May 1770, *ibid*. B 618.
173. *P.-v*. 13 June 1773, *ibid*. B 649.
174. *P.-v*. 12 June 1771, P. Marsal, *ibid*. B 628.   175. *P.-v*. 25 June 1784, *ibid*. B 795.

serious offence than one of the other aggravating circumstances it was supposed to clamp down on - begging with 'insolence'. The authorities preferred their beggars to adopt a humble pose befitting their station, and no doubt beggars found that it often paid them to be servile. The police depended again on the public to make complaints, and they only took action when a number of reports established a clear pattern of persistent rudeness to potential or reluctant donors. The Ste Foy brigade was persuaded to pursue two men knocking at doors 'with a proud and arrogant air' and demanding bread, wine, money, meat and linen. Some reports claimed the men had refused bread, and even 3s., and insisted on linen, and it transpired that the beggar Villepontoux did in fact need linen for his girlfriend, who was seven months pregnant. As he felt that such a situation was unlikely to evoke much sympathy, he claimed to be a sailor collecting clothes for a convey of injured colleagues mutilated by pirates.[176]

Insolent beggars were difficult to find, but it was impossible to find an armed beggar. Indeed the very poor were the only section of the population not standing in the serried ranks of those who were disarmed by the *maréchaussée*. The companies of the Auvergne and the Guyenne found only two vagabonds with firearms - Lacoste, whose indiscreet pistol shot in the forest had brought about his arrest, and Pierre Marty, who was found to have a pistol after he had been arrested in an inn for trying to make off with a couple of handkerchiefs. It is difficult to see Pierre as a dangerous criminal - when challenged by the innkeeper's wife, he returned the stolen articles, and begged her not to say anything about the incident.[177]

The *maréchaussée* appeared to take very seriously indeed the injunction to beware of *attroupements* of four beggars or vagabonds. It was part of the ritual of interrogation, as crucial and inevitable as the name and age, to ask beggars what company they kept, what associations they had formed, what 'band' they belonged to. Even the dimmest or most awestruck prisoner knew what to reply. But the *maréchaussée* found it very difficult to conceive of a 'troop of beggars', since they assumed that associations were formed to use violence, rob and steel. The brigades therefore organised pursuits of bands of robbers, on one occasion using the four brigades from Issoire, Lempdes, Brioude, and Ambert with the assistance of 150 local men in a painful manoeuvre through the thick undergrowth of the forests of St Anterme; the band turned out to be 'a few beggars brought together by their poverty', hardly dangerous enough, despite the regulations, to be worth the effort.[178] There was no general alarm when more than four beggars came together - the existence in 1771 of a band of 'seventeen or eighteen tramps' in the Périgord, accused of threatening arson on a reluctant host who discovered

176. *Interr.* May 1768, Mar. 1769, *ibid.* B 597.
177. *P.-v. de capture* Brantôme brigade 5 May 1788, A.D. Gir. 11B 15.
178. *P.-v.* four brigades, 15 May 1777, and intendant to Minister, 24 May 1777, A.D. P. de D. C 1547.

that his barn was their traditional home after he had bought the property, only came to the *maréchaussée*'s attention when he also charged them with theft.[179]

It was entirely typical that a beggar be arrested by the *maréchaussée* only because of his implication in some other more serious offence. Between the storms which passed through the sky after the publication of new legislation, beggars would usually go unmolested unless they supplemented their income with smuggling, counterfeiting, or theft. Jean-Antoine de Villard, a 39-year-old nobleman from Langres without profession who begged with insolence, was arrested when he was suspected of both theft and of being a minister of the Reformed Religion.[180] Henriette Repella, who had begged her way from Bordeaux to Brantôme and back, keeping company with beggars, sleeping in the barns frequented by tramps, was finally arrested as a thief in Cadillac when a butcher recognised the sheets she was trying to sell.[181] When in 1768, in the midst of the onslaught on mendicity, Marie Charbonnel was sent to the St Flour *dépôt* as a beggar, she had in fact been arrested for what the *maréchaussée* regarded as her real sin, theft; 'begging with her is not a regular fault', it was 'a pretext' seized upon to rid the Langeac area of a thief who remained unconvicted only because of lack of evidence.[182]

The concern with theft was such that an important robbery, or series of robberies, had the same effect as a new piece of government legislation – it galvanised the repressive forces of the ancien régime into life. The shadow of the indiscriminate round-up would descend again on the *prévôt*'s 'prey'. The *prévôt* himself set the pace: when a band of ten men and two women accused of numerous crimes in Bordeaux was reported to have taken to the countryside, the *prévôt-général* instructed his brigades to arrest everyone they did not know or who could not be vouched for.[183] With commands from *prévôts-généraux* and expeditions mounted by lieutenants to lead the way, the brigades followed suit. François Rozet who combined an 'evil face . . . apparently having considerable disposition to vice' with an unsatisfactory leave certificate from the Foreign Regiment of Dunkirk which was in three pieces and failed to indicate the bearer's age or that his face was pockmarked by smallpox, who had no passport and had neglected to follow the direct route to his native village, would never have been arrested had the Sarladais not been restless after a number of thefts: 'They are shouting Stop Thief on all sides' the *brigadier* explained, 'and the public would have

179. *P.-v. de capture* 30 Aug. 1771, A.D. Dord. B 629.
180. *Interr.*, lieutenant in Périgueux, 12 Mar. 1754, A.D. Gir. 11B 12.
181. *Audition prévôtale* 27 Apr. 1761, *ibid.*
182. *Subdélégué* in Brioude to intendant, 1768 *état des mendiants*, A.D. P. de D. C 1096.
183. It was important to keep track of them, as they aimed to dispose of a servant girl who had witnessed some of their evil-doing. *Mémoire* from the *prévôt-général* circularising the description of the twelve criminals, 10 Apr. 1763, A.D. Gir. C 2245.

shouted against me if I hadn't arrested him'.[184] The *cavaliers* in Blaye arrested Gabriel Simon Bureau on suspicion of desertion from the army, though he had every appearance of being a sailor, 'but as there are a lot of thefts just now in our area they thought they were justified in arresting him'.[185] The injunction to arrest 'à la clameur publique' was interpreted by the *maréchaussée* not just to mean pickpockets seized by angry peasant hands at markets and fairs, but almost anyone accused by public opinion in one of the periods of alarm. When a number of horses disappeared in the Ste Foy area, Labé, 'a peasant working his own land' was dragged in for questioning by the local brigade, because 'rumour' had it that he often changed horses.[186]

The police always knew where to find their *gibier*, where beggars preferred to stand to catch the attention of potential donors, which barns the wandering poor slept in. When the Périgueux brigade needed to find a particular thief, or a scapegoat, they checked first the barn of the *métayer* Migeon, in Cassel aux Tenières, at daybreak.[187] The Ste Foy brigade was stirred into raiding the barns in its area only by a murder in Bergerac and ever increasing complaints of damage to churches; one of them gave shelter to four beggars who were promptly arrested even though the local population insisted they had done no harm to anyone – the barn-owner and his wife were happy to lodge them as they spent the day patching up their clothes and boiling their 'little pot', and when they came home from town, they had nothing but pieces of lard and bread.[188]

The Marmande brigade further underlined the deficiencies of this crude technique when they held a round-up after the theft of a trunk containing clothes, silver plate and chandeliers. Ten were arrested, and the only one to be convicted was Lac, who had been brought in by the local peasants; the rest so uselessly harassed included four children and a peasant recently ruined by hail, all picked up without effort in a *métayer*'s barn, 'which has always lodged all the tramps, vagabonds and beggars who pass by way of Faugerolles'.[189] The long drawn out trial and imprisonment of all the accused was in itself an indictment of the *maréchaussée*'s *rafle*. Six-year-old Magdeleine died four months after her arrest, and she was followed to the grave six months later by Marie Mongaston, a pathetic case of a girl arrested by the *maréchaussée* the day after the theft as she stood watching the dancing at the fair; she was 'consumptive', racked by fever and diarrhoea for the last four months of her life, while being treated as mad because she constantly

184. *P.-v. de capture*, and accompanying letter to intendant, 4 Apr. 1764 – *ibid*. C 2175.
185. Blaye *brigadier*, in accompanying note with *p.-v. de capture*, 24 Apr. 1775 *ibid*.
186. *Brigadier* to intendant, 28 Aug. 1764, *ibid*., C 2175.
187. E.g. *P.-v.* 19 July 1765, A.D. Dord. B 565.
188. *P.-v. de capture* 26 Dec. 1736, A.D. Gir. 11B 3.
189. Aug. 1785 – June 1786, *ibid*. 11B 13.

refused confession. By the end of June 1786, the peasant too had died, from a malignant fever caught in prison.

The injustice inherent in a system of a sudden massive and indiscriminate arrest of potential thieves was perhaps greater than the hardship involved in the equally violent and periodic repression of mendicity. Of course mistakes were made: Henrion de Bussy, the director of the Riom *dépôt* complained that the *maréchaussée* was wasting its time dragging in categories of beggars the authorities were prepared to tolerate – workers on their way home armed with passports, soldiers on leave making for their native parish.[190] The vigour of the royal Ordinances was hardly intended for a certain Perceval, a tailor arrested by the Montaigut brigade who had in his possession 35L. an account book, pieces of cloth, and the tools of the trade.[191]

There is no evidence that abusive arrests were made systematically or even frequently. It was fairly common for beggars to claim that they had asked for alms the day of their arrest for the first time in their life. Pierre Guillotte, who had come up to Clermont from St Ours, a distance of four leagues, tried to persuade the lieutenant that never in the eighty-two years before the moment of his arrest had he resorted to mendicity, and he was released when he promised to return to his job as a farm labourer.[192] But very few denied they had begged at all. The stevedores in Bordeaux who got drunk and were arrested asleep, ostensibly for begging, seem to have had a foolproof alibi.[193] A smelter-engraver arrested in Clermont could at least claim to possess the moulds to make enamel buttons, crosses and medallions, and thus be able to earn a living, even if he had no merchandise.[194] When a mistake was clearly made, it was acknowledged – in the case of Jean Tibard, for example, an 11-year-old boy who came into Belvès to fetch a farrier for his father's bull and was arrested on the flimsy and unsubstantiated grounds that 'he had just been begging', the *cavaliers* had met him while returning home with a convoy of newly-arrested beggars, and arbitrarily taken him along for good measure.[195] In the majority of (the very few) disputed cases it was simply a question of the policeman's word against the prisoner's, resolved in all cases by the inevitable sentencing to the *dépôt*.

Many of the aggrieved prisoners changed their stories under interrogation: Marie Lavergne, a 16-year-old spinner, was told not to lie when she tried to assert she had never begged; the *assesseur* knew she had left her parents after 'maltreatment' a month before, and she soon agreed that she needed to beg to live.[196] Pierre Constantin, the same age as Marie, at least took the trouble

190. Poitrineau, *La vie rurale*, vol. 1, p. 585.
191. Letter from Perceval to Riom dépôt, 7 Aug. 1768, written in Paris after his escape from the dépôt, A.D. P. de D. C 1117.
192. *Etat* of arrests Jan. 1769, *ibid*. C 1109.
193. *Etat* of arrests Oct. 1778, A.D. Gir. C 4643.
194. *P.-v. de capture* 21 May 1769 A. Aursay, A.D. P. de D. C 1109.
195. *P.-v. de capture* 23 Mar. 1774. Jean was freed the same day, A.D. Dord. B 658.
196. *P.-v. de capture* 16 Apr. 1769 and interrogation 20 Apr., *ibid*. B 610.

to suggest an alternative source of income – he 'borrowed' a *liard* or two from people he met in the street, though he found it difficult to think of anyone to whom he had repaid the money.[197] There was a more serious difference of semantic approach between the police and the poor when a number of prisoners insisted before the court that they had not 'begged', i.e. they had not taken the positive step of *asking* for alms or bread. They had simply *accepted* bread and charity when it was offered. One of the Périgueux *notables* who handed out bread to the poor was the Sr du Plancher, and the Périgueux brigade only had to be on hand when the distribution was made at Plancher's door.[198] It was another operation of this type – arresting the crowd gathered for a pre-arranged handout – that led to the only beggar riot in the province.

The occasional abusive arrest must be set against the tolerance habitually accorded to the *gibier du prévôt*, and the fact that when the officers and men of the *maréchaussée* did permit themselves to step up the flow of arrests, the principal complaint of the authorities was the 'frequent discharges which they permit themselves to grant'.[199] The Auvergne intendant was not amused when he took the trouble to send to Strasbourg for a detailed report on the background of a beggar from Alsace, only to discover when the information came through that the lieutenant had already released her. He laid down specific instructions that in future all beggars who were not also vagabonds were to go to the *dépôt*, and he would take upon himself the responsibility to release them.[200]

Negligence and incompetence, success and failure

The policemen of the Guyenne were clearly held in better repute than their counterparts in the Auvergne; they also had an easier task. They were not on the whole harassed by accusations of corruption and they did not divert their energies to part-time jobs; they were spared the greatest difficulties of communication and the most intractable of peasant communities. It is consistent with these factors that they were also spared systematic accusations of neglecting their duties. In the Auvergne, on the other hand, no complaint was made so regularly against the *maréchaussée* as 'negligence', or 'laziness'. But whereas corrupt practices could at least be measured by some kind of objective standard – in nearly all cases the exchange of a few *livres* – there is no simple way to analyse the nature and extent of this alleged 'negligence'.

Failure to make an arrest was the favourite contemporary justification for these charges – 'I have never stopped telling the *maréchaussée* to leave no

197. *P.-v. de capture* 9 Jan. 1775, *ibid.* B 668.
198. *P.-v.* 11 Feb. 1769, *ibid.* B 610.
199. Intendant's note on *état de gratifications* 1769/70, A.D. P. de D. C 1113.
200. Montyon to Riom lieutenant 28 July 1768, *ibid.* C 1095.

stone unturned to have him arrested', intoned the Murat *subdélégué*, faced
with the continuing liberty enjoyed by Guillaume Traverse, who had stabbed
a neighbour to death,[201] and it was the continued freedom of Eyrand which
drove the intendant to confront the Langeac brigade with reports from 'trustworthy persons' of similar 'negligence' in the execution of orders.[202] When
the same brigade caught only one of two young men involved in some eighteenth-century gang warfare in the parish of Siangues – fighting not 'with
their fists, as peasants usually do' but with knives, bayonets and pistols –
the *subdélégué* lamented that 'to tell the truth, this brigade is very casual in
the way it carries out the tasks it has been charged with, particularly if there
is some trouble to be taken, or the slightest risks to be run'.[203] The same
brigadier had been given the intendant's order to arrest a forger, with 'the
strongest exhortations' on the secrecy and diligence of the operation; a
fortnight later he had done nothing, 'the order remains in his wallet and it is
very much to be feared that it expires'.[204] The Montaigut *subdélégué* had
similar difficulties with his *maréchaussée* when faced by the problem of
capturing Jear Guy, a former *milicien* who had escaped from Clermont
gaol after being sentenced to the galleys in perpetuity for repeated desertion. In 1759 he returned to the parish of Colombier, threatening arson if
neighbours took steps to have him arrested. As usual the initiative, even with
regard to the technical problem of how to capture him, was in the hands of
the *subdélégué*, who advised the *sous-brigadier* to surprise him at night with
his girl friend – 'but it is difficult to persuade the *sous-brigadier* to operate
at night'.[205]

The *subdélégués* were the most informed of the *maréchaussée*'s critics,
and to see the charges of negligence in perspective, it is important to note
that only three *subdélégués* accused their local brigades of laziness when in
1732 they had the chance to catalogue in secret all the failings they could
think of, with no necessity of justifying allegations or providing proof.[206]
The *subdélégué* in Aurillac, who prefaced his remarks by noting that the
cavaliers were 'exact' in their attendance at fairs, permitted himself to record that the *exempt* de Fontette, who had previously made his patrols in
the countryside with commendable enthusiasm, had shown slackness 'for
some time'. In Chaudesaigues the *cavalier* Barbe was trustworthy, but lazy;
Hautebesse was firm, but slow and lazy, 'and makes short absences'. Only
in Montaigut was the problem of serious dimensions with a *brigadier*, Legay,
who was 'as lazy mounting his horse as he is diligent going hunting'. The
subdélégué constantly found that the brigade had to be 'spurred on to do

201. Murat *subdélégué* to intendant 1735, *ibid*. C 1527.
202. Intendant to *brigadier* Dantry, *ibid*. C 1523.
203. Langeac *subdélégué* to intendant, *ibid*. C 1530.
204. *Ibid*.
205. Montaigut *subdélégué* to intendant 26 Dec. 1759, *ibid*. C 1552.
206. *Enquête*, 1732, *ibid*. C 6177 *passim*.

some work', and that after his denunciations of their 'nonchalance' he was told to mind his own business. The *brigadier* and *cavaliers* were frequently absent on leave and when the *brigadier* and two *cavaliers* went home for a holiday, 'those who remain at the barracks regard themselves as dispensed from service'.

Three brigades is not much to convict a whole company and it is possible to rescue the Auvergne *maréchaussée* from blanket charges of negligence. In Ambert, the intendant was told, hoodlums and libertines were free to roam the streets beating drums and making scandalous rendezvous in the cemetery, because, it was alleged, of the brigade's failure to mount patrols.[207] This was clearly the sort of letter to be read and discarded. The authorities habitually ignored such denunciations of parochial vice, while the singing, shouting and brawling in the streets of Ambert were no more than the traditional leisure activities of the local youth. It is difficult to see what one brigade of *maréchaussée* could have achieved if it had been foolish enough to intervene.

Perhaps only in the Mauriac district was there a general degree of public agreement on the subject of the *maréchaussée*'s negligence. *Subdélégués*, local officials like the tax receiver, local notables like the seigneur and landowner, the abbé de la Valette, relatives of murder victims, all contributed to the *exempt*'s reputation of 'lacking in courage and resolution'.[208] Certainly the brigade laboured under difficulties – in the 1740s there were only three *cavaliers*, including one detached from St Mamet and another too ill to carry out his duties, and the effectiveness of the brigade was not improved when one of its horses was stolen. Nevertheless there was a consistent pattern of delay in the execution of orders, lack of initiative, and 'nothing more pitiful than the way they make escorts';[209] two *cavaliers* rode together far behind or in front of the tax-receipts coach, and the *subdélégué* confirmed the receiver's criticism when he paid forty *sous* a day to four cavalrymen from a regiment stationed in Mauriac to escort the coach as far as Tauves. The authorities were even more convinced of the negligence of the Mauriac brigade by the catalogue of anarchy drawn up by the abbé de la Valette: when his own servants revolted against his cheese-making projects; when local peasants threatened to beat up the seigneur; when his neighbourhood saw six or seven murders go unpunished M. de Valette was driven to conclude that when the *maréchaussée* passed by on its regular patrols, 'insolence did not raise its head so often'.[210] For once the *prévôt-général* was reminded of his responsibilities. 'The brigade have got very slack in your company [the

207. Curé of Ambert to intendant, 17 Jan. 1759, *ibid*. C 1543.
208. Mauriac *subdélégué* to intendant, on Fontfreyde (1750), *ibid*. C 6185.
209. Correspondence between Dorinière, *receveur*, Sadourny, *subdélégué* in Aurillac, Vignier, *subdélégué* in Mauriac and intendant, 1739 and 1746, *ibid*. C 1529.
210. La Valette to intendant, 5 July 1735, *ibid*. C 1527.

intendant wrote]. Please order them to make more frequent appearances either to prevent these assaults or to arrest the culprits'.[211]

As yet it was a mild rebuke, administered to the brigade indirectly through the *exempt*'s commanding officer. Nothing changed however, and the abbé de la Valette was soon able to send the intendant a memorandum listing over a dozen unpunished murders or outbreaks of arson (including the shooting of a man at the Mauriac fair by Royer, the local *cavalier* of the *maréchaussée*). On this occasion the intendant wrote straight to *brigadier* Fontfreyde himself, heaping on to his puny shoulders the whole weight of a terrible sentence designed to shake him out of his complacency and sloth:

It is certain that if the *maréchaussée* took the trouble to show itself in its district from time to time to find out about the disorders taking place in its parishes, to draw up reports about them, to make use of its authority, not to say its obligation, to arrest scoundrels and others convicted or suspected of crimes without waiting for a judge to sign a warrant, it would be doing its duty, making itself feared, establishing the reputation it is supposed to have, and by its extreme vigilance preventing an infinity of crimes.[212]

The letter must have been of limited effect, for accusations of negligence were as rife twenty years later. The *cavaliers* regarded by the *subdélégué* as the most experienced and intelligent of the brigade were ordered by the intendant in May 1759 to arrest Audebert, the murderer of the Sr de Saignes; weeks went past as the *cavaliers* gathered 'precise information', and when they finally struck on 14 July Audebert was not in; on 17 August the murdered man's widow complained that Audebert was still quietly living at home. 'All this is proof of unpardonable negligence' commented the *subdélégué*, who warned the brigade it was not good enough to forget about an order if it had not met with instant success. As villains often escaped when they heard of the approach of the *maréchaussée*, the *subdélégué* recommended disguise as an infallible operational technique, but his advice was in vain. Audebert disappeared, apparently to Bordeaux, and the *subdélégué* was left to reflect that his local brigade was good for capturing criminals 'put straight into their hands'. It would never be 'cunning enough' nor 'conscientious enough for the duties of the force'.[213]

211. Intendant to *prévôt-général*, 1735, *ibid*.
212. Intendant Rossignol to Fontfreyde, 11 Nov. 1737, *ibid*. C 1528. The *maréchaussée* did not have a blanket authority to arrest anyone on sight. The *maréchaussée* made arrests after a specific order by authority of an arrest warrant issued by a court; *in flagrante delicto* (including beggars, vagabonds and deserters whose very existence was a permanent offence) and 'à la clameur publique', by public demand. The latter two clauses may have appeared to confer powers capable of wide interpretation, but there is no sign, as in fact the intendant appears to complain, that the *maréchaussée* went about making indiscriminate arrests. Rossignol's successor Ballainvilliers, as we have seen, made more of the fact that the *maréchaussée* did *not* have sufficient powers of arrest on its own authority to 'subdue the people, who are by nature so gross'. Ballainvilliers to controller-general, 6 Aug. 1760, *ibid*. C 6186.
213. Letters from Mauriac *subdélégué* to intendant, 17 Aug. 1759 and 23 Dec. 1759. When the unfortunate brigade did capture another murderer on Christmas Eve, 1759, he escaped on Boxing Day, letter from *subdélégué*, 31 Dec. 1759, *ibid*. C 1552.

The intendant however did not put all the blame, or even the major part of the blame, for the lawlessness in the Mauriac district on the failures of the *maréchaussée*. Better than his subordinates and local dignitaries the intendant could see how facile were accusations of police negligence in a province so mountainous, backward and isolated, accustomed to traditions of suspicion and violence, a province which furnished the *Parlement* of Paris with a third of its annual total of criminal prosecutions. It is clear that neither the intendant – whether Rossignol in the 1730s or Ballainvilliers in the 1760s – nor the government expected the *maréchaussée* to take entire responsibility for law and order in the Auvergne countryside. They knew the nature of the terrain, the character of the inhabitants, the small numbers of policemen, and realised that whatever the theoretical duties of the *maréchaussée*, whatever the potential of an omniscient royal police force, the incursion of royal power into the province was too recent for the police brigades to have displaced the old system of social control. In short, if disorder reigned in the Auvergne, it was reasonable to blame the inadequacies of seigneurial control, to point first of all to the inaction of seigneurial courts.

By the eighteenth century, the central government did not regard seigneurs or the tamed and well-behaved rural nobility as enemies – they were rather allies, with a common interest in repressing the criminal activities of the peasants. In the Guyenne, as we have seen, this alliance took the practical form of the police disarming the populace, in the name of public security, of weapons which were generally used to shoot game. In the Auvergne, the alliance between state and seigneur took the form of an attempt by the government to revive seigneurial interest in crime prevention by forcing seigneurial judges either to prosecute, or, if they could not afford the expense of prosecution, to denounce the crime and hand the case over to whichever of the royal courts – *sénéchaussée* or *prévôtal* – was competent to deal with it.[214] This was the culmination, in 1771, of a campaign initiated by Ballainvilliers in 1758 when he arrived in the Auvergne as a newly appointed enthusiastic intendant anxious to bring law and order to the province.[215]

In view of Ballainvilliers' understanding of the geographical and social realities of the Auvergne, and of his awareness of the encouragement given

214. It prescribed that if the seigneurial court took the initiative and prosecuted for a criminal offence, all expenses would be borne by the Crown; if however the royal court had to initiate charges, the entire cost, including all the expenses of appeal, would be borne by the seigneur. A. Poitrineau, 'Aspects de la crise des justices seigneuriales dans l'Auvergne du XVIIIe siècle', *Revue historique de droit français et étranger* (1961), 552ff.

215. With the support of the Chancellor, who also expressed his disapproval of the negligence of both seigneurial and royal judges, the procurators fiscal of all seigneurial courts were instructed to provide *subdélégués* with a list of all crimes committed each quarter in their area of jurisdiction. For a journalistic account of Ballainvilliers' *intendance*, see Vigouroux, 'Ballainvilliers, intendant de justice 1758-1767' in *Bulletin Historique et Scientifique de l'Auvergne*, LXXXI (1961), 126-33.

to crime and disorder by judicial negligence, we have to take note when he issued such a scathing indictment of the Auvergne *maréchaussée* as 'a troop which is the finest, the best mounted, the best fed, and the laziest in the kingdom'.[216] At this point the inventory of the *Fonds de l'Intendance* stops. Ballainvilliers himself however placed a comma after 'kingdom', and the rest of the sentence makes it clear that the remark related to the specific political situation in 1760 when, as we have seen, he was engaged in a bitter conflict with the *prévôt-général* for control of the *maréchaussée*. In 1760, therefore, the Auvergne company was a troop 'which, annoyed with being forced to obey my orders, will turn up but arrest no-one'. It is the bloody-mindedness displayed by the police force in 1760 that Ballainvilliers sought to illustrate by the failure of the Clermont brigade to arrest a soldier who had stabbed someone to death in a city street in broad daylight, and who was seen a-round the town at least three times later the same day. 'You can imagine, Monsieur', he wrote to a government official, 'the help which can be expected *at the moment* from this troop'.[217] When Ballainvilliers spoke the following year of 'the slowness and indeed total inaction of the *maréchaussée* of this province',[218] it was again to make the deliberate point that the force had to be directed by the intendant. It was because the *maréchaussée* 'no longer obeys the intendants' that it failed to carry out 'any kind of service'. To underline the point, the intendant cited the example of the two villains who had murdered their mother and father in a mountain village a year previously. No one would denounce them till they were arrested, the Clermont magistrates were afraid to venture into the hinterland, 'the *maréchaussée* made some useless moves and the crime remains unpunished'.

Despite isolated cases of negligence, therefore, in the carrying out of arrests or daily patrols, no sustained indictment was made out against the *maréchaussée* even by those best placed to do so. It is obviously indicative of the authorities' own attitudes and expectations that the 'negligence' implied by the spasmodic observance in both *généralités* of mendicity and vagrancy legislation should have attracted so little comment. It was much easier to pass judgment on the effectiveness or competence of the efforts the *maréchaussée* did make than on those they failed to make, even if it neither was nor is easy to draw up a balanced account of the efficiency of

216. Ballainvilliers to d'Ormesson intendant of finance, 20 Aug. 1760, A.D. P. de D. C 6186.
217. *Ibid.* [my italics] A dispute between du Deffan and the *officiers* of the Clermont *sénéchaussée* had equally disastrous, but temporary, results for the service of the *maréchaussée*: out of 150 prisoners, not 10 had been arrested by the *maréchaussée*, and *cavaliers*, it was claimed, were being called as witnesses to crimes tranquilly committed in their presence. *Mémoire* (n.d.) by *officiers de la sénéchaussée, ibid.* B 00384.
218. Ballainvilliers to St Florentin 28 Aug. 1761 *ibid.* C 7231.

eighteenth-century policemen. In the Guyenne, the most complete sources are those of the *prévôtal* court, which record the successful capture of all *prévôtal* prisoners, combined with complaints of unsolved crime in which an arrest was attempted, or the occasional bland certificate left by *cavaliers* that the suspect had disappeared. The failures were those of detection, for which ordinary *cavaliers* bore a minimum of responsibility. In the Auvergne, on the other hand, the crucial source for police operations is the correspondence between intendants, *subdélégués* and *prévôts* in which far more noise was made by more people about the *maréchaussée*'s failures than about the routine accomplishment of its tasks. Any quantitative computation of success and failure would therefore be bogus, but it is possible from the qualitative evidence at our disposal to strike a balance between success and failure, and assess the limits of the *maréchaussée*'s capabilities.

It does not detract from the *maréchaussée*'s reputation that they were so often able to profit from the assistance afforded them by their prey. After 3 prisoners had escaped from Riom gaol, the first was recaptured as he wandered down the main road to Clermont; the second on the road only one league from his native village, the third at home in bed.[219] A Breton sailor who robbed and murdered his aunt and escaped from Dinan prison, had the sense to move to Bordeaux, but after moving in with Mme Laporte, got his parents to send him money at his new address.[220] Jean Monseinguilhem, a 15-year-old *valet* in Bordeaux who walked out with 25 *louis d'or* his master had been foolish enough to leave lying around, was known to come from the Béarn; the *cavaliers* therefore turned south, and met the thief sixteen leagues from Bordeaux, walking down the main road to Bayonne.[221] The *maréchaussée* in Murat could hardly fail to suspect that it was Moissier who had murdered Valadier when he refurnished his house with Valadier's possessions.[222] The Aurillac brigade had little trouble recapturing a vagabond who had escaped from prison before he could be dragged to the galleys; the *cavaliers* found him behind a hedge by the roadside, 'where he was resting, as he could no longer walk'.[223] Half the beggars arrested by the Bordeaux brigade in 1778 were 'drunk, and asleep beside the river'. Suspected vagabonds were commonly arrested asleep on a pile of straw in a barn. A brigade's tally of beggars was boosted by women thrusting infants into the *cavaliers'* arms. Most of the deserters arrested by the *maréchaussée* were found wandering down the main road in their uniforms; and the *cavaliers*, as ex-soldiers, could be expected to have a keen eye for any 'individual who by his clothing and

219. *Etat de captures et traductions* 1788, Pont du Château, *ibid.* C 6256.
220. Arrested by the Bordeaux brigade, 30 May 1776 – one of the rare examples of interregional cooperation. A.D. Gir. 11B 12.
221. *Audition*, 12 Sept. 1738, *ibid.*
222. Murat *subdélégué* to intendant 1737, A.D. P. de D. C 1528.
223. *Etat des galériens* 1767, *Présidial d'*Aurillac, Verdier, *ibid.* C 1595.

bearing looked to us like a soldier'. The Sauveterre brigade, ordered to arrest the deserter Jouan, found him by accident already in prison in Libourne.[224] When Cazenave, *cavalier* in Langon, was having his hair combed at the barber's, he passed an innocuous comment that the wigmaker's assistant who was serving him had a good height and was a likely-looking chap for the army; the lad was 'troubled', and finding that he could no longer contain his guilty secret, told Cazenave that he had engaged in the régiment de Piedmont, received eighteen *livres*, and decamped.[225] Jean Mercier knocked at the door of the Bordeaux *maréchaussée*, and declared himself a deserter 'repenting of his crime and begging us to arrest him'.[226]

By the very nature of their profession, beggars made life easy for the *maréchaussée*, as they could not hide themselves away in out-of-the-way places if they hoped to live off public charity. Reports of the arrests of beggars, therefore, show the brigades of the Périgord in operation on the main roads; usually the brigades did not even have to stir out of town – the Bergerac brigade arrested in the main street of Bergerac, the Ste Foy brigade in the rue St James, and in Périgueux we can follow the *cavaliers* from the 'Place de la Cité near Périgueux' to the Porte Taillefer, into the town up the rue Taillefer to the Place de la Clautre, then past the cathedral to the hub of commercial and social life, the Place du Coderc, and on through the throng of people in the rue Limogeanne and the rue de l'Eguillerie.

Life was of course made easier for the *maréchaussée* to the extent that the overwhelming majority of beggars were not the dangerous men who constituted a real threat to public security, but children, the infirm, and the very old. In St Flour for example, at the height of the repression in 1768, the brigade brought in six beggars from the parish of St Saturnin, all 'infirm', and aged 92, 64, 75, 60 and 70, while other parishes provided an infirm peasant woman with four children, an infirm cowman with six little children, and two orphan girls aged 7 and 3.[227] The following month the brigade arrested only beggars born and resident in St Flour and conveniently listed by the curé: eleven of the twelve adults were aged between 60 and 78, four were 'impotent', two were 'imbecile', one man had a paralysed arm, seven were 'invalids', two were epileptics, two men were blind, and three were in their dotage. Children under 16, the aged, those certified as 'too old to work' and the infirm made up over three-quarters of the total arrests in the Périgord in 1769; of the remainder, there were twice as many women as men. Over the century as a whole children made up at least half the total, and men reckoned to be fit never reached a higher proportion than a fifth. The Bordeaux brigade

224. 'For some misdemeanour committed on his way home from grape-harvesting.' *P.-v.* and *Audition*, 25 Nov. 1747, A.D. Gir. C. 4637.
225. *P.-v. de capture* of Jacques Frelon, 18, 20 Oct. 1774, *ibid.* 11B 12.
226. *P.-v. de capture*, 18 Oct. 1780, A.D. Gir. C 2183.
227. *Etat* in A.D. P. de D. C 1111.

in 1778 arrested only twenty-nine healthy beggars, compared with thirty-four with twisted limbs or racked by pain and disease; no less than seventeen had venereal disease, and the rest were 'crippled', short of sight or 'broken by age', subject to rheumatism, scabies, epilepsy, ringworm, and mental derangement.[228]

If more subtlety was required than was usually necessary for arresting the halt and the lame, the policemen were on occasion able to produce it. There were *brigadiers* who were not without a certain cunning: 'informed of some assault or murder, he ignores it at first, lets a few days pass, makes his arrangements and then, moving at night, falls on his prey'. Another *brigadier* in Ambert, Meynial, who was ordered to arrest Passemart who had absconded with sums of money belonging to various *consuls*, followed the same technique, by studiously giving no sign of life in the hope of allaying suspicions and encouraging Passemart to return to Ambert.[229] Brigade commanders could sometimes devise stratagems on the spur of the moment. Lacoste, the Aurillac *exempt*, was patrolling the fair at La Capelle Barres when his suspicions were aroused by a weather-beaten ruffian who claimed to have arrived from Paris and had lots of money; though he called himself Baptiste Micalandie, his appearance fitted the description of Jacques Attrait, who was wanted for a number of robberies. The *exempt* needed time to make inquiries, so he got one of his *cavaliers* to buy a mare 'Micalandie' had for sale, on condition he came to Aurillac himself for the money. Attrait duly presented himself at the *maréchaussée*'s door, and soon found himself behind bars.[230]

In the last decade of the ancien régime at least, the *maréchaussée* could on occasion show some flair in their repression of vagabonds. At the 1784 Bergerac fair, the *brigadier* Peyrou got two *cavaliers* to 'dress up as bourgeois', and in this disguise to 'go through the fair. . .secretly detecting pickpockets and other suspect people'. The vagabond to be pulled in under suspicion was a wool-carder with a 'pair of iron compasses, with sharpened points', which, the *cavaliers* noted, was not an instrument necessary for the profession.[231] In uniform or disguise, *cavaliers* could also keep their ears open. The Bergerac brigade arrested Marie Vincente 'having recognised from her accent that she did not come from the Auvergne' as she had claimed.[232] Patrolling the Périgueux to Thiviers road, the *cavalier* Dubois met a 'suspect' claiming to be from a village 'half a league from here', which was immediately treated as a lie 'because in our district we speak *patois*'.[233] These were not perhaps very subtle deductions, but it is impossible not to be impressed by the Montignac

228. *Etats* in A.D. Gir. C 4643 and C 4644.
229. Ambert *subdélégué*'s tribute to his *brigadier*, in intendant's *Enquête* of 1732, A.D. P. de D. C 6177; and letter to intendant 8 Mar. 1751, *ibid*. C 6185.
230. Lacoste to intendant, 24 June 1767, *ibid*. C 1546.
231. *P.-v.* 13 Nov. 1784, A.D. Dord. B 768.
232. *P.-v.* 30 Aug. 1784, *ibid*.
233. *P.-v.* 9 Oct. 1783, *ibid*. B 756.

brigade's sources of information on the movement of vagabonds within its district. Jean Muratel arrived in Montignac at nine in the evening, and later that same night, the local *brigadier* knew that a stranger had put up at the inn, that he had a mare and two passports, and a sailor's leave-pass instructing him to retire to Carcassonne until further orders – all this despite the fact that the pass was 'hidden in his breeches'.[234]

The police records of the eighteenth century record a number of arrests made in the face of great difficulty. The Murat brigade captured a burglar and his wife who had taken refuge in the woods, even though it took six days; the brigade in La Tête de Buch caught up, after six days and nights, with the three robbers who had pillaged La Chapelle d'Arcachon.[235] A man who had stolen a mare and fled the Montaigut area was arrested when he reappeared ten years later.[236] The *exempt* in Périgueux needed less time to get his man when informed on the evening of 6 October (1779) of a highway robbery which had taken place on the Limoges road two days before: he took a *cavalier*, and they rode all night towards Limoges; at dawn a peasant redirected them towards Bordeaux, and the thief was caught at nightfall, five leagues from Périgueux, and still with the stolen property.[237] The Pauillac brigade snatched a deserter off the *Georgette* as she rode at anchor in the Gironde waiting for a fair wind for America.[238] Two *cavaliers* in Bordeaux, on duty at the Place St André near the *Hôpital Général*, and aimlessly watching the cart trundling corpses to the cemetery, recognised the driver as a felon they had escorted to the galleys, supposedly for nine years, five years before.[239]

The *maréchaussée* often remembered the faces of their regular clientèle, the professional beggars and petty thieves who had passed through their hands from time to time, but the Langon brigade had no more than the eighteenth-century identikit, the verbal description contained in the *signalement*, to work on when they arrested 'Jean', an apprentice with 4s. 8d. in his pocket, on suspicion, subsequently confirmed, of being Jean Larmitrie, wanted for the theft of 300L. and a gold ring.[240] The Marmande brigade was even more successful when they retrieved 3,977 L. of the 4,000 stolen from a Bordeaux banker; like all the other brigades they had no more than the thief's description, and became interested in 'a young man we did not know' riding across the town square. When they saw him again wandering the streets, the *cavaliers* followed him to the Inn of the Golden Lion; the *brigadier* stationed his men to prevent an escape, entered the young man's room,

234. *P.-v.* 12 Oct. 1788, *ibid*. B 821.
235. *Courses extraordinaires pour 1789*, A.D. Gir. C 3729.
236. Montaigut *subdélégué* to intendant 1746, A.D. P. de D. C 1533.
237. *P.-v.* Guy, 6 Oct. 1779, A.D. Gir. C 2182.
238. *P.-v. de capture* of J. Perrot, 4 Apr. 1782, *ibid*. 11B 12.
239. *P.-v.*, *ibid*. 3 May 1782, 11B 12.
240. *Ibid*. 11B 10.

seized the startled suspect's sword, and demanded to know if he was not Castes, wanted for theft. The prisoner did not try to deny it.[241]

To these successes must be added an explanation of, and justification for, many apparent failures. One of the most embarrassing – an incident which provoked rebukes from the Bordeaux intendant and the Minister of War – was the messy recapture of Calasson. He had first been arrested by the Villeneuve brigade at the fête in Casseneuil. When the brigade, with the added support of the 'bourgeois patrol', attempted to transfer him to Agen, the *cavaliers* abandoned their prisoner under a hail of stones and one of the patrol had his finger cut off by a billhook wielded by Calasson's sister. When two brigades were sent by the *maréchaussée* to arrest Calasson at home, they found that the family had barricaded themselves inside the house and were firing on all fronts. The *cavaliers* on this occasion not only faced violent opposition and the communal hostility of neighbours who ultimately forced the *maréchaussée* to withdraw, they were also plagued by bad luck and by bad equipment – one of the *cavaliers* had such a poor gun that it went off at the slightest knock and almost killed Calasson.[242]

It was more difficult to make excuses for the *maréchaussée*'s failures in the Auvergne when the brigade arrested the injured victim instead of the aggressor in a pub-brawl,[243] or made such a clumsy, well-publicised manoeuvre that the intended prisoner was scared off and not seen again.[244] Of course it is difficult to estimate how typical such failures were, but we are permitted to doubt that any police force might be generally efficient when it was capable of missing an arrest because it looked only in the suspect's house and forgot to look in his barn.[245]

There was no more apparent failure than a rebellion against the *maréchaussée*, not only because of the defeat which the *cavaliers* inevitably suffered at the hands of *force majeure*, but also because of the fact that revolt had taken place at all. It is clear however that in many heated circumstances when riot threatened, an acceptance of defeat was the wise policy, indeed that flight was usually the only possible policy. As will be seen, most rebellions against the *maréchaussée* were not provoked by police insensitivity or incompetence, but by the obligation the *maréchaussée* was under to apply the law, whether it entailed giving assistance to court officials, collecting young men for the militia, disarming the populace of illegal weapons, or inviting the revellers at a parish fête to stop their amusements and go to church. There were undoubtedly occasions at fairs and markets when the *cavaliers* stirred up trouble after drinking too much, but these episodes are outnum-

241. *P.-v. de capture* 18 June 1749, *ibid.* 11B 4.
242. *Procès-verbaux* October 1782, ibid. C 2187 and A.N. Z^IC 399.
243. Aurillac *subdélégué* to intendant, November 1731, A.D. P. de D. C 1522.
244. Mauriac *subdélégué* to intendant, 2 Nov. 1760, *ibid.* C 1544.
245. Thiers *subdélégué* to intendant, 1730, *ibid.* C 1519.

bered by the instances of deliberate provocation to which the policemen were subjected. There is copious documentation on the occasions when revolt or riot did occur, and only fragments of evidence to recall the happy days when rebellion was averted. The unfortunate Fauchey de la Combe, who so bungled the capture of a gang of thieves, was yet able to restore calm to a crowd of 4,000 when he walked amongst them, accompanied by a *brigadier* and a *cavalier*, promising to have bread made and distributed at seven *liard* the pound.[246] The Casteljaloux *brigadier* made a rousing speech when the 'rabble' wanted to take the corn for nothing, and lectured the mayor, the town council and the 'élite of the citizens' on how to organise its orderly sale.[247] The Langeac brigade, in the parish of St Cirques to enforce a decision of the bishop of St Flour to suppress the fête of Ste Julitte, argued so effectively with the crowd that they gradually dispersed.[248] Loriette, the *sous-brigadier* in Pont-du-Château deprived of any help from his *cavaliers* who were patrolling in the countryside, prevented even the beginnings of an *attroupement* over the impending departure for Orleans of four boatloads of corn, simply by visiting the militants and warning them not to do anything stupid.[249]

The final piece of evidence to the credit of the *maréchaussée* is again most evident in the Guyenne – the appreciation which the force enjoyed from its contemporaries. The most striking tribute to the effectiveness of the brigades in imposing their presence on the countryside is the ever-increasing willingness on the part of all sections of the community to come to the *maréchaussée* to denounce crimes of theft and violence.[250] It is true that the recovery of stolen property continued to be regarded as too important a matter to be left to the police, and that there were other factors contributing to the transformation of attitudes, but in the Périgord at least, the presence of brigades of *maréchaussée* certainly helped the peasants to overcome their communal reticence and fear of intimidation.

The Guyenne company was adept at exploiting this willingness to cooperate by getting private citizens to supplement the understaffed and overworked brigades in their routine service. As early as 1761 the brigades of Sauveterre and Créon were able to arm peasants and make use of their assistance to track down the murderers of the Dlle Dudon.[251] The Créon brigade had exceptionally good relations with the local populace for its expense claims in 1767 casually note that a thief had been captured 'with the aid of a number of peasants', and later the same year, when Jacques and Marie Gaussin tried to escape with their stolen property by plunging into

246. Caraman, 'La disette des grains', p. 304.
247. *P.-v.* 18 May 1773, A.D. Gir. C 1338.
248. *P.-v.* 1787, A.D. P. de D. C 6204.
249. *Mémoire* by Loriette, October 1768, *ibid.* C 6187.
250. See below, chapters 5 and 6.
251. *Etat de service extraordinaire*, 1761, A.D. Gir. C 2179.

a wood, the *brigadier* had them tracked down by peasants and their sheep dogs.[252]

In the Auvergne, on the other hand, it was not a question of the police organising assistance for itself. Reports describing Auvergnat peasants mounting their own patrols and guard-watches suggest that the *maréchaussée* enjoyed rather less than the entire confidence of the population. In 1755, for example, villages along the Velay border lived in fear, the peasants frightened to come out of their houses, any passing stranger regarded as a thief, and as if to rehearse 1789, 'These men keep watch with a lamp burning all night, afraid of the approach of thieves'.[253] Twenty years later in 1774, the timorous light in the window had given way to vigilante patrols and by 1777, the curé of Royat, in the outskirts of Clermont itself, was setting his parishioners to 'make patrols and set up guard posts' every evening against a band of thieves.[254]

The *maréchaussée* of course was even thinner on the ground in the forested lands which straddled the road from Ambert to Lyon on the frontier with the Forez. When in 1777 therefore the local inhabitants heard of fires being lit in the forest to roast livestock stolen from the fields, and of groups of men, women and children armed with knives and swords descending on isolated farms or hamlets to demand their subsistence, they organised the pursuit with no outside help other than to send for two *cavaliers* of the *maréchaussée* to lend them a hand. Seven prisoners were taken, and when neighbouring parishes decided to continue the hunt, it was again a question of the locals inviting the *maréchaussée* to give them assistance: four brigades turned up to join the 150 local men in the operation. The *cavaliers* were of no help whatsoever, 'encumbered the whole time by their horses' in the thick undergrowth.[255]

The cumulative effect of such incidents was a clear lack of government faith in the operational skills of the Auvergne force. A thief who was an expert at picking locks did appear at home from time to time, but made 'such brief appearances' that the *maréchaussée* could hardly be expected to keep up with him.[256] A band of brigands was systematically pillaging the Mauriac district of its horses and mares, but as they preferred not to stay too long in one place, 'it does not seem possible that the *maréchaussée* will be able to arrest them'.[257] When the government was anxious for the operation to succeed, it did not leave the arrangements to the police. The more villainous the criminal, the more forcefully were the *cavaliers* instructed to follow the

252. *Etat*, 1767, *ibid*.
253. Langeac *subdélégué* to intendant, 10 July 1755, A.D. P. de D. C 1552.
254. Correspondence 1774 *ibid*. C 1547, and De l'Arbre to intendant, December 1777, *ibid*.
255. Report from du Deffan to intendant, 13 May 1777, *ibid*. C 1547.
256. *Etat des crimes*, Clermont divisions 1749, *ibid*. C 1554.
257. Mauriac *subdélégué* to intendant, June 1752, *ibid*. C 1537.

instructions of the *subdélégué*, and the more ready the authorities to call in the assistance of regular troops.

Even the Auvergne company however was not universally decried. The abbé de la Valette himself paid a retrospective tribute to the effectiveness of the force: 'When the *maréchaussée* passed every month through the parishes calling on seigneurs to inquire if there were any rogues, insolence did not raise its head so often, and the effects of the interruption of such a commendable practice are obvious'.[258] Despite the abuse heaped on the Mauriac brigade and on the *brigadier* Fontfreyde in the eighteenth century and since, the *subdélégué*, faced by an outbreak of theft attributed to an influx of 'poor strangers' could think of no way to redress the situation other than by 'the operations and the vigilance of the *maréchaussée*', and by getting Font-freyde to divert the strangers to pastures new and encourage the others by arresting a few of their number.[259] This sort of praise of the *maréchaussée* was clearly interested, and there were many people with an interest in the effectiveness of the *maréchaussée*. Despite all its faults, it was the only viable police force around, and towns and municipalities without brigades clamoured for their establishment, or sent petitions if they lost a brigade. When the intendant of the Auvergne made trenchant and quotable criticisms of the uselessness of the *maréchaussée*, the whole tenor of his argument and his campaign was to underline the fact that he could not do without it: 'This police force, wisely administered, has so far held in check, in the Auvergne, rude and coarse people who know nothing to restrain them but the *maréchaussée*'.[260]

The local agents of the central government were the men who were most aware of the value of the *maréchaussée*, just as they were the men who most keenly appreciated its limitations. It was the local government officials in both provinces who most keenly regretted the *maréchaussée*'s lack of men and money and who were most eloquent in demanding more of both. It was after all the authorities themselves who drove the *cavaliers* into debt by forcing them to buy their own horses, and imposing burdens of irregularly paid 'extraordinary' service, just as it was the authorities who did not always provide decent accommodation, and even decent equipment, such as a rope strong enough to detain a sturdy 20-year-old beggar.[261] It is the reports of government officials which provide us with some of our most graphic illustration of Auvergnat violence, so they could hardly blame the *maréchaussée* for incompetence when it failed to effect an arrest in the face of such virulence.

From the point of view, therefore, of government officials aware of the handicaps imposed on the police force and painfully conscious of the social

258. La Valette to intendant, 5 July 1735, *ibid*. C 1527.
259. Mauriac *subdélégué* to intendant, Mar. and Apr. 1753, *ibid*. C 1527.
260. Ballainvilliers to St Florentin, 22 July 1760, *ibid*. C 6186.
261. *P.-v.* Langeac, March 1769, A.D. P. de D. C 1111.

problems of their localities, the *maréchaussée* could ultimately be regarded as a success in both the Guyenne and, with obvious reservations, the Auvergne. Such an optimistic conclusion can at least be justified by the standards of the ancien régime, for despite the hopelessly unrealistic intentions of the legislation the *maréchaussée* was supposed to implement, despite the very creation in 1720 of a police force supposed to keep the countryside in tutelage, intendants and *subdélégués* continued to share the modest assumptions of a pre-industrial and a pre-Beccarian system of law enforcement. They persisted in using the *maréchaussée* to serve a system of justice that did not have the means to deter crime by the certainty of punishment, and so could only hope to discourage by example. When the intendant told the *maréchaussée* to arrest an individual, he did not do so for the good of the villain's soul, or even in the spirit of social retribution; he almost always made it clear that the *cavaliers* would be issuing a warning to others.

Time and again the *maréchaussée* of both provinces was reminded of the need for 'examples'. After turbulence and emotion in the cantons round St Geneix, the *subdélégué* wanted 'striking examples'.[262] When rowdy youths in Thiers swaggered out of a *cabaret* and rolled a passing merchant down the gorge, the *subdélégué* wanted only one of them arrested, to 'make an example to subdue the great number of libertines'.[263] Examples were useful to encourage people to pay their taxes, and discourage them from insulting *consuls* and *sindics*; the scapegoat in Riom, in 1756, was to be the wife of an artisan, and not her husband, for his arrest would cause the abandonment of the property, and he would be punished by the very imprisonment of his wife, 'especially as it is more often the wives of artisans who indulge in these excesses', and at a time when tax collecting was getting difficult, 'an example seems indispensable'.[264] Faced with widespread grain disturbances in 1778, culminating in the establishment of road and river blocks around Domme by a troop 150 strong, Gigounoux de Verdon wrote that it was essential to 'make an example to intimidate the leaders of the riot'.[265]

Nowhere was this disparity between the absolute aspirations of the central government, and the restricting force of reality in the field, more apparent than in the repression of begging. The Declaration of 18 July 1724 had been made possible, Paultre tells us, by the reorganisation of the *maréchaussée* in 1720:[266] the force was to arrest all beggars and have them consigned to the *hôpital général*. But at no time were the resources of the *maréchaussée* or the *hôpitaux* sufficient for such a task. The Auvergne town of Montaigut had characteristic difficulties applying the law – its *hôpital* was

262. *Mémoire*, n.d., by Chabron (1738), *ibid*. C 1529.
263. Thiers *subdélégué* to intendant, 1740, *ibid*. C 1530.
264. Riom *subdélégué* to intendant, 11 Sept. 1756, *ibid*. C 1540.
265. Verdon to intendant, A.D. Gir. C 485.
266. Paultre, *La répression de la mendicité*, p. 325.

in no state to contain even local beggars, and with the nearest suitable *hôpital* in Riom, it would have been ruinously expensive and time-consuming for the *maréchaussée* to escort them such a distance. Monteloux who served as *subdélégué* and *lieutenant criminel* simply released a vagabond without a passport arrested as an 'example' to his 'Moorish' companions by the *maréchaussée*: 'It is astonishing how many of these people pass this way. . . if the *maréchaussée* arrested them all, the prisons would not be able to contain them'.[267] The *maréchaussée* was told to arrest only 'the ones whose appearance or speech suggests they are to be feared' who would suffer an exemplary punishment; if the others missed the point, the *maréchaussée* was to 'teach them a good lesson by throwing them out the town'.

The *maréchaussée* stuck to this restricted interpretation of their rôle – in the Guyenne, for example, the Coutras *brigadier*, protecting public security 'with all his might', arrested only one of the numerous beggars who cluttered the main road from St André to Libourne and Castillon: 'that will terrify the others and perhaps make them stay more in line'.[268] De la Crompe was appalled when the judge in Guitre tried to pass on to the *maréchaussée* a beggar/vagabond who had got drunk and found himself arrested by the bourgeois patrol: all the brigades of *maréchaussée* in the kingdom would not suffice if every court took it into its head to arrest beggars 'on the pretext of handing them over to the *maréchaussée*'.[269] The rôles were reversed but the logic was the same in Langeac, where the *brigadier* of the *maréchaussée* arrested two beggars '*sans aveu*', and the royal judge released them, 'saying it was enough to intimidate them'.[270] De la Crompe was interested only if the beggar was accused on a 'real' *prévôtal* crime; the Langeac royal judge was interested in the beggars only if they were implicated in theft. Similarly in Périgueux, the *assesseur* of the *maréchaussée* released a man, a fit young beggar, on the grounds that 'he can be charged with nothing but poverty' (having, by implication, no connection with the band of masked armed men who had held up a grain convoy on the Ribérac-Mussidan road).[271] The acceptance, therefore, by local officials in the courts, the *intendance* and the police, of the simple fact that given the resources of the ancien régime state, only a tiny proportion of law-breakers could be caught and punished led on the one hand to the notorious structure of brutal punishments inflicted in public, and on the other hand to a general tolerance, only spasmodically interrupted by special circumstances, of such 'victimless crimes' as mendicity and vagrancy.

267. Correspondence between *subdélégué* and intendant, 1732, A.D. P. de D. C 1523.
268. De la Crompe to intendant, 12 Mar. 1764, A.D. Gir. C 2175.
269. De la Crompe to intendant, 21 Oct. 1763, *ibid.*
270. Cristal, *brigadier*, to intendant, 27 July 1755, A.D. P. de D. C 1539.
271. *Interr.* of Jean Deschamps, 22, parish of Alleman, and 'summer valet' at the end of what must have been a long hard winter, 25 Apr. 1764, A.D. Gir. C 2175.

Rather than waste their limited time and energy on a futile attempt to keep up with government legislation, eighteenth-century policemen preferred to concentrate their efforts, either by paying token obeisance to the new laws which concerned them, or by organising a brutal riposte or concerted action to deal with a particularly serious situation. This, as we have seen, usually involved the grouping together of several brigades to control a menacing and disaffected population as in Bergerac in 1773, or to meet the threat posed by reports of large bands of thieves or smugglers. Whatever the distress caused by sporadic round-ups to the down-and-out population, and whatever the success of large-scale expeditions in harassing the brigands and even preventing the consolidation of organised bands, a reliance on such 'extraordinary' methods only served to underline the failure of the 1720 reforms which had sought to elevate a sense of security into a permanent way of life. Despite the multiplication of 'examples', it did not require a Beccaria to remind the public of the inadequacies of a system of law and order based on so intermittent an imposition of authority. The spasmodic enforcement of the law, the occasional passage of a patrol (with even that comfort withdrawn when trouble threatened at the other end of the province) were not calculated to bolster the confidence of the public in the protection afforded by the *maréchaussée*. And when the brigades were not off chasing brigands at the far end of the province, they were devoting their attention to the supreme military offence, desertion. In the 1770s and 80s, more than half the prisoners who passed through the *prévôtal* gaol in Bordeaux were deserters, and in the course of the American War, the proportion was more like three-quarters.[272]

This was a limited comfort in a period when economic conditions had begun to deteriorate. It was not surprising that despite the rearrangements in the police force, or perhaps because of rearrangements which increasingly deprived policemen of informal contact with the public, the populace continued to feel nervous. It was a time when more and more were being pushed into the ranks of the destitute and the incentives for crime and civil disturbances were multiplying. In their increasing alarm, the established, domiciled population was forced into cooperating more with the police, and into taking more steps to look after themselves. Social order however was enforced not only by *cavaliers* on police duty in the field or even by vigilante patrols, but also by the punishment of law-breakers in the courts. The *maréchaussée* had always retained these two complementary dimensions to the protection of 'public security' – the sword of its policemen, the robe of its judicial officers. For the *maréchaussée* these two rôles were complementary to the extent that the court depended on the police for the detection and capture of criminals; for the public, to the extent that its willingness to cooperate with judicial

272. In 1781, 73 deserters from a total of 95 prisoners; in 1782, 55 prisoners from 97. The highest proportion of deserters however was in 1788 – 60 out of 69. *Registre d'écrou*, A.D. Gir. 11B1.

investigations might well depend on its confidence in the physical protection afforded by the police brigades. From both these points of view, therefore, the *maréchaussée* was an indispensable part of a system of law enforcement which also included its judicial arm, the *prévôtal* court.

CHAPTER 4

The *prévôtal* court

The reputation of ancien régime criminal justice has never recovered from the Calas Affair. The subsequent victory of Voltaire and Beccaria seemed like the triumph of good over evil, the recognition of the rights of the individual in the face of a system which resorted to the most diaphanous of hearsay evidence, an inquisitorial procedure designed to produce a conviction, the threat of perjury charges to dissuade witnesses from changing their minds, torture, and a dreadful execution. It is easy, however, to overdramatise the clash between the 'enlightened' principles of our own day and the barbarism of a benighted ancien régime. Both then and now, courts have had the double function of ascertaining the guilt or innocence of an accused, and of helping to maintain law and order in society at large. Both then and now, a balance has had to be established between the protection of the individual suspect and the protection of society as a whole. The operations of the *prévôtal* court will therefore have to be measured against two standards. In so far as it can be assessed from the transcript of the trials – the same evidence, after all, which was before the court – how fair and reasonable were the decisions of *prévôtal* magistrates? And in what ways, and how effectively, did *prévôtal* justice contribute to the defence of law, order and public security?

Competence

Of all the institutions of criminal justice in ancien régime France, the *prévôtal* court was the one most heavily weighted on the side of public security, the one which offered the least protection to the individual suspect. It was a court of summary justice which had grown out of military tribunals used to combat the depredations of marauding soldiers and vagabonds. It was a court presided over by an ex-army officer who had no legal training, who brought into the courtroom the sweat of a long patrol and the dust of country lanes. Worst of all, the *prévôtal* court was a tribunal from which there was no appeal. The morbid atmosphere of finality hung over the prisoner virtually from the moment of his arrest, for he had to face an interrogation within twenty-four hours and the lieutenant or his legal adviser, the *assesseur,* was obliged to warn him at the outset that he would be judged 'in the last resort' before the *prévôtal* court. The security of the state was clearly the justification for this loss of a most important individual right – the *prévôté,* according to Jousse, dealt with crimes 'which demand prompt punishment',[1] not those which had inflicted the greatest loss or suffering on an individual subject of the king, but those which most directly threatened the public domain.

The most obvious military threats to social order were clearly established as *prévôtal* crimes in the Ordinance of 1670: the 'oppressions and excesses . . . of the military' which had always been the *maréchaussée's* concern: desertion, or any activity which tended to encourage desertion such as buying a soldier's uniform;[2] 'raising a private army', a dead-letter in the eighteenth century; and duelling, which had far from disappeared in the eighteenth century, but was in a state of sad decline. The Edict of 1731 confirmed the return of the nobility to the fold, royal recognition that they were no longer regarded as a threat, by specifically denying the *prévôtal* court all right of jurisdiction over nobles, as well as judicial officers, priests, and *secrétaires du roi.* Most crimes of *lèse-majesté* were not *prévôtal,* and the nearest the *prévôt* got to dealing with a specific threat to the kingdom was the absurd prosecution of a Protestant merchant in Bordeaux who had English and Genevan connections, and who was accused in 1762 of 'conspiring to commit high treason against his prince in favour of the enemies of the State'.[3]

Prévôtal competence to deal with 'armed illegal assemblies' or the riots labelled as 'popular seditions and emotions' was clearly designed to deal with the threat from below, and even the more subtle interpretation of the principles underlying *prévôtal* competence implied by 'the fabrication, alteration or use of counterfeit money' involved the *maréchaussée* in the repression of what was essentially a crime of the poor. The ancien régime forger was not a skilled artist reproducing complicated banknotes, backed up by the resources of modern technology and an organised system of distribution; he was a peddler or artisan who applied a chemical solution to a copper coin and hoped that a gullible innkeeper or harassed shopkeeper would accept it as silver.

The *prévôtal* conception of public menace was essentially an open-air one: soldiers or deserters making their way across the countryside, riots in the street, false coins circulating in the marketplace, highway robbery, and 'theft aggravated by *effraction,* the carrying of arms and public violence'. This 1670 formulation was clarified in 1731 when the *prévôté* was directed to prosecute two types of theft with *effraction:* those accompanied by arms

1. D. Jousse, *Nouveau commentaire sur l'ordonnance criminelle du mois d'août 1670* (Paris 1763).
2. After interrogation, however, the deserter was escorted to his regiment for sentencing by a *conseil de guerre.*
3. Rocaute, 36, 1st Lt., Compagnie des Volontaires de Bordeaux, A.D. Gir. 11B 7.

and public violence, and 'when the *effraction* has been made in the outside walls, doors and windows or in the roofs of houses, even when there had been no arms or public violence'. The *maréchaussée* was denied any interest in robberies carried out without breaking in – when, for example, the thief climbed in through an open window, or walked in through an unlocked door, even if the resulting theft was 'accompanied by interior *effraction,* as to the chests and cupboards inside the house'. The theft by a servant of his master's property, a crime which was as potentially destructive of the social order as a burglar who passed in the night was hereby excluded from the rigours of *prévôtal* justice. Breaking into a church, on the other hand, was *prévôtal,* in the curious category of 'sacrilege with *effraction*'.

If the authorities were quick to designate the dangerous kinds of theft, rather more hesitation was shown over crimes of violence. There was no problem about dismissing ordinary outbreaks of spontaneous violence, 'assault [*excès*] committed in a simple brawl' as too trivial to waste the *maréchaussée's* time, even if the assault had been fatal. To constitute a public danger the violence had to be premeditated. It was not one of the happier clauses of the 1670 Ordinance, for almost invariably the degree of premeditation was a matter of dispute, even in the mind of the assailant himself. 'L'assassinat prémédité' – which means no more than 'premeditated assault' – not surprisingly became 'the commonest source of conflicts of Jurisdiction'.[4] Another justification for reform sprang from the obvious fact that murder carried the sanction of the death penalty, 'and the life of men is so precious that there should only be a small number of cases in which it is made to depend on a *Prévôt des Maréchaux* [or *prévôt-général*] who has no academic training, or on a few legal officers of the *Présidial,* who often have not much more'.[5] The *prévôt* or lieutenant and *assesseur* decided cases with five other judges recruited from local courts, the *bailliages* or *sénéchaussées* and d'Aguesseau found it a chilling thought that anyone's life and honour should be confided to such a small number of officers and lawyers, when it took ten judges in the *Parlement* to consider the most frivolous lawsuit. In 1731, therefore, premeditated assault, whether murderous or merely painful, was removed from *prévôtal* ken and violent physical assault occupied the *maréchaussée* thereafter only if it was incidental to another *prévôtal* crime; murder on the king's highway threatened public security only if the corpse had been killed *en passant,* in the course of being robbed.

Thus even from the point of view of the crimes considered *prévôtal* by the nature of the offence, the threat to public security was assumed to come from below, and this was made even more explicit by the categories of charges

4. H. F. d'Aguesseau, *Oeuvres*, vol. 8 (28 March 1731), p. 314.
5. *Ibid.*, p. 312.

Table   *'Prévôtal' crimes, Périgord 1720–1790*[6]

	Charge	No. of cases	Percentage
Prévôtal 'by the quality of the accused'	vagabondage	261	26.8
	theft by a vagabond	98	10.1
	gypsies	4	0.4
	repris de justice	6	0.6
	theft by *repris de justice*	15	1.5
	escaped galley-slaves	6	0.6
	bris de ban	3	0.3
	deserters	97	10.0
Prévôtal 'by the nature of the crime'	theft with exterior *effraction*	170	17.4
	highway robbery	60	6.1
	miscellaneous theft	73	7.5
	counterfeiting	8	0.8
	fraud	7	0.7
	assault	147	15.1
	arms plus menaces and insults	35	3.6
	arson	6	0.6
	riot	16	1.6
	duel	6	0.6
	escape	6	0.6
	perjury	1	0.1
	seduction	2	0.2
	total	1,027	105.2
	overlap of cases counted twice[7]	51	5.2
	therefore total number of cases	976	100

which were *prévôtal* through the nature of the offender, 'by the quality of the accused'. The Ordinance identified people whose very existence constituted a threat to law and order: beggars, anyone previously convicted of any crime [*repris de justice*], vagabonds and *gens sans aveu*. No one wept tears over their exposure to arbitrary justice – Jousse dismissed them as 'vile and contemptible persons . . . unworthy of the favour of an appeal'. The repression of beggars was a case apart, more of a police than a judicial matter as a

6. Excluding 'political' trials of the Revolutionary period – the *attroupements* to burn pews and the like, which are discussed in chapter 8; and excluding beggars, who were not subjected to a *prévôtal* trial.
7. Unavoidable as many cases involved a combination of charges – 37 of the 60 highway robberies, e.g., were committed with violence.

beggar's incarceration did not involve the *prévôtal* court – all that was needed was a stroke of the lieutenant's pen. The court however was kept busy by ex-convicts and vagabonds. There was not only the charge of *being* a vagabond, that is anyone who had not had a job for six months and who could not persuade some respectable member of the community to testify to his good character, there were also the crimes committed by vagabonds. This involved the same muddled approach to competence as 'premeditated' assault – it rested on a premise which had to be proved, and more *prévôtal* time was lost when prosecutions were begun and had to be abandoned to another court when it was decided the thief was not a vagabond.

The *maréchaussée* and the *prévôtal* court – the sword and the robe – combined to form an intimidating instrument of repression of the lowest orders of society. 'Vagabonds' provided the largest single group of *prévôtal* prisoners, being involved in more than a third of all the investigations by the Périgueux *prévôté* between 1720 and 1790. The majority of *prévôtal* suspects, however, did not come from these 'marginal' classes — they were ordinary peasants who deserved a minimum of protection against judicial tyranny.

The most important safeguard was the refusal to allow the *maréchaussée* to determine on its own account what constituted a *'prévôtal'* offence. No prisoner was tried by the *prévôté* without the permission of the royal *Présidial* court in whose area of jurisdiction the crime had been committed, and the recognition of *prévôtal* competence, the *jugement de compétence*, was no formality. Naturally the *maréchaussée* did not usually waste time investigating what were obviously non-*prévôtal* cases, and yet the Périgueux *Présidial* saw fit to refuse the *maréchaussée* in seventy-three cases. One has to ask, therefore, if the *maréchaussée* was being deliberately hampered in its law enforcement capacity, either through professional jealousy or in the interests of the prisoners.

The *Présidial* courts were themselves competent to try *prévôtal* cases if they started proceedings before the *maréchaussée*, and there were certainly complaints in other *sénéchaussées* that the *maréchaussée* was being prevented from carrying out its repressive duties by being unreasonably denied competence by the *Présidial*. Maupeou protested to the Agen *Présidial* that it was too quick to deprive the *prévôté* of cases;[8] forty years before, d'Aguesseau had complained of similar abuses.[9] The Bordeaux *prévôt* Barret de Ferrand and his lieutenant Danay alleged that the officers of the Bordeaux *Présidial* wished to restrict the *maréchaussée's* competence to cases which were *prévôtal* 'by the quality of the accused', the vagabonds and other 'marginals', while reserving cases *prévôtal* 'by the nature of the crime' for itself.[10] They

8. A.D. Lot et Garonne, B451.
9. D'Aguesseau, *Oeuvres*, vol. 8 (21 Sept. 1734), p. 92.
10. Danay to the Chancellor, 7 Apr. 1753, A.D. Gir. C 4638.

were however unable to provide sufficient evidence to convince the Chancellor that *Présidial* decisions had not been legally justified.[11]

The *Présidial* and the *Prévôté* in Périgueux cooperated in an exemplary fashion, in fact sixty-three of the seventy-three declarations of incompetence had been requested by the *procureur* of the *maréchaussée* himself, after preliminary investigations had indicated that the prisoner was not a vagabond, or that the assault had not been premeditated, or that the thief had not broken any of the house's external fabric. In the few cases of initial disagreement, it might be the vexed question of the status of a 'vagabond', particularly in the early years when the *maréchaussée* was far from certain as to the degree of control they had over the wandering poor. They were told in 1728 by the *Présidial* that it was not enough for a thief to be 'of no fixed abode' in the sense that his profession of peddler obliged him to travel; it was understandable, however, for the *maréchaussée* to regard Laurent Langlois as a vagrant as he had no merchandise.[12] Nor did a suspect become *prévôtal* because he was a receiver of goods stolen by vagabonds,[13] or because he had the reputation of a thief who gave shelter to gypsies.[14] The *prévôtal* court, in short, was not being denied reasonable access to those who had committed *prévôtal* crimes by the non-cooperation of local magistrates, and the task of the court was further eased by the repeated intervention of the Council of State, and a stream of injunctions designed to prevent potential conflicts of jurisdiction and to cut through the tangle of confusion created by ancien régime judicial geography.

The Council of State issued an *arrêt* to prevent long legal wrangles when there were difficulties about deciding which local court was competent to try a case. The ordinary royal court, the *sénéchaussée* of Périgueux, for example, was instructed to proceed against a burglar when the circumstances of his break-in were confused,[15] whereas the *prévôté* was empowered to prosecute a group of thieving soldiers when it was not clear whether or not the culprits had been on an official march, which had since 1661 been the only *prévôtal* interest in the depredations of the military.[16] A more controversial *arrêt* consigned the innkeeper Bibie and his family to the mercies of the *maréchaussée* for their attack on a recruiting sergeant – an interpretation of *prévôtal* competence, to deal with 'enterprises contrary to the service of His Majesty', regarded by the *Parlement* of Bordeaux as over-generous.[17]

The Council also intervened when a subsidiary charge, such as suborning

---

11. Chancellor to Bacon (*procureur* in Bordeaux *maréchaussée*) 22 May 1753, *ibid*.
12. *Jugement d'incompétence*, 24 Sept. 1728, A.D. Dord. B 363.
13. *Jugement* on Valeureux, 8 Oct. 1721, *ibid*. B 323.
14. *P.-v.* 1 Sept. 1721 Robert, *ibid*., B 322.
15. *Extrait des registres du Conseil d'Etat*, 10 Mar. 1747, *ibid*. B 459.
16. Danay to *procureur général*, 25 Jan. 1761, A.D. Gir. 11B 4.
17. *Extrait* 8 Oct. 1769, subsequent correspondence, A.D. Dord. B 608.

Map 4. The *sénéchaussées* of the Périgord. (Based on the map of the *sénéchaussées* of the *Périgord* in G. Lavergne, *Manuel des études périgourdines* (Valence 1947).)

of witnesses, arose out of a *prévôtal* trial,[18] but the most useful rôle of the Council of State was to save the *maréchaussée* most of the confusion and expense implied by the legal formalities of *prévôtal* procedure in relation to two basic tenets – that the *jugement de compétence* be made by the *Présidial*

18. *Extrait* 12 Aug. 1766, *ibid.*, B 578.

in whose area the prisoner had been arrested; and that the prisoner be then judged by magistrates in the judicial area – the *bailliage* or *sénéchaussée* – in which the crime had been committed. Of all the administrative nightmares of the ancien régime, none was more notorious than the map of *bailliages* and *sénéchaussées*. In the Auvergne it forced the St Flour *maréchaussée* to trudge the long mountain roads escorting prisoners back and forth to Aurillac, Clermont and Riom.[19] Even within the relatively uncomplicated Périgord, the Périgueux *prévôté* covered a number of *sénéchaussées* (see map 4), and so for the lieutenant and *cavaliers* of the Périgueux department there arose the spectre of endless transferrals of prisoners between the towns of the Périgord and neighbouring provinces. The central government was not power-ful enough to effect a fundamental restructuring of the judicial map, but it could systematically bypass the Ordinances with *arrêts du conseil*. A few lines in the Register of the Council of State were enough to cut through the tangle created by the arrest, for example, of Jeanne Bâtarde in the area under the Sarlat *Présidial*, the arrest of her accomplice Arnard in the Libourne area, and their transference to the Périgueux *prévôté* to be tried for thefts com-mitted in the *sénéchaussées* of Périgueux, Sarlat and Libourne, not to mention the prospect of other associates being arrested in a fourth or fifth *sénéchaussée* somewhere else in France.[20] Arrests of vagabonds accused of theft were particularly frequent in the Ste Foy area on the road from Bordeaux, but this area of operations fell under the *sénéchaussée* of Libourne and numerous *arrêts du conseil* were required to save the *maréchaussée* the round trip of 110 miles between Libourne and Périgueux. Arrests of criminals wanted in Périgueux were made in the judicial areas of Bordeaux and Angoulême, but without *arrêts du conseil* this emerging rationale of drawing on the services of a national police force would have looked derisory beside the spectacle of the judicial proceedings moving back and forth between all the towns of south-west France.

The Council of State clearly allowed the *prévôtal* court to operate more efficiently, and the rationalisation was not achieved at the expense of what was virtually the only right the prisoner had – the right to have his case independently assessed as *prévôtal* or not. The Council of State bypassed the *jugement de compétence*, but with the contested exception of Bibie, it did not in practice abandon to the *prévôté* any suspect who was not clearly *prévôtal*.

19. Both Dastier and Brisson complained about this arduous chore and coloured their argument with allegations that the roads were blocked with snow half the year and dangerously exposed to the violence of the people. The town of Maurs in the furthest corner of the Haute-Auvergne, for example, related not to Aurillac but to Clermont, a good ten days' ride away. (Correspondence between Trudaine, Dastier and Dauphin, 1732, A.D. P. de D. C 6179; *Mémoire* by Brisson, *ibid*. C 7686; *Avis de l'Intendant*, *ibid*. C 6178.)
20. *Extrait* 19 May 1769, A.D. Dord. B 607.

Procedure and evidence

The *prévôté* was different from the other royal courts in only two respects – the lack of appeal, and the necessity of having the *Présidial* decide the *maréchaussée's* competence. As we have seen, the prisoner had to be interrogated within twenty-four hours of arrest, in the presence of the *assesseur,* the legally trained officer of the *maréchaussée,* who had to warn the prisoner it was intended to judge him in the *prévôtal* court, with no right of appeal. While the *habeas corpus* implications of this requirement had an obvious importance, it is hard to see how such a grim warning would help the accused in any practical way. The first interrogation, carried out when the prisoner was still confused and distressed by his arrest, having just spent his first uncomfortable night in a prison cell, was often the crucial interrogation, when it was expected that the prisoner's powers of resistance were at their lowest. It was at their first interrogation that Anne Besse and Catherine Perier admitted that their husbands had been responsible for the thefts they were accused of.[21] To begin this harrowing procedure, therefore, with the warning that their fate was sealed 'in the last resort' could only have added to the prisoners' despair.

Many *prévôtal* prosecutions, of course, did not begin with a prisoner. Apart from vagabonds and other thieves arrested *in flagrante delicto,* the investigation of robberies and assaults began with a complaint from the victim, who nearly always appeared in person. The *maréchaussée* itself could take the initiative at the demand of the *procureur,* who would 'request' an investigation into a crime or a series of offences he had heard about. This method of getting cases off the ground became common after the arrival in Périgueux of Gigounoux de Verdon, when the *maréchaussée* was no longer prepared to sit back and wait for an enterprising private citizen to prod them into action. Whoever initiated the investigation, however, prosecutions for crime were carried out in the king's name and paid for by the state. At the request of the *procureur* or the plaintiff, the lieutenant, the clerk of the court, an escort of *cavaliers* (and sometimes also the *assesseur*) moved to the scene of the crime, heard the victim's story and began to interview witnesses. The victim might well name a few names, of those he thought were guilty, but the arrest would not be made until a few witnesses had been heard. 'Witness' should not be understood in too literal a sense. It was exceptional for the 'witness' to produce concrete evidence which contributed materially to the case; their usual rôle was to suggest a suspect, establish his reputation. If two or three witnesses agreed on a suspect, he would be arrested.

It is difficult to see what else the *maréchaussée* could have done. Any police force would have to question a suspect accused on all sides, particularly in a village community where it could reasonably be assumed that individuals

21. *Interrs.* 8 Mar. 1739, A.D. Dord. B 438.

were acquainted with their neighbours' affairs. But the *maréchaussée* could not adopt an informal procedure and invite someone to help them with their inquiries. Even witnesses were not cross-examined – their testimony is presented in the *information* as a single paragraph encapsulating all the witness knew which was of relevance to the crime in question. There does not seem to have been much prompting, or unrecorded suggestions the witnesses concentrate on one aspect or another, for the depositions are full of material irrelevant even by the lax standards of the eighteenth century, while witnesses were allowed to repeat each other to a soul-destroying degree. The *maréchaussée,* therefore, did not hesitate to arrest (and so charge) anyone with a more or less direct connection with the offence. After many cases which ended happily with the conviction of the accused, a number of prisoners were released who had been arrested not as real suspects but as potential sources of useful information on the prisoners the court was genuinely interested in. It was a cynical device, used most effectively against a suspect's wife and children.[22]

Once he had testified the witness was for all practical purposes finished with the *prévôtal* court. In principle there were still two stages that concerned him – the *recollement,* when after the *information* had been completed, each witness had to listen to his deposition and indicate if he wished to change or retract anything. No one ever did so, perhaps because of the fear of being charged with perjury, which so many commentators on ancien régime justice have laid stress on, but also because so few witnesses ever contributed any damaging testimony. It would be difficult to prove malicious intent in a statement to the effect that the witness had heard that the suspect/prisoner had an evil reputation. It is a fact that practically no one who was accused of a *prévôtal* crime had a saintly public image. Nor could many charges of perjury be brought against witnesses who confined their testimony to recounting to the court how they themselves had been robbed eight months or eight years before, with the added comment that they had always suspected the accused. It was an unchanged testimony, therefore, which was read to the prisoner in the presence of the witness – the *confrontation,* another procedure almost entirely useless. It was no doubt diverting for the magistrates, as the prisoner would invariably seek not to dispute a particular point or argument in the deposition, but to discredit the trustworthiness of the witness himself. One thief had the gall to object to a witness on the grounds that he was a bankrupt – 'The accused is wrong', the witness replied, 'to reproach me for a misfortune of which he is the principal cause'.[23] In

---

22. Pierre Flourat, aged 10, was asked after his arrest how long he had been 'associated with his sister'; his 13-year-old brother was told his sister was the 'concubine' of Delage, one of the main suspects, and asked if Delage brought her stolen property. The testimony of the two boys helped to convict their mother of receiving stolen goods. *Ibid*. B 620.
23. Prosecution of Mouniasse, Aug. 1772, *ibid*. B 830.

no case could the *confrontation* possibly have affected the judges' decision. Convictions did not depend on a subjective impression of how the various parties reacted to the stress of such an unnatural situation, no matter how trenchant the character assassination performed by the accused. It can be objected that the confrontation was an outrageous procedure from the prisoner's point of view, as only at this late stage in the trial was he able to hear the evidence on which he was to be judged, while being expected to understand all the implications of what the testimony contained and on the spur of the moment refute any potentially damaging phrases. In practice the force of this criticism is weakened by the fact that testimony was usually too vague or irrelevant to be dangerous, and more importantly by the fact that if any serious allegation had been made, the prisoner would already have been questioned on it in an interrogation.

It was the interrogation which was the essence of the *prévôtal* trial. All the relevant material to emerge from the plaintiff's charge or the *information* was laid before the accused in the course of two or three interrogations. It is not important that officially he was not told what offence he was charged with. The officers of the Périgueux *prévôté* always opened proceedings by asking the accused if he had committed the crime in question. Vagabonds were asked about their movements and employment and, in a disarmingly straightforward way, if they had committed any thefts. There were those who replied yes. Fichequartier had not even been asked if he was implicated in theft, but why he carried a pistol: 'To defend himself and avoid being arrested', he explained, 'because he had carried out a big robbery in Bourdeilles at the end of June.'[24]

Fichequartier was hanged for this confession, but was only one of many prisoners who would have benefited from some legal advice. *Prévôtal* prisoners, like the other prisoners of ancien régime justice, faced the intimidating apparatus of a court of law entirely alone. There were those who reacted with bravado – Charles François, a deserter and vagabond reproved the magistrates for asking 'shameful questions', and told them that they were not there 'to lay down the law to him';[25] a former judge demanded to know who had denounced him,[26] and even a 19-year-old woodcutter indignantly retorted that any money he had had been earned 'by the sweat of his body', and explained that the thefts he had committed were 'the unfortunate effect of youthful imprudence.'[27] But in the vast majority of cases, the natural nervousness resulting from an appearance in a criminal court was compounded by social alienation, typified by a farm-labourer's confusion when referred

24. *Interr*. 11 Jan. 1741, *ibid*. B 432.
25. *Interr*. 8 Jan. 1767: François, day-labourer (Picardie), *ibid*. B 575.
26. *Interr*. 25 Nov. 1772: J. Laigne de Barade, *archer garde en la Connétablie, juge de Salon*, ibid. B 626.
27. *Interr*. 29 Apr. 1773, J. Jammes, *ibid*. B 648.

by the judge to a precise date, 29 March, instead of to a saint's day.[28] There was the added humiliation, just before the final judgment, of the 'interrogation on the *sellette'*, a 'shameful formality' which forced the accused to sit on a wooden stool and was abolished in 1788 when it was finally recognised that it offended the principle that the prisoner should be regarded as innocent until convicted, 'and leads him to lose the tranquillity of mind which he needs to defend himself'.[29] Counsel were not provided for prisoners until October 1789, although the accused who were to face the *prévôtal* court in the last year of its existence did not benefit much as the lawyers assigned by the court to defend them did not bother to turn up.[30]

Before 1789, there had been a few better-off, educated prisoners who were able to organise a *supplication* on their own behalf – Henri de Soudonne, Sr de la Grelière, for instance, accused on a counterfeiting charge – but the general lack of defence counsel was really highlighted in the prosecution of Jean Simon, an apprentice tailor, and Jean Laval, merchant, and his son, all local residents, for the 'sacrilege with *effraction'* of the church in Lalinde.[31] The *maréchaussée's* public operations – their arrests, the public identification of the tools found at the site of the break-in – were enough to tell the curé on what grounds the prosecution was proceeding, and he made a spirited and successful intervention, in a private letter to the lieutenant, making all the points a defence lawyer would have made. All the residents of Lalinde knew that the ostensory and processional cross were not made of real silver and gold, yet the thieves had stolen them with the more valuable silver-gilt chalice and the silver ciborium. It was ridiculous to suppose, the curé asserted, that if the owner of the tools had carried out the theft he would have left them to be discovered, when he could easily have disposed of them in the Dordogne, just over the cemetery wall. The curé also prepared his answers if the *maréchaussée* had argued with uncharacteristic subtlety that such obvious clues could have been planted deliberately to divert *prévôtal* attention from residents of the town. Jean Laval son, he assured the lieutenant, was too stupid to plot such a successful robbery; his father had been thirty years in the town, and built up a profitable business. Yet this solid citizen was the man charged by the *maréchaussée* with clambering through church windows and committing burglary. All three suspects were 'quite incapable' of such an outrageous crime, and the curé's testimonial

28. *Interr.* 24 May 1769, *ibid.* B 607.
29. Declaration of 1 May 1788, *ibid.*, B 832.
30. *Lettres patentes en forme d'Edit* (8–9 Oct. 1789): the prisoner could choose a Counsel (art. X); the witness to testify in the presence of the accused (art. XV); witness not to be accused of perjury if he changed his mind (art. XVI), A.N. Z^{IC} 412. See chapter 8.
31. *Procureur*, 25 Feb. 1772, on receipt of letter from Sr La Palice, curé of Lalinde, *ibid.* B 637.

was backed by a certificate from the 'seigneurs, nobles and bourgeois *vivant noblement'* of Lalinde.

Deprived of any legal advice, the *prévôtal* prisoner in Périgueux could at least have been assured that there was only the slimmest chance that he would be tortured, and that he would certainly not be convicted on evidence or confession extracted by torture. However systematic its use in the fight against group banditry,[32] torture made a minimal contribution to eighteenth-century judicial processes in less critical areas. The *prévôtal* court in Périgueux resorted to the 'question' in only nine cases between the 1720 Reform and the Revolution and not at all after 1772.[33] It was an exceptional measure used in particularly difficult circumstances: four of the instances of judicial torture date from the economic crisis of the early 1740s, three from the crisis around 1770. Those unfortunate prisoners who were put on the rack were not convicted on the strength of evidence or confessions extracted under torture, for in virtually every case the decision to use torture was made at the same time as the decision to convict, when the judges were already convinced of the accused's guilt by a heavy weight of circumstantial evidence.

Jacques Beausson had been seen in the company of Pierre and Jacques Marty, in the act of striking Jean Lafage, who died of his injuries; the torture merely served to tidy up the details of which of the three was responsible for the fatal blow.[34] Le Frejon had already been sentenced to be broken on the wheel, on evidence provided by his wife and the wives of his two accomplices, when he was tortured to establish the innocence of a fourth suspect.[35] In the case of the robbery and murder of the curé of St Pardoux la Rivière, it had been proved that since the theft, Antoine Boussarie had had large sums of money in his possession – his cousin Jean had even brought to the police a bag of gold hidden in the Boussarie house; it had been established that Antoine had had a pressing motive to do the deed: 'I want to take my wife back, now that I'm more able to support her than when we separated.' The interrogation under torture, therefore, was only concerned with examining Antoine's claim that he had robbed but not killed the curé.[36] The police were in no doubt who had murdered the Sr Clervaux, master pewterer, for although he had been robbed of 16 *écus*, he had left a widow, the local innkeeper Catherine Alliban, who was thought to be the lover of the estate manager of the Comte d'Aydie, a Spaniard known as 'Don Miguel'. 'Kiss me', Miguel had told Catherine before all her customers, when Clervaux was away

---

32. O. Hufton, *The poor of eighteenth-century France* (Oxford 1974), p. 283.
33. 'In the last third of the century, *prévôtal* justice only tortures with regret and without conviction.' P. Crépillon, 'La maréchaussée de Caen', *Revue historique de droit français et étranger* II (1968), 366.
34. A.D. Dord. B 346, 1724.
35. *Ibid.* B 438, 1739.
36. *Ibid.* B 422, 1740–1.

on a previous business trip. 'I'm a married woman', Catherine laughed, 'but if I become a widow . . .'.[37] As Miguel disappeared after the crime, it remained only for the *maréchaussée* to pull in his valet and his hired thug and torture them when they persisted in denying that they had done more than watch their employer do the deed. Their testimony under torture was particularly important in that it did not implicate Catherine herself, who was accused of complicity in the plot. The torture of Robinet and Le Maréchal, two of a band of thieves which had descended on the widow Robin at dead of night to rob her of handkerchiefs, shirts and spoons, was supposed to help the police identify those of the band who were not already under arrest or who had taken care to decamp; torture would also, it was hoped, confirm the band's participation in other unsolved thefts which had taken place in the area.[38]

In only one case did the authorities resort to torture in an attempt to make up for lack of evidence from other sources. Pierre Gourseau, a *métayer* in the parish of Goust, had been robbed of the 90L. he was foolish enough to keep in a kitchen drawer; at the time of the burglary Gourseau himself was detained in his barn by Jean Reynaud, who had been trying to persuade him that he needed an extra servant. Reynaud was arrested on the strong suspicion that he had acted as a decoy, presumably for his older brother and brother-in-law, Jean Faure. Although none of the stolen money was found, and no evidence produced to implicate Reynaud the elder and Faure, the court thought their involvement sufficiently probable to justify torturing all three. As all three persisted in denying their involvement, the younger Reynaud went to the galleys for life for what could have been a dreadful coincidence, and the other two were released.[39]

They were however able to walk out of prison as soon as the sentence was handed down, the day after being tortured. This discrimination in the application of torment was accompanied by a respect for formalities. The thief Donnadier had a fever when stretched out on the rack, and the surgeon insisted he could not be tortured; he was therefore hanged instead, two days later.[40] *Prévôtal* magistrates also took into account their presumption of guilt or innocence. Prisoners convicted on evidence acquired through regular channels had their legs encased in wooden planks, and wedges were driven between the wood and the flesh; this was followed by a spell on the mattress in front of the fire. Faure and the elder Reynaud, who could not easily be presumed to be guilty, had a much less painful experience – the wedges were not driven in, and they were not left in front of the flames.

The final decision on the guilt or innocence of the prisoner was taken by

37. *Inform.* 44th witness (a labourer), *ibid.* B 459.
38. *Ibid.* B 626, 1771.
39. *Ibid.* B 433, 1742.
40. *Ibid.* B 638, 1773.

a panel of seven judges, two of whom would be the lieutenant or *prévôt-général* and the *prévôtal assesseur*. For an anonymous Revolutionary admirer of the institution, this was the ultimate in protective devices for it meant that just as police strength was more façade than reality, so *'prévôtal* jurisdiction is, so to speak, a fiction',[41] a name designed to inspire terror among evil-doers while preserving the right for them to be judged by regular civilian magistrates. Given the procedural iniquities, it was on these judges that everything depended, and it is on their decision that the final estimation of the *prévôtal* court must be based. It is from the evidence left in the transcript of the trials that we must judge whether or not the final conviction or acquittal was reasonable.

The prisoner had certainly cause to worry if he was accused of *assassinat* for most victims of assault, having come into physical contact with their aggressor, were not usually in two minds about his identity. Such prisoners, however, had the consolation of expecting a comparatively light sentence – perhaps just the financial arrangement which could have been made privately – or, after 1731, of being sent to a less notorious court. The prisoner however who had most reason to despair of his future was the man or woman arrested *in flagrante delicto* or in a hue and cry, or with apparently stolen property – the vagrant, for example, caught picking pockets or making off from a peasant's cottage with a loaf of bread and a sheet. In most prosecutions which resulted from arrests of this kind, the accused did not long delay his confession of guilt. Jean Lavaux, a vagabond accused of theft, and arrested by the inhabitants of La Rochebeaucour, tried to deny his guilt, but a parade of respectable witnesses – the seigneur de Vigneras, the seigneur de Razac – testified that Lavaux had at some time been in their employ until he disappeared with their possessions, and the police also managed to find the innkeeper who had bought the stolen property.[42]

While those prisoners who were accused only of being vagabonds were judged, as we shall see, on the simple objective test of whether or not they could provide some kind of reference from someone accepted as 'trustworthy', even thieves dragged in by the populace were not convicted automatically. Jean Nadal had no date or place of birth, no domicile, he had been seen to 'prowl around M. de Briançon's chateau' the day a saddle was stolen from a chest in the stables, which he knew back to front from his days as a groom and 'vine-grower' in Briançon's employ. He was arrested 'hiding furtively in a *métairie*', and his captors could see a brand mark V on his shoulder only a year old. As the interrogating magistrate summed up, there was 'every appearance that he was the thief'. The *prévôtal* court, however, did not convict on appearances, and Nadal was acquitted.[43] The situation had looked equally

---

41. *Précis important sur les maréchaussées.*
42. Oct. 1767 – May 1768, *ibid.* B 587.
43. *Ibid.* B 720, 1780–1.

black for Michel 'The Rat', arrested by the *maréchaussée à la clameur publique* - the raucous clamour of his neighbours who 'shouted to us that The Rat was a professional thief' and who charged him with the burglary of oil belonging to Jean Guichard. They testified in court that they had seen the oil in his kitchen, that they had seen him fleeing from the scene of the crime, that his axe had been left behind at the scene of the break-in. The Rat's defence could not have sounded convincing: the oil was his own, bought in Périgueux; it was his axe, but he had lost it the day before the theft. The *procureur* asked the court to convict and hang, but The Rat was freed and he returned to a bleak welcome in St Jean de Cole.[44]

The *maréchaussée* often made arrests, like that of Michel, on the strength of a dreadful local reputation, but such market-day gossip was not enough to ensure a conviction. This was true even when the importance of the theft intensified the pressure for an expeditious, exemplary punishment. The *prévôté* could acquit even when thieves made a haul of twenty bushels of wheat, 200 pounds of nut oil, thirty to forty pounds of pewter plate, a lamp, tablecloths and napkins. The public was united in accusing Page and his accomplices Lapraye and Birlet, but much of the evidence was hearsay: '[Page] eats out extravagantly in inns; for a long time he was a butcher, although he did not have the means to set up shop or buy meat . . . twelve years ago Lapraye and Birlet robbed my cousin of 5s.'[45] A neighbour accused Page of highway robbery 'because he has often heard his door being opened and closed two or three hours before sunrise'. A ceremony to identify grain from Page's stock as the stolen wheat, and above all his own disappearance, allowed the court to convict Page himself, but the accomplices in custody were acquitted.[46]

There were of course cases where the court could not fail to convict as the accused's reputation was so richly deserved - to judge not from gossip but precisely documented incidents, often described by more than one witness: Bonnamy, Martinie and Lacroix, Grifoul.[47] A conviction would follow just as effectively if the reputation was justified by solid evidence of a single misdemeanour. Antoine and Barthelemy Gayet did not attend the Christmas mass during which Fourieu was robbed, and only reappeared in St Vincent d'Excideuil three days later; when they did turn up, they spent their time at the *cabaret* spending freely with coins 'of the old kind' - the sort of coins which were most likely to have been stored away by years of saving until returned to circulation by a burglar, the kind of easily recognisable coins which proved the undoing of more than one Périgord thief. The suspects were arrested and admitted their guilt at once.[48]

44. *Ibid.* B 647, 1773.   45. *Ibid.* B 596, 1768.
46. The police did not capture Page himself, but they did arrest his 70-year-old mother and charged her with burglary and highway robbery. She too was freed.
47. *Ibid.* B 576, 1766; B 578, 1766; B 599, 1768-9.
48. *Ibid.* B 328, 1721-2.

One of the most detested individuals to appear before the *prévôtal* court was Jean Chignac, called Mialette. His was the only trial in which the accused's wife appeared as a witness, to confirm enthusiastically that her husband was regarded by everyone as a thief and a scoundrel. The evidence for the charge of murder was paper-thin: Mialette had sold a strange hat and a pair of stockings just after a man had been found murdered in a local wood (it was an unidentifiable corpse as the face was so slashed with knife wounds); his wife had not seen her husband for the two days before it was found. Mialette was hanged not as a murderer but as a thief, and for his thefts the evidence was considerably more reliable. The first witness declared that Mialette had robbed him at bayonet-point on the highway of his horse and 20L. worth of truffles, and other witnesses confirmed the story. Other charges were made, but there was enough to convict.[49]

Jean Rousseau called Pinquet might conceivably have squirmed out of the circumstantial evidence, dismissing envious testimony from neighbours that his family ate meat every day (they had a small piece of fish or beef, he replied, on fête days), and explaining 'how he managed to have white bread made from the purest wheat while his equals could hardly afford the coarsest black bread'; he described as malicious lies a report from two neighbours that they had met him carrying a sack from which came the distinctive sound of a sheep sneezing. He had to admit, however, that he had been caught in the act of stealing half a bushel of flour.[50]

In the one case of a 'public thief' convicted on less than absolute proof, it is probable that the combination of circumstances would have persuaded a modern jury to convict – the 'premeditated assault' of Lacotte by his rival Faurichon. There was a well-established motive – Lacotte's marriage with Marie Dubreuilh, the girl Faurichon had intended for himself. There was the long-term background of intimidation inflicted on the *métayers* who tried to lease Marie's land, an escalating campaign which threw vivid light on Faurichon's frame of mind. The *information* produced a succession of witnesses who had not seen the shooting for which Faurichon was on trial, but who clearly established the disposition to violence which had always been an element in his character. Finally there was the actual event: if Faurichon had had a strong alibi he might have saved himself, but he was seen by two shepherds approaching the scene of the crime with a rifle shortly before the shot was heard.[51]

It was inevitable that most cases which were not neatly sewn up by an arrest *in flagrante delicto* or by the prisoner's confession would be resolved by a more or less subjective analysis of circumstantial evidence. The archives of the Périgueux *prévôtal* court leave no trace of any legalistic disputation

49. *Ibid.* B 411, 1736–7.
50. *Ibid.* B 619, 1770–1.
51. *Ibid.* B 322, 1720–1.

as to what constituted a complete proof. The Périgueux magistrates adopted what can reasonably be called a commonsense approach to doubtful cases. If the suspect seemed almost certainly guilty, judging by appearances and past behaviour, he was convicted. If he was possibly, or even probably, guilty, there might be a delay for a *plus amplement informé*[52] – but he would eventually be released.

The *maréchaussée* in fact had repeated failures in its attempts to obtain a conviction for the theft of grain. Aubin Mignot had to be acquitted when the evidence consisted of assurances 'that he had threshed grain at home at night, although he had no land'.[53] Pierre Tentier, a farm-labourer accused of the theft of considerable quantities of grain, largely owed his survival to his own presence of mind in the courtroom: he explained in detail how many bushels of grain he produced each year, and how it sufficed to feed himself and his family (there are no reports to suggest the *maréchaussée* went to verify his claim); and he made a virtue of the necessity of explaining why he had been selling grain at dead of night, 'so as not to be distracted from his work'.[54] Securing a conviction required the wealth of evidence which condemned Giraud, called Grand Bouvier, for the theft of eight bushels of maize and rye, eighteen bushels of wheat, and one and a half of beans from the seigneur's *fermier* in La Chapelle Gounaguet. This time there was the trail of corn and beans leading straight to Grand Bouvier's meadow; there was the twenty bushels of wheat found in his house; his servant testified that his oxen 'which they did not usually take out at night' were soaked with sweat the morning after the robbery, while his cart was covered with wet mud. When a hoard of grain was discovered buried in the suspect's barn, he confessed.[55]

It is difficult to imagine present-day police forces functioning without fingerprints, locks of hair, blood samples or chemical analyses of tread marks, but the eighteenth-century police were rarely able to produce such solid evidence. In the course of the trial of the band of thieves who intruded on Marie Robin, however, the lieutenant produced an old hat which had been left at the scene of the crime and triumphantly recorded that it fitted the head of the prisoner, Bernard Moreau.[56] The same trial also underlined the *maréchaussée's* inexperience in dealing with material evidence, for the *assesseur* was just finishing the interrogation of Jean Chambonneau when, of

---

52. A provisional sentence handed down when the court was convinced of guilt by circumstantial evidence or reputation, but was far from having proof, in the vain hope more evidence might turn up, or to avoid the necessity of having to release a potentially dangerous criminal; usually for six months or a year.
53. *Ibid.* B 639, 1772-4.
54. *Ibid.* B 627, 1771.
55. *Ibid.* B 609, 1769-71.
56. *Ibid.* B 626, 1770.

his own accord, the prisoner produced one of the stolen handkerchiefs from his pocket.

The *maréchaussée* had every right to be surprised that the thief had not got rid of the stolen property. Stolen property was clearly the best possible sort of evidence, but the police rarely had the good fortune to find it in the hands of the thief. Even when the item could be clearly identified, the thief had ample opportunity to sell it. If theft filled any social function in the Périgord of the eighteenth century, it was to redistribute a considerable quantity of property from those who possessed something to those who possessed less, not just to the thieves themselves, but to the bulk of the population for whom thieves, fences and peddlers brought a cheap supply of chickens, lard, plates, clothes and linen. The conviction of Jean de la Forge and Pierre Gautier, therefore, was exceptional in that the police managed to find someone who had bought the stolen goods after 47 witnesses had nothing to contribute except the vague impression that the suspect had a good time without doing any work: a Nontron merchant told the court he had bought the stolen copper-pan from the two accused for 9L. This was the only testimony to be brought up in the final interrogation on the *sellette,* and though the prisoner had been charged with multiple robberies, the sentence listed only the theft of the copper-pan.[57]

In one *prévôtal* crime at least it was impossible to do without material evidence – prosecutions for counterfeiting and distributing false coins. The police found in the possession of Henri de Soudonne, Sr de la Grelière, fifty pieces of copper, beaten to look like *sous;* even more suspicious in the eyes of the *cavaliers* who came to arrest him was the reaction of Mme de la Grelière – she seized a piece of paper and swallowed a mysterious black powder. A subsequent *supplication* from Soudonne did not fail to pour heavy sarcasm over the detective efforts of the *cavaliers;* what the *cavaliers* thought was the most important piece of evidence was, he assured the court, a spoonful of jam. There was certainly beaten copper, but, as the accused disingenuously pointed out, no hammer or other instrument suitable for producing *sous.* Soudonne's most telling point, however, was his argument which admitted he had spent false coins but which denied he had done so 'knowledgeably'. As he pointed out, no witness had explicitly accused him of deliberately using false coins or that he and his household had made them. A large part of the *supplication* was devoted to proving that it would be impossible to manufacture false coins in his house: no one had heard hammering, there were only two rooms, no cellars, no courtyard, even, to separate the house from the village – all practical details which any competent police force would have investigated on its own account. It was an

57. *Ibid.* B 617, 1770-1.

effective *supplication,* for he was convicted of no more than the literal truth, 'being found in possession of' false coins marked to the value of 6 *liards.* [58]

The *prévôtal* court was still in the middle of this case when reports came in that another criminal Rousseau 'makes and distributes false *écus* of 6 *livres'.* There was no technical evidence – only angry scenes in *cabarets* to indicate that Rousseau had spent the coins 'knowledgeably' and so he was convicted for the use rather than the fabrication of the coins. [59] It was crucial in this case – and in the conviction of Jean Defarge [60] – that witnesses could testify to the accused spending their counterfeit coins over a period of time, for though there was no doubt that Pierre Sauveau de Lhourmade had a pile of false *écus* and although three innkeepers, a blacksmith and a miller assured the Castillonnès *cavaliers* that he had used them the day of his arrest, he was able to claim that he had never used them before he sold his horse, a couple of days previously. This argument, combined with his status as the owner of 30,000 *livres* worth of property, produced the court's only acquittal on a charge of counterfeiting. [61]

Of all the cases resolved by the *prévôtal* court between 1720 and 1790 there are only three in which the transcript of the trial does not prove the guilt of a convicted prisoner beyond reasonable doubt. They were cases in which it was vital to take account of any reasonable doubt, for the verdicts which resulted condemned two men to spend the rest of their lives in the galleys and sent two men to be broken on the wheel.

This dreadful punishment was inflicted for the murder and mutilation of Jean Lalliot. [62] Although the two suspects were tried and executed within seven months of the murder, there was no direct evidence of any kind at any stage of the trial. The first 26 witnesses were restrained in their depositions, suspecting the men Lalliot had been drinking with and showing his money to the day before his death – 'the dead man always had money on him which he kept showing to everyone'. As he had spent the entire day drinking the *maréchaussée* baulked at the sheer number of potential suspects, and arrested only two friends of the victim who were known to have spoken to him at some length. One of them, Bonnard, who was Lalliot's cousin, had a 'bad reputation'; the other, Pierre Gaillard, had been heard to say, 'Well, well, you'll see.' The disquieting fact is that after the arrests, which were made after the twenty-sixth witness, the tone and content of the statements changed dramatically. Witnesses remembered much more incriminating remarks, particularly on the part of Bonnard. He had stopped suspiciously in

58. Apr. 1769 – Jan. 1770, *ibid.* B 608.   59. June 1769 – Apr. 1770, *ibid.*
60. Defarge, 40, *métayer* (Sarzac), convicted of using three coins of blanched copper, supposedly worth 30s. 4d. Apr. – Aug. 1728, *ibid.* B 362.
61. *Ibid.* B 708, 1779–80.
62. *Ibid.* B 578, 1766–7.

mid-sentence when describing how the mutilation must have been interrupted by dogs coming on the scene; although the body could hardly be seen from the road, Bonnard had immediately recognised it as his cousin, and made 'exaggerated and affected exclamations on the tragic death'; Bonnard's recognition of the corpse from the clogs was suspicious as the clogs were like all the other peasants' clogs; a 12-year-old boy remembered seeing some congealed blood in Bonnard's hair; the Dlle de la Serre discussed the affair with Bonnard and remembered how he was 'extremely pale, disturbed and embarrassed'; Bonnard had been present at the special service held for his cousin, and according to the curé, his 'extraordinary pallor made everyone, even the most pious, suspect that he was guilty'. There was an almost total silence on Gaillard, except for allegations of a previous highway robbery; *monitoires* in five parishes produced the information that as he was being arrested, Gaillard remarked that it was nice weather to be hanged, 'and this intrepidity was criticised by all present'. There were in short only two pieces of substantial evidence, both against Bonnard. There was blood on his clothes, but he was a butcher and claimed to have been cutting up liver. Most damning of all, and what was certainly responsible for the conviction, was the testimony of the seventy-eighth witness, a servant who was sleeping in the same room as Bonnard and who told the court that Bonnard had not come to bed till 4 a.m. The accused offered no explanation other than to say he had gone out for a walk.

In the case against Léonard Desplat called Marcin, convicted of the premeditated murder of his fellow miller Aubin Durand, there was no doubting the history of personal antagonism between the two men. Again, however, there was little evidence relating to the night of Durand's death. The damning testimony was provided by a *laboureur* who thought he heard Durand crying three times 'Hey poor Marcin, finish me off', but the 'witness' went on home, and his wife told him it was drunks having a joke. Even after Marcin's arrest witnesses managed to keep an open mind when referring to the day Durand was killed, 'or drowned himself'. Marcin was one of the very few illiterate prisoners to get a *supplication* presented on his behalf, claiming that witnesses could testify to seeing Durand staggering home incapably drunk and frozen long before the prisoner left the *cabaret,* and arguing that if he had been really guilty he would not have stayed at home waiting to be arrested. 'It cannot be said that Marcin did not know where to go, like most peasants, for he had served as a soldier under the Sr Tourtes de Preyssinat and would have been welcomed back'. It seems that the judges retained a measure of doubt, for had they been totally convinced that Marcin was responsible for the murder of Durand it is unlikely they would have let him off with a condemnation to the galleys.[63]

63. *Ibid.* B 352, 1726-8.

The third conviction was dubious enough to provoke the intervention of the *Garde des Sceaux,* the only time the central authorities found fault with the Périgueux *prévôté*. The case concerned an old friend of the *maréchaussée,* Alexis Faye, a stone-cutter who had talked his way off the roof of the house he was accused of robbing by pointing out that the witnesses had made no mention of a ladder.[64] Seven years later he was caught on the roof of a house occupied by François Guinot, father-in-law of the Seigneur de l'Age; a crowd of peasants arrested him, and the Thiviers brigade arrived to take him away. The *brigadier's* report accused Faye of the theft of the 31L. 4s. he had in his pocket. Alexis however insisted the money was his own, and obtained a certificate of payment for the sum of 31L. 15s., for work carried out for the Sr Villard de Pontignac, as well as character references and testimonials for work faithfully accomplished from the chevalier de Monclard, *Lieutenant des Maréchaux de France.* Alexis went on to denounce the corrupt troop of witnesses – notably the Thiviers *brigadier* – who had arrested him. The court duly convicted him 'of being found in possession of 31 *livres* 4 *sous* stolen with exterior *effraction* from François Guinot'. Three weeks later, a letter from Versailles informed the court that the judgment was quite unsatisfactory. There was no mention of Faye's responsibility for the theft, or his participation in the break-in or how he had acquired the money.[65] This was more than legalistic criticism of the form of the *sentence* – it highlighted the gaps in the court's knowledge of the sequence of events. Anxiety that Faye should not escape again so easily as he had done seven years before may perhaps have contributed to the court's anxiety to convict, and its apparent failure to adhere to standards which in so many other cases were demonstrably fair and reasonable. For the overwhelming majority of prisoners, brought in for their first interrogation, had had good reason not to despair. Of the 1,090 prisoners charged with a *prévôtal* offence in Périgueux between 1720 and 1790, only 324 were convicted.

Punishment

In the eighteenth century, as in the twentieth, rules of competence, procedure and evidence were firmly established. As in the twentieth century, these rules involved a certain class bias in the administration of justice, but at least they were applied consistently and with an evident degree of rationality. As in the twentieth century also, the arbitrary nature of judicial power was most evident in the penalties handed down. More than at any other stage of the trial, the *prévôtal* prisoner could not be certain of what to expect as

64. *Ibid.* B 620, 1771.
65. Dufour to Périgueux *procureur,* Dufaulx, 21 May 1778, *ibid.* B 684.

he stood before his judge for sentencing. It is nevertheless just possible to discern the outlines of the 'normal' punishment for any particular crime amidst the host of exceptions and anomalies, and it is possible to see if magistrates in the Périgord were following the example of their colleagues elsewhere and reacting in a spirit of fear and insecurity to the increasing rate of theft and the proliferation of vagabonds in the difficult last decades of the ancien régime.[66]

While rather too few to be statistically convincing, punishments for highway robbery in the Périgord were on the whole fairly lenient: six banishments and three sentences to the galleys. The banishments were certainly for trivial offences: the theft of 30 *sous* and a spoon; a 'theft' which was less a theft than a disputed contract; a passive accomplice; a 'robber' who had made ineffectual appearances by the roadside without ever persuading any travellers to part with their money. But other forms of theft apparently just as trivial were not to enjoy such indulgence, and even within ancien régime terms of reference the sentences were hardly consistent with the affront to public security which highway robbery was always proclaimed to pose. When a heavier penalty was imposed, the terms of the sentence imply that the thief was going to the galleys not so much for stealing a large sum of money, or aggravating the theft with assault, as for his 'perfidy in assaulting a man with whom he had just had a drink'.[67]

With a total of 62 convictions for burglary, the *prévôtal* concept of punishment emerges with greater force, a concept which was chronologically consistent and characterised by extreme severity. Throughout the century, *prévôtal* penalties maintained a balance of terror between the galleys and the gibbet. In the first two decades of the reformed *maréchaussée*, 5 burglars were hanged, 9 went to the galleys for the rest of their lives, and 5 others served as galley-slaves for a total of fifty-five years. In the three middle decades, 1 man was banished, 6 died on the gibbet, and 7 went to the galleys (6 for life, 1 for nine years). In the last two decades of the ancien régime, 3 women were branded and banished, but 9 men died by hanging, and 13 went to the galleys, 10 of them for life. These latter figures apparently indicate a slight secular trend to the greater use of the death penalty, but the nine executions were almost entirely due to the bloody repression in the year 1771 which alone accounts for seven hangings. It was a grim warning of the power of the state in the midst of the economic crisis, when the *maréchaussée*

66. N. Castan, 'La justice expéditive', in *Annales E.S.C.* 31e, no. 2 (1976), 331–61, and A. Farge, *Le vol d'aliments à Paris au XVIIIe siècle* (Paris 1974), both describe a 'hardening' on the part of the judges in this period, longer and longer spells in the galleys, more and more corpses hanging from the gallows.
67. Sentences against J. Perier, 18 Jan. 1727, A.D. Dord. B 352, and A. Nanzelle, 22 Aug. 1767, *ibid*. B 586.

had all but suspended its repression of mendicity to devote its energies to the more serious offenders. Two years later there were two more executions for burglary, but in the reign of Louis XVI none at all.

One might say, therefore, that the standard punishment for burglary was galleys for life, the sentence for a single theft of reasonable importance – 800L. or two horses, or any offence committed by a recidivist. In cases where more than one thief had participated in the robbery, the perpetual punishment was reserved for those who were regarded as most responsible, and the others let off with fifteen, or ten, or nine years. A certain Guillabeau, for example, got nine years as he was convicted of the theft of only a mule, an insignificant part of a large trial involving quantities of sheets, shirts, napkins, *écus,* bread, oil, hemp, thread, pigs, geese, poultry, flour, apples and chestnuts which his fellow prisoners were unsuccessfully accused of stealing.[68]

It was appropriate that the death penalty – the most exemplary of all punishments, designed for a weak pre-Beccarian system of law enforcement – was in fact used in cases which must have reminded the authorities of their weakness, and in particular of the *maréchaussée's* feeble attempts to contain burglary. For hanging was the fate of those persistent and often intimidating thieves who had been allowed to escape retribution until it was too late for them to be saved for the galleys – Rouveilhac; Fichequartier; Bessont and Beaussont; Bouthieyroux, Magnieux and Gourdon; Lacroix and Martinie; Aymon; Mialette, Page, Toudaud and Patas; Fossemaigne; Pinquet; or the leaders of the band which robbed Mme Robin and the *fermier* in Vanxains.[69] But just as some kind of pattern begins to emerge, the exceptions crowd in from all sides. And while, as we shall see, the anomalies in the sentencing of vagabond thieves tended to greater leniency, the exceptions in the cases of burglary usually erred on the side of greater severity.

Why was Louis Besse, the standard *repris de justice,* who had stolen twenty-nine bushels of grain, sent to the gallows? He was 63 at the time of his execution; perhaps the court felt he would be unlikely to survive very long in the galleys and could provide a more useful example by dying quickly and publicly in the town square than in the obscurity of the hulk.[70] The execution of François Gouneau, a 25-year-old tile-maker, and Pierre Donnadier, a weaver of 32, for the burglary of Sr Burière de la Sicardie is even more indefensible. The stolen property amounted to a pathetic 'quarter of lard', four pots of fat 'with pieces of goose', some butter, a tablecloth and two pieces of black bread – a nice meal for two. Donnadier had, however, cast

68. *Sentence* 21 Aug. 1771, *ibid.* B 620.
69. Sentences respectively on 30 May 1722 (B 334); 14 Mar. 1741 (B 432); 17 Aug. 1739 (B 438); 25 June 1754 (B 558); 12 July 1766 (B 578); 9 Mar. 1768 (B 587); 9 Feb. 1737 (B 411); 10 Sept. 1768 (B 596); 24 May 1771 (B 617); 5 Jan. 1771 (B 618); 8 Aug. 1771 (B 619); 25 June 1771 (B 626).
70. *Sentence* 21 June 1727, *ibid.* B 358.

himself in an unfavourable light by escaping half-way through the trial (to be recaptured a few months later); he also made the worse mistake of continuing to steal in prison, which clearly established his unrepentant, incorrigible character.[71] Grifoul, who had carried on a career of repeated violent thefts and brutal intimidation, earned life in the galleys, but Le Frejon died in agony on the wheel for two or three small thefts.[72]

It is not surprising to find that death by hanging was the normal penalty – in seven cases – for murder. What is surprising is the fact that galleys for life – the standard punishment for burglary – could also be the penalty for murder. In such cases there is, however, at least the hint of mitigating circumstances. In the conviction of Beausson for the premeditated murder of Jean Lafage, for example, it is possible, if not probable, that the victim had played a major rôle provoking the disturbance; he had certainly helped to envenom the underlying dispute by giving refuge to a servant girl his assailant had sacked and providing her with the means to sue her former employer. It could also be said on behalf of the accused that he was only one of three to attack Lafage, and apparently restricted his participation to providing the ammunition. The gun had been loaded with buckshot designed for rabbits, and therefore, their defence lawyer would have argued, not intended to kill.[73]

It clearly had not been a calculated plot for vulgar financial gain; two other prisoners who were involved in such a murder – that of the pewterer Clervaux – were also sent to the galleys, as menial accomplices 'convicted of having organised and plotted the murder of Clervaux' along with the principal suspect and sole beneficiary, Don Miguel, who escaped. Yet in the same case, another of Don Miguel's lackeys, apparently no more responsible than the other two, was sentenced to be broken on the wheel, a verdict which seems to have been inspired as much by desire for vengeance as by the dispassionate demands of justice.[74] Such a vicious punishment was, however, inevitable in the case of the murder of the curé of St Pardoux; Antoine Boussarie met the common fate of sacrilegious murderers: after torture, the payment of costs and a derisory 3L. fine, he was led out to make public penance, to have his hand cut off, and to be broken on the wheel.[75]

For no *prévôtal* criminals were the punishments so bewilderingly diverse as for counterfeiters. In the Périgord there was none of the repetitive resort to the death penalty which was the practice of the *maréchaussée* of Langres.[76]

71. *Interr.* 16 June 1773, sentence 18 June, *ibid.* B 638.
72. Sentence 12 Aug. 1769. *ibid.* B 599 and sentence 17 Aug. 1739, *ibid.* B 438.
73. Sentence 29 Aug. 1724, *ibid.* B 346.
74. Sentences, 2 June, 26 June, 11 July 1743, *ibid.* B 459.
75. Sentence 14 Jan. 1741. His two associates, or *confidantes,* were hanged. *Ibid.* B 421.
76. 'The repression of the principal culprits was inexorable: the gibbet (Desvignes, Tierce, Richard, Barjon, Hance), or the galleys for life (Savoye)'. A. Garnier,

Only one of the Périgourdin counterfeiters was put to death – Jean Rousseau, who was convicted of distributing false *écus* 'knowledgeably'.[77] The wording of sentences for this offence reveals the *prévôtal* court in the last stages of scholasticism, for de la Grelière was let off with the derisory punishment of five years' banishment for simply 'being in possession' of false coins.[78] Jean Defarge was also 'found in possession' of 30 *sous* 4 *liards* worth of false coins, yet his three-year banishment was preceded by a flogging and a branding (V).[79] Even this sentence did not exhaust the possible range of penalties, for something had to be found that was appropriate for an offence more serious than being in possession of a paltry sum, and spending large sums in false *livres* and *écus*. The crime was provided by Pataud – 'convicted of having whitened one-liard coins and of having passed them off as 12 and 24 *sous*'; the penalty was provided by the infinite resourcefulness of the *prévôtal* court: neither the gibbet nor banishment, but nine years in the galleys.[80]

In the repression of one *prévôtal* crime – that of being a vagabond – a 'hardening' was imposed on local magistrates by government legislation. Before 1764, vagabonds were sentenced to more vagabondage, perpetual banishment from the province of arrest and a 3L. fine. The Declaration of 1764 itself recognised the absurdity: 'We acknowledge that the penalty of banishment is incapable of restraining people whose life is a sort of voluntary, perpetual banishment, and who, chased out of one province, pass with in-difference into another.' Thereafter convicted vagabonds departed for the galleys, or the *hôpital général*. The court had not much more freedom of manoeuvre when dealing with the 11 convicted women of the 35 charged with *prévôtal* theft – a flogging, a branding and banishment or occasionally detention in an *hôpital général* which persistently complained that it did not have the means to prevent the escape of anyone who tired of the accommo-dation it provided. Detention for life was reserved for Catherine Grandpierre, recidivist, escapee, beggar and vagabond.[81]

The court did have more latitude when dealing with the archetypal prisoners, the vagabonds who were also convicted of theft. The magistrates of this 'booted justice' could be expected to take the opportunity to wreak havoc among their ranks to set a dreadful example to other idlers and the thieves and brigands they spawned. It is immediately obvious, however, that the range of penalties inflicted on vagabond thieves were on the whole much

76. cont'd.
    'Histoire de la maréchaussée de Langres', *Mémoires de la Société pour l'Histoire du Droit* XIII (1951), p. 248.
77. Sentence, 31 Mar. 1770, A.D. Dord. B 608.
78. Sentence, 13 Jan. 1770, *ibid.*
79. Sentence, 28 Aug. 1728, *ibid*, B 362.
80. Sentence, 22 Jan. 1773, *ibid.* B 636.
81. Sentence, 8 Apr. 1769, *ibid.* B 599.

less terrifying than the executions and life sentences which were the common lot of burglars. Only 2 were actually hanged, and 11 went to the galleys for life, but most got nine, five or three years. This lower scale can perhaps be explained by the fact that vagabonds were so much more easily apprehended by public or police, and so were usually charged with the theft of much more trivial items. Nevertheless a number of vagabonds did receive very heavy sentences; for most of them the reason was their previous record. It is not surprising that many vagabonds were also ex-convicts, that banished thieves and ex-galley-slaves had to take to the road and carry on stealing to keep alive. Pierre Dupont, a boatman of 22 who had been branded V in Bordeaux for stealing a shirt he found drying on a hedge,[82] went to the galleys for fifteen years for his part in stealing a mare, though his accomplice got only five years.[83] François Mazière, who three years previously had been whipped and branded by the Bordeaux *Parlement* for stealing 'a few clothes' went to the galleys for nine years for the theft of a pitiable coat and two sheets.[84]

The usual penalty for a vagabond thief, as established by the Declaration of 1764, was five years in the galleys, but the sentence was bound to be lengthened, usually to nine years, if the vagabond aggravated the offence by the direct challenge to public security and *prévôtal* competence implied by committing the theft on the highway or by breaking in, or if the vagabond had committed more than one theft. The size of the theft was also important; if 100L. was worth nine years in the galleys, 356L. was worth a life sentence.[85] The difficult *conjoncture* of 1769 seems, however, to be the only factor which might help to explain why the vagabond Pierre Morance should be hanged for 'theft and assault on the highway', for what had been no more than a drunken attempt to grab three 12-*sous* coins from a woman he had met on the road outside Mussidan.[86]

The *prévôtal* magistrates did come to realise that such severity was unnecessary, once they understood that the Périgord had nothing to fear from the 'vagabonds' who wandered in the province. The handful who suffered from excessive harshness were grossly outnumbered not only by the hordes of suspects the courts released, but also by vagabonds who were convicted of theft, who even admitted their guilt, but who were not made to pay for their crime: those vagabonds who went to the galleys for only three years, when the Declaration of 1764 demanded five; those vagabond thieves whose penalty was commuted by royal grace and favour, or those who were simply forgiven and released.

82. The *prévôtal assesseur* (Taratin) disputed the fact that he could have been branded for so trivial an offence, but the prisoner insisted. *Interr.* 3 June 1767, *ibid.* B 585.
83. Sentence, 3 Sept. 1767, *ibid.*
84. Sentence, 1 Sept. 1778, *ibid.* B 697.
85. Sentence, 7 June 1777, *ibid.* B 667, and Sentence, 24 Jan. 1779, *ibid.* B 698.
86. Sentence, 6 Apr. 1769, *ibid.* B 607.

A three-year galley sentence was the most common form of *prévôtal* indulgence. The first beneficiary was a farm-labourer called Jean who stole only a tablecloth without any kind of *effraction*, having found it left out to dry.[87] The triviality of the object stolen was the usual criterion for a three-year sentence – two chickens as the haul of a labourer with no bread or money;[88] a jacket found in a barn by Mathieu Breuil, who took it 'because he was naked.'[89] It was however the last decade of the ancien régime which was to be marked by an increasing reluctance on the part of the *prévôtal* court to condemn vagabonds to an extra two years of servitude for a relatively minor theft. Eight of the 12 vagabond thieves who were let off with three years were sentenced in the 1780s; and the articles they had stolen tended to be more substantial than the trivia which alone qualified for clemency in the 1770s. Jean Pradier took a pile of stockings, shirts, four pounds of thread, bonnets and sandals – virtually all the possessions of a miller's boy, and the vagabond Jean Fretillère got three years even though he had compounded his theft of a sack of grain with breaking and entering.[90]

Even if a sentence of five years did result from a robbery committed by vagabonds, the *prévôtal* court might restrict the full rigour of its retribution to only one of those responsible. Georges Bleygeas (who was 26) got five years were sentenced in the 1780s; and the articles they had stolen tended gether pilfering in a barn.[91] It was lack of years and responsibility which saved François Elie, the typical juvenile delinquent of the Périgord. Brought up in the Périgueux *dépôt de mendicité,* he escaped at the age of 14, and for the next two years lived by begging and pilfering whatever he could get his hands on until the Périgueux *cavaliers* responded to the complaints against him. He was now 16, old enough to go to the galleys;[92] he admitted he had often stolen fruit in the market-place, but he was freed, 'accused of no crime'.[93] It was in fact regular policy to send teenage boys convicted of theft to the *hôpital* even when 16 or over, and even when certified fit to serve on the galleys. In 1789 itself, all vagabonds who admitted thefts were sent to the *dépôt.*

The most spectacular sign of judicial clemency was a royal intervention to reduce the severity of a sentence. The central authorities were very much in the hands of local magistrates in cases of potential commutation, if only

87. Sentence, 10 July 1767, *ibid.* B 574. The Périgueux magistrates were clearly not impressed by the argument that the greater the ease of the theft the greater the deterrent should be.
88. Sentence, 1 Sept. 1770, *ibid.* B 618.   89. Sentence, 18 Feb. 1777, *ibid.* B 684.
90. Sentence, 14 Mar. 1783, *ibid.* B 735, and Sentence 3 Feb. 1787, *ibid.* B 806.
91. Sentence, 15 June 1767, *ibid.* B 575.
92. Art. III of Declaration of 1764 specified that 'hommes valides' from the age of 16 to 70 inclusive were to go to the galleys.
93. *P.-v.* Chousserie, Dubois, Reveilhac, 21 July 1776; freed by Lt., 2 July 1777, *ibid.* B 684.

because the local court had to stay the hand of the executioner, wielding rope or branding iron, for longer than the customary twenty-four hours. Of the 6 individuals who were allowed to benefit from a commutation, 5 were vagabond thieves. In the case of the 17-year-old day-labourer Mangonneau and his 21-year-old accomplice, the sailor Jacques Laforce, the prisoners had stolen just two pieces of bread, two shirts and a pair of woollen stockings. Mangonneau explained they had been driven by hunger, that the stolen bread was mouldy and that he had been unable to resist the temptation to steal a shirt 'as he had nothing on his back but a shirt which was practically rotten and completely falling to bits'. Their five years in the galleys was commuted to five years' banishment from the Périgueux *sénéchaussée*, as there were no 'aggravating circumstances' and the prisoners were 'sincerely repentant'.[94] The property stolen was not so trifling, and there were no mitigating circumstances, in the case of Jacques Vergnes called Marchandou and Pierre Cavard. They staged a brawl on the Bergerac to Issigeac road, and when the gardener Pierre Bonnamy intervened to separate them, they turned on him, robbed him of 42L. and left him with serious head injuries. They were duly sentenced to be hanged, and then reprieved for service on the galleys.[95]

Far from following the panic-stricken example of their colleagues elsewhere, and launching a campaign of repression against the swelling ranks of the 'marginal classes', the Périgueux *prévôtal* magistrates moved hesitantly in the opposite direction. In the last decade of the ancien régime, the *prévôtal* court neither tortured nor executed a single prisoner. It can be said that the authorities at least were setting a course which led away from the violent procedures of the past. It will be seen in chapter 6 if this lead was being followed by the mass of the population.

The court's clientèle and the treatment of vagabonds

One important element of the modern criminal trial was conspicuously absent in most cases which occupied the Périgueux *prévôté:* that is, motive. This was because it was taken for granted given the poverty of the *prévôt's* usual clientèle. There was no great social divide between those charged with burglary and highway robbery, crimes of peasants and rural artisans of all kinds, and the shoddy peddlers, shoeblacks, farm-hands and labourers who faced charges of *vagabondage*. In the early years of the century, when representatives of the upper classes still resorted to violence to settle their disputes, the *prévôté* dealt with more elevated members of society. After

---

94. P.-v. Reveilhac 8 June 1772; *Interr.* 9 June; sentence 5 Mar. 1773; ratification of commutation 23 Apr. 1773, *ibid.* B 638.
95. Sentence, 23 Aug. 1786. *Entérinement*, 9 Feb. 1787, *ibid.* B 782.

1731, when the *maréchaussée* was no longer competent to deal with pre-meditated assault, it had to assume a crass material motive in every crime, for it could not charge an assassin unless he had also robbed.

The resident peasants and artisans who were suspected of burglary and highway robbery were certainly at least one step above destitution – they still had a roof over their heads. In the case of Grifoul, however, his house had collapsed and he lived in a shack 'constructed of firewood leaning against the remains of a chimney'.[96] *Prévôtal* thefts were committed because someone needed something to eat or something to wear. When Jean Ramond committed a burglary in the suburbs of Périgueux, part of the booty was a pair of shoes to put on his feet; peasants caught Jean Durand, a day-labourer, stealing two jackets, a waistcoat, a shirt and a 'pair of shoes which he already had on his feet'.[97] Delfe, farm-labourer, had helped to build the barracks in Libourne, worked on the vineyards of the Pères Chartreux in Bordeaux, trained in a tile-works in Pont de la Souze, but reached Donzillac without a sou and was arrested stealing a chicken.[98]

It was not only 'vagabonds' who went hungry. How many witnesses came before the *prévôtal* court to denounce a suspect because all of a sudden he had been able to afford the luxury of a few drinks at the *cabaret,* or had been able to pay off some of his debts, or was rumoured to eat white bread? Antoine Bessont, a basket-maker, and Beaussont, a farm-labourer, resisted the blandishments of their friend Le Frejon until he reminded each of them 'that he was poor and needed the money to feed his family'.[99] *Prévôtal* prisoners found it natural to explain away the nocturnal transpor-tation of property as a simple removal to a neighbour's house to avoid having it confiscated for the tax collector or for some other debt. Jean Beaussont, a ditch-digger, remarked that his belongings had been seized so often that he no longer knew what was behind each confiscation.[100] When a friend suggested robbing the château de St Martin, Pierre Lamouroux agreed at once as he had been *métayer* on the estate and could make nothing of it, and now, 'having no work and no bread, he would be glad to have a bushel of corn to live on'.[101]

Although there were relatively few grain riots in eighteenth-century Périgord, large quantities of grain disappeared surreptitiously from chateau granaries, merchants' warehouses and bourgeois cupboards. When the day-labourer Pinquet tried to steal some grain from the Sr Peytoureau, his wife and child had had nothing to eat for three days.[102] Veyssinayre, a carrier,

96. *Inform.* Jan. 1769, *ibid.* B 599.
97. *Ibid.* B 821, 1784 and 1788.
98. *P.-v.* Girodel 7 May 1770, *ibid.* B 618.
99. *Interr.* 8 Mar. 1739, *ibid.* B 438.
100. *Interr.* 19 Apr. 1724, *ibid.* B 346.
101. *Interr.* 8 Mar. 1729, *ibid.* B 367.
102. *Réponses* 8 Aug. 1771, *ibid.* B 619.

robbed a mill 'because for five days he had had neither bread nor flour nor any means to live'; it was the same simple answer as the explanation given by 'Jean', a young farm-worker who had stolen 13L. 'because he had nothing to live on'.[103] The highly successful robber who got away with 84L. from a house in the *bourg* of Nazac took the risk of stopping to eat five waffles.[104] More striking still is the image drawn by the 10-year-old son of the notorious Lacroix, who got home in the middle of the night with three or four loaves and the whole family – aunts, sisters, mother – got up to eat it, as they had had no dinner.[105] The *maréchaussée* may have been reluctant to incarcerate beggars in the years of greatest economic distress, but such charity had the advantage of leaving their hands free to deal with those who used even more illegitimate means to supplement their income.

One of the crimes which had Grelety whipped and branded was the theft of a coat from a master who did not feed him well, paying him only 5s. a day until he ran out of money altogether.[106] One *métayer* of the Périgueux *brigadier* Reveilhac blamed his theft of corn on 'the callousness of his master who would not provide him with corn to live on'.[107] The lieutenant of the *maréchaussée* might prompt the prisoners, and ask them 'if it was need which forced them to commit the theft'.[108] The *maréchaussée* filed a complaint in 1775 from the prior of the abbey in St Jean de Cole that 'idlers' and 'good-for-nothings' who spent the night at the *cabaret* filled the ranks of the thieves 'who prowl every evening round about' and had destroyed 'public security' to such a degree that he could no longer get out at night to see the sick and dying; but even the prior, Vopart de Nargis, recognised that 'it is obvious that it is poverty and the high price of food which give rise to these misdeeds'.[109]

To understand the economic plight of the *prévôtal* prisoner requires only a glance at the jobs which they claimed to depend on for a livelihood (appendix 2). The variety of 'professions' represented are a tribute not to the heterogeneity of the *prévôtal* clientèle but to the endless resourcefulness of the poor, from the 'maker of flywhisks to put on the heads of cattle and of game-bags for huntsmen' or the 'soot maker' to the courageous 'skinner of animals killed by disease'. Nothing is so indicative of the economic desperation of the 'game' hunted down by the *maréchaussée* as the number of prisoners who had been forced to move from one employer to another, one job to another: the sawyer who had been a glass-worker, a mason and a gelder; the

103. *Réponses*, 29 Apr. 1773, *ibid.* B 830, and *P.-v.* Greilh Gontier, 11 Sept. 1781, *ibid.* B 735.
104. *P.-v.* Lt., 1 Mar. 1770, *ibid.* B 617.
105. *Inform.*, 13 May 1766, *ibid.* B 578.
106. *Interr.* 17 Aug. 1765, *ibid.* B 565.
107. *Interr.* 29 Jan. 1770, *ibid.* B 609.
108. *Réponses*, 30 Mar. 1770, Izabeau Garteau, *ibid.*
109. Letter from Vopart de Nargis to Lt., 31 Jan. 1775, *ibid.* B 668.

lace-maker who had been a navigator on merchant ships before going from parish to parish to sell the 'cords and belts for priests' he had made. Most *prévôtal* prisoners who had been street-porter or stevedore at some time did not survive long on the job, or had taken it up after failing as a shoeblack, a farm-worker or a builder's-labourer. Shoeblacks were failed postilions or herdsmen or rag-and-bone merchants or upholsterers; the unskilled labourer was a failed groom who was a failed stonemason; a tailor resorted to taking merchandise by boat down the Dordogne, and after that to herding cattle; a youthful button-maker had already tried his hand as a metal worker and cutler. Most *prévôtal* prisoners worked on the land at some part of the year, and a straw-dealer would bring in the harvest alongside a tailor, a household servant, a boat-master or a tobacco smuggler. Many claimed to have no profession, which could mean anything from herding pigs to selling devotional pictures. A number of prisoners were not surprisingly confused about their principal occupations. One sailor who was simultaneously a miller's boy and a wool-carder concluded he was 'without a positive profession'. An honest vagabond described himself as 'without a profession, of all trades, and at present a beggar'.

The most varied and insecure jobs were held by the poorest of all, those who were picked up by the police as vagabonds. Vagabonds more than any-one knew the dire poverty which had driven them to take to the road. The father of a young spinning-girl had a letter written to her in Périgueux prison urging her to explain to the court that she had left home 'because there was no work in this area and with my poverty I was unable to support you'.[110] Two young Limousins picked up by the Bergerac brigade convinced the lieutenant they were not vagabonds: Jean Boisseau because his parents were *métayers* 'who had had the misfortune to see their crops ruined by hail two years in a row', Jean Mons because he had been 'forced by poverty' to leave the Limousin for the grape harvesting in Bordeaux.[111] After leaving the army, Pierre Rougier went home to the Périgord to make haystacks and take jobs as a gamekeeper or a groom till the low wages forced him to leave.[112] Jean Bezy, a 15-year-old straw-dealer from the Haute-Auvergne, combined two popular reasons for leaving home: 'poverty and maltreatment from his stepmother'.[113]

That the French provinces in the eighteenth century were full of wicked stepmothers and a few hostile sisters-in-law is just another painful testimony to the strains placed on the social fabric by poverty and the struggle for

---

110. *Interr.* 3 Nov. 1764, Jeanne de la Maisonneuve, 21 (Rufet en Angoumois), *ibid.* B 597.
111. *P.-v.* and *interr.* 25 Aug. 1771 – Boisseau, 18 (Hautefaye), and Mons, 18, (St Pierre en Limousin), who had left home eight months previously; *ibid.* B 628.
112. *Interr*, 21 Sept. 1772, *ibid.* B 639.
113. *Interr.* 22 Oct. 1772, *ibid.*

survival. The struggle was ceaseless, and even those in relative comfort had no cause to relax. François Bompierre had been a grocer with a stock worth 150L. but had to take to the road after going bankrupt and was picked up in a run-down inn in Bergerac with a few scissors and ribbons.[114] Léonard Lizois, a nail-maker, had had his own business, but debts piled up and he had to sell it; his son died, he was left resourceless at the age of 58, and set off to look for work in other people's shops.[115] Jean-Antoine Radeau lived in Tonneins for twenty years until forced to leave by a ruinous lawsuit.[116] Marie de Laval and her husband were ostensibly involved in the textile trade in Libourne, while carrying on a more profitable but illegal sideline in spirits until obliged to leave town when bankrupted by heavy fines.[117] The *maréchaussée* picked up those who had been felled by the disasters of daily life – pregnancy for an 18-year-old girl who was overcome by her shame and left home; shipwreck for a sailor, left with only a few torn rags; a broken leg for a stevedore.

It is not surprising how many of these casually employed, underfed vagabonds struggled with medical problems, which in turn made them more difficult to be employed. Jean Genouilh had been a wool-carder, but could never find work at his own trade because of a 'fluxion' in his thigh, the result of falling off a roof, and had to resort to the usual expedients of the destitute; in the course of his wanderings he was five months ill in the Paris 'Autel-Dieu', and in the Saintonge his wife lay ill in a barn for weeks on end.[118] Antoine Gerauc progressed from town to town, and from hospital to hospital; he had taken to begging after being struck by some kind of paralysis, spent five months in hospital as the result of a fever; worked in La Rochelle for a time cleaning out ditches, which put him in hospital for six months, and in Bordeaux again where he caught another fever in an inn in the rue Ste Catherine and spent another three months in hospital.[119] Yet Antoine had left home at the age of 19 with high hopes of earning his living as a paver, and for the first two years he was employed in a tile-works in Poitou before taking work as a stable lad and resorting to digging the unhealthy ditches.

Like most of the vagabonds who were arrested in the Périgord, Antoine Gerauc had confined his wandering to the south-western provinces of France. Almost half of the suspected vagabonds came from the Périgord itself, a quarter from the equally poor and neighbouring province of the Limousin; there was another large contingent from the Quercy, backed up by a number of wanderers from the western side of the Massif Central, and even from the

114. *Interr*. 18 Nov. 1769, *ibid*. B 689.
115. *Interr*. 1 Aug. 1769, *ibid*. B 688.
116. *Interr*. 22 May 1771: Radeau, 52, *ibid*. B 638.
117. *Interr*. 22 Oct. 1772, *ibid*. B 639.
118. *Interr*. 25 June 1743, *ibid*. B 459.
119. *Interr*. Oct. 1741, *ibid*. B 432.

poor Atlantic province of Brittany, but only isolated, intrepid individuals from further afield. Very few came inland from the Bordelais, which was not surprising as even the police of the Périgord regarded their province as a benighted backwater and could not understand why Etienne Miremont could leave a town of opportunity like Libourne to come to the Périgord. Jean Brand was a farm-worker from Cardeleque near Blaye, and the last question he faced before leaving for the galleys was why he had ever left the Blayois, 'an area where he would earn twice as much as in the Périgord'.[120]

For almost all the vagabonds who crossed the Périgord, the Mecca of decent wages, employment, or even just a passage to the Indies, was or had been Bordeaux. It is well known how the population of the city was expanded by immigration from the hinterland in the course of the century, but for those who left the inland provinces to make their fortune in the metropolis life was hard, working a few days here, a day or two there. The *maréchaussée* of the Périgord was there to pick up those who did not make it in Bordeaux. When the Périgueux court asked Jacques Laurent why he had left Bordeaux when he would find much less work in the countryside 'than in Bordeaux where there is always some kind of work to be found', it learned that it was not at all easy to get work in a city where so many competed for every casual job.[121] Jean Cassan could turn his hand to most things – he had been brought up to work for stonemasons and thatch roofs and saw wood to make barrels and haul boats on canals, but having hurt his arm, he followed three shoemakers to Bordeaux to earn his living as a shoeblack; he left the city after thirteen days as shoeblack and stevedore, 'since there were so many of them'.[122] Charles Cloche, an ironmonger, lasted a day longer in the city – two days helping a butcher, three on the quayside, and nine picking grapes.[123]

At this level of the social scale, the wandering in search of work was permanently confused with the search for alms, and a wool-comber who left Montauban in search of work used his passport to get twenty-four-hour begging permits, which in itself meant he had to keep moving on: 12 August 1779 – Montauban; 18 August – Toulouse; 20 August – Castelnaudary; 22 August – Carcassonne; 25 August – Narbonne; 27 August – Béziers; 31 August – Agde; 1 September – Cète; 3 September – Montpellier; 6 September – Gignac; 7 September – Lodève; 10 September – Milhau; 13 September – Rodez; 16 September – Villefranche de Rouergue; 18 September – Caussade; 8 November – Moissac; 11 November – Agen; and he was arrested in Bergerac on 13 December.[124]

Such a brief glimpse of Laforêt's career suggests an unadventurous itinerary confined to the Languedoc until his unfortunate foray into the Périgord.

120. *Interr.* 10 Dec. 1765, *ibid*. B 566.
121. *Interr.* 6 June 1767, *ibid*. B 585.
122. *Interr.* 28 Aug. 1767, *ibid*. B 586.
123. *Interr.* 9 Nov. 1784, *ibid*. B 768.
124. *P.-v.* Peyrou, 13 Dec. 1779; Jacques Laforêt, *ibid*. B 709.

Yves Lorgane, however, a house-painter from Brittany, had been on the move since the age of 10: five years in Quimperlay as scullion, three years in the port of Lorient, eighteen months in the Indies. His return to France ended his period of relative stability, for he took to the road and saw Nantes, La Rochelle, Libourne, Toulouse; he was a cook in Alais for three months; he went to Avignon to get a job as 'commissaire à l'Hôtel de St Omer' before going across the sea to Corsica as the servant of an army surgeon. On his return to the continent he met up with 'Martin' who 'displayed strange animals' in Toulouse, and drummed up custom for him. He left Martin near Albi and was arrested in the Périgord in the company of a button-maker who displayed 'a mechanical device'.[125]

It was not only the uncouth and unskilled who had to keep in perpetual motion to find work. There was no profession so insecure as the dancing master, and Jean-Bernard Gautier and his wife Louise were obliged to move from town to town, looking for pupils. Like Laforêt, they started from Montauban: 28 April 1765 – Montauban; 7 June – Auch; 5 July – St Flour; 16 July – Riom; 22 July – Moulin; 31 July – Gien; 3 August – Châteauneuf; 6 August – Yenville; 8 August – Chartres; 15 August – Evreux; 17 August – Caen; 22 August – Rouen; 28 August – Pontaud; 30 August – Honfleur; 3 September – Caen; 12 September – Angers; 16 September – Evreux; 27 September – Aubigny; 17 October – Gueret; 22 October – Limoges; and they were arrested in Périgueux on 1 November.[126]

Most of the wandering poor found work at least intermittently. One group of travellers treated by the police as vagabonds, however, never found the time to stop and work. Despite strong official disapproval, pilgrims continued to beg their way to and from Rome, Santiago de Compostella and their home parish. They were immediately recognisable on their return from Santiago, with shells on their hats or on a scarf over the shoulder. Pierre Martin was on his way back to Fontenay le Comte, having fulfilled a vow to God and the Virgin made during a serious illness that if he recovered he would make a pilgrimage to Rome and Santiago.[127] Jean Maguelin, a maker of silk belts from Bourg-en-Bresse, his wife and child, had taken six months to get to Santiago and five months back as far as the rue Limogeanne in Périgueux, happily unaware of laws 'which forbid all the King's subjects to leave the kingdom on the pretext of a pilgrimage without the permission of a Secretary of State'. The family was released when the court received the most condescending of references from their curé: they had always been good servants, but 'people like them' often regarded 'these sorts of pilgrimage' as one of the most meaningful acts of religion.[128]

125. *Interr.* 4 Apr. 1772, *ibid*. B 637.
126. *Interr.* 2 Nov. 1765, *ibid*. B 566.
127. *Interr.* 7 Feb. 1772, *ibid*. B 637.
128. *P.-v.* 9 Sept. 1768, Mage and Reveilhac. *Certif. légalisé par Lt. gén. de police*, 12 Jan. 1769, *ibid*. B 598.

All travelling members of the general public who were not sufficiently upper class to be above harassment by a policeman were required to carry a 'passport', to name its holder correctly, and guarantee that the holder was required to travel by his job. The 'passport', which does not seem to have been described or defined by legislation, usually took the form of a certificate of good character and statement of occupation by a municipal magistrate. A number of travellers carried an extract from the record of baptism which favourably disposed the *maréchaussée*, but did nothing to indicate the holder's occupation or whereabouts in the previous six months. The police would however accept a certificate signed by a curé that the holder's house had been burned down, and that he had been driven despite his good character on to the road. There is ample evidence in other provinces of the ease with which false documentation could be obtained, but the Périgord *maréchaussée* managed to find only one suspect, arrested for theft, who admitted to carrying a forged document: Jean Jeamine had a certificate that he was a poor farm-labourer who had lost all in a fire, signed by the curé and *consuls* of La Chapelle Monrival (Quercy), a certificate which had cost him a bottle of wine.[129] There was also the case of Guillaume d'Anvin who on being questioned by Greilh, the Mussidan *cavalier*, produced a Neapolitan passport; as he had already said he came from Coutances in Normandy, the *cavalier* soon deduced he was using someone else's passport.[130] Any foreign passport, in fact, was treated with suspicion in the Périgord, and Jean Mariaux was able to get from Santiago only as far as Sarlat with a passport signed by Francisco Gonzalvez Valdes, 'substitute general of the French Consul in the Principality of the Asturias'.[131]

The essential requirement of a passport, however, was to confirm the holder's good conduct in the previous six months (in accordance, obviously, with the terms of the Declaration of 1764 against vagabonds), and it was almost always the date which was the object of *prévôtal* concern, no matter where or by whom the passport had been issued. The Périgord *cavaliers* seem to have been conscientious in arresting anyone with a passport more than six months old, whether it had lapsed for a few days or a few years. Procedures for obtaining the passport in the first place, however, seem to have been less rigorous. An apprentice monumental-mason from Switzerland had no trouble obtaining a certificate issued by the *'Consuls, Conseillers et Lieutenants-Généraux'* of Aix-en-Provence, testifying that the holder was an honest ironmonger and requesting 'all Consuls, Bridge guards, ferries and tolls to give him free passage, entry and unhindered commerce'. How was this impressive document obtained? The consul signed blank passports and left it to his clerk to fill in the names; any peddler could apply for one – it

129. *Interr.* 16 Feb. 1772, *ibid.* B 637.
130. *P.-v.* 16 Aug. 1772, *ibid.* B 639.
131. *Interr.* 22 Nov. 1768, *ibid.* B 598.

was known in the trade as a 'rolling ticket' – if he could name a local merchant or tradesman he had done business with.[132]

There was no passport at all in the vast majority of charges against 'vagabonds' who had to prove they had had a job in the previous six months or get themselves a character reference from a 'trustworthy person'. Right from the start the *prévôtal* court twisted the terms of the Declaration to exclude from *vagabondage* not only those who had actually been at work in the previous six months, but those who could prove that there was some kind of work they could do. This did not provide a loophole for the majority of suspects as the sort of person arrested by the police as a likely vagabond usually had a suspiciously meaningless occupation – peddler, street porter, the unskilled agricultural labourer, the occupations which required a minimum of merchandise and even less training and which provided most recruits for the ranks of eighteenth-century 'vagabonds'. For a few individuals, however, it saved a lot of time and effort. It was accepted that Guillaume Segelon was a genuine tin-founder as he carried a spoon mould.[133] Claude Maréchal admitted he 'had no profession other than displaying a kind of monkey . . . and selling a few pictures'; he was arrested because his three passports were all out of date, but released within a fortnight because he did have a handful of pictures, a trumpet, and a monkey.[134] Of all the peddlers arrested by the Périgord police, only three could provide receipts for the purchase of merchandise. Françoise Mas was freed on the strength of a single undated receipt 'which proves that she is a merchant'.[135] Aubin Arbelot and his 'concubine' Jeanne Biarre had receipts for the purchase of goods worth a total of 24L. covering the period of eight years between 1764 and 1772.[136]

For the great majority of 'vagabonds', therefore, it was a question of organising references, with regard either to their character or to their profession. Jean Peyrinet, the conjugal peddler of ironmongery arrested in a Ste Foy *cabaret*, summed up the predicament in the letter to his wife:

If they don't get a passport sent within three months they are branded by the executioner and led off to the galleys for three years. That would be a real disgrace for me. I must tell you, my dear wife, that I had the honour to write to M. the curé to ask him to be kind enough to make out a certificate for me and get it signed by the principal residents of the parish. I'll be out of this prison as soon as you've sent me a certificate.[137]

Peyrinet could not sign his name to the transcript of the trial; it will be immediately clear that it was no easy matter for an illiterate peddler or shoeblack in a prison cell to acquire documentary proof of his good character –

132. Case of C.-F. Martinoly, *ibid.* B 577.
133. *P.-v.* Reveilhac 1 May 1773, *ibid.* B 648.
134. *P.-v.* arrest 13 Dec. 1770, *ibid.* B 627.
135. *P.-v.* by *procureur*, 10 June 1767, *ibid.* B 586.
136. *P.-v.* arrest 7 May 1772; *jugement d'incompétence* (on the charge of vagabondage the equivalent of an acquittal), 10 July 1772, *ibid.* B 638.
137. Written in Périgueux prison, 5 Oct. 1766. *ibid.* B 574. See pages 105–6 above for first half of letter.

a reference usually from the curé but in all cases to be countersigned by a local magistrate. The onus of proof of innocence was left on the prisoner, which was particularly unfair now that the authorities had a national police force at their disposal. The police of course were already overworked, but in a matter of this importance, with a sentence to the galleys in the balance, the authorities could surely have used their resources as a matter of course to check on a prisoner's claim that he hailed from a certain parish or had worked for a certain employer.

Peyrinet's letter mentions a delay of three months – this was an exaggeration designed no doubt to encourage relatives and referees not to waste time. The *prévôtal* court was prepared to wait six months, on average, before deciding that the postal service was not going to produce the letter that would clear a suspect's name.

The prisoner was told at the first interrogation to arrange for someone to write on his behalf, but the 'vagabond' was usually so intimidated that it was only at the second interrogation two or three months later, when no letters had arrived and the *Présidial* had passed a *jugement de compétence* that prisoners admitted to practical difficulties. At their second interrogation, after three months in prison, prisoners would tell the court that they did not have writing materials, or did not know to whom they should write, or whom to ask to write on their behalf. They were directed to charitable prison visitors. The problem of communicating with isolated villages was compounded by financial difficulties; how could a roof thatcher get in touch with the village of Lascours in the Quercinois parish of Lavresse, or an old employer in Vettenoux, both places 'far from the postal service . . . with no money to stamp his letters'?[138]

It was therefore the most elementary good sense of the *prévôté* to advise prisoners to write to a judge, or a curé who, even on a stipend, could afford to collect his mail. Peyrinet, however, was not the only 'vagabond' to write to his family. The shoemaker René Blanchard had left home near Nantes to do his *tour de France*, but left his baptismal extract behind; after his arrest his sister sent it on:

I send you what you ask for, but take good care not to lose it for it cost a lot. You know we're not rich but we're honest, thank God . . . Mother has begun a novena for you to ask the Good Virgin of Contegoist to do you the grace of getting you out of that evil place.[139]

René's sister had been worried by his failure to send news for so long. One touching benefit of an arrest by the *maréchaussée* was that it often forced 'vagabonds' to get in touch with their families again:

Your uncle George died nine years ago . . . Your aunt urges you to be an honest boy . . . Let me know if you intend to stay in Périgueux and what you intend to do there, what

138. *Interr.* 17 Nov. 1767, *ibid.* B 586.
139. May/June 1766, *ibid.* B 578.

your present situation is and if you need some money. Goodbye, brother. Your very humble and obedient servant, George Maurice.[140]

The *prévôtal* court could also serve as an employment agency. When Pierre Gaunoid, an architect in Belvès, heard that the *maréchaussée* had arrested the entire Callet family – father, a house-painter, wife Marie, upholsterer, sons Pierre and François, both painters, and Louis, apprentice painter, and daughter Marguerite, also upholsterer, he asked the court to release them after he promised to find work for them.[141]

The conviction or release of most 'vagabonds', however, depended on the parish curé. Many suspects were allowed to go free after they had found a curé who had known them, and the *prévôté* asked no further questions about the suspect's way of life in the previous six months. Marguerite Serre was aggrieved at the injustice of her fate when she had to tell the court that her native parish had changed curés three years before, and so the 'new' one would not know her.[142] The curé of Villard admitted he did not know Gabrielle Grangier, but after making inquiries he was able to include a reference from the Montignac postal director which brought about her release on the grounds that at an undisclosed time in the past she had been a wet-nurse to his children.[143] The curés often complemented their own moral authority with a submission of the 'principal residents' of the community: the Bordeaux sailor Livet received a testimonial from his curé, a judge, a *procureur général,* a canon, a clockmaker and a host of neighbours.[144] The references from the curés themselves usually assured the *prévôtal* court that the prisoner came from a poor but honest family, had fallen perhaps into bad company, but was more in need of moral exhortations than judicial punishments (and they often included the exhortations in a separate letter to the prisoner). The curé of Ambert, however, was forced into a more pragmatic defence of his parishioner Jean Ansedat by the severe economic difficulties of the town: the paper industry had been virtually closed down by 'the price of food and the tax on paper'. In these circumstances, young paper workers had no alternative but to go in search of work elsewhere.[145]

For 'professional' as opposed to 'character' references the suspect vagabond did not usually rely on the church. Merchants could be 'reclaimed' by their colleagues, seamen were ordered to their home post by the navy administration; tradesmen could be authenticated by employers and clients. A tapestry-repairer from Aubusson spent only a week in the *prévôtal* prison

140. 2 Mar. 1766, *ibid*. B 576.
141. Arrested 19 Mar., freed 24 Mar. 1774, *ibid*. B 658.
142. *Interr.* 16 Apr. 1771, *ibid*. B 627.
143. Letter from curé of Villars, 11 Apr. 1779, *ibid*. B 698.
144. Freed 2 Feb. 1785, *ibid*. B 768.
145. Certificate arrived in Périgueux 15 July 1773, and suspect released the same day, *ibid*. B 649.

before being allowed to continue to a chateau near Jumilhac where he expected to find work.[146] When Pierre Gouni, a *scieur de long* from the Haute-Marche, was arrested as a vagrant suspected of horse-stealing, the Dame de Cablan came to his rescue, complaining that his continued detention was holding up the work he was doing for her.[147] Pierre Robert, a 47-year-old silk-worker who had left Lyon in January 1768 because of the unemployment, provided impressive certificates from the *Maîtres fabriquants en étoffes d'or d'argent et soye* and from the *Maîtres Gardes Inspecteurs et Contrôleurs jurés de la Communauté des Fabricans en Etoffes d'or d'argent et soye,*[148] but even at the lowest level of the social scale it was possible to gain professional recognition. There was not much lower than the shoeblack, yet the *maréchaussée* were able to verify that Louis Roux 'had drawn lots for the militia in Bordeaux with the porters and shoeblacks last year, 1767, which proves that Roux exercised these professions immediately before his arrest'.[149] Antoine Laborie was certified by the coachman of the *prévôt-général* himself: 'I knew him . . . as he was always cleaning my shoes and running a thousand errands for me and many others.'[150] Evidence of any kind of occupation was accepted by the *prévôtal* court, therefore, from every kind of source. Even a conviction for trying to defraud the internal customs was accepted as proof of a genuine profession as a merchant. Gilberg Jullien, a young haberdasher, was saved from the galleys by a certificate he obtained from the Libourne customs that they had caught him trying to smuggle a box full of ironmongery into the town.[151]

In their approach to the question of *vagabondage,* the magistrates of the Périgueux *prévôtal* court had, in short, taken seriously the advice they had received from the Chancellor Maupeou when he sent them a copy of the 1764 Declaration, and drew their attention to the severe penalties – galleys or *hôpital général* – now prescribed for vagrants and vagabonds: 'It will be easy for you to appreciate how important it is to be very circumspect in the application of such a serious penalty . . . Special and local circumstances should have a great influence on your decisions.'[152] The Périgord was not what Castan calls a 'turntable' of vagabondage. The *cavaliers* found only legitimate artisans and small-time peddlers who still had sufficient links with the community to be accepted as part of it, and verified as no threat to public order. The Périgord was a province which did not have the problems posed by expansion and change, like the Bordelais or the progressive northern provinces; yet it was not a province like the Auvergne preserved in atavistic

146. Arrest, 19 July 1772, freed 25 July, *ibid.* B 639.
147. Arrest and *interr.* 10 May 1773, freed 15 May, *ibid.* B 596.
148. Arrest 14 Mar. 1768, freed 12 May, *ibid.* B 596.
149. *Procureur* 14 Mar. 1767, *ibid.* B 587.
150. Freed 30 July, *ibid.* B 585.
151. *Certif.* 16 Sept. 1771, *ibid.* B 624.
152. Letter from Maupeou, 15 Apr. 1765, *ibid.* B 683.

patterns of violent behaviour. It did not have to suffer the bands produced by different geographical and economic reasons in the Beauce or the Forez or in Brittany. The Périgord was the quiet province in between, and when Gigounoux de Verdon asked the three British travellers what on earth had brought them to the Périgord, or wondered how the day-labourer from Blaye could have left the Gironde for the Dordogne, he was only too aware that the Périgord was off the beaten track, and for that the lieutenant of the *maréchaussée* had reason to be grateful. The authorities in sixteenth- and seventeenth-century Périgord had to fight the armies of the *Croquants;* the eighteenth-century police picked up the aimless wanderers, the strays.[153] No one headed deliberately for the Périgord – there were a few *scieurs de long* working their way down towards the Bordelais from the Limousin or the Auvergne, but the Périgord itself had little to attract the seasonal migrant. Migration to Bordeaux indicated that there were already too many Périgourdins to get in the grain or grape harvest, and the province was not on any of the major axes of communication. There was not enough commerce or traffic or wealth to attract the most undesirable of brigands on a permanent basis, and so the lieutenant had the leisure to mount his ostentatious operations of propaganda. It was a province with no discernible organised crime, and no bandit leaders more terrifying than the violinist Anjou. There was a worrying increase in the number of unsolved thefts, but so long as bands could be held as scapegoats, the wandering poor had nothing more to fear than police harassment, a few weeks in prison, and release. Local circumstances in the Périgord permitted the *prévôté* to adopt such a relaxed attitude to the vagrants and wanderers who were arrested by the police or by suspicious residents that 5 were banished (before 1764); 22 women went to the *hôpital général,* with 24 male *invalides;* a derisory 14 went to the galleys, and 230 were freed.

The *prévôtal* court no more allowed itself to convict as vagabonds suspects with a scruffy appearance and a lack of identification than to condemn as thieves those with a reputation as 'public thieves'. The failure of Périgueux judges to 'harden' their outlook, their failure to torture prisoners on any scale, their willingness to find virtually any pretext to release a suspected vagabond, all underline one of the major characteristics of eighteenth-century law enforcement – its ability to take account of local circumstances. Maupeou's advice to judges on the application of the 1764 Declaration against vagabonds was clearly kept in mind over the whole spectrum of criminal law. Far from being crude and hamfisted, law enforcement in eighteenth-century France was conspicuous for its flexibility. If he avoided the few really dangerous

153. The 'vagabond' and deserter Henri Laboissière, returning from the Atlantic provinces of Spain after an amnesty, had been heading for Bordeaux when arrested in Périgueux – 'because the peasants did not know the way to Bordeaux'. *Interr.* 21 Aug. 1730, *ibid.* B 372.

provinces and the big cities made nervous by the strains of uncontrolled immigration, the individual prisoner had a reasonable chance of a fair hearing.

Such a conclusion is less surprising when we take into account the fact that law enforcement in France, unlike in England, was entirely in the hands of professionals. Throughout the provinces, the great majority of judges had at least a university degree in law, and in the *prévôtal* court the one 'military' outsider had a legal adviser at his side. Alfred Soman has recently shown that at the height of the witch-craze at the turn of the sixteenth and seventeenth centuries, magistrates in Paris made drastic revisions to the sentences of provincial courts solely on the grounds that the prisoners had been convicted on insubstantial evidence.[154] It is at least feasible that in over a hundred years, local magistrates should have been accustomed to respect for professional standards even in so distant a province as the Périgord. They were undoubtedly encouraged in this direction by the centralised supervision of their activities. The Chancellor's office received copies of provincial court records and, as we saw in the trial of Alexis Faye, the Périgueux *prévôté* could be taken vigorously to task for sloppy work.

Given the willingness of ancien régime justice to allow its prisoners a reasonable hearing, however, there is still the problem of the effect this fairness had on efforts by the authorities to keep law and order in the community at large. It was certainly a policy that was not without risks. The sight of so many villains 'getting away with it' might produce resentment in the village communities which had come forward to denounce their local thief. The escape from retribution of so hated a character as Michel 'The Rat' might well have encouraged some of his neighbours to consider the possibilities of thieving on their own account. The release of prisoners known to their communities as 'public thieves' may conceivably have been one of the factors behind the indisputably rising theft rate, even if one of minor importance beside other deep-seated social and economic forces. But if the over-generous treatment of suspected thieves did in some way add to the crime rate, it was a small price to pay for its contribution to one of the major aims of government policy – the acceptance of central government institutions in local affairs.

It was essential for the royal government to break down *esprit de clocher,* hatred of outside interference in the village community, particularly in the field of law enforcement which had so long been the preserve of local interests and private vendetta. The 1720 reform of the *maréchaussée,* rather more than the Criminal Ordinance of 1670, was slowly bringing the *prévôté* into the village community. It was the regular appearance of the *cavaliers* of the *maréchaussée* which helped persuade even peasants not to keep their troubles to themselves, no longer to suffer violence and intimidation from

154. A. Soman, 'Les procès de sorcellerie au Parlement de Paris, 1565–1640', *Annales E.S.C.* (1978), 790–814.

the local thug or local *notable*. The daily sight of all those 'thieves' and 'vagabonds' freed on lack of evidence may well have encouraged this trend by persuading people that it was safe to cooperate with the royal authorities: the poor wretches they saw from time to time being branded or whipped or executed or led in chains to the galleys could safely be assumed to be guilty. The 'fairness' of ancien régime justice therefore was not contradictory but complementary to the occasional terrible example in the struggle to maintain law and order. The harsh public punishment was still useful as a deterrent, but the presence of those who had been freed was a permanent reminder, even in villages which rarely or never saw the passage of a police patrol, of the existence of the king's *prévôté*. And *prévôtal* justice was not only trust-worthy – it was also less subject to the delays and complacencies of the lower royal and seigneurial courts. Jeanne Goulpière, the wife of a rag-and-bone man, went to the *maréchaussée* after waiting in vain for six months for local judges to investigate the five men who broke up her wine shop;[155] the clerk Cournil was obliged to come to the *prévôtal* court as 'the local prestige' of a surgeon who had assaulted him 'interferes with the course of justice'.[156] Marthe Bastide, the widow of the shoemaker, went to the *prévôté* months after her husband had been stabbed by his apprentice; since the assault, the murderer Georges Marty 'appears every day and the ordinary court in Cléran has not started proceedings'.[157]

Whatever the rôle of local courts in providing a cheap service for the settling of peasant disputes, therefore, village communities now had both policemen and released suspects to remind them that for matters of criminal justice, there was an alternative that would be certain to take action and that would cost them nothing. The *prévôtal* court, a police court of summary justice which respected conventional legal standards, was both the spearhead and the very epitome of royal enforcement of the law: a system which until near the end of the ancien régime sought to be fair to the innocent and utterly merciless to the guilty.

155. *Plainte* 28 May 1728 (original *plainte* 2 Nov. 1727), *ibid*. B 362.
156. *Plainte* July 1728, ibid. B 363.
157. *Plainte* Apr. 1730, *ibid*. B 372.

PART II
Crime and disorder

CHAPTER 5

Theft

No crime or offence preoccupied the *maréchaussée* so much as theft: in no less than 416 of the 976 affairs before the Périgueux *prévôté* between 1720 and 1790. And no crime or offence was less tolerated by the population as a whole. While a physical assault could be settled out of court, and while the vast majority of beggars and vagabonds were allowed to go on their way, no mercy was shown to the vagabonds suspected of theft. Not content with handing them over to the police – and practically all vagabonds convicted of theft had been arrested by private citizens – the public exacted its own immediate retribution. When caught in his second burglary, Alexis Faye was stoned and beaten with clubs; Georges Petit, caught running out of a house with piles of linen under his arms, was 'seized by several people who struck him numerous blows with sticks and bellows'.[1] Grelety stole a ploughshare and went to sell it at market in Le Bugue, but the owner turned up, tore it from his hands and used it to beat him.[2] Even the presence of a brigade of *maréchaussée* could not protect the thief caught *in flagrante delicto*. Pierre Geneste, arrested by the Mussidan brigade at their local market when a *métayer* caught him picking his pocket, subsequently had the greatest difficulty walking to the *prévôtal* court in Périgueux, 'as he was set upon by the crowd of peasants'.[3] The usual ritual was to strike the thief on the side of the head with the club of his intended victim, after which the crowd cut off the hair on one side of the thief's head.

The value of the stolen property was immaterial: attachment to property was so ferocious that the local populace went to all the trouble of making the arrest, taking the prisoner to the authorities, giving their testimony, confronting the accused, for a shirt and a pair of breeches as well as for larger sums of money or livestock. No matter who had stolen his property, the victim was prepared to go to extreme lengths to recover it. Not all arrests were made *in flagrante delicto*, or when a suspicious character aroused fears which had immediately to be appeased. A number of thieves were captured by the civilian population and handed over to the police after con-

1. *Interr.* by *juge* of Ribérac, 7 June 1724, *ibid.* B 341.
2. *Interr.* 17 Aug. 1765, *ibid.* B 565. Alexis Faye, caught in the act of burglary, was stoned and beaten with clubs – *Interr.* 17 Oct. 1776, *ibid.* B 684.
3. *P.-v.* 4 June 1746, and *Inform.* 8 June, *ibid.* B 459.

siderable delay and what was for a private individual an enormous effort of investigation. The Sr Nicolas Alexandre, goldsmith of Paris, was able to follow the trail of the two thieves who had robbed him of silver buckles and diamonds, one to Rochefort where he was caught with two trunks full of the stolen property about to embark for Port-au-Prince, the other, despite changes of name to 'Des Plantes', 'des Isles', and the 'Chevalier of Chartres', to a *cabaret* in Périgueux.[4]

The extent of do-it-yourself detection merely underlines the fact that the loss of property was far too grave a matter to be left to the police. Pierre Goursat, a master-tailor robbed of a few pieces of clothing and two loaves, took five days to find the thief, who was caught trying to sell the articles at the Bars fair.[5] When money was involved it was advisable to catch the thief before he got too far away: Marie Darblade, an innkeeper in Libourne who lost 92 *écus*, had the thief followed and arrested just outside Bordeaux.[6] The loss of livestock, too, with all that animals represented in terms of economic survival, could spur victims to extraordinary efforts. The victims at least had the advantage that animals were more difficult to dispose of quickly than money, and would have to be driven long distances before they could be sold, hopefully leaving a trail that could be followed. Bernard Monribot, a *laboureur*-cattle merchant from Rouffignac, at a difficult pass in his business affairs, helped himself to two head of cattle in the fields, but found himself pursued by friends of the victim into Quercy, and finally was arrested at the fair in Ourliac and brought back with the 64L. 9s. which was all that he had left.[7] On their return from the Quercy, the *métayer* who had lost his cattle was so angry that he kept the thief at home to exact private retribution and private compensation. This, however, was quite exceptional. Although many victims of theft were not confident that the overworked police force was likely to capture the thief or recover the stolen property, once the villain had been apprehended they were prepared to entrust his punishment to the courts.

There is no doubt that an important element in this willingness to assist the authorities was a community desire to protect itself against strangers. There was bound to be more cooperation with the police in the Guyenne than in the Auvergne for the simple reason that there were far more strangers around in the broad river valleys of south-west France than in the remote and inaccessible villages of the Massif Central. The increasing number of prisoners handed over to the *maréchaussée*, or denounced for their suspicious presence, eventually accustomed the countryside to cooperating with external forces, but it had not always been intended in that spirit. The eighteenth-century

4. *P.-v.* 25 Mar. 1787, *ibid.* B 807.
5. *P.-v.* 13 Mar. 1772, *ibid.* B 637.
6. *Plainte* 11 Feb. 1751, to *juge* of l'Ormon, A.D. Gir. 11B 11.
7. *Interr.* 26 Sept. 1789, A.D. Dord. B 833.

citizen's arrest was to a large degree a reaffirmation of the strength of the local community, a closing of ranks before the rising threat from outside. The same suspicion of outsiders, the same persistence of *esprit de clocher* which can be seen in the denunciation of harmless deserters long since safely employed,[8] or of the three respectable British travellers who wandered off the beaten tourist track as far as Périgueux,[9] is apparent also in the arrests carried out by the populace themselves. Even the turgid police reports drawn up after the event convey something of the community spirit which enlivened the capture of a thief and the procession which escorted the prisoner to the nearest seat of authority. This was one occasion when it was permissible to form an *attroupement*. Cries for help, 'au voleur', assembled three, four or a dozen neighbours, the culprit was seized and delivered to the *maréchaussée* by 'the populace', 'all the inhabitants' of an entire community. All sections of the community participated in this active protection of property, and police reports paid homage to the vigilance of tanners, millers, *métayers*, gentlemen and bourgeois.

It was easy for any community to feel an outraged solidarity when the thief was a destitute stranger, one of the poor who wandered the provinces of France in search of their daily bread. It was much more difficult to know how to react when the thief came from within the community itself. The problem might be resolved by a stream of verbal abuse and the usual well-aimed blows. If the stolen goods were easily identifiable, pressure could be brought to bear on the thief to return them; if the goods were well hidden, the owner could resort to the use of bailiffs of the local courts armed with search warrants. If, however, the presumed thief was taller and stronger than his victim, or if ownership of property could not be proved, or the property could not be found, the victim had then to decide whether or not to call in outside help. Police reports in the Auvergne suggest that the peasants of the Massif Central preferred to settle accounts on their own.[10] In the Périgord, however, the records of the *prévôtal* court suggest that such intense community spirit was breaking down.

The horror of being robbed proved too overwhelming not to encourage

---

8. *P.-v. de capture* 22 May 1776 (Muret): Cornet, *dit* Sans façon, 25, *tailleur de pierre en plâtre*, A.D. Gir. 11B 11. *P.-v. de capture* 24 June 1783 (Castres brigade), *ibid.* 11B 12.
9. The three British tourists were interrogated under the official charge of leading a vagabond life: John Wear, merchant of Bristol, 22, in France to take the waters at Barrège; Edward Edwards, 36, archdeacon in Brechnaud, diocese of St David, in the 'Principality of Wales in England', who suffered from rheumatism; and James Fisher, 18, nobleman, 'native of London, student of rhetoric at Oxford'. The three had been to Toulouse and visited a number of Protestant friends in the Agenais, and the bulk of the interrogation concerned the religious implications of their tour. 13 Aug. 1768, A.D. Dord. B 598.
10. The police and *subdélégués* frequently complained that investigations were blocked by local 'fear or bad faith'.

victims to complain – and complain they did. Between 1720 and the arrival in Périgueux of Gigounoux de Verdon, the *prévôtal* court dealt with 78 cases of theft which did not involve a vagabond, and 63 were the result of a formal complaint or denunciation or citizen's arrest. With the new lieutenant, the proportions altered – there was far more police initiative, and the 15 cases initiated by the police between 1720 and 1764 rose to 124 for the period between 1764 and 1789. But the spirit of public cooperation in the denunciation of theft was only encouraged by greater police activity, and in the last twenty-five years of the ancien régime, the *maréchaussée* recorded twice as many complaints of theft as in the previous forty-four years.

Local thieves were subjected to the same rough treatment as thieving vagabonds, the same popular adaptation of the violence and public infamy of official retribution. The Brantôme brigade was summoned to the château de Puyguillem to take possession of a local miller caught by a *laboureur* making off with a blanket, coat, breeches and jacket; he was delivered to the police as it was his second offence, his face covered with scratches, 'and the public said it was the same man who had previously been caught stealing a horse . . . and who had been sent on his way after being well beaten'.[11]

Like the pilfering of vagabonds, many 'local' thefts were denounced to the police immediately. Marguerite Malet, a widow living in St Pierre de Chignac, walked to Périgueux after being robbed on New Year's Eve 1777/8 of twenty-five pounds of thread, seven pairs of stockings she had been given to repair, and two bushels of corn, 'all she had to live on'. She went to the *maréchaussée* precisely because, and not in spite, of the fact that she had heard that the goods were concealed in the village. Her complaint led to a decisive intervention in what was very much an internal community dispute, for three women robbers had organised the burglary 'to punish the plaintiff for warning the Sr du Debert that they sometimes used his land to collect firewood'.[12] It was not only desperate widows facing destitution who went to the police. A *laboureur* from the village of Pellicerie (parish of St Julien de Crempse), one of the many victims of the robbers who struck during the Christmas Eve mass, lost 36L., ten sheets, twelve shirts, three ells of linen and the usual lard; he had no difficulty telling the *maréchaussée* to direct their attentions to two weavers from the village who had left the church halfway through the service, and drunk themselves into oblivion on Christmas Day. They spent the following Christmas on the galleys.[13]

This is by no means to deny that the process of accepting police investigators into the community was exempt from hesitation. The arduous investigation in 1770 and 1771 into the robberies committed in 1769 in the

---

11. Lieutenant's *p.-v.* 21 Mar. 1729; *Inform.* 22 Mar. 1729, *ibid.* B 367.
12. *P.-v.* 11 Jan. 1778 and *Interr.*, *ibid.* B 697.
13. *P.-v.* 22 Jan. 1787, *ibid.* B 807.

Mareuil area revealed the disappearance of mountains of lard and butter, acres of sheets and handkerchiefs, and the delay in starting investigations was certainly attributable in part to the victims' failure to lodge formal complaints with the authorities. Four years before, however, the Sr Reydi had gone straight to the police on being robbed of corn, oil and pewterware, and a witness in the Mareuil case investigation drew the conclusion that was beginning to make its mark on public opinion: if the victims of theft had followed Reydi's example, perhaps they would now have news of their possessions.[14] The *procureur* in the Mareuil case started proceedings finally as a result of 'several verbal complaints';[15] far from battering their heads against a silent wall of hostility, the police were forced to intervene by an ever-growing public outcry. Even as late as 1789 there was still at least one individual who only had recourse to the *maréchaussée* after a series of thefts of wine and after he had personally put the thieves to flight with a shotgun.[16] But also in 1789 we find the outrage felt by the *métayer* Pierre Chinon when told by his neighbours to 'devour his disaster in silence' after being robbed, apparently by local thieves, of six bushels of wheat and eleven pounds of cloth.[17] After a second incursion by the burglars, successfully repulsed, Chinon went to the police; still his neighbours refused to identify the owners of the bags and the jug left behind by the thieves in the confusion of their flight. Such reluctance to involve the authorities (assuming it was not the result of the neighbours' own complicity) was increasingly rare in the eighteenth century, and the reasons for its persistence must be sought in more convincing factors than a sentimental attachment to the community.

If no official steps were taken after the victim had overcome the first moments of anguish and despair on the discovery that he had been robbed, it was because he, or his friends or neighbours, thought it was hopeless to try to do anything against the weight of practical difficulties which obstructed his path. He might well have a strong suspicion who the thief had been, but if he himself could not prove it, how would an outsider be able to identify the true owner of a sack of flour, or vegetables from his garden, or a sheet, or a pot of lard? There was the fear of incurring legal expenses, a fear which on occasion allowed even thieves caught in the act to go free.[18] Local judges refused to imprison thieves unless their captors promised to provide all of the prisoners' food for the entire duration of their captivity.[19] Most modern victims of theft or violence who bother to record

14. *Inform.* on theft from Sr Debrigeas, 5 Feb. 1768, *ibid.* B 546.
15. *P.-v.* 13 Sept. 1770, *ibid.* B 620.
16. *Supplication*, Despart de Puydarnac, 23 Mar. 1789, *ibid.* B 830.
17. *Supplication* (n.d., apparently July 1789). P. Chinon, *laboureur exploitant la métairie de Dlle Dubois*, parish of Bassillac, *ibid.* B 831.
18. (a) *P.-v.* Mussidan brigade, 16 June 1775, *ibid.* B 667. (b) 'The fear of being committed to legal expenses' allowed J. Aymon to rob his neighbours with impunity for a number of years in the 1750s, *liasse* on his trial in 1767, *ibid.* B 584.
19. *Inform.* against Grifoul, eleventh witness, a *métayer*, 16 Jan. 1769, *ibid.* B 599.

the event for insurance purposes, or because it is easy to lift a telephone, are well aware that the police have virtually no chance of identifying or capturing those responsible, and the peasants of the Périgord had no reason to have any more confidence in their police force. How many villages were there, in the vast districts of the Périgord brigades, which never saw a patrol of *cavaliers*? There was no risk involved in denouncing or arresting a vagabond who passed like a thief in the night. The *maréchaussée* could be expected to treat a vagabond's story with scepticism, and even if he were released, he did not have to be lived with afterwards. In numerous trials which brought unreported and unpunished thefts to light, when the victim had been quite certain who had robbed him, the silence is explained by one factor alone – intimidation.

Pierre Chinon himself claimed that his neighbours could identify the thieves, 'but have refused . . . as fear keeps them silent'.[20] Threats of violence and even more often of arson were common, and potential witnesses as well as victims were subjected to blows and insults.[21] The terms of *monitoires* specifically invited witnesses to overcome their fears and on occasion the police charged relatives of *prévôtal* prisoners with intimidation.[22] It was but one sign of the decline of the acceptability of violence in Périgourdin society (to be traced in the next chapter) that local professional thieves were no longer allowed to continue their careers of theft and intimidation after the 1760s. The Sr de Boisselin took over a year to pluck up the courage to denounce his tormentor,[23] but patience would snap in the end. The Sr Dambier put up with the minor depredations of Lacroix and Martinie, but when they got too ambitious, the *maréchaussée* was summoned within a week.[24]

The public willingness to denounce thefts of all kinds was further encouraged by the increase in thefts of all kinds which seem to have marked the last decades of the century. It would no doubt be difficult to find any police force which can be said, in any meaningful way, to be 'winning' its war against crime, but it is clear that even with one of the lowest crime rates

20. *Supplication* (1789), *ibid*. B 831.
21. E.g. *Supplication* of J. Verger (1734), B 392; *Inform.* against J. Lacombe (1764) B 586; *Plainte* from P. Escandeca (1769) B 609; *Inform.* (1725) B 346; *Inform.* against Lacroix (1766) B 578; Aymon case (1767) B 587; Bonnamy case (1766) B 576; in the case against Grifoul, a witness before the *prévôtal* court claimed that the *greffier* in the jurisdiction of Villefranche had capitulated to the threats of this notorious thief; the witness (one of Grifoul's victims) was then advised by a barrister to let the case drop for fear of provoking Grifoul. *Inform.* Jan. 1769, *ibid*. B 599.
22. E.g. Prosecution of J. Rousseau, June 1771, *ibid*. B 619.
23. *Plainte* against J. Bonnamy who had on various occasions robbed Boisselin of 150L., punched him and burned down his barn. June 1766, *ibid*. B 576.
24. On 9 May 1766, they stole fifty shirts, fifty-four serviettes, five tablecloths, six *linceuls*, five sacks, twelve aprons, three stockings, a skirt and fifty pounds of lard. *Inform.* May 1766, *ibid*. B 578.

in the country to contend with,[25] the *maréchaussée* of the Périgord were fighting a losing battle.

In the first thirty years of the reformed *maréchaussée,* the number of prosecutions which were capped by successful convictions was relatively high - 34 out of 81 reported cases of theft. The halcyon days were the twenties, when the newly reorganised police force set about securing convictions for a series of burglaries left over from before 1720. These trials accounted for a total of 890L. in silver and gold, plus linen used to decorate the alter of the church in St Martin de Ribérac, impertinently stolen from the curé of Bures while he celebrated mass on Christmas Eve.[26] The *maréchaussée* had some initial success with Christmas Eve burglaries after 1720 - the Gayet brothers did not long enjoy the 100 *demi-escuts* 'of the old kind' they stole from a neighbour.[27] Nor did the robbers who preyed on natural targets like travelling merchants escape all retribution - the police caught at least two young men who had profited from the peculiar habit of travellers in the Périgord of leaving their money in the pockets of a pair of breeches hung on the bedpost overnight.[28] But already in these early years of greatest *prévôtal* success it was clear that the bigger the haul the less was the risk of detection. The one successful conviction in the 1730s for a theft of reasonable proportions - the highway robbery of 2 *louis d'or* and 204L. from a Bergerac merchant by a young farrier - was not the result of police efficiency but of quick thinking by men working in vineyards near the road, and a spirited citizens' arrest *in flagrante delicto.*[29] The leader of a gang which unburdened a lace-merchant of four trucks containing 3,950L. and a large quantity of clothes in a Bergerac inn in 1721 was never caught, and the money was not recovered.[30]

In the 1750s, there was only one conviction for theft but only eight robberies had been reported in the whole decade. This apparent 'decline' of theft may reflect in part the economic prosperity of the mid-century, but it more obviously indicates the moribund state of the *maréchaussée* and the continued reluctance of the populace to report theft to the authorities. Investigations carried out in the 1760s and 1770s with a more cooperative public by a police force invigorated by structural change and an energetic lieutenant brought to light cases of theft unreported since the 1750s. The

25. The percentage of 'criminality' per head of population has been estimated at 1.64 per cent (the third lowest of all important judicial centres in France). Castan, 'La justice expéditive', pp. 331-61.
26. Prosecution of Lasfayas and Tournier, 1717-22, A.D. Dord. B 329.
27. Dec. 1721 to Jan. 1722, *ibid.* B 328.
28. Prosecution of Rouveilhac and Peruque, 1721-3, *ibid.* B 334.
29. Dec. 1736 to Jan. 1737, *ibid.* B 352.
30. The leader was 'Silvain', and the police caught only a minor accomplice, J. Boutier, 1725-26, *ibid.* B 351.

number of thefts dealt with by the *prévôtal* authorities rose dramatically from 8 in the 1750s to 80 in the 1760s, and 135 in the 1770s. However contentious the 'decline of violence', it is impossible to dispute that part of the 'theft-violence' syndrome which posits the obvious 'rise' in theft in the eighteenth century. It was not, however, rising as fast as the statistics suggest, for allowance must be made for the exaggeration produced by the greater willingness to report theft and by the greater zeal of the police in bringing thefts to light. Such qualification is particularly important in the Périgord, for the number of recorded thefts fell from 135 in the 1770s to 98 in the 1780s, most of which took place before the retirement of Gigounoux de Verdon on 18 February 1784.

Even he, however, had no more success than his predecessors in capturing thieves. In the last thirty years of the ancien régime, convictions were recorded in 77 out of 313 cases and, as in the 1720s, those who committed robbery on a decent scale made sure they were not caught. The scale was increasing all the time, and in the 1770s, the decade of Verdon's prime, over 23,000L. were stolen in gold and silver coins alone. The Lieutenant himself was in Bergerac when a draper's shop in the main street was emptied of merchandise – silks and muslin – worth 3,450L. The *maréchaussée* reacted the only way its limited imaginative faculties permitted, by turning to its traditional prey. *Cavaliers* raided a shanty on the river which had long given refuge to beggars and suspicious 'strangers', and one of its lodgers, Pierre Maumont, a 66-year-old beggar with counterfeit infirmities was picked up and charged with burglary. After eight months' imprisonment, he had to be acquitted on the principal charge, and the burglars had had ample time to dispose of the stolen silk and cloth.[31] The largest single theft recorded by the eighteenth-century *prévôté* in Périgueux fell in the middle of the reign of Gigounoux de Verdon – the theft in 1775 of no less a sum than 12,288L. from M. de Razac. Chambaudry, the Thiviers brigade commander, also reported that the thieves had taken gold earrings, two bottles of brandy and a pair of sheets.[32] Six months later, a vagabond arrested in Razac was asked if he had any knowledge of the theft of 12,288L. the previous autumn. It was a pathetic demonstration of the level at which the *maréchaussée* operated in its fight against theft. The vagabond they had succeeded in capturing – Mathieu Breuil – was charged with stealing 1L. 14s., a *linceul* and a child's jacket, which he had picked up in a barn as he had nothing of his own to wear.[33]

In a number of these successful robberies the victims suggested likely suspects – former servants, for example, or tradesmen who had done some work in the house. If they were the work of more organised professional criminals, such individuals were so organised that they succeeded in

31. Lt's *p.-v.* 3 Dec. 1778. Sentence, 5 Aug. 1779, *ibid*. B 698.
32. *P.-v.* 10 Oct. 1775, *ibid*. B 677.
33. *P.-v.* 10 Apr. 1776 and *Interr.*, *ibid*. B 684.

concealing every trace of their existence from the police. On only one occasion does it appear that a professional operator was applying a conscious formula for highway robbery. Thanks to the *maréchaussée*'s inability to capture the man himself it is difficult to be categorical about the degree of organisation, but within a period of six months two successful highway robberies of merchants were committed by suspects whose descriptions matched. The first netted 11 *louis d'or*, from a merchant who had exchanged silver coins for the gold in an inn on the road from Périgueux to Brantôme under the eyes of the stranger who robbed him a few miles further on. The second cost the merchant Dechene 2,004L. in silver, after he had accepted an offer from an 'amériquin' to change it for gold in the stables of an inn in Bergerac. The police did capture Jean Cavaillon, thanks to his earrings and his bonnet with red ribbons; this failed peddler from Nîmes, who was more of a hanger-on than accomplice, had 900L. in his pocket, but was unable to shed any light on the 'amériquin's' identity, and could only confirm the obvious fact of his respectable appearance, the very factor which made the two merchants trust him and which made the *maréchaussée* unable to find him.[34]

Whatever rudimentary forms of criminal organisation existed in the Périgord to carry out thefts or to distribute stolen property, the *maréchaussée* did not find, or even seek to find. They made no systematic attempt to keep likely 'fences' under surveillance, no search for the receivers of stolen goods. Many peddlers were picked up as suspected vagabonds, but as we have seen, they were automatically released if they found someone to vouch for them; instead of inspecting the merchandise they had for sale, or interrogating the prisoners on their sources of supply, the *prévôtal* court made every effort to get rid of the suspects the *cavaliers* had arrested. There was no systematic effort to keep watch on the places where stolen goods were bought and sold. The *cavaliers* happily patrolled markets until there was a riot or a pickpocket lynched by the crowd; they descended on inns and *cabarets* but questioned no one who had a scrap of paper testifying to his good character. Meanwhile burglaries were committed on all sides, the police ran helplessly from the scene of one crime to the next, faithfully jotting down the particulars of every item stolen to the very last stitch.

It is not just a question of the *maréchaussée* having insufficient resources to do anything more subtle than the basic tasks of patrol and the arrest of beggars and vagabonds and criminals for whom they had a warrant; the *maréchaussée*'s efforts to contain theft were determined by the institution's idea of itself as an essentially rural police force. In the Bordelais there was the excuse, provided by the *jurats*, that the *maréchaussée* was kept out of the city. In the Périgord, there was no effective urban police apart from the *maréchaussée*, but the *maréchaussée* could conceive of no type of criminal

34. March to July 1768, *ibid*. B 597.

organisation other than the *bande* – the band of vagabonds who lived in the open air and were capable of no form of criminal behaviour more sophisticated than holding up travellers on the highway or attacking farmhouses. *Bandes* haunted the Périgord *maréchaussée* all through the eighteenth century, but the nature of the threat varied from one decade to another.

The first sort of band – that of 'gypsies' – was inherited from the pre-1720 *maréchaussée* but troubled the new institution no later than 1721. The Brantôme brigade inaugurated its operations with a descent on the parish of Varaigne, 'where gypsies are usually out in force'.[35] The only arrest to result from the expedition was that of Pierre de la Braude, a dancing instructor in Varaigne, who had been branded and whipped for tobacco smuggling seven or eight years before. The Périgord was the scene of a considerable traffic in smuggled tobacco. Most of it seems to have been in the hands of small distributors, packmen or porters who found it a less dangerous and more socially acceptable way of eking out a precarious existence than theft. Large but elusive bands of smugglers were occasionally rumoured to be responsible for outbreaks of burglary, but if they did exist they caused no real alarm among the population until the murder of three *gabelous* in 1778 caused enough stir to inspire Verdon to mount one of his intimidatory *chevauchées*.

More substantial evidence of a band of thieves surfaced in 1758, when Jean Langerie, a *laboureur* in the parish of Rossignol, came to the *maréchaussée* to report that seven armed and masked men had broken into his house two hours after midnight, tied him up, and made off with all the portable goods he possessed: an indefinite number of *linceuls*, eight new *serviettes*, a linen tablecloth, three pewter plates and eleven spoons, his coat, hat, stockings and shoes; his wife's dresses, brassières and blouses; thirty pounds of hemp, fifteen pounds of tow, seven of wool; 51l.. in cash; and the fat, lard and salted meat of a sow. Such an account was a godsend to the *procureur* of the *maréchaussée* who was able to proclaim that numerous thefts committed on the highway between Mareuil and Brantôme, 'particularly the murder and robbery of a young man', were not a complete mystery to the *maréchaussée*, but the work of 'a troop of masked men'.[36] There remained the problem of finding them. It was only Gigounoux de Verdon who realised that there was in fact no problem, for having announced the existence of a band, patrols could be mounted against it, and even the inevitable failure to catch any member of the band could be hailed as proof that the resolute operations of the *maréchaussée* had dispersed the band and saved the Périgord from further pillage. The 1758 operation was one of only three occasions when a witness claimed to have seen a band of at least four together, and the question of the identity of the seven masked men remains open. Certainly nothing can be learned from the judicial aftermath in the

35. *P.-v.* Rudeau 7 Oct. 1721, *ibid.* B 323.
36. *Procureur's p.-v.*, 14 Feb. 1758, *ibid.* B 558.

prévôtal court, one of the most futile prosecutions of the century. The main suspect was a young paper-worker from the Auvergne, who was caught begging in his lice-infested rags and tatters; he was held for months, as he claimed at first to be part of the band and named as his accomplices a weaver called Jean and his three sons. The *maréchaussée* managed to find a weaver called Jean and his father, both respected members of the community against whom no evidence could be produced. The trial ended in squabbles between the legal officers of the *maréchaussée* over who was to blame for the prolonged detention and suffering of the prisoners.

It was twelve years after Langerie's experience before a band was sighted again. This time the victim was Mlle Morselve, whose house near Monfaucon was invaded by 'a small group' of men armed with pistols and daggers. They wrapped the servant up in a sheet, and bound her with ropes, 'then they surrounded the mistress and her servant with straw and set fire to it to burn them little by little until they admitted where they had hidden their money'.[37] So the *chauffeurs* were not entirely absent from the Périgord,[38] but not as a permanent organised troop; it is not surprising that the occasional passing vagabond or *repris de justice* resorted from time to time to such time-honoured techniques. Perhaps it was the noisy police patrols which encouraged those responsible to move on and singe their victims elsewhere. One can only speculate, for the *maréchaussée*, as usual, came up with totally inappropriate suspects – Léonard Bordas, a 76-year-old *laboureur* resident in a nearby parish, his son-in-law and three nephews – before whom the Lieutenant simply opened up his catalogue of recent unsolved thefts.

It was of interest for both the Morselve and Langerie incidents that in June 1770 the *maréchaussée* did manage to capture members of a 'troop of armed men' ten to twelve strong which had burst in upon the widow Robin. They carried rifles and daggers and carried off the same kind of booty as in Rossignol in 1758 – cloth, neckerchiefs, hats, a dozen pewter spoons, a pair of handkerchiefs. This time the victim did not imagine that a band of brigands had emerged from the dark recesses of the Périgord forest: 'there is every reason to presume that most of them were neighbours', led no doubt by Rousseau, the servant she had dismissed a fortnight before.[39] Mme Robin lived in the parish of St Sebastien (in the far north-west corner of the department), and her assailants were all local men: Rousseau, a day-labourer from La Chapelle Gresignac; Broudichou, day-labourer in St Martial de Viveyrol; Moreau and Pacomard, *laboureurs* from Nanteuil; Robinet, shoe-maker from Nanteuil, and his brother from Lajard, in the parish of Coutures;

37. *Interr.* Léonard Bordas, July 1770, *ibid*. B 619.
38. On the *chauffeurs* of the Beauce see M. Vovelle, 'From beggary to brigandage: the wanderers in the Beauce during the French Revolution', in J. Kaplow, *New Perspectives on the French Revolution* (New York 1965).
39. *P.-v.* Lagarde (*assesseur*), 5 June 1770, A.D. Dord. B 626.

Simon, 'Le Maréchal', a blacksmith in St Martial, and Pierre de la Roussie
was a farm-worker in the nearby village of Montignac. There were allegations
that individually or in pairs they had a number of robberies to their credit,
but as a group they had operated on only one previous occasion. Three years
before, the *fermier* of an estate in Vanxains was awakened in his barn by
eight thieves who covered his eyes with bundles of straw, threatened to kill
him if he revealed the theft, and carried off fifteen bushels of wheat and
eight *linceuls*. For three years he said nothing, until he was prepared to
identify three of the men on trial for robbing Marie Robin.[40]

The fact that the only successful repression of a *bande* revealed a collection
of neighbours supplementing their income with an occasional moonlight
sortie did not prevent an increasingly frenetic concern with *brigandage*, even
if the only band which seems to have had any reality was the troop of
smugglers vainly pursued by Gigounoux de Verdon. For the rest, we can
understand why such reports became common currency in an expanding and
restive population, and regret that the obsession with bands created an
atmosphere of insecurity culminating in the anguish of the Great Fear of
1789. For the population of the Périgord, the fear of bands revived ancient
folk memories of children being carried off to be eaten.[41] For the *prévôtal*
court and the officers and *cavaliers* on whom it depended, they meant that
the *maréchaussée* would restrict its efforts to chasing shadows. The whole
process of judicial investigation was distorted when it was accepted without
question that 'a troop of brigands' had broken into Pierre Marty's bakery to
steal lard, flour and fat.[42] No troop was found, but the possibility that there
might have been hungry or greedy neighbours was not considered. *Cavaliers*
shared the obsession as much as anyone. The Mussidan *brigadier* Greilh reported that 'a troop of brigands is pillaging and robbing in the Gratade wood',[43]
the Thiviers brigade learned of the depredations of a 'band of thieves' in and
around the parish of Negronde.[44] The result was not the capture or even
sighting of any band but the continued harassment of strangers and vagabonds
who all turned out to be isolated, lonely individuals. By the 1780s the
maréchaussée seemed incapable of dealing with anyone but vagabonds, for of
the 98 thefts which the Périgord *maréchaussée* investigated in that decade,
80 remained unsolved and unpunished; and of the 18 for which the *Prévôtal*
court managed to obtain a conviction, 17 involved theft by a vagabond.

40. *Inform.*, fourteenth witness.
41. 1771, *ibid.* B 628 and 629 *passim*.
42. Lt's *p.-v.* Bergerac, 10 Nov. 1771, *ibid.* B 630.
43. *Inform.* 5 Apr. 1781, *ibid.* B 735.
44. *P.-v.* 24 Aug. 1780, *ibid.* B 421.

CHAPTER 6
Violence

Vol-violence

The renunciation of violence by *prévôtal* magistrates, and the unabating, increasingly profitable activity of Périgourdin thieves, are both consistent with what is now received doctrine on ancien régime criminality, *vol-violence* – 'theft-violence'.[1] In the course of the eighteenth century, in other words, the theft of property replaced physical violence as the most common form of criminal activity. This 'Authorised Version' of ancien régime criminal behaviour, arising out of the urgent need to impose some kind of pattern on the confusing mass of incident which makes up the judicial archives, had the attraction of alliterative simplicity, and the advantage of adaptability both to *Annaliste* and to Marxist historiography. Violence could optimistically be labelled the characteristic form of criminal activity under an aristocratic, 'feudal' society, while theft became the characteristic crime of bourgeois capitalist society. The criminological pattern could be made to fit the general pattern of eighteenth-century social and economic development.

The *vol-violence* theory was built upon statistics culled from the systematic study of court records, a rich and rewarding source for social historians, but one fraught with limitations. If in the twentieth century cases in which prosecutions are initiated constitute only a fraction of the crimes which are actually committed, it is hardly necessary to stress that this distortion is an obvious problem for the period of the ancien régime, when the natural difficulties of communication were accentuated by community spirit and intimidation, and when police patrols made appearances in most parishes at

---

1. A complete bibliography of *vol-violence* would include virtually all recent work on eighteenth-century criminality – see the useful 'Répertoire sommaire des travaux d'histoire de la criminalité dans la France moderne (XVIIe-XVIIIe siècles)' in A. Abbiateci *et al.*, *Crimes et criminalité en France sous l'Ancien Régime* (Paris 1971). The leading disciples have been the pupils of Pierre Chaunu in Caen, and the seminal article, B. Boutelet's 'Etude par sondage de la criminalité du bailliage de Pont de l'Arche (XVIIe-XVIIIe siècles); de la violence au vol', *Ann. de Norm.* (1962), 235–62. The argument is taken up in Poitrineau, *La vie rurale*, vol. 1, p. 619; and in a number of *thèses de 3e cycle* of the University of Bordeaux, one of which has been published – M. Laveau, 'Criminalité à Bordeaux au XVIIIe siècle', pp. 85–144. The theory has met with less favour among Anglo-Saxon historians – Hufton's *The poor of eighteenth-century France* dismisses it by implication, and the latest French work has begun to express reservations: R. Muchembled, *Culture populaire et culture des élites* (Paris 1978), pp. 251–3.

long intervals. There are particular risks of distorted statistics in the field of violence, as the problem of persuading the people to cooperate with the authorities over such crimes was even greater than over theft.

The numerous victims of the 'muggers' who inhabit the streets of the modern city normally prefer their assailants to take their money and leave their bodies intact. Under the ancien régime however, these priorities were reversed. The great disaster for a peasant or even a bourgeois was not to suffer pain and discomfort but to lose his property; so it was not only lack of confidence in the police which drove victims of theft to pursue thieves for fifty or a hundred miles, or from Paris to Périgueux, to recover anything from an apron or a cow to a box of jewels. Physical assaults, on the other hand, were much more acceptable. So acceptable, indeed, that they rarely got as far as the courts, which is awkward for a historian trying to base his judgment of ancien régime criminality on the statistics provided by court records. Whereas the victim of an assault would now be expected to react with emotional distaste to the idea of further contact with his assailant, the ancien régime victim and his attacker would normally make a private arrangement – an *accomodement* signed perhaps before a notary – that the aggressor would pay the victim's medical expenses, plus a certain amount of compensation for loss of wages. An Auvergnat peasant whose head had been beaten by a clog, dropped charges when his aggressor agreed to pay 60L.;[2] in the course of a quarrel with a neighbour, the *laboureur* Garnier received five or six gun-shot wounds in the stomach while his young son got a bayonet in the kidney, but the curé of Saunaire managed to reconcile the two men, 'although it will cost the aggressor dear'.[3]

Far from being offended by their exclusion from a legitimate area of law enforcement, the authorities gave their blessing and encouragement to the process of private *accomodement*. When a number of peasants were 'severely beaten' in the course of a drunken brawl and their seigneurs made a private deal, the *archers* of the Aurillac brigade abandoned the search for the aggressors.[4] Even judges tried to persuade victims to 'accommodate': when the judge in Pujols heard that one of his neighbours was accused of assault and highway robbery by a fellow parishioner who had got home covered with blood and 12L. poorer, he went to see the aggressor: 'My friend, believe me, you must "accommodate" this affair . . . pay money . . . and everything will be settled.'[5]

If the affair did get to court, the authorities felt it incumbent upon them

---

2. Correspondence between Courpière *subdélégué* and intendant, 1731, on Lacrompt case, A.D. P. de D. C 1522.
3. Correspondence between *subdélégué* and intendant (1751), *ibid.* C 1536.
4. Letter from Sadourny, Aurillac *subdélégué*, to intendant, 21 Apr. 1724, *ibid.* C 6174.
5. The judge's own testimony – twelfth witness, *Inform.* 14 Nov. 1758, A.D. Gir. 11B 13.

to fill the gap left by the parties' failure to make a private arrangement: a conviction for assault did not lead to a public whipping or a spell in the galleys, it led to an order to pay the victim damages. Two *fermiers* of the Sr Bodin de St Laurent were subjected to violence and unlawful arrest by two *cavaliers* of the Périgueux brigade, and the *Connétablie* sentenced Reveilhac and Leyssenot to pay their victims 20L.[6] Even when a certain Roussel was 'overwhelmed by such a multitude of stones that he stayed all night under a heap of stones without moving', and it was recognised that 'this brutality' should not go unpunished, the fact that the episode took place on the highway was not enough to bring the assault within the public domain; it was only a brawl, 'and damages are all that is required'. In most cases of assault the authorities did not get involved at all until someone defaulted on his payments. Two peasants, on their way home from a wedding, who beat up some people they met and subsequently 'laughed at the treaty' by which they had agreed to pay 322L. medical expenses, were put in prison till they paid up. 'A lot of wine is drunk at weddings', the intendant admitted, 'but contempt for treaties is another matter', and allowing anyone to default could only 'encourage the others to do the same'. When a particularly vicious thug, paying compensation to several people, got behind with his instalments, the *subdélégué* ordered the *maréchaussée* to put him in prison for a week to remind him of his financial obligations.[7]

Despite the inadequacy of the court records of the Périgord however, and the almost complete absence of criminal records in the Auvergne – other than the convicts dispatched to the galleys in Rochefort from the *généralité* of Riom, usually as a punishment for theft or smuggling – there is sufficient evidence in both provinces to suggest that the *vol-violence* theory must be subjected to certain qualifications.

Violence in the Auvergne

Problems of documentation are particularly acute when the chronicle of violence in the province must be reconstituted from administrative correspondence. It is very tempting to select from the grey routine a few incidents of exotic brutality and endow them with unwarranted significance. At least two aspects of these sources however suggest that life in the Auvergne *was* more than usually brutal, that violence was more pervasive and socially acceptable than in more civilised provinces. There is first of all the shocked reaction of strangers in the province – travellers like Le Grand d'Aussy,[8] government officials fresh from Paris, or the rare example of an outsider

6. Sentence of *Connétablie*, 26 Mar. 1742, A.N. Z^{IC} 339.
7. Correspondence between intendant and *subdélégués* in Riom, Rochefort and Issoire – 1750, 1751, 1742; A.D. P. de D. C 1535, 1536, 6223.
8. Le Grand d'Aussy, *Voyage fait en 1787 et 1788*, vols. 1–3.

who came to settle in the province. All of these individuals illustrate the second qualitative indication of Auvergnat brutality: the casual origin of violent disputes, the triviality which so easily led to pain and death.

The abbé de la Valette arrived in 1734 to exploit the considerable properties of the abbey in the parish of Menet, Haute-Auvergne,[9] and for a cleric newly arrived from the capital, the peasants of the Haute-Auvergne were not easy to live with: 'The People of these mountains, Monsieur', he wrote to the intendant 'have an intractable character which those who have only seen the Court cannot easily understand.' Even the nobles and seigneurs in the region trembled before the landless peasant, made independent by a simple threat 'to beat and to burn'. The abbé's attempts to collect his dues, or to chase away goats grazing on his land, or to import cheese-makers from Switzerland in the hope of improving the quality of the local product, had all foundered on the peasants' violent resistance. To give the intendant a more convincing picture of the lawlessness of the Haute-Auvergne, the abbé listed a number of barns which had gone up in flames, interspersed with six or seven murders committed in the vicinity of the abbey in the year since his arrival. None of the murderers had been inconvenienced by official investigation, not even when a stonemason had been stabbed to death by one of his workmates while repairing the abbey itself, even though the murderer returned to the scene half an hour later to make sure his victim was dead. The abbé is perhaps intentionally vague on the question of the motives of the various murderers; the impression of senseless slaughter is all the greater. He does specify that a peasant working on his *corvée* duty used a scythe to kill a girl who had resisted his attempt to rape her; the local seigneurial judge, who had five barns full of highly inflammable hay, had failed to take any action. Even when a nobleman, M. d'Auzers, was killed in a duel by a bourgeois from Trizac, the relatives of the dead man were intimidated into silence by the common knowledge that his assassin went around with pistols in his pocket.

If strangers like the abbé de la Valette could not contain his outrage, local officials had a considerably more sympathetic attitude to the use of violence. The *subdélégué* of St Flour was merely 'surprised' that the Sr Bertrand, *avocat et premier consul,* should have dragged a recalcitrant tax-payer by the hair down the main street, kicking him in the stomach and banging his head against the wall; the king after all 'did not authorize *consuls* to beat up tax-payers'.[10] It was however no more surprising than the reaction of a *consul* in Muratel who took an axe to his neighbour in the course of a dispute

9. The considerable correspondence generated by his sojourn in the province is to be found in A.D. P. de D. C 1527, 1528, 1535, 2430, 7224 and 7226, and is used by M. Juillard, 'Violences et rébellions en Haute-Auvergne', *Revue de la Haute-Auvergne* (1931–2), ch. 6, 'Démêlés de l'abbé du Broc avec les habitants de Menet (1732–1752)', pp. 60–8.
10. Correspondence between Montluc and intendant, 1759, *ibid*. C 1543.

over the clearing of the commons.[11] At least these *consuls* from the Haute-Auvergne had grievances to provoke them; in the Issoire area of the Basse-Auvergne, the peace was constantly disturbed by the young men from Apchat, Ardes, and neighbouring parishes, 'who only go to the fêtes to have a fight'. According to the *subdélégué,* the fairground was 'their favourite battlefield'.[12]

It was not until 1760 that an intendant took serious steps to restore order. Ballainvilliers was forced to attend to the problem of the administration of justice by a number of crimes which were remarkable only for their brutality. The problem which faced the authorities was, as we have seen, not so much the negligence of the police force, though M de Valette had plenty to say about the conduct of the Mauriac brigade, as the collapse of seigneurial justice. The decline of this crucial aspect of 'feudalism' in the Auvergne was marked not by the growing importance of theft, but by the incidence of violence. Ballainvilliers was informed that a canon of the Clermont Cathedral chapter had stabbed to death the daughter of a *conseiller* in the *Cour des Aides* while having tea with the young lady and her mother, in a different social setting, Marguerite Paulet was hacked limb from limb by the young man she had not wanted to marry.[13] When steps were taken in 1760 to ascertain the extent of seigneurial negligence, the list of unpunished crimes painted a vivid picture of the cheapness of human life in the Auvergne.[14]

The Besse *subdélégué* reported that in the course of a riot in the summer of 1752, the servant of the Murol *procureur fiscal* had gone beserk, started lashing out at anyone near him and was himself killed; two others had received knife injuries 'without knowing why or from whom'. From Bort came the sparse memorandum that there had been seventeen murders and no arrests. The Rochefort report provided more details: a miller who had opposed the construction of a wall across his meadow – killed by a blow from a spade; an innkeeper – killed by a locksmith in a brawl on the way home from the fair; a court official – killed while trying to seize livestock for non-payment of debts; a man killed in a fight for a place at a gambling table; a girl killed by her brother when he applied to her head the shovel they were using to load manure on to a cart. There was endless variety in the reports of these bloody scenes which came from all corners of the province: from Aurillac, word came of a labourer killed in a field on receiving a blow from a hoe; from Langeac, of a postilion killed by another servant as they argued at table in the château de Chavagnac; near Issoire, the servants of a miller had

11. Correspondence between Mauriac *subdélégué* and intendant, 1759, *ibid.* C 1543.
12. The *subdélégué* wished to make an example of the two ringleaders, Belair and Frinquant, who led their gangs of 'satellites' round the fêtes of successive patron-saints in order to 'provoke brawls with all-comers'. Correspondence between Issoire *subdélégué* and intendant, 1763. *ibid.* C 1545.
13. Vigouroux, 'Ballainvilliers, intendant de justice', pp. 133–4.
14. Reports covering the years 1739–69, A.D. P. de D. C 1550–63, *passim.*

a quarrel, and the body of one was later washed up by the stream; from Ardes murders were reported which had been committed by *brigadiers* of the *gabelle* 'in pursuit of smugglers'; an Aurillac priest was indicted for rape, murder and arson; the Riom *subdélégué* reported a murder committed by Christophe de Panneyre, *écuyer*, an 8-year-old child; an aunt killed by her nephew, a woman by her father-in-law, brother by brother. A bottle of wine was often blamed: one peasant, fighting with a drunk neighbour received a knife blow 'which brought his intestines into the daylight'. No government official even attempted to analyse the state of mind of the persons unknown who had abandoned newly born babies to drown in ditches, or to be half-eaten by dogs on piles of garbage.

To this private death toll must be added the victims of communal violence.[15] This was occasionally contained within the confines of the parish, as in the 'bloody battle' between the inhabitants of the parish of La Queulhe who exchanged blows with pickaxes and shovels in a dispute over the division of brushwood. More often, the corpses littered the battlefields of inter-parish warfare. Again the motive for the violence is often obscure. In the case of Sauvagnat versus St Frome the *subdélégué* simply noted that this was the third Sunday in a row that the two parishes had fought it out. It was traditional for the parish of Madriat to send along a band of rowdies to the annual fête in Augnat – 'for the express purpose of disturbing divine service, maltreating and striking the residents'. Every year, the brigade of *maréchaussée* turned up to try to keep the parishioners apart. The inhabitants of the nearby parish of Chadeleuf 'form a little republic', and directed their energies against the inhabitants of Neschers to the north west, or Sauvagnat and Pardines to the east and south. There were continual battles in this direction, as the parishioners of Chadeleuf had many sheep and restricted grazing grounds, and constantly tried to usurp those of their neighbours. In 1756, two men died in these struggles, and the trouble broke out again two years later; the police did not intervene, and the curés of the parishes concerned drew up a peace treaty.

Although two other villages in the Issoire district fought a battle over a *corvée* dispute, no issue was so inflammatory as grazing. It was asking for trouble for the owner of a hillside and wood traditionally used by the parish of Fossat to give permission to some inhabitants of Valcivières to use them for grazing their livestock, even if only for a limited time. Fossat called to arms: pistols, guns, bayonets, pikes, iron pitchforks and clubs appeared, and chased the intruders back to Valcivières. The parish of Colamines was torn apart by civil war when the ancient grazing rights of the village of Longchamp were attacked by fellow parishioners from the village of Bourg. Bourg made

---

15. Correspondence between *subdélégués* and intendant, 1739–60; *ibid.* C 1530–1544, *passim.*

the mistake of launching the assault with insufficient forces, and it was repulsed. The inhabitants of Longchamp remained in triumphant possession of the battlefield. Bourg was uncowed, however, soon the tocsin rang out again, and this time at full strength the villagers of Bourg routed their neighbours, and pursued them all the way to Longchamp.

Those records of the Auvergne intendant which survive to provide the bulk of archival material on the persistence of violence are particularly rich in the first part of the eighteenth century, and it will be noted that none of the violent incidents which aroused the authorities' concern took place after 1769. If the attack on seigneurial negligence was as effective as Poitrineau suggests,[16] the greater likelihood of prosecution may have done something to discourage unnecessary assaults. This therefore raises the possibility that in the last two decades of the ancien régime, the Auvergne too fell into line with *vol-violence*. One crucial step to prepare the ground had certainly been taken with the 'domestication' of the nobility which resulted from the *Grands Jours d'Auvergne*. By the eighteenth century, there is scarcely a trace of noble violence to be found. Two of the very few Auvergne noblemen to get into trouble in the eighteenth century – the Sieur Falnard de la Verdière and his brother – were drunk, on the way home from a fair, when they attacked a couple of peasants, only to be put to flight by the flash of a scythe; they showed more spirit when they swore vengeance for this humiliation, but allowed themselves to be bought off by 50L. and 'lots of drink'.[17] The patience of the eighteenth-century government was not strained by an excessive need to use influence to protect wayward nobles.

There is however no evidence to prove that the new provisions covering seigneurial justice seriously affected the prevalence of violence in the peasant community, and two sources at least suggest that such a transformation was highly unlikely. One is the evidence of the violence which continued to be directed against the police themselves – the 'rebellions' for which we do have documentation, and which, as we shall see, showed no signs of abating in frequency or ferocity in the latter part of the century. The other testimony to the longevity of Auvergnat violence is an eye-witness, Le Grand d'Aussy, who travelled in the province on the very eve of the Revolution and found the same penchant for communal brutality that had so little distressed the *subdélégués* of earlier decades. For the peasants of the Monts-Salers, he reported, the favourite battleground – the setting in which to exact revenge for wrongs hitherto suffered in silence – was the wedding celebration. While daylight lasted, the guests ate, drank, and made merry. After dark, the assailant and his accomplices stationed themselves near the victims and beside the lamp; at a given signal, which might fall unexpectedly in the middle

16. Poitrineau, 'Aspects de la crise des justices seigneuriales', pp. 552ff.
17. Correspondence between Rochefort *subdélégué* and intendant, 1742, A.D. P. de D., C 1530.

of a dance, the light was extinguished and the victims set upon. While the women kept out of the way as best they could,

the victims and their aggressors strike and lash out aimlessly in the dark; and the place resounds to the noise of blows, the cries of the wounded, blasphemies and howls of rage. At last, when no one knows where to hit any more, the massacre ceases, the lamp is relit, the dancing starts again, and the injured retire – their faces bloody, their heads shattered, their bodies covered with cuts and bruises.[18]

There was no judicial sequence to these scenes. The victims would be patched up, and wait in silence for a favourable opportunity in which to 'repay with interest the blows they have received'.

A preliminary look, therefore, at violence within the community tends to suggest that reassuring theories about the decline of violence must be subject to severe regional qualifications. From the evidence available, it seems that the *vol-violence* theory does not survive the harshness of life in eighteenth-century Auvergne. In the Périgord, the documentation is more impressive, as the records of the *prévôtal* court are available. It is necessary to bear in mind that our statistical base is provided by a court whose contact with affairs of violence was drastically restricted not only by the habitual acceptability of violence on the part of the population, but also by government edict. The 1731 Edict deprived the *prévôtal* court of its competence to deal with pre-meditated assault; it also removed the nobility from *prévôtal* jurisdiction. Despite the reservations, however, a clear pattern does emerge, which will be confirmed by the pattern of rebellion against the police, a picture which indicates that life in the Périgord, at least in the later years of the century, was not quite as joyously brutal as in the Auvergne.

Violence in the Périgord

There was little sign of any impending change in the Périgord of the early eighteenth century. The *prévôté* had still to deal with the criminal violence of the upper classes. The Sr de Labrousse had been killed in 1717 on the very steps of Vanxains parish church by the *juge royal* of Ribérac;[19] in 1725, the Sr de Faureillères was struck on the head, as he stood on the doorstep of the church of La Chapelle Monmaureaud, by the Sr de l'Emberterie, *écuyer* – to his great surprise, since to his knowledge there was no cause for dispute.[20] So distinguished a Périgord noble as the marquis de l'Action resorted to blows with the butt of his pistol when he came across the Sr de Lafforest, bourgeois of Thiviers, carrying a gun on his way to mount guard in the bourgeois militia. The enforcement of disarmament regulations was, according to the

18. Le Grand d'Aussy, *Voyage fait en 1787 et 1788*, vol. 3, p. 335.
19. Trial, A.D. Dord. B 334.
20. *Plainte* 3 June 1725, *ibid*. B 346.

victim, only a pretext for the attack: the marquis really 'wished to teach him to sign petitions against the marquis de l'Action'.[21]

Right up to 1731 indeed, the *prévôtal* court was primarily concerned with crimes of violence. In 1730, ten of the cases which came before the Périgord *prévôté* involved physical assault, compared with only 4 charges of theft. As in the Auvergne, the violence was inflicted with astonishing nonchalance. There was a murder in a *cabaret* after the victim objected to his assassin's company.[22] The soldier Aubin Arthia attacked his enemy, the servant of the Sr de la Dersse, because his victim had talked publicly about finding him under a hedge with one of his female relatives.[23] In this early decade of violence, human life was as cheap in the Périgord as in the Auvergne. Raymond Aubertie was shot for building a wall across a commonly used path, which forced the cattle of the village to make a detour through the cemetery. In the same year, 1726, the corpse of a miller, Aubin Durand, was fished out of the river after he had 'poached' a miller's *valet* from his colleague. The sawyer, François Metre, died in an argument among three of his colleagues and a *métayer* about the value of a pair of cows; Jean Duguilhen was killed when an enraged *laboureur* caught him stealing his brushwood (and thereby gave the newly reformed *maréchaussée* its first *prévôtal* case).[24]

After the 1731 Edict deprived the *maréchaussée* of direct interest in premeditated assault there was inevitably a dramatic decline in the number of cases involving physical violence to appear before the *prévôtal* court, though it was still of course concerned with violence when it accompanied other *prévôtal* crimes, such as highway robbery. Between 1720 and 1730, the Périgueux *prévôté* dealt with 24 murders; between 1731 and 1741, only 2. Many crimes of violence, however, continued to find their way before the *prévôtal* magistrates – and not only in cases where the violence was incidental to some other *prévôtal* offence. After 1731, theft was to be the primary concern of the *prévôtal* court, following a rhythm which depended on the economic circumstance and the enthusiasm of the law officers, but despite the fading memory of a pre-1731 competence, violence remained a *prévôtal* preoccupation and the revival of the *maréchaussée* in the 1760s and 1770s was marked by an increase in the number of assaults to attract the force's attention as well as by intensified prosecution of vagabonds and thieves. Indeed the statistics of the Périgueux *prévôtal* court indicate a deterioration in the province's pattern of violence to the extent that robberies were com-

21. The petition signed by Lafforest in his capacity as *consul* had argued against l'Action's request to be exempted from providing oxen and carts to transport army equipment. *Supplication*, 17 Mar. 1721, *ibid*. B 323.
22. *Supplication*, Jan. 1729, P. Simon, *ibid*. B 367.
23. *Inform*. Sept. 1726, *ibid*. B 341.
24. *Plaintes*, 1721-6, *ibid*. B 322-352.

mitted with more, and not less, brutality. Before 1731, barely one theft a year was accompanied by physical violence; in the decade after 1766, the *prévôtal* court dealt with 29 robberies with violence. Nor are statistics the only evidence that violence in the Périgord was not 'declining' in quite the manner prescribed by *vol-violence*.

It was not till 1766 that the court was confronted with the most brutal of the cases it had to deal with in the eighteenth century – the highway robbery, murder, and mutilation of Jean Lalliot, a servant-*métayer* from St Léon de Grignols. When the lieutenant of the *maréchaussée* was taken to the body lying in a field of rye, he was obliged by the deformity of the corpse to put the official seal on an exposed thigh, rather than on the forehead; the head was covered in wounds and the scrotum and testicles were found in different directions a few yards away.[25] Long after 1731, the Périgord shared the alcoholic ferocity endemic in the Auvergne. In 1775, a *métayer* having a drink in an inn in Thiviers was stabbed in the stomach by a tiler who escaped and was never seen again.[26] The court was faced with assaults as brutal and trivial as in the Auvergne – the Sr Delmas left unconscious 'swimming in his blood' for taking his time to repay a debt of 20s;[27] the same inter-parish hostility, which coalesced in the attack by the blacksmith Bridat and his acolytes from the parish of St Médard, on Pierre Denoyer and his family, inhabitants of the parish of St Laurent des Pardoux. Like the Auvergne, the Périgord continued throughout the century to be plagued by parish hoodlums, the local 'terrors' whom the Riom intendant was so willing to consign to administrative detention. The Périgord parish of Montren suffered in the 1760s from the militiaman Labrandette, who exploited his fearsome reputation to keep his larder stocked with eggs and poultry; he finally overstepped the bounds of popular tolerance by helping himself to the 2s. which the young children of a local poor family had begged in St Astier.[28]

As in the Auvergne, there was the same gratuitous viciousness against soldiers. Jean Labrousse, a dragoon in the Régiment du Roi making his way home to Pannac from Le Bugue, at nightfall, was struck on the head by a hail of stones from five or six individuals, apparently for the pleasure of it. There was no attempt to rob him, even though 1771 was a year of great economic distress.[29] Recruiting was one of the most dangerous occupational hazards of the eighteenth-century army sergeant. Antoine Condoin ironically

---

25. *Liasse* in B 578. The *prévôtal* court showed no interest in the motivation for the brutality, asking simply, 'Has the act been established and is it punishable? . . . Who committed it?' rather than 'To what level or to what field of reality does it belong? Is it a phantasy, a pyschotic reaction, a delusional episode, a perverse action?' (Foucault, *Discipline and punish*, p. 19).
26. *P.-v.* 7 Dec. 1775, A.D. Dord. B 667.
27. *Plainte* 4 May 1740, *ibid.* B 421.
28. *Plaintes* 26 and 27 May 1766, *ibid.* B 578.
29. *Plainte* 25 Nov. 1771, *ibid.* B 630.

called Bienaimé (Wellbeloved), a corporal in the Vieille Marine regiment, had hardly begun to sing a war song in a Le Salon *cabaret* when the daughter of the innkeeper threatened to smash a bottle in his face. The corporal, anxious for an extra signing, rejected the innkeeper's advice to leave the *cabaret,* whereupon the other customers and the innkeeper's family locked the door, plied the soldier with blows, and relieved him of his pistol and three enlistments which had been finalised.[30] Soldiers foolish enough to provoke the local population, of course, had always taken their lives into their hands. St Germain and another *cavalier* from the Clairmond regiment, stationed in Lalinde, were already under the influence of alcohol when they crossed the river (the Dordogne) at Badefol; when they found the inn in Drojand locked and everyone asleep, they banged on the door and threw stones against the innkeeper's window, shouting for a drink. Soon the whole parish was roused, the tocsin was rung, and a crowd of three hundred peasants armed with guns, halberds, iron pitchforks and batons descended on the unfortunate soldiers. When St Germain's body was dug up a week later, it was covered with wounds caused by stones, bars, and clubs.[31]

Until the final decades of the ancien régime merchants and other travellers continued to make long detours to avoid the Forêt Barade, whose dreadful reputation was enhanced by the discovery in 1772 of a body hanging by a red garter from a tree, robbed of its shoes and breeches. Only a few miles away, it was said, someone had found the putrefying hand of a corpse; in another direction some skin from the head of another corpse had been found, covered with black hairs. These stories were soon supplemented by reports that a young man had been stabbed with a hunting knife for the 4L. 10s. he was carrying, while a merchant had been stoned to death, leaving 'in the middle of the Forest . . . the entrails of a rotting corpse'.[32] Rumours of violence spread in the wake of theft – they were not mutually exclusive. The gamekeeper of the Forêt Barade who was confronted with such a trail of rotting flesh was also accused of the robbery of 14L. from a citizen of St Léon de Vézère, pilfering from a *scieur de long* he found asleep in the shade, and the theft of 4L. from an old man too feeble to offer resistance. It was inevitable that reports of a band of thieves operating in the Belvès area – after the disappearance of a barrel worth 40L., of 17L. in a highway robbery, and numerous sheep, turkeys, chickens, pigeons and a pair of cattle – should be pursued by reports of violence. An impressionable young *cavalier* – Ferey – recorded them for posterity. He faithfully transcribed the clichés of peasant nightmare – the inn which lured lonely travellers to their doom, the faithless woman who poisoned her husband and family to run off with her lover.[33]

All of this evidence – the widely-believed rumours of brigands and brutality,

30. *Plainte* 6 Aug. 1769, from A. Condoin, *ibid*. B 608.
31. *Inform*. 25 Dec. 1730, *ibid*. B 372.
32. *Ibid*. B 637, *passim*.
33. *P.-v.* 23 July 1780, *ibid*. B 721.

the parish 'terrors', the violence against soldiers, the violent highway robberies, the mutilation of a corpse – warn against a facile assumption of any rapid disappearance of violence in the warmth of eighteenth-century civilisation and economic progress. But it does not invalidate the *vol-violence* theory as effectively as in the Auvergne, for despite the policeman's irresponsible retelling of gossip, it is clear that the accounts of robberies in these closing years of the ancien régime were precise and substantiated, while the rumours of large bands and of violence were wildly distorted. By the second half of the eighteenth century, theft was an everyday fact; violence was largely a myth. Early in the century physical violence had been common and real. A great change had come about, in spite of the evidence we have seen of the persistence of certain forms of brutality – particularly violence inspired by hatred of soldiers, by drink and by greed – to the very end of the ancien régime.

The transformation began with the abandonment of violence by the upper classes. *Notables* disappear almost without trace from the ranks of those accused of premeditated assault (and accusations continued to be made despite the 1731 change in *prévôtal* competence), illustrating the same process of 'domestication' made evident by the increasing acceptance among the eighteenth-century nobility of the social value of merit and competence, and the abandonment of 'honour' and the military ethic.[34] The decline of violence can be seen clearly in the bastardisation of duelling as a means of solving disputes.Whereas the seventeenth-century duel would be concerned with the lands, titles and distinctions which made up a family's patrimony, its eighteenth-century namesake was likely to be a drunken brawl over girls or gambling disputes fought by army officers bored by the routine of life in a garrison town in the provinces.[35] In the Périgord, there were more challenges than actual fighting, petty disputes which could hardly be dignified with so reasonable a grievance as losing a girlfriend or cheating at cards. The Sr de Lanousillère was challenged to a duel when he complained that the Sr du Reclaud was flicking crumbs over him at lunch in the Inn of the Three Merchants in Nontron.[36] Pierre Chasseloup de Lombat felt obliged to draw his sword when he felt insulted by an army captain who raised his wig to him in public.[37] The only case to lead to a full trial again concerned mere provocation, the Sr de Malibas, bourgeois, accosting his cousin with 'obscene and abominable' songs in the presence of ladies, challenging him to fight, promising death at his hands; no reason for the animosity which existed

34. G. Chaussinand-Nogaret, 'Aux origines de la révolution: noblesse et bourgeoisie', *Annales E.S.C.* (1975), 265–77.
35. F. Billacois, 'Le Parlement de Paris et les duels au XVIIe Siècle', in *Crimes et criminalité en France sous l'Ancien Régime, 17e–18e siècles* (Paris 1971), pp. 33–47.
36. *Supplication* (n.d., between May and August 1740) from Sr de Lanousillère; the plaintiff did not accept the challenge. A.D. Dord. B 421.
37. *Supplication* 5 Feb. 1781, from P. de Monferran de St Orse, *ibid.* B 735.

between the two cousins was suggested at any stage of the denunciations, interrogation, *information* or confrontation.[38] This dramatic change of lifestyle by the upper classes evidently produced a temporary social cleavage as profound as that created in the seventeenth century by the educated classes' abandonment of superstition and witchcraft. As with superstition, however, the lead away from violence being set by the social élite would sooner or later be followed by the rest of the population. Sooner in the Guyenne, later in the Auvergne.

An equally positive sign of a change in attitude to violence in the Périgord is found in the example the *prévôtal* court set, not only by restricting its resort to torture and the death penalty, but also by a new unwillingness to bow meekly before a private *accomodement*. The *prévôtal* court sent for trial the soldier who had taken a bottle and a sword to the woolcomber Chaumande, even though his victim had accepted 35L. as *accomodement,* and even though the aggressor was only captured four years after the assault.[39] The *prévôtal* magistrates and police officers reserved their greatest efforts for serious crimes against the person, which the *procureur* himself unreservedly described as 'atrocious'. The investigation into the murder and robbery of Jean Charouchey, a soldier in the Viennois regiment involved the questioning of ninety witnesses;[40] the comparatively modest total of forty-nine witnesses in the murder case which resulted from the love affair of Catherine Alliban and Don Miguel were dealt with at such length and detail that their testimony filled 138 closely written pages.[41] But what is particularly important in the inquiry into the murder and mutilation of Lalliot is not so much the fact that the *maréchaussée* saw fit to interview seventy-eight witnesses, as the attitudes towards the crime conveyed in their testimony. Although mutilation was part of the ritual of 'peasant furies' in the sixteenth and seventeenth centuries, the witnesses in this trial – peasants, shopkeepers, artisans – express their horror and disgust. One of the accused themselves described the assailants as butchers; the fiftieth witness spoke of their extreme inhumanity; the twenty-ninth witness commented that 'it must be really cruel people to have made him suffer more'; the seventy-fifth witness, 'those who had mutilated the dead man were devils'.[42]

This popular revulsion against violence is confirmed in the most important way possible – an increasing willingness on the part of all sections of the community to come to the police or the judicial authorities and denounce an act of violence. In the second half of the eighteenth century, it was no longer a question of the upper classes only calling on the resources of the

38. *Inform.* 11–17 Aug. 1767, *ibid.* B 586.
39. *Interr.* of Chataignon 20 Aug. 1735, *ibid.* B 392.
40. The entire *liasse* numbered B 769.
41. *Ibid.* B 459.
42. *Inform.* 3 June – 9 July 1766, *ibid.* B 578.

state to punish the uncivilised and obstreperous poor. Marie Reydit, the wife of a *métayer,* went to see the lieutenant of the *maréchaussée* when her husband was assaulted by a barber's apprentice on the road from Périgueux to Lisle; nor was this her first hesitant contact with the law; when the same apprentice had fought with her husband three months before, she had gone straight to the *lieutenant criminel* in Périgueux.[43] A servant came to see the lieutenant of the *maréchaussée* within minutes of being jostled and cut to the bone of the elbow by the sword of a grenadier, when buying a lettuce in the Place de la Cloche in Périgueux.[44]

In matters of physical violence, as in cases of theft, the population did not reserve its appeal to the police for cases which involved strangers. Practically all the *plaintes* identify the assailant as someone known to the victim, and there was no reluctance to denounce a son-in-law or brother-in-law. The conviction of Antoine Boussarie for the murder of the curé of St Pardoux was assured by the treachery of Boussarie's cousin, who had been entrusted with the bag of money.[45] Is it conceivable that an Auvergnat peasant in this situation would have gone straight to the police? Another direct indication of the decline of violence in the community is that so many of the charges of robbery aggravated by assault and battery turned out on investigation to involve more the threat of violence than violence itself. The soldier Jean Sceleries had been glad to cooperate when the barrel of a pistol was pressed into his stomach, and handed over the signed enlistment of Raymond Faurie; yet the charge was 'violence with firearms and premeditated assault followed by theft on the highway'.[46] No blows at all were exchanged when the merchant Sr Jean Bassuet was accosted by Antoine Rouchon, who carried a large club and demanded his money or his life.[47] In many complaints of theft, the victims mention *en passant* that they were assaulted, or that the robbers wielded clubs, but it is difficult to believe they were seriously damaged when they were able to trudge to Périgueux to present themselves to the police immediately after the 'assault'. The claim by P. Breteuil that he had lost most of his hair in the attack launched by a gamekeeper and two accomplices was in fact directly contradicted by several witnesses.[48] The *assassinat* and attempted rape of Anne Morlande were found to refer to an incident in which her assailant had made off with the ribbon of her brassière.[49] We have seen assaults of real brutality, but it is clear that these were exceptional cases, where the official documents lingered on the violence because it was so unexpected. The general public did not usually go to the trouble of making a

43. *Supplication* July 1785, M. Reydit, parish of Beauronne-de-Chancellade, *ibid.* B 782.
44. *Plainte* 24 Jan. 1740, Jean Lambert, servant, *ibid.* B 421.
45. *Inform.* Sept. 1740, *ibid.* B 422.
46. *Plainte* 8 Apr. 1740, *ibid.* B 421.
47. *Supplication* Jean Bassuet, 3 Oct. 1789, *ibid.* B 608.
48. *Supplication* 22 Dec. 1769, and *Inform.* 2 Jan. 1770, *ibid.* B 617.
49. *Plainte* 23 Mar. 1773, A. Morlande, servant, parish Morssac, *ibid.* B 648.

citizen's arrest except to defend their property, but they were capable of handing over to the *maréchaussée* a *scieur de long* who had attempted to rob a fellow *scieur de long* from the Limousin, and their prisoner was labelled an assassin, not a thief, as they were concerned above all by his excessive brutality. He had 'rained blows on the head of an unknown man' and left him 'covered with blood'. The aggressive sawyer whose violence exceeded the bounds of tolerance of the Périgord community came from the parish of Pombiac, near St Flour, in the Haute-Auvergne.[50]

In most cases where violence was used in the cause of theft, just enough blows were delivered and received to persuade the victim of the folly of resistance, and the necessity of handing over the money. The 'knee blows' in the stomach suffered by the day-labourer Henri Lestrade when losing 24L. did not prevent him shouting with all his force that he was being murdered and robbed.[51] It was not unknown for would-be highway robbers and assassins to use so little force, so ineffectively, that they themselves were put to flight with nothing to show for their trouble. When a stranger seized the *laboureur* Jean Pursat crying 'Your money or your life' and directing a kick towards Pursat's stomach, the assailant himself received two blows from the victim's club, turned on his heels, and fled.[52] This highway robber, however, was not so incompetent as Bertrand Preignac, a day-labourer from the village of Mare who took a spade along to his attempt on the purse or the life of Léonard Feyteau. Léonard had just sold cattle for almost 250L., and coolly told Bertrand to take his life as he had no purse. As Bertrand was perplexed by this unexpected answer, Léonard seized the spade and cried, rather unnecessarily, for help.[53] There were of course cases of real violence in the eighteenth-century Périgord, but except in the very early decades of the century, they were employed as a rational device to steal large sums of money. Five hundred *livres* were at stake when François Fargau was waylaid by Labrousse and his two sons, who demanded a receipt for the money they still owed him.[54] The bag of money stolen by Antoine Boussarie from the curé of St Pardoux was worth a total of 281L. 6s. 4d. Jacques Laforest, a *métayer* of the Dame de St Sulpice, came home to find that his wife's throat had been cut for the 200L. they had kept in a cupboard.[55] Burglars usually preferred to break into houses when and where it was known, or could be expected, that the house would be empty; with highway robbery, and the unavoidable physical contact between robber and robbed, the risk of violence was greater. It was not only for the fair hand of Catherine that Clervaux

50. The case was dispatched between 24 June and 22 Aug. 1767, *ibid*. B 586.
51. *Plainte* 3 June 1736, *ibid*. B 411.
52. *Plainte* 2 Mar. 1772, *ibid*. B 639.
53. Plainte 24 Dec. 1766, *ibid*. B 575.
54. *Supplication* 13 Jan. 1740, *ibid*. B 421.
55. *Plainte* May 1768, *ibid*. B 597.

succumbed to the highway attack organised by Don Miguel – the Spaniard promptly disappeared not with Catherine (who was left behind to face charges of complicity) but with the pewterer's 16 *écus.*[56]

It is consistent with the obvious regional differences in the pattern of violence that even rumours in the Périgord were less brutal than those which tormented the Auvergne. Whereas the hills on the border with Le Velay echoed to tales of an *auberge rouge,* worthy of the Fernandel film, which could hardly find room for the number of corpses it had to dispose of, suspicions in the Belvès area were all on a small scale. The innkeeper was reported to have buried a single arm, and sold off combs, fifes and the pathetic wares of a peddler.[57] Even the Forêt Barade declined in notoriety; by 1784, the *maréchaussée* had to investigate a report that there was a solitary thief in the forest making passers-by pay up, in other words sending them on their way after taking their money.[58]

The population of the Périgord was increasingly quick to reach the threshold beyond which the incidence of violence was unacceptable. Who in the Auvergne would have tried the patience of the police with a denunciation of a shirt torn in a street brawl,[59] or a report of idle threats and insults? Jean Jay wanted the *maréchaussée* to arrest Henri Trassagnias for shouting from a window that he would blow Jay's brains out.[60] It is difficult to imagine the repose of an Auvergne *cavalier* being disturbed of a dark winter evening by an unknown member of the general public 'who had diligently rushed to inform us that two vagrants and vagabonds had just committed an assault'; it is in fact difficult to imagine the victim of the assault – a lady merchant dealing in salmon, cod and salt – travelling round isolated country houses in the Auvergne with no other company or protection than her niece.[61] It is equally doubtful that an Auvergnat merchant would have invoked the retribution of the *prévôtal* court for being *almost* stoned by an irate butcher, a 'murderer' who was intimidated just in time by the arrival of two pewterers.[62] Only in the Périgord could a dramatic charge of 'ambush on the highway with firearms, assault and public violence' apply to a nuisance like the Sr Dervieux, who was in the habit of calling the Sr Vincent a tramp, or a rogue, and Vincent's niece a whore; he had occasionally thrown stones against Vincent's window, and was now accused of 'stationing himself armed on the

56. *Procureur's p.-v.* 2 Jan. 1743, *ibid.* B 459.
57. *Interr.* of G. Breton, innkeeper, 52, parish Rouffignac, 10 Feb. 1781, *ibid.* B 721.
58. *P.-v.* 10 Oct. 1784, *ibid.* B 768.
59. *Plainte* 20 Mar. 1787, G. Roux, *practicien,* 21, whose shirt had been torn by a student in the rue Taillefer the night before, *ibid.* B 830.
60. *Supplication* 3 Apr. 1739, Jay, *practicien,* village Le Masouille, parish St Astier, *ibid.* B 437.
61. *P.-v.* Mussidan, 29 Jan. 1769, *ibid.* B 607.
62. *Supplication* 23 Feb. 1769, F. Valbousquet, draper in Bourdeilles, *ibid.*

road', and waiting for his enemy. He had made no attempt to use his weapon and had merely watched the plaintiff go by.[63]

Police violence

The use of judicial violence by the courts had always been a recognition of weakness in the authorities' prosecution and containment of crime. It could perhaps be expected that the police too would be driven to violence by an overwhelming sense of their own feebleness and frustration. There is always the difficulty of finding evidence of police brutality committed within the four walls of the police station, but it should be remembered that eighteenth-century police investigations had rather less need than their twentieth-century colleagues to resort to unlicensed savagery – if the inquiry ran into difficulties they could always wait for the controlled, official torture. There is evidence of only one case of violence applied to a prisoner in police custody: in the judgment which sent Jean Daniel to the stocks for two hours after he and his master, the Sr de Segonhac, had rebelled against the *maréchaussée* and injured the Montaigut *brigadier,* two cavaliers were reprimanded for the violence they had inflicted on Daniel inside the prison.[64] And while a number of prisoners died from disease or old age while in a *prévôtal* prison, only one died as a direct result of police violence – François Ragoubat, from a rifle shot fired by the Bordeaux *cavalier* Mensac, while allegedly trying to escape from the court-house yard.[65]

In exposed situations where the twentieth-century police would have imposed its authority with brute force, the eighteenth-century *maréchaussée* had to temporise or beat an undignified retreat. The Bordeaux brigade was given a painful reminder of the dangers of attempting to use violence for an arrest on warrant when they tried to capture Lordellot de Bellegarde inside the shop of his brother-in-law, a perfumer in the rue Judaïque. A crowd formed at the door to watch Lordellot, his sister and brother-in-law struggling with the *cavaliers,* and allowed Lordellot to escape, after dragging the *cavaliers* off him by the hair. It had however been the *cavaliers'* brutal technique which had drawn down popular wrath upon themselves. The policemen were disguised as bourgeois, as Lordellot had escaped on several previous occasions, and they were determined he should not escape again; they passed a rope around his neck which practically strangled him and a *valet de chambre* was not the only passer-by to agree with the spectator who commented aloud that the police should not resort to such brute force to make

---

63. *Supplication* 1 June 1769, P. Bardon, innkeeper, in St Vincent de Connazac (Neuvic), *ibid.*
64. *Jugement deffinitif,* 22 Dec. 1767, and preceding documents, A.N. Z[IC] 369.
65. *Jugement deffinitif,* 1738, *ibid.* Z[IC] 337.

arrests.[66] What appeared to be a violent rebellion against authority turns out to be a popular protest against violence, an indication of the declining acceptability of violence in the community. Yet the *cavaliers* were only too aware of Lordellot's facility for escaping, and they had to face not only his violent resistance but also that of his relatives.

There was no such excuse for the brutality of the Mauriac *brigadier*, Fontfreyde, denounced by the local judge himself, when arresting a certain Barret: the judge alleged that the *brigadier* had beaten the prisoner with a sword in his presence, before throwing Barret into a cell for the night with his wounds left untreated.[67] The *brigadier's* behaviour on this occasion was according to the judge no isolated exception to his general pattern of behaviour, and it almost brought about his dismissal. The intendant decided instead to tell Fontfreyde to pay his victim's medical expenses.[68] It was the same brigade which many years later provided Juillard with his sole example of the 'revolting brutality' which was supposed to characterise the *maréchaussée's* method of operating.[69] The episode in question was the arrest of Rougier, a man regarded by local *laboureurs* as an incendiary with such hostility that the *cavaliers* of the *maréchaussée* did not have to initiate the violence, they merely had to allow it. Rougier was 'violently beaten' by the two peasants who arrested him; his brother-in-law added a wound to his forehead, apparently in the presence of the two Mauriac *cavaliers,* who, with no regard for the condition of their prisoner, had him bound and led off on a horse to prison. They had not gone half a league when the prisoner died.[70]

Whatever the disadvantages of the suspicion which the national institution of the *maréchaussée* aroused in local authorities, it did mean that local judges did not hesitate to prosecute *cavaliers* at the merest hint of abuse. They themselves were incompetent to deal with the charges against the *maréchaussée*, but the very act of initiating a prosecution obliged the court which was competent to remember its obligations.[71] The *Tribunal de la Connétablie et Maréchaussée de France* tried *cavaliers* for abuses committed while on duty, as it dealt with rebellion against the *maréchaussée,* and was jealous of its prerogative in both fields. Numerous local courts began proceedings when a local *cavalier* was involved in violence, but the *Connétablie*

66. Sixth witness in *Inform.* by the lieutenant, 26 Apr. 1782, a week after the *cavaliers' procès-verbal de rébellion*, A.D. Gir. 11B 2.
67. Letter from Chaviale to intendant, 20 Oct. 1731, A.D. P. de D. C 6177.
68. Intendant to Fontfreyde, 1731, *ibid.*
69. M. Juillard, 'Violences et rébellions en Haute-Auvergne', *Revue de la Haute-Auvergne* (1931–2), 174.
70. *État,* Mauriac, 1754, A.D. P. de D. C 1555.
71. I have found only one allegation before a local court which on surviving evidence was not taken up and investigated by the *Connétablie*: the Courpière *brigadier* Bompard was accused of viciously maltreating one Brugier and imprisoning him for two nights, because he had been insulted by Brugier, (1734) A.D. P. de D. C 1526.

stepped in and 'evoked' the case to itself. The Bordeaux *Parlement* itself was forcibly overruled when it opened proceedings against Mensac, the *cavalier* who had killed a prisoner in the *Parlementaire* courtyard.[72] The *Connétablie* however was never given any startling evidence by the Bordeaux *jurats,* despite their anxiety to prosecute *cavaliers* for their 'habitual brutality'. The municipal *procureur* could only come up with 'violent incursions of *cavaliers* of the *maréchaussée* into houses in the town', by which he meant a nocturnal raid by four *cavaliers* on a lodging-house near the St André hospital, in an effort to find four apprentice shoemakers who had beaten up the *prévot-général*'s valet. The residents were alarmed to be woken up at 9 p.m., and a number of the ladies professed to have been shocked by the *cavaliers'* military vocabulary, but no blows were exchanged and no one was arrested.[73]

The constant vigilance by judicial authorities in the provinces produced a relatively small total of cases of police violence, and not in sufficient numbers to cause any serious interruption to the parade of rebellions against the *maréchaussée.* Given the regional variation in patterns of behaviour, it is hardly surprising to find that *cavaliers* of the Auvergne company of *maréchaussée* were involved in more than twice as many violent incidents as the more numerous *cavaliers* in the Guyenne. Between them the two companies managed only 34 incidents, ranging from proven cases of brutality to flimsy allegations – 23 in the Auvergne, 11 in the Guyenne. And only in the Auvergne was there an example of such unprovoked criminal brutality as the attack on Claude Bourgade, *laboureur,* insulted by three *cavaliers* of the Thiers brigade in a *cabaret,* dragged outside, robbed of 25 *louis d'or,* and stabbed to death with a bayonet.[74]

There were other violent deaths at the hands of the *maréchaussée,* but in both provinces the impression left by official documents is that the victims fell foul of their own folly or brutality; the least that can be said for the police contribution to the violence involved is that there were mitigating circumstances. The Auvergne *cavalier* Compagnac was actually given a gratuity of 200L. in lieu of the pay he had lost when sacked for killing a man 'he had come across cutting a woman's throat'.[75] Clearly peasants who

---

72. The *Connétablie* took note of the *arrêt du Parlement de Bordeaux* of 6 June 1735. A.N. Z^{1C} 337.

73. *Inform.* 14 Dec. 1752 by Léonard Despiant, 'avocat en Parlement et jurat', A.D. Gir. C 2188.

74. *Jugement de la Connétablie* 15 Sept. 1745, condemning Michel Rougerie *dit* Clermont, and Antoine Renouard *dit* La Jeunesse, to be hanged for 'deliberate murder, and not in self defence'; their colleague, P. Bard *dit* Lapierre, was banished for three years for making a false *procès-verbal de rébellion* alleging insults and violence by the peasants of Ecoutoux, A.D. P. de D. C 6184. *Décret de prise de corps* 3 Oct. 1744 A.N. Z^{IC} 341. *Jugement* reprinted in Serpillon, *Code criminel ou commentaire sur l'ordonnance de 1670,* vol. 1, pp. 353–4.

75. The *cavalier* was pardoned and reinstated: Correspondence, A.D. P. de D. C 6174.

carried weapons and resisted disarmament did so at their own risk. No twentieth-century policeman would have had more than administrative explanations to make for the deaths, after 'armed rebellion', of a deserter from the militia and his cousin.[76] It seemed equally inevitable that one day someone would be seriously hurt by the violent confrontations which punctuated the fêtes of the ancien régime. The Agen *cavalier* Delpont had the misfortune to intervene in a dispute among peasants, brought out his sword, and one of the assailants fell dead on the town square.[77]

A good proportion of the deaths and other physical assaults inflicted by *cavaliers* in the Guyenne were confined to their colleagues within the *maréchaussée,* who provided, perhaps, an unwilling but useful safety valve for old soldiers unable to give free rein to their aggressive instincts when dealing with the general public. The authorities were often perplexed as to the cause of a dispute. No explanation was offered as to why Elie Cherchouly, the Nontron *cavalier,* was lured by his colleague Lacombe behind the Cordeliers at 6 a.m., and critically injured by a sword thrust.[78] It is known however that in both the Guyenne and the Auvergne *cavaliers* got violently drunk, and their colleagues were often the first bodies they stumbled across. In Tauves the quarrel between Imbert and Dionnet broke out 'under the influence of wine'; the two *cavaliers* retired behind the barracks, where Imbert killed his colleague with his sabre.[79] Murder under the influence of alcohol was a pardonable offence, and Imbert was forgiven, as the *cavalier* Passerieux was forgiven for killing his colleague François Peycher when both were 'heated with wine'.[80]

It cannot be denied that both companies had a small number of individuals who were unpleasant even when sober. Chapus, a Bordeaux *cavalier* killed by his colleague Bremont, had been 'the most violent man in the world', and had previously been imprisoned by the *prévôt* for two months for knocking a peasant senseless.[81] The Ambert *brigadier* Duplessis suffered greatly from the presence of his insubordinate *cavalier* St Amour, who had been forced to leave the army for the police force for striking his sergeant and who was eventually imprisoned for striking the *brigadier* himself.[82] But on the whole the inhabitants of the Auvergne and the Guyenne had little to complain about. In matters of physical violence the *maréchaussée* was more sinned against than sinning. In St Flour, capital of the Haute-Auvergne, in 1733, a year when the province was prey to the incursion of armies of smugglers,

76. *P.-v. de rébellion*, 6 July 1745 A.N. Z[IC] 342.
77. *Evocation* 28 Sept. 1742 A.N. Z[IC] 339.
78. *Plainte* by Pierre Cherchouly to Lieutenant, 23 May 1767, A.D. Dord. B 585.
79. The 'murder' had taken place on 7 Apr. 1774, A.N. Z[IC] 389 and from the King's *Lettres de grace*, 6 Mar. 1778, *ibid.* Z[IC] 390.
80. From *procès-verbal* (n.d.) by E. Cherchouly, *ibid.* Z[IC] 443.
81. *Prévôt-général* to intendant 21 Apr. 1755, A.D. Gir. C 2189.
82. Letter to intendant, 1736, A.D. P. de D. C 6183.

the worst that could be said against the *maréchaussée* was a complaint from Delmas the innkeeper, whose wife had 'impertinently' asked Lieutenant Dastier to pay off his outstanding bills; the Sr Dastier 'gave her a kick on the backside'.[83]

The restraint shown by the Auvergne policemen sprang from a sense of their own weakness; the police force of the Guyenne had no more freedom of action, in the midst of a population increasingly less willing to tolerate gratuitous violence. It is the regional difference which is important in establishing eighteenth-century patterns of criminality, rather than any putative town–country dichotomy within a region. Despite the town's contempt for the country, violence was declining in the Guyenne countryside too, preparing the way for the bloodless uprising against the seigneurial system in 1789. The similarity of rural and urban patterns of behaviour is hardly surprising considering the fact that the great expansion of towns in the Guyenne in the course of the century was largely due to immigration from the countryside. It is difficult to imagine a scenario in which the savage rustic was tamed and refined by the struggle for survival in the overcrowded slums of eighteenth-century Bordeaux. The 'civilising' of the masses – rural or urban – was a slow and hesitant process. Even Laveau, an eloquent partisan of *vol-violence,* admits that the character of Bordeaux criminality in the late 1780s was still 'rough, tough and virile' even if 'non-violent'.[84]

Even such a modest claim cannot be made for the Auvergne and if the regional contrast in the pattern of violence is a valid one, we must expect to find it also in the violent resistance the population offered to the authorities, and above all to the front-line representatives of authority, the police force. When violence was turned against the police the crude physical assault became rebellion.

83. Dastier did have a considerable bill to pay – 126L., *Etat des plaintes contre des cavaliers de maréchaussée* (1732–3), *ibid.* C 6180.
84. Laveau, 'La criminalité à Bordeaux' p. 144.

CHAPTER 7

Rebellion and riot

'Rebellion' in eighteenth-century France was much less serious than 'riot', as it involved physical resistance to the authorities by only a handful of people or even a single individual. 'Rebellion' in fact was as devalued a term as *assassinat*, and was always supplemented in police reports and judicial charges with references to aggravated circumstances: 'rebellion with insults and threats'; 'rebellion with violence and assault'; 'armed rebellion' even if the accused had only carried a pistol or shotgun. If at least four people had been involved in the resistance, it became 'rebellion with *attroupement*'. If so many had taken part that the authorities had seriously taken fright, it became a 'sedition'. A full-scale riot was usually described as a 'popular emotion'. For greatest effect, these various charges would be compounded, so that a grain riot became an *'attroupement* and popular emotion with insults, threats and violence likely to prevent the grain trade'.[1]

Despite the apparent gravity of these charges, it is clear from the lenient, even trivial, sentences imposed by the magistrates that the eighteenth-century authorities were not so alarmed for the safety of the political and social fabric as their vocabulary suggested. Throughout the century in fact, the authorities displayed the complacency and over-confidence which led to disaster in 1788/9. Since small and scattered brigades, a make-believe police force, had sufficed for so long to control make-believe rebellions and seditions, the government found at the outbreak of the Revolution that it did not have the means to control a real rebellion. Yet they had been warned, considering that the peasant revolts of 1788 and 1789 'could not have burst so suddenly from a cloudless sky unless previous conditions and detailed rehearsals had prepared them'.[2] The pattern of these rehearsals is only beginning to be sketched:[3] a mountain of judicial records will have to be taken down off the shelf, read and absorbed, from the workings of the seigneurial courts to the *Eaux et Forêts*, or the *Aides*. This study can be concerned only with popular resistance to the operations of the

1. *Plainte* 5 Sept. 1768, J. J. Lamarque, A.D. Dord. B 598.
2. P. Goubert, *L'Ancien Régime*, vol. 2 (Paris 1973), p. 213.
3. E. Le Roy Ladurie, 'Révoltes et contestations rurales en France de 1675 à 1788', *Annales E.S.C.* (1975), 6–22.

maréchaussée,[4] within the prescribed geographical limits. But when the full story can be told of the great divide between the seventeenth-century *jacqueries* and the Revolution, it will not be a heroic tale of pitched battles, desperate sieges, and provinces ablaze. It will be a surly catalogue of stubbornness and uncooperativeness, erupting from time to time into guerilla warfare.

A rebellion was bound to occur when the forces of authority pushed the people a little too far, or outstepped the bounds of the activities which the people were prepared to tolerate. These bounds were not unduly restrictive – for the *maréchaussée* they encompassed such essential duties as the repression of thieves and vagabonds, and most beggars and deserters. The general public was prepared to let the *maréchaussée* get on with its job when it was a question of the control of those classes of people who represented a threat to the great majority of the resident population. A significant section of the community could expect to have to resort to begging at some time in their lives, but the police must have acted with discretion for the two provinces under consideration produced only one rebellion against the *maréchaussée* when it was engaged in arresting beggars. This incident took place in May 1769, when the *maréchaussée*'s drive against mendicity was at its height. The Périgueux brigade had been warned that alms were to be distributed to the poor, to mark the funeral of the seigneur de Crévoiseret, and the entire brigade was not enough to arrest the crowd of about fifty who gathered for the distribution. Only local residents were involved, and the *maréchaussée*'s clumsy shuttle service to the prison gave their friends and relatives opportunity to intervene. The *cavaliers* were forced to give up the beggars, though by drawing their swords they were able to drag the 'ring leader', the baker La Baraquette, to prison through the crowd and a hail of stones. By interrupting a previously announced commemorative distribution of charity to the local poor the *maréchaussée* had clearly exceeded the limit of public tolerance.[5]

If of course the beggars were strangers in the area, or reputed to be in contact with a band, the police could expect general cooperation and assistance. The same is also true of deserters from the army, who were often difficult to distinguish from ordinary vagabonds. Even when they were identified as deserters, and even when they were local men, they were not always welcomed back with open arms. Deserters from the army did not

4. Rebellion against the *maréchaussée* was dealt with by the *Tribunal de la Connétablie* in Paris (which also dealt with police corruption), whose records are kept in the *Archives Nationales*, series Z[IC]. G. Le Barrois d'Orgeval, *Le Tribunal de la Connétablie* (Paris 1918) dips eclectically into this series, and reproduces one or two *jugements* – pp. 175–9, and *Pièce justificative* no. 69.
5. A.N. Z[IC] 373 and 439, La Baraquette case.

bear the full stigma of the hated soldiery, but their military service had contaminated them, put them irrevocably beyond the pale of the village community. There were deserters who were denounced to the police; there was not a single rebellion against their arrest. The corollary of this attitude, however, was that riots broke out to prevent a man being sent off for service in the militia. It also meant, as we have seen, that collective action might be taken to disrupt the work of recruiting sergeants - violence which became rebellion when the police were foolish enough to interfere. One of the most effective rebellions against the *maréchaussée* involved the action taken by foundry workers against the forced engagement of one of their mates, who had been 'signed up' with the connivance of the Mussidan brigade.[6] The success came from the heart-warming unanimity found among the witnesses to the recruit's incarceration - the wig-maker, the student and the bourgeois - and the blacksmiths and cannon casters who formed the spontaneous *attroupement* which routed the *cavaliers* of the *maréchaussée* in the streets of Mussidan.

With or without the support of the local population, soldiers and suspected deserters were themselves able to give the *maréchaussée* a great deal of trouble. The *maréchaussée* had a list of every soldier, *cavalier* and dragoon in the department, and all soldiers had to check in with the police on their arrival in town, and carry identification and leave-passes at all times for the *maréchaussée* to inspect. Soldiers however had enough bravado, and possibly a weapon, to make them resent cow-towing to the country policemen, who were only old soldiers like themselves. The *cavaliers* of the Auvergne met far fewer deserters, but it was the Auvergne which provided the most violent confrontations, and the only one which proved fatal.[7] A few men in uniform had sufficient lack of respect for authority to be bloody-minded when asked to show their leave-pass - their spirit of independence is statistically insignificant. The *maréchaussée* arrested hundreds of deserters, and questioned thousands of soldiers, only a few allowed themselves to be exasperated by the *maréchaussée*'s zeal.

While soldiers were particularly insubordinate to police authority, they were not the only individuals who decided from time to time that they had been pushed around long enough. Beggars and vagrants did not cause trouble - they knew the insecurity of the tolerance the police afforded them, and had to take whatever the constables offered. Members of the resident population, however, were not always so subservient and might react against a brusque police injunction to stand aside or move on. The resulting altercation or exchange of blows could lead to a charge of rebellion, but on the whole it

6. Mussidan 1760. The trial lasted till 1763, and documents from the case are scattered across A.N. Z^{IC} 357, 358, 361, and 434.
7. A *cavalier* from Brioude killed by a deserter encountered by chance on a routine patrol, *P.-v.* 4 July 1775, *ibid.* Z^{IC} 384.

seems to have been reasonably safe to bait the *maréchaussée*. The son of the Montaigut prison concierge who threw stones at the *cavaliers* was imprisoned for only one week.[8] These examples of rebellion, some of which were serious but more of which were trivial, hardly constitute a groundswell of opposition. When three or four peasants refused to move aside for the Aurillac *exempt* and forced him into the ditch, it was the policeman who resorted to violence and applied a few blows with his whip, while the peasants restrained their rebellion to verbal insolence.[9]

No doubt many trivial or abortive attempts at resistance to the police went unrecorded. It was not always worth bringing a charge of rebellion, which required transferring the prisoner to Paris, when the punishment would almost certainly be less than the penalty for whatever offence he was being arrested. An individual's resistance to arrest only became rebellion when the *cavalier* was killed or seriously injured – most often in a disarmament operation – or when the wanted man received support from his friends and relatives. In the Guyenne this was a comparatively rare event – small consolation for the Villeneuve brigade which had to arrest Calasson for causing a disturbance at the Casseneuil fête. They had to take into account his wife and sister, who even in pregnancy were 'more terrible than Calasson himself'. A member of the bourgeois militia had his finger cut off by a bill-hook wielded by one of these women, who later did sterling work fighting off the two police brigades; after Calasson was wounded, their tearful grief and bitter accusations almost succeeded in setting off a general revolt.

The spontaneous, desperate efforts by Auvergnat families to protect one of its members provided even more serious episodes. When the Tauves and Besse brigades tried to arrest a murderer, they had to face his sister-in-law, a shrew who defended her house against the police by throwing pots of boiling water over the *cavaliers*.[10] The most spectacular family rebellion took place in the parish of Anglard, part of the district of the long-suffering Mauriac brigade, as late as 1786. It was a large-scale operation involving the brigades from Mauriac, Aurillac, Maurs and St Martin under the command of the Aurillac *sous-lieutenant*, and the objective was to capture the five ringleaders of a rebellion which had marred the Mauriac fair. The police arrived after dark to find that three of the five had decamped, but Didier, father and son, were at home. After breaking in, the *sous-lieutenant* and his men found that they had overcome only the first line of defence, for the entire Didier family had retreated to the attic and were hurling stones down the narrow staircase, and through a hole in the ceiling made by lifting a few planks from the attic floor. The Didier family fought off the *maréchaussée* with stones, spades,

8. 1734, A.D. P. de D. C 1523.
9. *P.-v.* 11 May 1737, A.N. Z^{IC} 336.
10. *P.-v.* 1760 A.D. P. de D. C 1544. The scene is imaginatively described in Juillard, 'Violences et rébellions' (1931-2), 80-2.

pitchforks and scythes from 11p.m. till 5a.m. the following morning, when shots were exchanged, and the family overpowered. As dawn was breaking, and the rest of the village beginning to stir, the police left with its prisoners 'without daring to procure witnesses, and on the verge of provoking a general revolt'. Didier's father had been injured in the hand - it was in fact permanently maimed; one of his younger sons had been shot, and died the following day.[11]

In both the Calasson and Didier arrests, the *maréchaussée* had narrowly avoided provoking not only the wanted man's family but also his friends and neighbours into rebellion. In both cases, the police had beat a precipitous retreat when it looked as if community spirit would take over where blood ties had left off. The *cavaliers* did not need to be told how disastrous such an intervention could be. When the Issoire *cavaliers* descended by night on Bourg to make arrests after the village's triumph over nearby Longchamp in the course of their grazing dispute, the policemen managed with great difficulty to capture and bind a certain Dieudonné, only to find that they stirred up what the *maréchaussée* tried at all times to avoid, a general riot. The tocsin rang out again, the whole village assembled 'tumultuously', stones rained down. The *cavaliers* released their prisoner, and took refuge in a stable. Not to be thwarted the inhabitants of Bourg led by Dieudonné took the straw off the roof and continued the bombardment. On being hit on the head the *cavalier* Brun was provoked into firing his rifle. With Dieudonné hit and seriously injured, the brigade fled into the night, abandoning horses and equipment.[12] Not for the last time the *maréchaussée* had knocked its head against the wall of village solidarity. Family solidarity was to be expected, and usually the *maréchaussée* could cope with it. The small numbers of the force made it powerless when the entire community was prepared to act together to prevent a mission being accomplished. Theft and personal assault were not acceptable to the community and so, at least in the Périgord, the population gave their support to the authorities in the repression of what were universally regarded as crimes. A 'rebellion' came into being when the authorities oppressed individuals or repressed activities not popularly regarded as criminals or crimes. It was at this point that the 'community spirit', which had been strengthened by the appearance of wandering, destitute, strangers, but so frayed by internal theft and violence, came into its own again. The *maréchaussée* persistently underestimated the degree of public sympathy which could be evoked by the plight of an unfortunate individual - the attempt for example to take a deaf-mute off to a monastery[13] - but the

11. The family's defence in court was considerably more feeble than their resistance to the police - they had not recognised their assailants as policemen, they claimed, *P.-v.* 13 July 1786, A.N. Z^IC 466.
12. *P.-v.* 30 Sept. 1755 *exempt* of Issoire brigade, A.D. P. de D. C 1539.
13. Attempt by St André de Cubzac brigade to arrest Gaston, May 1777, A.N. Z^IC 389.

'rebellions' which resulted were of passing concern compared with the numerous situations where the police regularly faced the most intransigent hostility.

Main-forte

The *cavaliers* of the *maréchaussée* made many arrests in their capacity as auxiliaries to court officials or other agents of law enforcement. They provided an extremely limited assistance for the collection of royal taxes or the constraining of tax-payers indebted to the government: the occasional sortie against smugglers in conjunction with the *Ferme*, the occasional escort of upper-class individuals or garrison upon a family in arrears. In any case, it would appear that the natural reluctance to part with hard-earned money did not in the eighteenth century escalate into rebellion. The administrative records of the period contain only brief and passing mention of disturbances provoked by the *taille*, and only in the Auvergne. When trouble did break out, it was usually directed at a specific individual who, it was felt, was not paying his fair share of the *taille*. The peasants of Vic-le-Comte sent a deputation to the intendant; in St Amant a few walnut trees were cut down and there was a lot of shouting and bell-ringing.[14] From the meagre evidence at our disposal, it is possible to draw the conclusion, confirmed by the events of the Revolution, that eighteenth-century peasants were more antagonistic to seigneurial dues and, in certain circumstances to the tithe, than to the *taille*. From the evidence provided by royal sources, dues and the tithe were at least responsible for rebellions worthy of the name, when real and not verbal blows were physically applied.

We know from appeals for aid addressed to the *prévôtal* court that there was constant resistance to the seigneurial monopoly of wood. Those who helped themselves to the seigneur's wood had not yet perhaps acquired the full consciousness of the political and social significance of their defiance which Balzac describes in his novel *Les Paysans,* but it was not a crime which was committed with a guilty conscience, and peasants reacted violently when caught in the act of deforestation. It was not unknown for the Haute-Auvergne peasants to attack and beat up their seigneur when he found them carrying off stolen wood.[15] In the Périgord, in the parish of St Angel, near Nontron, Roger Martin, *écuyer*, was the victim of a 'sedition, popular emotion and armed *attroupement*' when he came across four women stealing wood on his brother's estate, and was foolish enough to follow them to their village, La Grezille. He was attacked by thirty men and women armed with rifles, sticks and clubs, crying 'Kill, kill, we must kill him', but he escaped

14. A.D. P. de D. C 1526.
15. Juillard, 'Violence et rébellions', pp. 57–8; 1737, village of Creyssac. M. d'Auzers was the victim.

with bruises on his shoulder left by a blow from a spade. The local charcoal-burner was too concerned for his own health to tell the owner who had participated in the rebellion.[16] The inhabitants of Tremoulat did not waste their time pilfering a little wood from time to time – they organised expeditions 'to cut down the big oaks'. When disturbed by the Sr de Melefon and his *métayers* they had already carted off five trees, the smallest of which was twenty feet long.[17] All of these cases were referred to other courts to deal with – the theft of wood was not a concern of the royal police. The *maréchaussée* did however become involved in the protection of the seigneurial system when peasants who had refused to pay their dues or the tithe forcibly resisted the attempts of bailiffs to compel them.

The most violent hostility to seigneurial dues was displayed in the Auvergne, more specifically in the hills on the Velay border, and in the mountains of the Haute-Auvergne.[18] The parish of St Privat d'Allier which, under Louis XIV, had refused to pay the *taille* on the advice of a notary subsequently hanged, under Louis XV rebelled against court bailiffs sent to collect dues owed to the seigneur. In the Langeac department, the parish of St Jean de Nay repeatedly proved awkward about paying its seigneurial dues; in the 1730s and 40s, peasants repeatedly inflicted injuries on estate managers or anyone else sent to collect the money. The eventual appearance of five brigades of *maréchaussée* intimidated the peasants, not, unfortunately, into paying up, but into taking to the mountains. The intendant at least was far from anxious to pursue these rebellious vassals and encouraged the *fermier* to come to some sort of an arrangement with the peasants; however 'reprehensible' the rebellion had been, the state had more important concerns: 'It is a long time since I wrote how much damage is done to the collection of taxes by the desertion of villages.'[19] Successive intendants were equally accommodating and conciliatory towards the parishes of the Haute-Auvergne which used a variety of obstructionist tactics, passive resistance and violent rebellion, to avoid paying their dues to their seigneurs.[20] Although the

16. *Plainte* (n.d.) and *Inform.* 1741, A.D. Dord. B 432.
17. *Plainte* 31 Dec. 1729, *ibid.* B 367.
18. Le Roy Ladurie, in his 'Révoltes et contestations', pp. 19–20, lists the Auvergne as an area of comparative torpor, as the peasants were spared the threat of agricultural progress and of contact with restless new ideas. His evidence comes from Poitrineau's study of the Basse-Auvergne, but there was considerably more violence and contestation in the Haute-Auvergne. Juillard explains this by the clear mountain air which made the Haute-Auvergnats more healthy and vigorous than the depressed inhabitants of the swampy Limagne ('Violences et rébellions'). Poitrineau shows too that the mountain peasants had a more varied diet than those of the plain, and blames the apathy of Basse-Auvergne peasants on chronic undernourishment.
19. Correspondence between intendant, the Langeac *subdélégué* Talemandier, and the marquise de Crussol, 1737–1743 A.D. P. de D. C 1528 and C 6184.
20. Juillard, 'Violences et rebellions' *passim*. Practically all the seigneurs to suffer violent resistance were *abbés*.

peasants of La Rodde and of Tremouille St Loup fell behind in their payments to the abbés of Port-Dieu, between 1703 and 1748, to the tune of
14,000L. the intendant's sole concern was to 'avoid the ruin of these poor
people'.[21] The village of Chassagne, in the parish of La Nobre, stopped
paying dues in 1734 until such time as the seigneur, a 9-year-old *abbé in
commendam*, proved the validity of his titles to the *seigneurie*. When the
fermier arrived with bailiffs, they were quickly put to flight by the inhabitants of the village armed with pitchforks, scythes and stones. A second
detachment, protected by the *maréchaussée* from Ussel in the Limousin,
met with a similar disaster, and again the intendant intervened with the
moderating generosity of the central government. The Bort *subdélégué* was
instructed to 'terminate the affair and get the inhabitants to acknowledge
their responsibility to pay something'.[22]

It says something for religious loyalties among the peasants of the Haute-
Auvergne that while so many *abbés* had to fight to hang on to their profits,
the church had little trouble collecting the tithe. In the Périgord, however,
peasants had to feel that they were getting value for their money. Rebellion
against those who were sent to collect the tithe could break out when the
people were angry at the deficient service provided by their curé. When
Sicaire Bleynie, *fermier*, accepted the job of collecting the tithe from the
Périgord parish of St Léon on behalf of the abbé de St Astier, du Carteron
de Valereuil,[23] the parish had been without a curé for some time, and the
parishioners had warned the abbé, their seigneur, that they would pay the
tithe only on condition they were given a priest and refunded the money
they had paid to temporary replacements. Crowds of women soon put the
fermier to flight and when the Périgueux *cavaliers* themselves appeared, a
display of clubs, poles and stones brought about their early retreat. On the
eve of the Revolution, a riot erupted when a locum curé failed to turn up to
serve the parish of Chaleix, near Thiviers. The previous curé had recently
died, and his father, Robadan, had organised a rota of replacements. Several
hours after the curé of the parish of St Pierre de Cole failed to appear
Robadan was disturbed at dinner in the company of some parish *notables* by
a furious crowd of peasants who broke into and pillaged the presbytery. As a
result, 'nobody dares to collect the tithe'.[24]

It was only the following year that the *maréchaussée* was the victim of a

21. Correspondence between intendant and M. de Mallesaigne, 1733, A.D. P. de D.
    C 2775.
22. Police reports and correspondence, 1735, *ibid*. C 1527.
23. *Inform*. July 1722, A.D. Dord. B 329.
24. *Plainte* 11 June 1786, *ibid*. B 795. Curés were also expected to conform to the
    standards of their ecclesiastical status. There was little sympathy for the curé of
    Brochaud, shot in the back, for 'if he had gone straight home instead of going to
    visit females (the Dlle la Picaudie in particular), it would not have happened to him'.
    Inform., July 1788, *ibid*. B 830.

more significant rebellion against its protection of ecclesiastical vested interests. While most rebellions in Périgourdin churches were inspired by the peasants' anxiety to retain their traditional patterns of worship, or were inspired, as we shall see, by traditional superstitions such as hostility to *monitoires*, the parish of Donzillac in 1787 staged a revolt against the *maréchaussée* which was a presage of Revolutionary things to come. Mr Joseph, Chevalier de la Grave, a magistrate in the *Parlement*, had obtained the concession of a private pew in the parish church in return for an annual contribution to the church fabric, but his right to such a status symbol was disputed and after he and his wife had endured insults, and been 'troubled in the enjoyment' of the pew, he had summonses issued against the ring-leaders. This action enraged the parish, and in a dress rehearsal for 1789, the offending pew was carried out of the church and burnt. The *lieutenant criminel* in Périgueux changed the summonses to arrest warrants, and his bailiff was left to organise police support. Although unrest in the parish had prevented the holding of divine service for four months, he took only the Périgueux brigade and one *cavalier* from Montignac, striking quietly at night. When three of the eight accused had been taken, the prisoners began to shout 'Fire! Stop thief! "A l'assassin!"',' and in the lurid light of flaming straw torches, the *cavaliers* saw the peasants assemble with their shotguns, pitchforks and clubs, issuing cries of 'Strike, kill this swine.' They fled with their three prisoners to the safety of the château of the local seigneur, the marquise de Talleyrand.[25]

Both provinces, then, were prepared in different circumstances to resist the enforcement of seigneurial or ecclesiastical rights. This was a different issue from the enforcement of warrants issued by the various courts of the realm for arrest or seizure of property on criminal or debt charges. In this area of *main-forte*, the authority of the whole judicial system was at stake. *Main-forte* had always been a favourite occupation of *cavaliers*, as it was paid extra as *service extraordinaire*. Such operations did however have one disadvantage – they were particularly liable to meet violent resistance. The very fact that the bailiffs did not feel strong enough to act on their own was a warning to the *cavaliers* of the controversial nature of the manoeuvre. In the backwoods of the Auvergne, indeed, court officials were content to allow the *maréchaussée* to take their place, particularly if a seizure of property was contemplated. Usually, however, the *cavaliers* were present only to protect the bailiffs. The bailiff would already have paid one unsuccessful call on the person who was to be arrested or whose property was to be seized, or who was to be forced to pay debts or dues. A court order would then be issued authorising the bailiff to take an escort of 'sufficient numbers of policemen to ensure victory'.

25. *P.-v.* Jan. 1788, A.N. Z^{IC} 470, and A.D. Gir. C 3729.

The rôle played by the *maréchaussée* in this system again underlines the fact that respect for the law was more evidently lacking in the Auvergne than in the Guyenne. In the one year 1744 the *maréchaussée* faced rebellion when providing *main-forte* for the *bailliage* in St Flour, the court in Besse, and the municipal jurisdiction in Brioude. In the first episode, the brigade was particularly vulnerable as it led away twenty-five cows and a mare, whose owners organised a troop of about forty neighbours in the parish of Lascombes to attack the police with the usual array of guns, scythes, hoes, clubs and other implements. The Besse disturbance was a minor affair involving only two *laboureurs* and a servant; the Brioude revolt, the entire village of La Bugy.[26] The following year, the Tauves brigade had to retreat from assisting at an arrest when rifles were trained in their direction, and the Murat brigade was put to flight at the fair in Riom-ès-Montagnes, when protecting a bailiff trying to arrest a man for debt.[27] It is therefore possible to understand why a royal court bailiff in Brioude took along three brigade commanders and eight *cavaliers* on an expedition to arrest two peasants and their wives.[28] When the detachment reached the village of Chaudecol, in the parish of Bousselargues, a crowd of about eighty people were waiting, stones at the ready. The bailiff himself took flight at once, and the *cavaliers* were forced to shoot their way out.

As well as vigorously resisting the *cavaliers* when they happened to turn up in the wake of court ushers, the peasants of the Auvergne were also prepared to take preventive action. The question of *main-forte* lay behind the notorious ambush which the parish of Cassaniouze laid for the St Mamet brigade. The 68-year-old *brigadier* Lasalle and his four *cavaliers* were innocently patrolling the Calvinet fair when a group of peasants staged a fight: the *cavaliers* were obliged to intervene, and found themselves surrounded by a menacing crowd of two hundred peasants armed with batons. The *brigadier* just had time to catch sight of the *lieutenant-général* of the Calvinet court scuttling away in fright – he had been responsible for a number of arrest warrants issued by the *lieutenant criminel* in Aurillac against several inhabitants of Cassaniouze. The peasants had assumed the *maréchaussée* was present at the fair in order to give him *main-forte* to put these decrees into effect. By the time the brigade was allowed to take its leave covered with blood, it was in no condition to arrest anyone. Nor was the parish of Cassaniouze nervous about the possibility of official retribution: 'It is a kind of Republic which fears neither judge nor justice and which has announced that even if six brigades of *maréchaussée* come to the parish to arrest any of its citizens, they would soon be destroyed.'[29]

26. *P.-v.* A.N. Z^IC 341.
27. *Ibid.* Z^IC 342, and correspondence in A.D. P. de D. C 1523.
28. *Jugement deffinitif* 20 Mar. 1772, A.N. Z^IC 378.
29. *P.-v.* 23 Apr. 1755, *ibid.* Z^IC 378.

It is a sign of popular acceptance of the judicial authorities – consonant with Périgourdin willingness to involve the police in community disputes over theft or assault – that rioting against the police engaged in *main-forte* was practically unknown in the Guyenne. On one occasion, however, they confirmed the example of the Auvergne in a demonstration of the popular refusal to regard indebtedness as a crime. Tonneins, in the Garonne valley, half-way between Bordeaux and Toulouse, was the setting in 1784 for a revolt involving a crowd variously estimated at two to eight hundred against a decree of the *Parlement* of Bordeaux. The man to be arrested was Hebraan Beaudon, and when the bailiff seized him, Beaudon coolly replied that he would not be taken far, as he already had been arrested three or four times and each time he had been delivered by the crowd. 'We must fight against these f... rogues and rescue M. Beaudon', the mob shouted, 'otherwise we must blind them with lumps of sand, or bash them senseless.' The *cavaliers* sensibly agreed to give up their prisoner, and so the revolt was accomplished without a single blow exchanged.[30]

This rebellion in the Guyenne, like most others, was accompanied by less gratuitous violence than was usual in the Auvergne. It involved only as much physical constraint as was required for the specific purpose in mind, when no other course of action was available, and this pattern was confirmed when the *maréchaussée* attempted to assemble young men for their militia service.

Militia operations

The *maréchaussée* was able to keep control at the actual drawing of lots; it was more difficult to contain the spontaneous upsurge of animosity which the *cavaliers* provoked when they arrived to drag a fugitive away. 'Help me, friends! You surely won't let me be taken away!' Barbarin cried as he threw his arms around a tree and hung grimly on as the Langon *sous-lieutenant*, Le Maître de Chancelée, tried to pull him free. It was not very clever of the *sous-lieutenant* to undertake such a clumsy arrest in the middle of the Sainte-Bazeille fair. A crowd of peasants gathered, armed as always with their clubs and cattle-prods, uttering the usual menaces and imprecations. It was a little more cunning of the police officer to offer to release the prisoner if the crowd left their names and addresses, it was at any rate a change from the moral exhortations with which Guyenne police officers loved to harangue the populace. No one answered, some of the crowd moved away. When the *cavaliers* began to lead Barbarin himself away, however, the peasants returned to the attack – *cavaliers* were punched in the stomach, and the fugitive was allowed to go free. The ringleaders – a miller, a mason, the son of the sacristan, a bailiff – were all from Barbarin's own parish, Couturère.[31]

30. *Inform.*, *ibid*. Z^{IC} 460.
31. *Inform.*, June 1782. A.N. Z^{IC} 456.

If village solidarity could operate at a distance, one would expect it to be all the more effective on the spot. But where the militia was concerned, as Barbarin almost discovered to his cost, there was a certain hesitancy which is not found in other sources of popular rebellion. In two operations in the Sarladais in which the *maréchaussée* had acted on the word of the *milicien* himself, the crowd stood and watched for some time until shamed into action by an angry woman or a curé.[32] While there was general sympathy for the young men who did not turn up to draw lots, the sympathy was clearly not shared by those who had turned up, and particularly by those unfortunate enough to draw the wrong token. It was therefore possible for the authorities to play off one section of the community against another. The Brioude *subdélégué* made it his policy to organise a troop of about twenty of the bravest lads from those who had turned up, and to use this force to help the *maréchaussée* find the fugitives. 'In this way I set the boys of a parish against other boys from the same parish.'[33] The recruitment of the militia under the ancien régime was a system which bred violence in the community. But in every case of resistance to the arrest of a fugitive, there were those who were prepared and anxious to support the law and establish order. Militia disturbances were not so much popular rebellions as civil war. It was a system which could lead to the sort of bloody confrontation which occurred in the village of Croze (Périgord), in June 1729.

Pierre Baullard, a *practicien* from Nanteuil and organiser of the draw for the militia in Nanteuil, had heard that one of his eligible young men had taken refuge in the village of Croze in the parish of Millac. Accompanied by six relatives and friends, he made a surprise expedition to Croze, where they found their man, Jean Favard, lying in a meadow. They were just leading him away when they were spotted by the seigneur's daughter, who began to shout 'Help! They're taking away our valet.' The whole village appeared almost at once, men, women and children brandishing clubs, stones and guns and crying 'Kill, kill.' The party from Nanteuil held on to their prisoners, someone in the crowd fired, and Baullard's cousin was hit in the chest: 'I am dead', he said, and in fact he died on the spot.[34] It was soon established that the fatal shot had been fired by one Laliette, a tenant of the Sr de Croze, but the *prévotal* court did not accept that a mere *métayer* could be the spirit and 'motor' of the *attroupement*. It was de Croze himself who stood to benefit by the retention of his valet, and it was his daughter who had first raised the alarm. His wife and daughter were arrested and he himself disappeared with Laliette. Laliette had of course to be sentenced to death (in his absence), but another peasant from the village, Lagrave, was banished for

32. *Plainte* 28 Aug. 1766, *ibid.* Z[IC] 367; *Plainte* 27 July 1766, *ibid.* Z[IC] 436.
33. Letter to intendant, Aug. 1781, A.D. P. de D. C 5296.
34. *Plainte* 8 June 1729 from Baullard, A.D. Dord. B 367. It was a fête day, and the village was already assembled to dance.

six years and the Sr de Croze sentenced to pay expenses.[35] Five years later, a
bailiff was sent to collect outstanding debts from de Croze, amounting to
540L. 8s. 8d. The house was deserted, and any remaining movable property
was seized. The spontaneous militia revolt had led to one death and disaster
for four households – for the widow and children of the dead man, and for
the families of three men forced into flight and exile, Laliette, Lagrave and
the Sr de Croze.

All this agony because a gun had gone off, a gun held by an ordinary
peasant. There was no hope of sending violence into retreat while the civilian
population carried arms. Yet the individual in France had always had to carry
arms to guarantee his own safety. With a collective memory firmly impressed
by the lawlessness of marauding troops, brutal *jacqueries*, civil war, and
foreign invasion, the French populace would not readily entrust its security
to the sporadic appearances of the police. The disarming of the civilian
population, therefore, on the scale undertaken by the *maréchaussée* under
the inspiration of the Marshal de Richelieu, could not be expected to proceed
smoothly. The loss of a gun or pistol was bitterly resented, and the very fact
of carrying a weapon made the act of rebellion that much easier. Disarmament
was clearly one of the most dangerous of the *maréchaussée*'s duties.

Disarmament

Popular hostility was made obvious in 1721 by the first attempt of the
Périgord police to implement the government disarmament Ordinances which
followed the conclusion of the War of the Spanish Succession. The *prévot-
général* provided the Mussidan brigade with a list of eighteen offenders, but
the *archers*' arrival in the *bourg* of Corgnac provoked a confrontation with
a crowd of thirty to forty people, including fifteen armed men. One of the
Mussidan *archers* was himself disarmed, wounded by a knife blow, and
dragged by the hair down the street. Shots were fired, and when the *archer*
Fauvel received a bullet in the stomach, his horse bolted, carrying the dying
archer all the way to St Jory.[36] Peace finally returned when the seigneur, the
marquis de l'Action, persuaded the crowd to disperse.

There was danger too in that most banal situation – a simple encounter
with a poacher. When three *cavaliers* from Bordeaux accosted two men
hunting with dogs on the moors behind Bruges, one of the *cavaliers* was shot
and the other two were content to let the two huntsmen run off and disappear
into a wood. Their comrade died the following day, and nothing was ever
discovered about the murderers.[37] It did not always have such serious
consequences, but resistance to the confiscation of a weapon and the impo-

35. *Sentence* 20 July 1730, *ibid*.
36. *P.-v.* 4 Jan. 1721. Murat *brigadier* A.D. Dord. B 335.
37. *P.-v.* 21 Jan. 1772, A.N. Z^{IC} 378; and *Inform.*, 27 Jan. *ibid*. Z^{IC} 442.

sition of the fine was virtually an everyday occurrence. The really violent incidents provoked by disarmament however were individual rebellions rather than general riots. When two men in the parish of Rufiac refused to give up their *fusils* to the Casteljaloux brigade, an *attroupement* formed which not only prevented any hope of confiscating the guns, but removed from the hapless policemen a gun they had taken earlier in the day; it was enough, however, to jeer and mock the *cavaliers*, none of whom was actually hurt.[38]

In the context of disarmament in the Guyenne, *maréchaussée*-baiting was a spectator sport. In the Auvergne, on the other hand, it was a communal activity. The Brioude *exempt* had to shoot his way out of an *attroupement* formed when his men arrested two peasants firing off pistols at the fête in the parish of Notre Dame de Grace. Although the prisoners were released, the *exempt* was knocked from his horse by a hail of stones, and after a heated hour of exchanging insults and threats, with the hostile mob closing in, the *exempt* fired his musket. A peasant was killed, and the brigade was allowed to go home.[39] This scene of pistol shots and provocation on a public holiday was a recurring nightmare for the Auvergne *maréchaussée*. They knew the unpopularity of disarmament, and they knew that a general riot was most likely to occur at a fête or market, with large crowds assembled, and much drinking. Yet what could the *cavaliers* do? How could they maintain a semblance of respect for law and order if they allowed peasants to swagger round town with pistols?

The Besse brigade had mixed success in this situation. They were bruised at the fête in Chaix by their intervention in a brawl when they disarmed a group of combative peasants of four knives, a bayonet, a six-inch dagger, a razor, and a boulder.[40] But the same brigade later took effective action at the fête in Courgoux when someone started firing a pistol. The brigade was at the time taking refreshment in the house of the local seigneur, who had expressly forbidden pistol shots in the village if only because it was the middle of summer and the houses had inflammable straw roofs. *Cavaliers* tried to pursue the offender, but the peasant responsible managed to get rid of the powder and pistol, passing them from hand to hand through the crowd. The seigneur sent his servants to help the *maréchaussée*, and their combined efforts succeeded in capturing a few of those who had threatened the *cavaliers*.[41]

Pistol shots – attempt to find and arrest or disarm the offender – rebellion: the classic progression of an Auvergnat fête. This was not quite the harmless

38. *P.-v.* 10 Jan. 1757, *ibid.* Z[IC] 335 and 432.
39. *Jugement d'entérinement de lettres de grace* – for Pissis, 1 Sept. 1778, *ibid.* Z[IC] 391.
40. *P.-v.* 15 Aug. 1762, *ibid.* Z[IC] 473.
41. *P.-v.* 13 Aug. 1776, *ibid.* Z[IC] 387.

ritual of Guyenne youths sticking weapons in their belt before swaggering round the town; Auvergnat pistols were carried and shot in the air not with any desire to kill, but at least in the expectation that a brawl would develop in which the police force would be injured and humiliated. When, for example, the St Flour brigade, on duty at the fête in Corvin, heard shots coming from a house in the late afternoon, the *cavaliers* tried to approach the house, but had to fix bayonets and retreat under a hail of stones.[42] It was pistol shots from a barn that prompted the intervention of the Murat brigade at the fête of St Jacques in the parish of Valenjol. The *cavaliers* disarmed Rocher, innkeeper, of a pistol and powder, and arrested him when he demanded the return of the weapon. The arrest led to the usual hail of stones, and shots were fired in the air by 'a crowd of young men'. The *cavaliers* fled for refuge to the curé's house where they were besieged, but the youths sent an emissary, the servant Jean, to negotiate the surrender of the pistol. Treacherously the brigade seized Jean and made a dash for the church, where the curé himself was still in the middle of the evening service. The *cavaliers* did not reach the church. They were hopelessly outnumbered, pistols were trained on them, it seemed as though they would be 'entirely massacred'. Salvation came from the church – the curé ran from the pulpit, 'crying to his parish to give assistance to the *maréchaussée*'.[43]

The police were never in any doubt as to the deliberate nature of this provocation by firearms: 'in order to defy us, several pistol shots were fired'. No sooner had one man been disarmed than other shots were heard, 'always on the opposite side'. When the *cavaliers* tried to investigate they were always obstructed by the crowd. Unidentified voices would cry out, 'Get out of here', or 'These buggers will have to leave'. Stones would fly, but before the situation got out of hand, the local representative of law and order, the *procureur* of the seigneurial court, might come to the *maréchaussée*'s assistance, sometimes by accompanying the brigade round the town to forbid innkeepers to sell any more wine. Popular reaction to such a draconian move would hardly be favourable – more shots, and barely concealed plans to ambush the brigade on its way home. Finally the curé would intervene – haranguing the crowd in the main square, winning promises not to ambush the *cavaliers* in return for the brigade's immediate departure.[44]

Rebellion at the fête

As the *cavaliers* of the Auvergne company apparently only attempted disarmament when driven to it by a display of public bravado, the closure

42. *P.-v.* 24 June 1753, *ibid.* Z^IC 350.
43. *P.-v.* 25 July 1756, *ibid.* Z^IC 352, *Jugement* 6 Sept. 1758 Z^IC 355 and *Inform.*, Z^IC 437.
44. The *procès-verbal* of the Tauves brigade, 29 June 1771, describes such a scenario, an episode at the fête in Bagnols, when the *cavaliers* had arrived at 6 p.m. and been obliged to leave thirty minutes later, *ibid.* Z^IC 376.

of the *cabarets* was only a formal recognition of the interrelationship between alcohol and illicit weapons, rebellion and the popular fête. With or
without the aggravating presence of pistols or guns, the loss of inhibitions,
the heightening of courage and of tension by the wine and the crowd made
the fête the most popular scene for both individual and collective acts of
violence. The *cavaliers* went the round of the fêtes expecting trouble and
invariably finding it. It was, in a word, the essence of the *maréchaussée*'s
duties to keep order when the popular classes set about amusing themselves.

There were of course those who caused more trouble than others. 'Youth',
'young people', 'the boys': the term varies according to the report, but
everywhere in the Auvergne the *maréchaussée* saw as its principal enemies
the gangs of youths who regarded themselves as the local toughs. For the
Langeac brigade, it was the youths of the parishes of Siangues, St Jean de
Nay, St Privat près le Velay, Vissac, Anteyrac, Chanteuge, and others in the
neighbourhood. These eighteenth-century tearaways adopted the usual
ancien régime forms of provocation: pistol shots as the *maréchaussée* went
by at the fête as a mark of derision, followed by a hail of stones when the
cavaliers tried to put a stop to their insolence.[45] The *maréchaussée* of the
Guyenne did not have quite the same problem: the Agenais brigades did
complain about the bands of young men from the parishes of St Hilaire,
Coulayrac and Monbran, for example, who went to local festivities to have
a fight. They however did not bring firearms and intended only to fight
amongst themselves.[46]

In both provinces, the fête was the main source of popular entertainment,
the only time peasants had an opportunity to relax, and so in both provinces
the obstreperous youths did the rounds of the fêtes in the neighbouring
parishes. The curés facilitated this practice by holding the parish fête not on
the precise date specified by the calendar for the celebration of the patron
saint in question, but on the nearest Sunday. While such flexibility had the
advantage of avoiding interruptions in the normal work of the week day, it
created a law enforcement problem as the crowd at every village fête was
swollen by visitors from every parish within walking distance. After a particularly fierce skirmish in Vissac, therefore, when the Langeac brigade was put
to flight by a crowd of youths who had been drinking in a barn, the
maréchaussée suggested that each parish commemorate its patron saint on the
proper day. The proposal does not appear to have been taken seriously.

The *maréchaussée*'s numerical weakness meant that it had real problems
not only when too many people attended one fête, but also when two fêtes
fell on the same day within the district under the supervision of one brigade.
There was no option but to split forces. The Agen *brigadier*, for example,
took himself and a *cavalier* to the fête in the parish of St Cirq held on the

45. Letter from Marie to *brigadier* Cristal, 28 Oct. 1755, A.D. P. de D. C 7229.
46. *P.-v.* 25 July 1774, A.N. Z[1C] 403.

25 July, and sent two *cavaliers* to the parish fête in St Cristophe. He found in St Cirq at the 1784 fête that the usual crowd of young people had gathered, and in an effort to compensate for his obvious lack of *force majeure*, the brigade commander and his solitary companion strolled up to join the dancers, and amicably told them the police would be delighted if they had a good time, quietly. The two policemen were of course unable to intervene when later in the day one young man was held down by other youths and pummelled by their fists.[47]

Whenever it became obvious in the course of a fête that the populace had tired of the presence of the police, the *maréchaussée* had the simple alternative of retiring discreetly, or of fixing bayonets and threatening to shoot unless allowed to retire. The Mauriac *brigadier* Fontfreyde denied himself this range of choice on one occasion, when he and his brigade turned up at the St Luc fair with no weapons at all. The Haute-Auvergne, needless to say, was not ready for the sophistication of an unarmed police force; the peasants did not regard the experiment as a conciliatory gesture, and did not hesitate to exploit the situation: the *cavaliers* were forced to swallow an even greater dose of humiliation than usual: 'the drubbing they took from whips and clubs is not of a nature to be made public'.[48]

In this instance, the *maréchaussée* fell victim to the Auvergne's gleeful and gratuitous brutality. Usually, however, the *cavaliers* were able to say why they had been threatened or beaten, and in both provinces they came to learn the danger which would result from any attempt to interfere in popular festivities. It was the *maréchaussée* which had to bear the brunt of popular anger in the parish of St Cirques at the decision of the bishop of St Flour to suppress the celebration of the fête of Ste Julitte, when two hundred people assembled in front of the church to form an '*attroupement* to dance'.[49] The Besse brigade knew they had been stoned at the Brion fair in 1740 for trying to assist the *sergent* of the Campoix court to make an arrest;[50] there was clearly no diminution of communal violence in this area for the lesson was repeated verbatim in 1786, when the same brigade was stoned at the same fair for trying to arrest two men who had been fighting.[51] On both occasions the forces of authority retreated in disarray, without prisoners, for fear of a 'general riot'; in 1740, the *cavaliers* were injured on the head and arms, in 1786 they received facial injuries.

Fêtes in the Auvergne were marred by a variety of distasteful forms of amusement in which the *maréchaussée* felt obliged to intervene. In Thiers the young paperworkers entertained themselves by splashing water from a

47. *Ibid.*
48. Letter from Dauphin to intendant (1760) A.D. P. de D. C 1544.
49. *P.-v.* (n.d.) Langeac brigade – 1782, *ibid.* C 6204.
50. *P.-v.* 7 Aug. 1740, A.N. Z^{IC} 338.
51. Besse *subdélégué* to intendant Aug. 1786 A.D. P. de D. C 6191.

stream over the people dancing nearby; when the *maréchaussée* failed to be amused, the result was another riot, and one of the apprentices was injured by a *cavalier's* sword.[52] A more unpleasant Auvergnat pastime was the harassment of strangers. When a group of travelling merchants set up their stalls in Pleauzac, the local bullies came along and broke their merchandise – pistols of all things.[53] The *sous-brigadier* from Veyre tried to persuade one of the vandals to pay for the damage, only to be insulted, seized by the mob, and threatened with death. The brigade was eventually allowed to leave, and to escort out of town the merchants who had requested police protection.

Provincial borders provided their own source of antagonisms. The Maurs brigade was asked by a local innkeeper to throw out two peasants who were brawling in his *cabaret* in the course of a fête. The *cavaliers* found however that not only did the two men, both from Quercy, proceed to turn on the police, they also stirred up 'sedition' among their compatriots – no less than two hundred *Quercinois* armed with clubs.[54] If there were no strangers around to cause conflict, the next best thing was a dispute with visitors from neighbouring parishes. The inhabitants of the parish of Anglard attended all the fairs and markets at Mauriac, and invariably started fights with local people, or with another parish; hardly a week went by without the *maréchaussée* having to do the rounds of the inns and drag out the peasants of Anglard.[55] This parish was perhaps particularly notorious – 'there is no area so bold and so little policed, where father and son daily fight amongst themselves' – but in the exuberant atmosphere of the fête, other parishes too, even in the Périgord, did not need much of an excuse for a brawl. When the peasants of Azerat were having a dance in a local *cabaret*, and a visitor from Thenon began to play the pipes out of time with the dancing, a general mêlée developed, with the *cavaliers* of the *maréchaussée* in the middle. The Montignac *cavalier* Gontier tried to restore order by striking the 'rebels' over the fingers with the sheath of his sword – he emerged from the fray with all the hair torn out from one side of his head.[56]

It was the *maréchaussée's* misfortune that the law of the land insisted that popular amusements had to cease, at least temporarily, when it was time to go to church. There was a certain poetic justice in the outcome of the Besse brigade's attempt to interrupt the dancing at the local fête: they retreated under a hail of stones to the curé's house, all the windows of which were smashed.[57] The Murat brigade thought they had discovered a simple device

52. *P.-v.* and *inform.*, on Thiers *cavaliers'* day at the fête in St Georges, 1774. A.N. Z^{IC} 384 and 444.
53. *P.-v.* 3 Oct. 1775. There were several pistol merchants at the fair; it is hardly surprising the *maréchaussée* had such trouble with disarmament; *ibid.* Z^{IC} 393.
54. *P.-v.* 7 June 1764, *ibid.* Z^{IC} 393 and 451.
55. *P.-v.* 18 Oct. 1785, *ibid.* Z^{IC} 461.
56. *P.-v.* 15 Aug. 1775, *ibid.* Z^{IC} 385. *Inform.*, *ibid.* Z^{IC} 445.
57. *P.-v.* 26 July 1750 A.D. P. de D. C 1568.

to put a stop to the dancing – they confiscated the pipes at the fête in St Antoine. Angry peasants, however, surrounded the brigade on all sides brandishing clubs, stones and pistols, and the *cavaliers* had to fix bayonets, and retreat.[58]

While the Auvergnat peasant on holiday passed the time between drinks by dancing, brawling, or firing pistols, the population of the Guyenne devoted a considerable part of their fêtes to gambling. The curé in Clérac formally requested the help of the Sauveterre brigade of *maréchaussée* to put a stop to the games during divine service; the first *cavalier* to be sent along was beaten up, and when the *brigadier* and other *cavaliers* came to his assistance, a general riot developed which put the brigade to flight.[59] Two *cavaliers* from Coutras – Mestreau and Gendreau – were not so lucky when they tried to stop a ball game at the fête in St Sulpice-de-Faleyrens, a mile or two to the south of St Emilion. Yet they had displayed a good measure of festive spirit, having drunk plenty of wine, 'entertaining themselves with fife and drum', even giving rides to children on the backs of their horses.[60] Such amiability was lost on several bowlers whom the *cavaliers* disturbed in the middle of a game, and who were urged to enter the church. The *cavaliers* themselves attended the service, but when they emerged to find the game still in progress, the players refused to disperse, 'and threw themselves on to us shouting that no one could prevent them doing what they wanted, not even the King, because it was a fête day.'[61] The stones, clubs and lethal agricultural implements, which were always so readily to hand at ancien régime fêtes, made their appearance; there were, significantly, no firearms, as a voice from the mob cried 'We'll make you pay dearly for the *fusil* you took from us some time ago'.[62] The tumult grew, with the *cavaliers* crying desperately but in vain for assistance, while the crowd shouted that they should be killed like mad dogs. Mestreau managed to reach the *sindic*'s house, where two armed soldiers stood over and protected him. His colleague Gendreau fell under a blow from an iron bar, and was beaten to death.

Rebellion at church

From as early as 1750 therefore, and from the backwoods of the Auvergne as from the valleys of the Guyenne, there was evidence of a profane preference for dancing, gambling and bowling even when driven to church

58. *P.-v.* 18 July 1751, A.N. Z^{IC} 348.
59. *P.-v.* 1 Sept. 1777, *ibid.* Z^{IC} 447. *Inform.*, Z^{IC} 389, *Jugement deffinitif* 20 Aug. 1779, Z^{IC} 393.
60. *Inform.*, Sept. 1754, nineteenth witness, an innkeeper's daughter, A.D. Gir. 11B 4.
61. *Rapport* 18 Feb. 1755, to *Connétablie*, A.N. Z^{IC} 351, and *P.-v. de rébellion*, 1 Sept. 1754, A.D. Gir. 11B 4.
62. *Inform.* second witness (Mestreau himself).

at the point of a bayonet. The *maréchaussée* itself was capable of treating the church like a marketplace – it was, after all, a useful place to make arrests. The attempt of the Clermont brigade to arrest a man at his own wedding met with such general disapproval that obstruction of the *cavaliers* in the aisles enabled the bridegroom to escape into the vestry, and so 'an arrest became impossible, given the nature of the locale'.[63] The unseemliness of such scenes, however, did not approach the disorders caused by the hated institution of the *monitoire* – the threat of excommunication placed on anyone who withheld information on a specific crime from the judicial authorities.

It was a sure sign of desperation when the police were forced to resort to this method of obtaining a lead to the criminal. After the *maréchaussée* had obtained permission from the diocesan authority, the *monitoire* was read aloud from the pulpit on three successive Sundays, and *cavaliers* attended the services if the curés thought they needed protection. The reluctance of the *prévôtal* court to resort to the *monitoire* was certainly not due to a shortage of unsolved crime; it can be explained partly, perhaps, by a desire not to devalue the threat of excommunication, but also by the fear of the violent opposition which it invariably aroused in rural parishes.[64]

Both sides prepared carefully for a *monitoire*. When the curé of Tourtoirac, the Sr La Jugie, was due to deliver one, he called in the entire Périgueux brigade; the congregation made sure that everyone was warned in advance to bring clubs. Several of the women of the parish came to the service with supplies of cinders, sand and lime, which they threw into the *cavaliers'* eyes. While the men broke the woodwork, pews and balustrades apart, the women broke into the chancel, and were pursued by the *maréchaussée* to the foot of the altar. Faced with vandalism and brawling in the middle of the church, the brigade decided not to encourage the sacrilege by their presence, and fled.[65]

Small wonder that when it was decided to publish *monitoires* after the murder of the curé of St Pardoux in 1740 the curé of the parish of Abjat got out of it on the pretext that he fell within the jurisdiction of the *Officialité* of Limousin, and not that of the Périgord, which had authorised the *monitoires*. The curé of St Saud simply refused to comply, in view of the revolt he expected from his parishioners. In this case, however, the police had a prime suspect and did not insist. They were in no such happy position over the notoriety of the Forêt Barade. The gamekeeper they had hauled in had been questioned about all the murders and thefts which had occurred, or

63. *P.-v.* 5 Feb. 1788, A.N. Z^{IC} 410.
64. The examples I have found are restricted to a limited area in the Périgord, but the superstition which provoked the riots was not a purely local one. H. Hours finds one example of a riot induced by *monitoire* in the Lyonnais – 'Emotions populaires dans le Lyonnais au XVIIIe siècle', *Cahiers d'Histoire* (1964).
65. *P.-v.* 5 Aug. 1753. *Jugement*, 22 Jan. 1753. A.N. Z^{IC} 350, 351, and 430.

which were reported to have occurred in the area but there was absolutely no proof of his complicity in any of them. The *procureur*, therefore, requested that *monitoires* be read out in all the parishes in and around the forest – Thenon, Fossemagne, Auriac, Rouffignac and Bars. There is no record of how the *monitoires* were received in Auriac and Rouffignac – nor of any witnesses coming forward. In Thenon, the women and the girls made a great row and threatened to kill the curé on the altar.[66] The *exempt* Reveilhac reported back from Fossemagne that the reading of the *monitoire* had been greeted with 'cries and howls'. But it was in Bars, in the very centre of the forest, that the rebellion went furthest.[67]

On 22 November 1772, the curé made his first attempt to deliver the *monitoire*. His parishioners stormed the chancel and tore the *monitoire* from his hands. For the second attempt, on 13 December, the *exempt* from Périgueux, the *brigadier* from Montignac and three *cavaliers* were present: the previous scene was repeated, and both the curé and the *maréchaussée* were forced to retire before mass could be said or the *monitoire* read. Warrants were issued for the arrest of 5 men and 7 women. Three of the women were arrested, 2 of whom, in the course of their long detention, presented a petition for their freedom. They were ignorant of the law regarding opposition to *monitoires*, they claimed; their sole motive had been the popular fear 'that the publication of the *monitoires* in the church would infallibly bring down the scourge of hail upon the parish'. Everyone knew that *monitoires* meant the destruction of crops by hail for seven successive years. This explanation for a series of sacrilegious disturbances of the peace was accepted without difficulty, but with contempt, by the *prévôtal* court. The peasants were 'blinded by a vulgar superstition', a superstition, as the *procureur* nicely put it, 'both impious and contrary to reason'. His impatience is understandable, for resistance to *monitoires* and drunkenness at a fête were practically the only situations of revolt which made the Périgourdins of the later eighteenth century forget their allegiance to *vol-violence*. Not even the vexed question of grain supplies provoked so much physical violence.

Grain disturbances

The *maréchaussée* had a triple connection with grain disturbances: it took action to prevent or forestall rioting when the food situation became critical; it took repressive action as a police force when rebellion finally broke out; and as a judicial institution it punished those who had rebelled. When they

66. Report from Thenon curé to *procureur* 27 Nov. 1772, *ibid.*
67. Most documents relating to the case are in A.D. Dord. B 637; there is also the *p.-v.* of 14 Dec. 1772 in A.N. Z[IC] 380; appeals and interrogations, July 1773, *ibid.* Z[IC] 381; sentence, 8 Feb. 1776, Z[IC] 382; late arrest and interrogation, 24 Mar. 1775, Z[IC] 384.

did have to take action the police had at least the comfort of knowing that they would not be harassed by the petty rivalries and squabbles of jurisdiction which plagued their activities in other fields, at other times. For the problem of grain supply was such a potential threat to public order that for once all the authorities of the kingdom were prepared to cooperate.

It was a sure sign of crisis for the *maréchaussée* to be involved at all in the policing of grain supplies beyond their routine patrol of markets. Their most constructive contribution was to 'oblige those who had greater supplies of grain than they needed to take them to market to help feed the poor', duties assumed by virtually all the Auvergne brigades in a year of famine like 1739.[68] The Aurillac *cavaliers* saw their task as one of preventing 'the transportation of grain to other provinces' and of forcing carters to take it to local markets, or as the St Flour *brigadier* succinctly put it, 'to bring out the grain'. The Chaudesaigues brigade commander took the initiative of stopping a convoy of grain, and selling it off at a much cheaper rate than the economic price.

The crisis of 1750 hit the Auvergne less harshly than neighbouring provinces, where as a result prices were higher. The Riom intendant therefore forbad all export of grain from his *généralité* and the *maréchaussée* set up frequent patrols to watch the frontiers and enlist the aid of peasants to man guard posts on roads leading out of the province. The *cavaliers* put themselves to a lot of trouble running all over their departments, poking their noses into barns, cellars and cupboards, depriving themselves of the relative comforts of the barracks for weeks on end, but all for precious little result. The patrols by night and day which the St Flour lieutenant inflicted on his brigade brought only modest gain – forty *setiers* – 'but what a pathetic amount for such a number of starving people'.[69] Only a large import from outside the province could make a substantial improvement in the situation and by July three hundred *setiers* had arrived in the Haute-Auvergne from the Limousin and been distributed efficiently with the aid of the *cavaliers*.

When calling on fortunate individuals to persuade them to sell off excess grain for the common good, the *maréchaussée* enjoyed public support, but other aspects of their grain policing were less appreciated. The escort of grain convoys carried the permanent risk of rebellion. When the carters transporting grain were attacked by men, women and children carrying pitchforks and sticks, *cavaliers* were no protection against a populace desperate for seed to sow for the next year. Neither the presence of the *maréchaussée* of Brioude, nor the intervention of a detachment of *cavaliers* of the regular army prevented the parish of St Jean de Nay from stopping a grain convoy. The women and girls who had been sitting at their lace work drove the

68. Claim for expenses, 1739, A.D. P. de D. C 6223 and C 6192.
69. Brisson to intendant, 13 June, *ibid*. C 871.

cavaliers back with stones.[70] There was always insecurity and the threat of violence on market day, when large numbers of hungry people were unavoidably gathered together. It was only natural that as the first line of defence against civil disturbance the *maréchaussée* – as separate brigades in routine patrols, or grouped together by the lieutenant in special circumstances – should be involved in the control of grain riots.

A more important indication of the nervousness which such rebellion caused among the authorities was the fact that the *maréchaussée*'s court of summary justice was made competent to try cases which involved disruption of the grain trade. The Ordinance of 1670 (article XII) had merely specified 'popular emotions' as a *prévôtal* offence provided the peace had been disturbed outside the town where the court sat. Such provision was reckoned to be inadequate in times of crises, as in the hungry years of 1739–40, or on the eve of the Revolution. The opportunity was then taken to reinforce the authority of the *prévôté* by issuing *arrêts du conseil* designed on the one hand to prevent disputes over competence, and on the other hand to encourage the officers of the *maréchaussée* to prosecute.[71] In the Périgord, the 1739 *arrêt* was immediately followed by the *prévôtal* trial of 13 grain rioters from Ribérac.

A full-scale trial – even before a *prévôtal* court without appeal – was the heaviest, most unwieldy and most expensive instrument of repression the authorities had at their disposal, and it was used with the greatest discretion. The Périgueux court dealt with only six grain disturbances between 1720 and 1788, and all of them at a time of great local or national distress – 1739, 1758, 1764, 1768, 1770 and 1773. Most of the disturbances broke out in the classic riot months of spring – three in May (1739, 1764 and 1773), one in April (1758) and one in March (1770). They were naturally very much concerned with the price of grain – it is not necessary to draw up logarithmic graphs, for both the witnesses and the accused described to the court the discussion of prices which invariably preceded a riot and the fierce attempts by the poor to haggle the price down to a level they could afford. A riot was not, however, a mechanical, computerised, reaction to a given price level: the wife of an innkeeper who witnessed the 1758 riot in Bergerac noted that at the time of the disturbance, 'a bushel of wheat weighing 150 pounds cost only ten *livres* whereas only a few years ago it was selling for twenty *livres* and nobody stirred'.[72] Special circumstances were needed to make the crowd angry enough to resort to violence.

70. *Chevalier* de Champelion to intendant, 31 Oct. 1750, *ibid*. C 1535.
71. *Arrêt du Conseil d'Etat* 19 May 1739: 'the King being informed that the high price of Grain is principally the result of seditious alarms . . . and wishing to stop the rumours and *attroupements* . . . makes the *Prévôts* of the *Maréchaussée* competent to try seditions or *attroupements* which might be caused by Corn or other Grains, even in the towns of their residence'. A.D. P. de D. C 6183.
72. *Inform.*, 24 May 1758, witness 22; A.D. Dord. B 523.

First and foremost came the prospect of losing grain to another locality. When hunger threatened, every province, every town, and every parish intensified the natural hostility it felt towards its neighbour. The 1739 rebellion in Ribérac, for example, was sparked off by the arrival in town of a deputation of grain merchants who had been authorised by the Nontron *subdélégué*, anxious to relieve the famine in his own district, to buy grain in Ribérac or Libourne. The carters, who suffered from greater occupational hazards than any other ancien régime profession with the exception of *gabelous*, as usual bore the brunt of popular wrath. The people of Ribérac seized the carters' equipment – their harnesses, bridles, saddles, ropes, even their clothes – and burnt it in the town square, while their horses were so maltreated that one died from the injuries it received. It was not just a question of the presence of 'strangers who had come to starve them', the innkeeper's wife was herself the object of popular distrust on account of the large purchases of grain she had made to feed her guests who were strangers by definition. Even worse 'she had furtively and secretly sent grain to her son in Nontron, and it was his stockpiling and trading in it which drove the populace to revolt'.[73]

The transport and distribution of grain was a constant provocation and temptation for the hungry populace. 'Every day, heavy carts loaded with corn and flour travelled the roads . . .How could anyone die of hunger when so much corn was on the move?'[74] Grain merchants in Bergerac had their grain driven out to the mill at Ponbonne every day, and the flour driven back to Bergerac every day, 'and they make several trips every day'. At 8 a.m. on the 10 April 1758, the inhabitants of Bergerac finally helped themselves; the *maréchaussée* later recovered the flour by following the trail the thieves had left, straight to the pocket of an apron, or to the bag hidden under the bed, or in the wardrobe in houses by the roadside.[75]

The 1764 rebellion in the village of Montrac involved an attack on a grain convoy, but it was a rather different affair from the Bergerac episode. It was one of the rare grain disturbances which were exclusively rural. The villagers seized four cartloads of wheat on their way to Mussidan, a move more obviously inspired by desperation than the Bergerac disturbance, when a witness had commented that grain prices were not particularly high: the village of Montrac had been reduced to destitution by hail, and the little grain that had been spared had, it was alleged, been transported elsewhere. The most articulate of the accused, a 26-year-old carpenter called Pierre

73. All the accused stated that they went to join the rebellion when they heard that the innkeeper's wife, Anne Quillat, and the Nontron merchants were buying up the grain. One of the two stonemasons to be accused (the only prisoners to sign their names) had feared starvation, as the unwanted competition on the market would have put grain beyond the reach of artisans. (Interr. of M. Plumenchie, 20) *Inform.*, *ibid.* B 437.
74. G. Lefebvre, *The Great Fear of 1789* (London 1973), p. 25.
75. *P.-v.* 10 Apr. 1758, Lt. de Sorbier, A.D. Dord. B 523.

Tamarelle, complained that his pregnant wife had been left to look after and feed their other children, with no source of income and no stock of bread, while he rotted in prison. The family had in fact had no bread for two months before the morning of the attack on the grain convoy.[76] The rebels had been 'armed and masked', it was alleged; in other words, one of the band wielded the club which he carried as a matter of course, several pulled the brims of their hats low over their faces, and one of the men wore 'women's *brassières* on their shoulders'.[77] It was no doubt because of these ludicrous disguises that Tamarelle was somewhat heartlessly asked if the theft had been inspired not by necessity and hunger, but by the desire for entertainment. It was a pathetic and feeble gesture and the fourteen sacks of grain were recovered intact by the *maréchaussée*, barely concealed by bushes near the roadside.

A rebellion was liable to occur when a community reached the threshold of exasperation. For a poor country parish, the threshold was the threat of starvation. For a town like Mussidan, exasperation was having to watch the repeated export of grain from or even through the town. Grain bought in St Astier by the merchant Sr Lamarque, got only half way to its destination, Menesteyrol, when it was stopped by the inhabitants of Mussidan. Twice (August and September 1768) the carters tried to get their carts rolling again, and twice the grain was forced back into Mussidan when the crowd threatened the carters' lives. For the third attempt, on 5 September, the owner appeared in person armed with a copy of the *arrêt du conseil* of 5 June 1739, and again the populace intervened, armed with stones and pitchforks, to prevent the 'export' of the grain.[78] On 13 October, two cartloads got as far as the suburb of St Médard; on this occasion the carters fled in fear when warned that a mad woman had been let loose who loved to carry millstones and carters on her back. This prolonged resistance to the transport of grain through the town was not motivated by desperate hunger; it was autumn and the crowd had not used its power to lay a finger on the grain. Popular anger was stimulated by the belief that most of the grain in question did not come from the St Astier area, but from the Mussidan area.[79] The rôle of local villain, fifth-column accomplice of foreign interests, played in Ribérac by the innkeeper's wife, was played in Mussidan by Lacoste, *sergent*, generally reckoned to be Lamarque's agent. He had taken the official measure round the countryside and bought up whatever grain there was to be found; he had employed relatives and servants to buy up grain at the Mussidan market. This had naturally forced up prices, and discontented the poor. The police inquiry did not establish beyond doubt that Lacoste had acted as Lamarque's agent

76. *Interr.* 8 June 1764, *ibid.* B 559.
77. *Interr.* Lacoste 16 June, *ibid.*
78. *Plainte*, 5 Sept. 1768, *ibid.* B 598.
79. *Inform.*, sixth witness.

or 'accomplice', but it did destroy the merchant's self-projected image of a total stranger in town, merely trying to pass through Mussidan on his way home to Menesteyrol. His was a familiar face at the Mussidan market, and whether buying or selling grain, was regarded as personally responsible for inflating prices. That the conflict led to an exchange of blows and grain rebellion was attributed by the accused and by witnesses as respectable as the *procureur* in the Monpon court to Lamarque's inflammatory promise to the poor of Mussidan that if they wanted grain at 2L. the bushel, he would make them buy it at 7L.[80]

In 1770, 'this time of calamity',[81] a band of fifty attacked the grain convoy leaving the parish of Paussac for the market at Bourdeilles. Without the delicacy of the townspeople of Mussidan, these *laboureurs* and farm-labourers, armed with axes and pitchforks, helped themselves to the grain – one bushel each. Yet this rebellion was no automatic reaction to high prices, or even to provocative transportation. For once the *maréchaussée* were correct to assume that the disturbance had not been the spontaneous result of hunger. There was a clearly identifiable ringleader, the standard-bearer who had taken not one bushel but eight. Françoise Ladoire was no plebeian harpy or starving widow – she was the daughter-in-law of the plaintiff whose grain had been pillaged. The rebellion was the result of a history of family conflict involving a mean father, a wicked stepmother, and a son and his wife thrown out of the family house and deprived of the inheritance left them by the father's first wife. Françoise Ladoire's father-in-law had paid only 12L. of the 100 which were due; in the economic difficulties of 1770, she naturally asked her father-in-law for another instalment. He refused, although his barns were gorged with hay, maize and vegetables of all kinds, preferring instead to sell most of it to some millers in the parish of La Chapelle Faucher and the rest of it at the Bourdeilles market. Françoise, it can be imagined, had no difficulty recruiting for the *attroupement* which interrupted this profiteering.

With the exception of the few rebels held after the 1773 Bergerac disturbance, all the prisoners of the Perigueux *prévôtal* court to be accused of sedition and *attroupement* over grain supply had committed their offences in the absence of *cavaliers* of the *maréchaussée*. Most of the grain rebellions had taken place in localities which did not enjoy the presence of an established brigade; the exception was Mussidan, where the Sr Lamarque, seeing trouble brewing, had gone to ask the *brigadier* for assistance, but found no one at the police barracks.[82] Grain disturbances did not after all cause nearly as much trouble to the *maréchaussée* in its police capacity as many other contentious or

80. *Interr*. Catherine Cellerier, 40, 14 Jan. 1769, *ibid*.
81. *Supplication* of Françoise Ladoire, the accused in the 1770 grain disturbance, *ibid*. B 608.
82. *Plainte* 5 Sept. 1768, *ibid*. B 598.

inflammatory situations. Yet paradoxically this was the problem regarded by the authorities as the greatest potential threat to law and order, and for that very reason, this was virtually the only activity in which they met nothing but goodwill and cooperation from local authorities. A threatening grain disturbance was one occasion when even the members of the bourgeois militia of the Guyenne took their duties seriously. In Bergerac in 1758, twelve years before the town had a resident brigade of *maréchaussée*, the riot ended when the mutinous troop of flour thieves was dispersed by regular troops and the town militia; in 1758, 1773 and 1775 many of the accused who eventually appeared before the *prévôtal* court were arrested in the first instance by the local militia and handed over to the *maréchaussée*. The rest followed the general pattern of the accused in a *prévôtal* grain trial: they were arrested by the *maréchaussée* not in the heat of the rebellion, but after the *prévôtal* investigation. One can therefore largely discount the well-known problems associated with identifying the social composition of the crowd from the background of the individuals arrested in the course of the riot. With very few exceptions, those prisoners accused of grain rioting never denied their interest in rebellion, but sought only to explain and justify their action. The only accused who denied, repeatedly and vociferously, that they had played more than a passive spectator's rôle in the disturbance were those who were arrested during the rebellion.[83]

Apart from these exceptional cases of (possibly) mistaken identity, it can be accepted that the rest of the accused were genuinely those who had participated in the rebellion, and so it is unfortunate that the investigating authorities were not really interested in examining in any depth the motives of the rebels or the mechanics of the progression from discontent to riot. They laboured under the assumption that the mass of 'rebels' had been incited, manipulated and exploited by a ringleader, a '*moteur*' of the rebellion, and all the court's efforts were directed at identifying this individual or small group of individuals. When the magistrates thought they had found him, as in Bergerac in 1758, the full weight of judicial retribution fell on his head: the sailor Jacques Riboulet, the only male in a long list of women who were accused and released, was given what was for grain rebellion the ferocious penalty of five years in the galleys.[84]

For the identification of troublemakers in a riot at which *cavaliers* had not been present, the *maréchaussée* was clearly in the hands of its witnesses. The shopkeepers and artisans who testified, however, were all masters of their

83. Several of the women before the court in 1758 and in 1773 had been present at the riot 'out of curiosity'; one saw a friend being led away crying 'Save me!' – she rescued the friend but found herself arrested. A weaver in the 1773 disturbance had objected to a *cavalier* waving his sword about and when he raised a club to ward off any stray blows, found himself arrested.
84. Sentence 29 May 1758, *ibid*.

trade; the bellringer was the only common worker at the Ribérac trial; peasants were isolated exceptions among the bourgeois and other *notables* who came along to name names. Where grain riots were concerned, unlike any other *prévôtal* trial, there was a firmly horizontal line of social distinction between the witnesses and the accused. It is hardly surprising that rebels who claimed to have acted out of poverty and hunger should prove to belong to the poorer classes. All the accused were illiterate and not one person among the 29 men and 31 women appearing before the court for participating in a grain riot could sign his or her name, including the only accused to have any claim to social respectability, Françoise Ladoire, the wife of a bourgeois. Fifteen of the 60 accused lived in the countryside, peasants or rural artisans; the rest were well-established residents of the towns: the one sailor involved was based in Bergerac and worked the river traffic no further than Bordeaux and back. The typical grain rebel, then, was the ordinary urban artisan or shopkeeper and his wife: the carpenter, the shoemaker, the pewterer, the stonemason, weaver, tailor, baker, the weaver-cum-ditchdigger; the wives of a hatmaker, innkeeper or gardener; the daughter of a sievemaker; the widow of a porter; a seamstress, a waitress in a *cabaret*. No masters of their trade were involved in a grain riot, nor the totally destitute and the vagabond; a stonemason's widow claimed as her accomplices 'all the poor of Mussidan', but those who lived on charity and never had to buy grain could clearly be excluded from consideration.

This class distinction was sometimes re-emphasised in a positive way in the actual course of the rebellion. The Ribérac innkeeper Simon d'Anguinan had been rescued from the crowd by the *procureur* of the local court 'accompanied by some of the most notable bourgeois'. When the unfortunate carters tried to leave town, the *procureur fiscal*, the comte de Ribérac, had to provide them with an escort against the angry populace, 'an escort of bourgeois and notable artisans'. The rebels themselves had complained 'bitterly and tumultuously . . .that Messieurs the bourgeois were against them but for strangers who had come to starve them' and warned that 'the bourgeoisie would not be the stronger party'.[85] It came therefore as something of a surprise to the interrogator when one of the accused, a peasant living in Ribérac, attempted to justify his part in the rebellion by claiming that several bourgeois had also participated; the only example he cared to quote was a wig-maker and his family. In the next round of interrogations another of the accused, a stonecutter, was asked 'if several bourgeois of the town, instead of preventing the disorder' – as was expected of them – 'had not encouraged it?'.[86] The prisoner had seen nothing of the sort, and no evidence was forthcoming of any bourgeois involvement on the side of the rebels.

85. Deposition of the Sr de la Chaume, *avocat*.
86. *Interr*. of Rivière, 14 Oct. 1739, *ibid*. B 437.

Atavistic patterns of violence weighed heavily on the eighteenth century; imperceptibly however the load was lightening, even in the most backward, primitive and brutal provinces. It is possible to discern the retreat of collective violence before the act of individual violence, a process described by Michel Vovelle in a telling phrase as 'the pulverisation of violence'.[87] There is a degree of poetic licence in the phrase – entire provinces were no longer roused in revolt but disarmament, militia, grain transportation, *monitoires* and gambling were all capable of stirring the community into action at least on the level of the parish, and even on the scale of a town the size of Bergerac. But they were not allowed to get out of hand, and they resulted in far fewer deaths than in the *jacqueries* of previous centuries.

Many ingenious reasons have been suggested as contributory factors in the decline of popular violence after the accession of Louis XIV: the economics of the 'glorious' eighteenth century, the beneficent influence of a better-trained clergy, the increasing effectiveness of the government in rushing in emergency supplies of grain, medicine, and troops, even the existence of a national police force; all perhaps more tangible factors than any greater propensity to steal brought about by the materialistic values encouraged by the 'Rise of Capitalism'. Perhaps the crucial factor lay in the fact that the upper classes had abandoned the brutal practices of their forefathers. Even in the Auvergne, as we have seen, the violent nobility of the seventeenth century had been 'tamed'. The eighteenth-century nobility made itself useful by denouncing criminals to the police, and complaining about the failure of government law enforcement: 'there used to be *cavaliers*, now there are none, and the whole nobility is complaining about it'.[88] By the eve of the Revolution even Le Grand d'Aussy, who had been so appalled by the ferocity of the local peasants, could appreciate the civilising influence this change had had: 'How times have changed since the *Grands Jours*! It was only then that the people of the countryside and the small towns began to get a secure hold on their liberty, on their property, on the fruit of their labour, on their very lives.'[89]

The decline of gratuitous violence was of course much more marked in the Périgord than in the Auvergne, and it is entirely in keeping with this pattern that the grain disturbances in eighteenth-century Périgord were so strictly limited to the seizure of property (and in Mussidan not even that). Only in the very first grain riot – in Ribérac – was the disturbance accompanied by unnecessary physical assault. By 1773, virtually the only casualty was the Lieutenant de Verdon himself, whose foot was hurt by a

87. In conversation with Olwen Hufton; my thanks to Professor Hufton for passing on the remark.
88. Abbesse de St Genest to intendant, 5 Mar. 1727. A.D. P. de D. C 1528.
89. Le Grand d'Aussy, *Voyage fait en 1787 et 1788*, vol. 3, pp. 263–4.

stone – an injury he bore with ostentatious stoicism.[90] The lack of violence which characterised the popular uprising of 1789 should not be seen as an astonishing departure from violent tradition.

The sporadic disturbances which did occur when the creaky system of grain distribution broke down followed a conspicuously less brutal course than the peasant or urban revolts of only a century before. The townspeople of Bergerac only threatened, in 1773, to exterminate the race of the grain merchant Gimet, only talked about wearing a piece of his skin on their rosaries, only speculated on how Gimet's liver would taste on a piece of his substandard bread. Even the peasant uprisings of 1789/90 against feudal and seigneurial dues were notable for the lack of violence, the restraint and even good humour shown by the peasantry after 'a thousand years of injustice'. The peasants of the Périgord made their revolution a festive occasion, provoking less anguish for the seigneur and his lady than among the domestic staff, who suffered the indignity of having to serve the mob food and wine; the maypole, decorated with the symbols of seigneurial authority, was a visible sign of their joy, and the bonfire of church pews helped to keep festivities warm through the chilly Périgord winter of 1789–90. But a revolution, even one carried through with bonhomie and restraint, was too much for the eighteenth-century *maréchaussée*.

90. On 24 May he sent for the surgeon at 4 a.m., because of 'the great pain in his toe'; three days later, he accompanied the *cavaliers* on their patrols, without wearing a boot on his injured foot.

CHAPTER 8

The *maréchaussée* in Revolution, 1789–1790

As an instrument of police control and judicial repression, the *maréchaussée* was an institution devoted to the maintenance of law and order, hence of the status quo. The Revolution was the ultimate rebellion against its authority, the *maréchaussée*'s ultimate defeat. *Prévôtal* justice was destroyed in a barrage of public execration; the very name *maréchaussée* disappeared for ever, apart from a few derisory appearances in student songs. Having had nothing more intimidating to face than sporadic interference from men emboldened by drink, or rioting by hungry women, the *maréchaussée* in 1789 soon found itself hopelessly inadequate to deal with a nation-wide uprising. This did not mean however that the normal service of the force was discontinued. Indeed a conscious decision seems to have been taken, with the blessing of society at large, to retreat into the daily routine while a thousand years of injustice crumbled round about.

The traditional clientèle flowed into the *prévôtal* prison in Bordeaux till October 1790.[1] The prisoners accused in May 1789 of *attroupement* were considerably outnumbered by a succession of beggars, vagabonds, petty thieves, escaped galley slaves, and in 1790 the Bordeaux prison had no 'political' inmates, only 2 horse-thieves, a boy suspected of theft, 2 escaped convicts from Rochefort, and 9 deserters. The *prévôtal* court in Agen dealt with no cases remotely concerned with the Revolution, and devoted most of 1789 to the prosecution, in his absence, of an unidentified Spaniard accused of the murder and robbery of a sheep merchant.[2] Although by 1790 the Périgord *maréchaussée* had become preoccupied with sedition, *attroupement*, forced contributions, church pews and may-poles, the Sarlat brigade still found time to complain about the cost of its routine escorts of taxes.[3]

Even in routine police matters, however, the *maréchaussée* played the passive rôle it was to adopt in most of its Revolutionary operations. Virtually all the thieves who appeared before the *prévôtal* court in 1789 were in fact

---

1. A.D. Gir. 11B 1 – Register of arrests usually made in the area covered by brigades in Bordeaux, Castres, Lipostey, Pauillac, Libourne, La Tête de Buch, 1770–90.
2. The last preserved record of *prévôtal* justice in the Agenais sent a 15-year-old boy to the Bordeaux *dépôt de mendicité* (*p.-v.* 29 Nov. 1789), A.D. Lot-et-Garonne B 554).
3. Letter from de Ronchamp to controller-general, 10 Mar. 1790, A.D. Gir. C 3729.

arrested by the general public, either by private individuals, or by one of the do-it-yourself police forces – variously called 'bourgeois militia', *'troupe nationale'*, or *'garde nationale'* – which were springing up all over the province. The *maréchaussée* proved more lenient than these self-appointed guardians of the law, and released the wandering poor who had fallen into their clutches. The lieutenant also insisted on the release of a thief on the grounds that no warrant had been issued for his arrest.[4] It is important to note respect for legal niceties being reaffirmed at the very start of the Revolution, when a flood of denunciations would compare the *maréchaussée* with an oriental despot and the bloodthirsty gods of antiquity.

The *cahiers* concentrated their fire on the concept of 'exceptional' tribunals.[5] The nobility of 43 *bailliages* took the uncompromising stand 'that the *prévôt*'s jurisdiction be abolished, so that every accused has the opportunity of an appeal'. Other *cahiers* sought at least to restrict the *maréchaussée*'s legal power, for example to peasants in cases of popular rebellion. Many *cahiers* would have reduced the *maréchaussée* to the rôle of a simple police force, uncovering the crime and the criminal, laying both before the court; others would have allowed the *prévôtal* court to issue warrants and subject the accused to his initial interrogation. At the end of the century of Enlightenment the *prévôté* provided altogether too rough a justice.

Popular prejudices against *prévôtal* justice could only be strengthened by royal decrees in 1789 which freed the *prévôt* from the *compétence* formality – and confirmed by the behaviour of some of the *prévôts-généraux*. In the Paris area there was no let-up in the catalogue of degrading punishments – stocks, branding, galleys – inflicted under the very eyes of the National Assembly.[6] Politicians in Paris also became concerned by the embroilment of the *maréchaussée* in the peasant unrest in central and south-west France, with *cavaliers* combining with detachments of bourgeois militia to fight pitched battles with the peasantry.[7] But it was the judicial repression of these disturbances that aroused most controversy. While Mirabeau waged his campaign against the 'cruelty' of the Marseille *prévôt*, Bournissac, the *prévôtal* court in Tulles was gaining public odium for the institution itself by its support of property-owners in the Corrèze. The two Limousins who were hanged by the judges of the *prévôtal* court became

4. 13 Apr. 1789, A.D. Dord. B 830.
5. 'Résumé des cahiers sur la réforme judiciaire établie par la Chancellerie', *Arch. Parl.* Annexe IV, art. 82; A.N. B^A 59, and Esmein, p. 407; E. Seligman, *La justice en France pendant la Révolution*, vol. 1 (Paris, 1901), pp. 173–4, 489–505.
6. *Ibid.*, p. 242.
7. *Histoire des brigandages commis dans le Limousin, le Périgord, l'Auvergne, le Rouergue, le Querci, l'Agenais, la Gascogne, et le Languedoc à la fin de l'année 1789 et au commencement de 1790*, by the 'Chef du Corps de Volontaires de Montauban', Paris, 28 Feb. 1790.

martyrs, fallen to 'the sword of the *prévôt* of the Limousin which is on the march, aimlessly striking off heads which may be innocent'.[8] Their fate led Durieux, the *tambour-major* of the *milice nationale* in Brive, who was himself arrested by the *prévôté* as the ringleader of the 'bandits' who had ravaged the château de Lissac, to compare French justice with 'these terrible gods of antiquity, who had to be fed with human blood'.[9]

The executions, and the rhetoric, contributed to the campaign against the institution whose essential feature was the combination of police and judicial functions. Its success was assured when the Assembly heard that 'the exercise of judicial and military power makes France the best-policed nation in Europe'.[10] This was precisely what made the institution for Robespierre 'a political monster',[11] and on the 6 March 1790 the execution of all *prévôtal* sentences was suspended; on 30 March all prisoners detained by virtue of a *prévôtal* sentence were released; decrees of 6–11 September abolished all 'exceptional' tribunals, including *prévôtal* justice. It was a harsh final judgment on a court which, while remaining within the limitations of a class justice, judged fairly and consistently with the evidence, inflicting the death penalty with discrimination, never condemning on evidence obtained by torture. Did the *maréchaussée*, then, show its true colours in the Revolution?[12]

The main source of public disorder in the Guyenne throughout 1789 was the dearth of grain. The *maréchaussée* was of course actively involved in the suppression of grain riots - it always had been. But it is somewhat unfair and certainly exaggerated to accuse the *cavaliers*, as Bussière does, of single-minded repression. When we examine the totality of the force's operations on the question of grain supply we can see that the *maréchaussée* found it expedient, in the interests of peace, to use the carrot as well as the stick.

8. *Mémoire des députés de la ville de Tulle, relatif aux troubles du Bas-Limousin, pour être mis sous les yeux de l'Assemblée Nationale* (n.d.). After the *maréchaussée* arrested 18 of those accused of 'opening up the dyke on the Favart pool', belonging to the Dame de St Hilaire, local peasants forced the lady to request the prisoners' release; in the subsequent confrontation, 80 members of the Tulle *milice nationale* stood alongside the *cavaliers*; 26 peasants were arrested, 16 released, 4 sentenced to the stocks, and a whipping, 4 to a year's imprisonment, and 2 to be hanged (*Jugement* of 20 Feb. 1790).
9. *Plaidoyer pour le Sieur Durieux* (n.d.): Durieux did not fall victim to the *prévôté*; in August 1790 he was transferred to the municipal prison in Bordeaux from which he was eventually released.
10. Speech by Mirabeau's antagonist, Manry, Seligman, *La justice en France*, vol. 1 p. 245.
11. Robespierre's speech on 29 Dec. 1790, *Moniteur*.
12. Of the areas we have looked at, by far the greatest volume of evidence as to the *maréchaussée*'s rôle in the Revolution comes from the Périgord; in the Auvergne, the institution sinks without trace in 1789. The *prévôtal* records of the Dordogne provide the material for much of G. Bussière's *Etudes historiques sur la Révolution en Périgord*, 3 vols. (Bordeaux 1897–1903); they are exploited to portray the *maréchaussée* as the sword-bearer of the forces of darkness, reaction and aristocracy.

The dual pattern to be followed emerges clearly from the 'Special operations for public tranquillity' ordered by the *commandant* of the province, particularly those undertaken by the brigades in the Bordeaux department. There was an unprecedented effort to keep order at weekly grain markets throughout the first half of 1789, and the spirit of the exercise was emphasised, if need be, by the presence of the cavalry of the Royal Pologne.[13] Combined with this intimidatory activity however went an effort to ensure that the markets were well-stocked with grain. The Créon brigade spent several days away from home going round the parishes of its district instructing all owners of grain to take to market whatever they did not need for their personal consumption, and while the *cavaliers* naturally indicated that they had unearthed all the grain there was to be found, the *procureur* of the royal court paid tribute to the effectiveness of the brigade in 'assiduous' efforts throughout 'the present year of calamity'. The *cavaliers* themselves distributed all the grain that had been brought in for sale, most of it because of their efforts, selling it off in half or even quarter bushels, 'so that each person who came to the market was able to get as much as possible for his subsistence'.[14] The hero of the hour seems to have been Mainvielle, *brigadier* in Castres. In a relief operation which occupied his time for twelve days and nights, he organised a grain dépôt in the town, sent carts out into the countryside to collect grain, personally advanced the money to pay anyone prepared to sell, and supervised the sale of the 617 sackfuls of corn which he had collected.[15]

In the Périgord, however, the operations mounted by the lieutenant directly recalled the expeditions of Gigounoux de Verdon to Bergerac in 1773 and 1775. Both 1773 and 1789 began with impassioned pleas from local authorities for help, especially against the threat from the countryside. As in 1773, the lieutenant got his brigades together, and progressed from town to town, supervising the sale of grain, reading aloud the *arrêts*, listening to individual complaints, combining occasional arrests with demagogic acts of kindness, such as to force a merchant who had sold rotten grain to contribute to the curé's fund for the poor. The lieutenant's patriarchal dispensing of justice on the market-square led to his being called upon to intervene in disputes over weights and measures, which was strictly the concern of the local authority. And as in 1773, Bergerac again: the same patrols with the bourgeois of the town, the same 'dissertations' from the steps of the Hôtel de Ville, the same appeals to Bordeaux for grain and soldiers.[16]

13. *Etat des courses*, 30 Dec. 1789, A.D. Gir. C 3729.
14. *Certificat* of the 'Procureur du Roy de la Grande Prévôté de Créon', 29 July 1789, *ibid*.
15. He was given a special gratuity of 158L. for his efforts in feeding not only Castres itself, but also Preignac, Barsac and other local markets. 'Ordonnance sur les dépenses variables de 1786', 12 May 1789, *ibid*.
16. Correspondence of Lieutenant, A.D. Dord. B 831.

It is noticeable, in contrast to the other areas of the Guyenne, that the Périgord brigades claimed expenses in 1789 only for inquiries and arrests resulting from 'popular seditions', which tends to confirm the depressing story told by Bussière of the *maréchaussée* 'hounding the starving poor'.[17] He fails to mention, however, the even-handed rôle the *maréchaussée* played when workers from the iron foundries at Ans, on the edge of the Forêt Barade, seized a grain convoy heading for Thenon. There was a long background of hostility between the foundry and the town with each doing its best to deprive the other of its grain supplies. The *maréchaussée*'s intervention to retrieve the grain and supervise its ordered sale at the market in Thenon ensured that the needy from both sides benefited from the distribution.[18]

Bussière does mention the action taken against the Périgueux baker Nicaud,[19] when the *brigadier* Paignon seized a convoy of forty-five sacks (128 bushels) of wheat, and had them sold cheaply at market. In Bussière's account, it was a solo effort by the *brigadier* who is not credited with charitable motives, but 'visibly yielded to popular pressure'; in fact the seizure was made in open country because, as Paignon put it, hoarding intensified starvation, and was contrary to the *arrêt* of 23 November 1788. Bussière describes how Paignon, panicked by mob rule, drove at once to the market and sold off the grain; in fact the grain was impounded under an official seal, the *procureur du roi* requested permission for it to be sold, and the decree was granted by the *assesseur prévôtal*. The actual sale took place three days later, at 7L. 5s. the bushel the first day (29 April) and 6L. 14s. for the second batch (2 May) not, as in Bussière, for 7L. 7s. It was sold in batches of one to three bushels, and many of the customers were peasants from neighbouring parishes – Château-l'Evêque, La Forse, St Laurent, Bassillac, Chancevinel, Cornille, Agonac – as well as servants, midwives, gardeners and *métayers* living in Périgueux itself.

Bussière entirely omits two other prosecutions of grain hoarders both initiated by the *maréchaussée* at the request of peasants with enough faith in the institution to walk to Périgueux to denounce M. de Chisan's estate manager (who had distributed his stockpile of grain among his *métayers* so that the *maréchaussée* would not find it), and the curé of Eyliac who, in contravention of the law that all grain be sold at market, had made a large private purchase from none other than M. Lagrèze, the *lieutenant assesseur* of the Périgueux *sénéchaussée*.[20] In both cases there was an immediate descent by the Périgueux brigade on all barns and hay-lofts in the two areas, and a seizure of large quantities of grain. The lieutenant duly informed the

17. Bussière, *Etudes historiques*, vol. 3, p. 78.
18. *Liasse* on Forgerons d'Ans affair, beginning with *p.-v.* 16 June 1789, A.D. Dord. B 831.
19. Bussière, *Etudes historiques*, vol. 3, pp. 80–1; *P.-v.* 26 Apr. 1789, A.D. Dord. B 831.
20. *Plaintes*, A.D. Dord. B 831.

commandant, Fumel, of the *maréchaussée*'s intention to prosecute for hoarding; the cases were transferred from the *prévôtal* court to the *sénéchaussée*, despite the implication of Lagrèze.[21]

There was, therefore, no official encouragement of prosecutions of grain hoarders from any level higher than the *maréchaussée*, and most of those caught with illicitly large supplies of grain were simply made to 'promise' they would take it to the nearest market. The *maréchaussée* in the Périgord found no evidence of organised hoarding by professional speculators, and just as in their pursuit of criminals, the *cavaliers* of the Périgord were only able to catch small fry: the transaction between Lagrèze and the curé of Eyliac involved only sixty bushels. Nicaud described himself as 'a poor baker burdened with seven children with no other source of income than his work and quite unable to keep large stocks'. It was only natural that in times of famine and shortage those with grain should try to hold on to it; the French are not alone in hoarding supplies with every rumour of shortage, even if there are French housewives still eating 1968 sugar. We should not therefore criticise the police too fiercely for not having greater success prosecuting a crime which was too natural a reaction to too many people to be regarded as an offence. It is perhaps more surprising that the authorities did have some success controlling prices and disrupting market forces than the fact that these forces could not always be denied.

It was no accident that the period of grain shortage coincided with the outbreak of the *esprit de clocher* patriotism associated with Federalism, and in the fierce disputes which resulted from the attempt of every parish to hang on to its grain, it was the *maréchaussée* which was called upon to arbitrate. The lieutenant was called in when the bourgeois militia of Périgueux sent soldiers to overturn the decision of the St Rabier committee to ignore the decision of the National Assembly to allow the unimpeded transport of grain, and when the parish of Corgnac prevented a Thiviers baker getting his usual supplies of grain.[22] All the *maréchaussée*'s qualities of tolerance and tact were required when it came to dealing with the local forces of law and order, the bourgeois militia, a hitherto moribund institution, which in 1789 and 1790 sprang to a vigorous new life and proliferated to an embarrassing degree. There is less evidence of *prévôtal* jealousy at its loss of control over the countryside and the towns to these upstarts, than of gratitude for their cooperation in handing over suspects. Overall, however, these local bodies caused the *maréchaussée* more trouble than they were worth, for despite the responsible exceptions, the majority of the militias sought to pay off old scores, fight among themselves, and call in the *maréchaussée* to pick up the pieces.

21. Lieutenant informed of decision 22 May 1789, *ibid*.
22. Correspondence of Lieutenant, *ibid*. B 834.

One of the most serious abuses of power was committed by the 'patriotic regiment' of St Georges-de-Monclard; it had no sooner been formed than it arrested Mathieu Séguin and his friend and associate Izabeau de Brie.[23] The *maréchaussée* accepted the victims' explanation for the fact that Izabeau was put in a pigsty for three days, while Mathieu was imprisoned for five days in a dungeon. For Mathieu and Izabeau had just won a lawsuit against the Sr des Bories, the commander of the 'patriotic regiment' and other prominent citizens of St Georges, including La Rivière, the regiment's lieutenant. When two *cavaliers* of the *maréchaussée* heard of the imprisonment, the *sous-lieutenant* from Bergerac, the *brigadier* Paignon and Lieutenant de Bellevaux himself went to release the prisoners, amidst general relief that decent constituted authority had been restored. La Rivière and des Bories were tried, though the latter was an old friend of the Lieutenant's, and told that the 'régiment patriotique' was only 'a troop formed to prevent *attroupements* and brigandage . . .by vagrants and vagabonds and to give assistance to legal officials to whom it must always be subordinate'.[24] The lieutenant's restricted view of the powers of the bourgeois militia was not shared by everyone, and the Monclard troop was not alone in arrogating to itself powers of arrest. Between the beginning of August and the middle of September 1789 22 local residents (and numerous vagabonds) were consigned to the dungeons of the château de Villamblard by order of the officers of the militias formed in neighbouring parishes.[25] De Bellevaux was moved to a forthright denunciation of 'this abominable harassment', committed in the main by Jacques Loreilhe, 'commander of the Douville militia', who had constituted himself 'police judge', military commander and even 'haute-justicier' - a revival of a term from the seigneurial court.

The *maréchaussée* continued to be called in to counterbalance the local 'tyrant', but by the beginning of 1790 the form of tyranny was changing. In 1789 the police had set itself up as the defender of the new order: it prosecuted a former judge for assuming police duties he had fulfilled for thirty-six years according to the instructions of the Duc de Richelieu; and it prosecuted peasants who had refused to allow nobles to sign the Celles adhesion to the Périgord Federation, a proclamation of 'peace, union and concord' which the police lieutenant saw as glowing achievements of the Revolution.[26] The *maréchaussée* in 1790 however was increasingly cast in the rôle of defender of the conservatives and persecutor of the radicals, a

---

23. *P.-v.* Lieutenant 7 Sept. 1789, *ibid.* B 831. The arrest was made ostensibly because they caused scandal by living together, and because Mathieu was alleged to beat Izabeau.
24. *Interr.* of Les Bories 4 Oct. 1789.
25. *P.-v.* Lieutenant, 17 Sept. 1789, *ibid.* B 834.
26. *Interr.* of Durand, *juge de la Baronnie d'Auberoche*, 11 Sept. 1789. The Lieutenant told Durand that Richelieu had been superseded by the States General. Cf. Lieutenant's *interr.* of Faye, *laboureur*, 20 Sept. 1789, *ibid.* B 833.

rôle which was less sought by the police than imposed upon it by the municipal 'committees' who had taken power and by the militias dominated by bourgeois and other *notables* who were increasingly hostile to the activities of their more plebeian colleagues. The commandant of the St Mesme militia, the Sr Mayme de Peyreyrol, in company with other local *notables*, ran in alarm to the *maréchaussée* when a miller, Janisson, organised his own 'band of seditious rebels' and collected contributions from the villages.[27] In this case prompt action prevented the militia's authority getting into the wrong hands, but in other parishes, rival companies were formed which would eye each other nervously across the village green.

There was, for instance, a sharp and unbridgeable gap between the rival companies formed in Cendrieux.[28] On one side was the troop organised by the enterprising innkeeper, Louis Chantal, a 'troop of farm labourers, *métayers* and servants', which had to face the hostile machinations of 'the soundest part of the parish', the mayor, the Sr Mareilland de Crespiat, the municipal council, above all the *commandant* of the rival troop, and first consul, the Sr Bernard de Senailhac de Durestal. Both sides looked outside the parish for support: Chantal to the neighbouring militia in La Cropte, commanded by a sympathetic basket weaver; Senailhac tried to involve the *maréchaussée*, with two *supplications* alleging that Chantal was a suspected highway robber, and had perpetrated 'violence' against 'citizens and their daughters'. Even worse, he had promised *métayers* in the area that there would be no more landowners, and that in order to advance the Revolution had exacted contributions, burned church pews, and carried a placard denouncing 'seigneurial rent', the remnants of the dues which had escaped the reforms of 4 August 1789. But it was not the *maréchaussée* which would run to the aid of Senailhac; and the *supplications* were of use only to the extent that they provided a convenient way to justify the execution and dispose of the corpse once Chantal had been destroyed by the bodies with real power in the Périgord in 1790. Firstly the militia of Vergt, the *chef-lieu* of the canton, then the *état-major* of the Périgord Federation[29] came to Senailhac's support; by mid 1790, the towns and the rural *notables* had joined hands to stem, and even throw back, the advance of the peasant revolution. The Federation decided, appropriately enough, to arrest Chantal at the fête on 14 July 1790, and he was duly delivered to the *maréchaussée*, labelled with charges of violence, *attroupements* and armed extortion. His brother Joseph and the basket weaver from La Cropte soon joined him in prison. The *prévôtal* court

27. Janisson was arrested after a *Supplication* from the lieutenant of the jurisdiction of St Mesme, the *sindic*, and the *procureur d'office*, and released after he agreed to pay compensation for pews he had burnt. *ibid*.
28. The Cendrieux affair fills the whole of A.D. Dord. B 846. For a blow by blow account of events, see Bussière, *Etudes historiques*, vol. 3, pp. 355ff.
29. The commanders from Périgueux, Bergerac, Nontron, Excideuil, Montignac, Ribérac, Belvès, Monpon and Mussidan.

had always been a useful instrument of class justice, and so although it had taken no part in the harassment or arrest of Chantal, it was not surprising that it found itself responsible for punishing him for his presumption. By 1790 the *prévôtal* court was too moribund either to drop all the charges and release Chantal, or to prosecute the case with vigour, and the affair was closed only in March 1791, by the Tribunal of the Périgueux district.[30]

The *maréchaussée* had been allowed to play an entirely passive rôle in the Cendrieux affair, but it was to find itself increasingly embarrassed by the necessity to make decisions as the radical militias broadened the scope of their revolutionary activities and aroused the passionate hostility of the conservative forces in society. After organising in 1789 a compromise between the rival militia companies, the *maréchaussée* was recalled in 1790 to Savignac-les-Eglises to deal with the political and social problems posed by church pews. The church pew, the very epitome of seigneurial privilege, became one of the *maréchaussée*'s greatest problems. For accepting its destruction was the shibboleth of acceptance of the Revolution itself, and when the municipality and national guard of Périgueux sent a circular round the department ordering the local militias to put a stop to the public ceremonies of immolation, the militias in Negrondes, Grun, Bourdeilles and Leyguilhac split along class lines. The officers called in the *maréchaussée* when the men refused to obey on the grounds that 'good citizens', such as *laboureurs*, had ended privilege and gained their freedom; those who wished to preserve pews wanted to 'preserve the ancien régime and forget the new Constitution'. The *maréchaussée* was invited to consider the gravity of the 1790 forms of sedition – forced contributions and telling the peasants not to pay the tithe. Even where the rebels had limited themselves to destroying pews (or, as in Leyguilhac, to auctioning them to the public and using the money to eat and drink) such behaviour constituted 'an attack on property' and could even be regarded as incitement to civil war.[31] It was clearly expected that the *maréchaussée* would know how to deal with these criminals from the countryside, its traditional sphere of operation, particularly as they came laden with further charges of sedition, armed *attroupement* and extortion with menaces.

Three of the Negrondes accused were released after a week in prison, as soon as they said they had to be back to get in the harvest; the fourth was

30. The Chantals were found guilty of undermining property rights and the authority of the law, less through evil intention than as 'a result of the spirit of the times', and released. [B 846]. The *maréchaussée* was also dragged into disputes between rival militias which did not involve a difference of social and political principle. In Savignac-les-Eglises the brother of the commander of one company was a major in the rival company, and the *maréchaussée* were called upon to arbitrate. (Lastours to lieutenant 22 Sept. 1789, *ibid*. B 833); in Mussidan, the problem was clash of personal ambition between a barrister and a notary [*ibid*. B 844].

31. *Supplications, ibid*. B 847.

released soon after, when he offered the derisory excuse that the pews had been thrown out of the church because the seat rent had not been paid, and because the roof was leaking. It took four weeks to process the Bourdeilles prisoners. In Grun, the commandant of the militia had not pre-empted the *maréchaussée* by handing over prisoners, and the lieutenant turned up a few days later with one *cavalier*, and a clerk. We must picture the sword-bearer of the bloody tribunal of the *prévôté*, come to investigate a 'seditious revolt', 'conversing with the armed mob',[32] who expressed the opinion that they would prefer their dog to Landurie (who had denounced them) as their commanding officer. After an amicable discussion on the merits of Landurie, the dog, and Jean the innkeeper, the lieutenant took his departure. In the Leyguilhac case, however, the lieutenant's hand was forced by the *procureur sindic* of the administrative district of Nontron, who presented him with a complete dossier and a petition from the members of the national guard 'admitting' they had carried off the pews; a report from the *commandant* denouncing the same confiscation; a report and a letter from the municipal officers denouncing the seizure; and a reminder from the *directoire* of the Nontron district that article 10 of the decree of 21 October 1789 prescribed the death penalty for any member of the 'national guards' who fomented sedition, and a three-year term of imprisonment for anyone who refused to obey the directives of the municipality. The form of a trial could hardly be avoided, and the *maréchaussée* laid on an impressive detachment of men to arrest the accused: the *brigadier* and three *cavaliers* from Thiviers, the *brigadier* and three *cavaliers* from Brantôme, four *cavaliers* all the way from Périgueux. The two ringleaders were not found, however: they presented themselves voluntarily on the 22 December and were released the same day.

There is only one instance of the *maréchaussée* yielding in any degree to the conservative pressures placed upon it, and taking action against recalcitrant members of the national militias, and on this occasion it was the *assesseur*, the magistrate assigned part-time to the *prévôtal* court, who received the original complaint from the curé of Laforce, and initiated proceedings.[33] It took the *prévôtal* court three months to unravel the tangled web of conflict between the curé, who had made no secret of his anti-revolutionary sentiments, and his parishioners, who had been insulted by the curé's refusal to say mass in the presence of the officers of the militia. Although the accused were in prison for only ten days, they were day-labourers and *laboureurs*, and complained that instead of wasting time on militia and respectable citizens, the *maréchaussée* should turn its zeal against the brigands and riff-raff who were pillaging the countryside. For the first time we have some echo of the nation-wide campaign against the *prévôtal*

32. *P.-v.* by lieutenant, 24 July 1790, *ibid.*
33. *Mémoire* and *supplication* from nine accused, 3 Mar. 1790, *ibid.* B 830.

court – a consciousness of *prévôtal* 'tyranny' which was produced or at least heightened by the strong element of shock that comparatively respectable citizens might find themselves before so degrading a court.

After national militias and church pews, the greatest headache for the *maréchaussée* during the Revolution was caused by maypoles. All across the Périgord liberty trees were planted, hung with the symbols of the ancien régime. Two *cavaliers* from Périgueux on a routine patrol in St Gerat came across one of the poles – shaped at the top to form a gibbet, and hung with two grain measures, a placard with inscription, a receipt for dues paid, and the seigneurial weather-vane. Looking on, M. de St Gerat, 'very sad'.[34] The planting of a may-tree was a positive act which altered the pattern of social relationships in the countryside. It was sometimes accompanied by more forceful demonstrations of social liberation – insults, threats, 'contributions' – and it always led to a queue of angry victims hammering at the door of the *maréchaussée*: 'certain to find safety in your authority and justice'.[35] The *maréchaussée* registered the complaint, ordered an inquiry, sometimes even interviewed a few witnesses, but never took the procedure further than the *Information*. When the parishes of Beauregard, Bassac, Fonteix and St Martin des Combes were subjected to the depredations of a crowd extorting forced contributions, again with the object of acquiring symbols of the abolition of the seigneurial system, the *prévôtal* court in the person of the *assesseur* issued a warrant for the arrest of the ringleader Chortal, and a clogmaker, but the cavaliers were unable or unwilling to capture them.[36] Only when the accused was literally handed over to the *maréchaussée* did the investigation go ahead, only to end in the 'provisional' release of the prisoner when the charges had been investigated, and tempers had been allowed to cool.[37]

The case against the *maréchaussée* as an important force in the repression of the Revolution in the Périgord must be limited then to the only prosecutions to be treated seriously – the trials which resulted from the displays of Revolutionary zeal in the Sarlat and Montignac area in the south-east of the department. The prosecutions led the Périgord *prévôté* to shed its only Revolutionary blood, and inspired the accused to make a Périgourdin contribution to the mainstream of Revolutionary demagogy. The feeble *prévôté* of 1789/90 was transfigured into 'the *prévôtal* inquisition'; the lieutenant who had scarcely lifted a finger was singled out for criticism as

34. *P.-v.* 31 Jan. 1790, *ibid.* B 844.
35. *Supplic.* e.g. of M. Bezenac, Sr de la Font, 5 Oct. 1789, *ibid.* B 833, or d'Abzac de la Douze, 9 Feb. 1790, *ibid.* B 844.
36. *Supplic.* of Antoine de Bonnal, seigneur de Beauregard, 26 Feb. 1790, and *Inform.*, 1 Mar. 1790, *ibid.* B 845.
37. T. Chaveron, *dit* Negron, handed over by two bourgeois from Vergt. *Supplic.* of Srs La Jarière, and Du Monteil, 5 May 1790; release 18 Sept. 1790, *ibid.* B 845.

'less anxious to know the truth than to find a culprit against whom he could direct . . .the cruelty which he has so often displayed . . .'[38]

The trials began when the municipality of Belvès arrested Repayré and two of his accomplices, Hugon and Soustre, and delivered them to the *maréchaussée* with five powerful denunciations hanging around their necks. It was in fact a carefully concerted campaign involving *notables* representing the law, the army, and the church, who wrote to the lieutenant in identical terms to demand action against the rebels and brigands.[39] Political pressure, which was also to be an important factor in Perier's case, was not however the only factor which led the *maréchaussée* to pursue these investigations to the limit. The burning of a church pew or the planting of a maypole, however loaded with symbolism, did not rank in the same category as pillaging a château or ransacking a curé's house between gun shots. The five accusers all had tales of forced 'contributions' – 20 *écus* from Sauret; 24L. and food and drink from the curé of Alès (on the pretext he had demanded 24L. for damage to his livestock fifteen years before); from the curé of Cabans, food, wine and the 30L. he had collected to repair the church steeple. All five added to these precise complaints stories of flaming pews, repeated menaces of untimely death to anyone foolhardy enough to pay 'seigneurial rent'. All singled out Repayré as the ringleader, and quoted his frequent assertion that he would kill thirty rich men with the greatest indifference. Repayré was sentenced to be hanged, and his two principal accomplices to five years in the galleys and one year in prison.[40]

A full-scale *prévôtal* investigation confirmed and clarified the charges relating to incidents at Thonac and Manegre for which Brunet, Chapgier and Jardel were held responsible.[41] In the first episode, the curé of Thonac was invaded by a crowd of around 300, from the parishes of Valjan, Sarzat, and St Léon, many of them armed with axes, rifles and halberds. After drinking the curé's wine, and making slurred threats to hang the curé from the maypole, or to split his head open with a stick, the crowd moved on to the church. The pews were dragged out to the cemetery and chopped up, but were only singed before the fire went out. The expedition 250 strong to the château de Manegre originated in a desire to find a M. de St Genies, com-

38. *Supplics.* of J. Perier, Labrousse *dit* Brunet, *ibid.* B 1689; J.-J. Escande, *Histoire de Sarlat* (Sarlat 1903) includes a brief survey of events.
39. Letters dated 3, 4 or 5 Feb. 1791 to Lt. from Sauret, capt. in Régiment de Poitou; Martres, curé in Alès de Badefol, the Chevalier de Boucher, the Sr Delisle de Fregere, *avocat*, and Camnon, curé in Cabans, A.D. Dord. B 1689.
40. These accusations are the only remaining source of information on the *attroupements* of the 27 Jan. and 1 Feb. 1790 in the parish of Cabans, and neighbouring parishes, until the Sentence (30 Apr. 1790, *ibid.* B 1701).
41. The curé in Thonac; the *homme d'affaires* of Président de la Borde; 2 *laboureurs*, a carpenter, a tapestry-maker and a painter (tradesmen from the town working on the castle); the cook and other servants.

pounded by the thought of laying hands on 'bread, wine and other eatables'. Despite the laying of tables in the courtyard, the crowd spread through the château; some linen was pilfered, a few hardy souls threw onions and cloves of garlic from the loft to their friends below; a few pigeons were shot, and confiscated rifles retrieved. This joyful scene was accompanied by the enactment of harmless fantasies: 'the masters themselves served the food and drink'. Two or three peasants asked M. and Mme de Manegre to indicate to them how they were now 'equal'; Monsieur clearly did not agree and provocatively held out his left hand. Madame, however, embraced them. The *maréchaussée* launched an extraordinary expedition to capture the suspects – a *sous-lieutenant*, 5 brigade commanders, and 18 *cavaliers*, reinforced by 8 *cavaliers* from the Royal Pologne.[42] The interrogation of the prisoners did help to place the two episodes in a wider context. The visit to Manegre appeared less as a punitive expedition than as part of the general anti-'feudal' movement. They had gone to Manegre to collect a weathervane for the maypole; there had been no violence, not even a pew broken, and the prisoners had all been released by the beginning of 1791.

Perier, however, did not fall into the usual rut of rural grievances. Urban politics fell far outside the normal sphere of *prévôtal* activities; that Perier fell into such hands was not the result of the *maréchaussée* spreading tyrannical tentacles where they did not belong, but clear indication of its weakness. Perier was sacrificed by the municipal council of Montignac, not by the sword of *prévôtal* retribution. He was not convicted and was also to be released in 1791. Even Bussière finally admits that after the initial denunciation of Perier, 'The *prévôté* hesitated a moment. But it was finally obliged by the growing authority of the new power to comply with its demands.'[43] Perier had to be removed as he had been so successful in disrupting the smooth functioning, under the *notables*, of local government in Montignac. One of his motions, which had proposed the fixing of the price of bread at two to three *sous* the pound, had led to such tumultuous acclaim that the *cavaliers* of the *maréchaussée* were called to arrest him; but true to their lieutenant's discretion the *cavaliers* demanded a written order, and the judge retreated before popular disapproval. The main count against Perier was his organisation of forced contributions: from the Sr Pomarel, a barrel of wine; from Sr Huzy, wood worth 60L.; 60L. from the widow de Gemes, 18 from Laroche. What was alarming to the Montignac authorities was the very organisation: as Bussière puts it in a felicitous phrase, Perier invested extortion with 'revolutionary dignity'.[44] A fund was set up, and a treasurer appointed. Receipts were given, signed 'Neker de Perier', and the money used to cover the expenses of the troop which was set up to patrol the streets at night and

42. *P.-v.* 15 Feb. 1790, *ibid.*
43. Bussière, *Etudes historiques*, vol. 3, p. 318.
44. *Ibid.* p. 270.

organise Revolutionary fêtes. Witnesses paid tribute to the troop's discipline – Perier had stopped the men firing on pigeons, or pillaging cellars, and reprimanded those who started to make a row. For preventing the very disorders which aggravated the charges against Brunet and Jardel, Perier came to be seen as all the more dangerous, and all the more liable for prosecution.

It was not long before the *maréchaussée* had cause to regret that it had allowed itself to be used for these prosecutions. The prisoners had petitions presented denouncing the lieutenant's vexatious abuse of power, and the dangers of being dragged before so 'anti-constitutional' a court. The magistrates of the Sarlat *Présidial*, in their capacity as judges of the *prévôtal* court, lost no time in declaring such charges 'impertinent and inadmissible',[45] accepting the lieutenant's own sibylline defence that the charges were disproved by the cessation of his functions. The prosaic mind of Bussière interprets the phrase to indicate that the lieutenant had been ill; perhaps it was a diplomatic illness to suit the *maréchaussée*'s fortunes in 1790. The 'cessation of functions' could conceivably refer to the National Assembly's suspension, on 6 March, of all *prévôtal* judgments, a reminder that whatever the court decided about Perier it would not be put into effect. It might be a straightforward allusion to the fact that the lieutenant had taken virtually no part in the prosecutions – the *information* which had led to the warrant against Perier had been conducted by the *assesseur*, as had virtually all the 'political' trials of 1789/90. The 'cessation' of the lieutenant's functions might simply be a disillusioned reflection on the waning prestige of the *maréchaussée* and of *prévôtal* justice just a few months before their final abolition.

The essence of the Revolutionary critique of *prévôtal* justice was the combination of robe and sword, and in the course of his account of this debate in Sarlat, Bussière asserts that the independence of the magistrature was vitiated by 'the presence of a man of the sword'.[46] The problem was in fact the reverse. What Chapgier and Perier were denouncing was not the presence of the lieutenant, but his absence. His hand-washing abandoned the accused to the tender mercies of the regular legal officers of the *Présidial*. And in this complaint their instinct was correct, for it was because of the weakness of the *maréchaussée* in 1790, not its tyrannical strength, that the accused found themselves in a *prévôtal* court in the first place.

The *maréchaussée* had never been regarded as a tyranny because of its brigades of policemen, and it is not surprising that when it emerged triumphant at the end of 1790 as the *Gendarmerie Nationale*, the crucial difference was not to be the change in name, a pleasant compromise which added a modern veneer to one of the oldest terms in the military vocabulary, but its increase

45. Decision of 10 Apr. 1790, A.D. Dord. B 1701.
46. Bussière, *Etudes historiques*, vol. 3, p. 321.

in numbers. This was to be the long-delayed recognition of demands made since 1720, and forcibly repeated in the *cahiers*.[47] From villages like St Pardoux Lastour (near Issoire) demanding brigades of *maréchaussée* in towns and villages off the main roads, to the nobility of the Agenais: 'It would be desirable for the tranquillity of the countryside that the brigades of *maréchaussée* be multiplied'; the Third Estate of Chateauroux, Chartres, Etampes; the nobility of Beziers, Bordeaux, Blois; the clergy of Amiens, Chaumont en Bassigny and Le Maine, all used identical terms to stress the importance of the *maréchaussée*'s service and the desirability of increasing its strength. The Third Estate of Bordeaux asked that patrols covering highways, roads and even isolated houses be more frequent; more frequent patrols necessitated more brigades, either on horseback or on foot. *Cahiers* which seemed to propose only more efficient placing of brigades in reality presupposed the augmentation of numbers. In the Auvergne, one brigade was requested for every town with any sort of court; for Châlons-sur-Saône the priorities were small towns and villages near forests, while the three Estates of Bordeaux wanted brigades of no less than 6 *cavaliers*.

For the Revolutionary detractors of the *maréchaussée*, it was all the more important that the bigger and better *Gendarmerie Nationale* shed its judicial connections. Victory was to be theirs, but only after bitter opposition, after the defenders of the force had tried to argue that the practical usefulness of the *maréchaussée* as a police force - which everyone agreed about - depended on the *maréchaussée* remaining both a military and a judicial institution.[48]

Part of the argument stemmed from the *cavaliers*' own self-esteem. The force's 'esprit de corps' needed the prestige of the magistrature to enhance the rôle of the ordinary policeman, whose duties would otherwise be harsh and degrading. To become the passive, mercenary agents of the courts would demoralise the whole police force. Perhaps some of the *cavaliers* did like to see themselves as humble members of the legal profession - in Montauban at least the *cavaliers* tried to pass as a legal and not a military body for the purpose of adding their contribution to the *Cahiers*.[49] It is doubtful if such pretensions on the part of 'hangmen's valets' made much impression on the public.

A much more important reason for the continued association of robe and sword was the very fact of this association of ideas in the popular mind: 'The

47. F. Mège (ed.), 'Cahiers des paroisses d'Auvergne' in *Annales scientifiques de Clermont*, ser. 2, fasc. 13 (1899); Mondenard, *Etudes sur l'Ancien Régime – les cahiers de l'Agenais*, p. 399; Desjardins, *Les cahiers et la législation criminelle* pp. 357–62.
48. *Précis important sur les maréchaussées*, anon. 1790; cf. also *Observations sommaires sur le tribunal des maréchaussées de France par un député de l'assemblée nationale* (Paris 1789).
49. V. Malrieu, *Cahiers de doléances de la sénéchaussée de Montauban et du pays et jugerie de Rivière-Verdun pour les Etats-Generaux de 1789* (Montauban 1925), p. 27.

intimidated evil doer sees in a flash the armed soldier arresting him, the judge interrogating him, the prison, the sentence without appeal, the punishment'.[50] In a natural chain of events, this healthy state of terror is communicated to other brigands, bands are dispersed, villains take to eternal exile. All France's criminological problems were solved 'by presenting to culprits at one and the same time the apparatus of justice and that of force, the dreadful uniform of the warrior, and the imposing apparel of the magistrate'.[51]

This psychological weapon was conceived above all to supplement the *maréchaussée*'s lack of numerical strength. The terror inspired by the *maréchaussée* was a fraud – 'the strength of the *maréchaussée* is moral rather than real'.[52] This is the real answer to the Revolutionary criticisms of the force. Its defenders agreed hopefully, optimistically, that 'booted justice' had the reputation of a sanguinary instrument of retribution. Such a reputation was of course unjustified, both because of the physical weakness of the force, and because of the judicial safeguards extended to the prisoners of the *prévôtal* court. But this dreadful reputation was the only factor which allowed it to function. The *maréchaussée* was a trick played on the populace by the ruling classes. Scattered across France in brigades of four – seven, eight or nine leagues apart – the *cavaliers* of the *maréchaussée* 'cannot offer any kind of effective resistance to schemes designed to undermine public order'.[53]

The bluff had been called by the uprisings in the earliest days of the Revolution. The *maréchaussée* of the Périgord had survived from month to month only by adopting the lowest possible profile. Now that 'this salutary error' had been corrected, now that the Revolution had torn away 'the veil of vulgar credulity which covered the constituent principles of the *maréchaussée*',[54] it was imperative to replace fiction and reputation with real strength. The days of an undermanned police force in France were over.

50. *Précis*, p. 15.
51. *Ibid.*
52. *Ibid.* p. 14.
53. *Ibid.*
54. *Ibid.* p. 1.

Epilogue

Since 22 December 1790, the *maréchaussée* has been known as the *Gendarmerie Nationale*.[1] It was at first sight only a change of name, a less radical reform than in 1720, when existing companies of *maréchaussée* had been abolished, and a new force created. Within the next few months, however, the opportunity was seized to make the crucial single change which everyone demanded: the *Gendarmerie Nationale* of 1791 was twice as big as the *maréchaussée* of 1790. To the former *maréchaussée* were added the old Parisian institutions which survived the 1720 Reform as well as about 4,000 entirely new recruits.[2] The *Gendarmerie Nationale* therefore started with almost 11,000 men, but numbers continued to grow and the Ministry of the Interior received no more complaints about lack of police strength. Since the end of the eighteenth century the population of France has only doubled, but in 1973, the *Gendarmerie Nationale* had over 68,000 men, while Paris and other cities were policed by a further 120,000.

The new Revolutionary police force was divided into Divisions, most of which grouped three of the departmental companies and corresponded to the former *généralité*. The Guyenne became Division Seven, with its three departmental forces of Lot-et-Garonne (Agenais), Dordogne (Périgord) and Gironde (Bordelais); the Auvergne *maréchaussée* however was split between two divisions: Cantal (the Haute-Auvergne) joined with Lot and with Aveyron to make up Division Twenty-four and thus parted company with the Basse-Auvergne, where the Puy de Dôme, the Haute-Loire (the southern part of the Basse-Auvergne, and the Velay), and the Creuze came together to form Division Twenty-five, an administrative rearrangement which implied no obvious rationalisation. No changes were made in the geographical distribution of brigades apart from the creation of new residences. The Department of the Gironde suggested transferring the Créon and Sauveterre brigades to Pompignac and Brannes, a proposal vigorously countered by the Créon and Sauveterre *communes*, which sent eloquent memoranda to the War Minister insisting on the need for the brigades to stay where they were. In the Cantal,

1. *Décret* of 6–11 Sept. 1790, *Moniteur National*, p. 1476.
2. The *maréchaussée* provided 5029 men, the other companies 1720, new recruits 4043, to create a *Gendarmerie nationale* of 10,792 men. The *maréchaussée* had had 945 brigades, the *Gendarmerie* 1560, *Tableau comparatif*, A. de G. X^F 9.

it was proposed to transfer the St Martin de Valmeroux brigade to Salers, to back up the district court - a priority which the *cahiers* had drawn attention to - but it was decided to leave the brigade where it was, on the direct route from Aurillac to Mauriac and therefore essential for the transportation of taxes.

The same pattern of continuity plus expansion was observed in the appointment of personnel to the new force. The only members of the old *maréchaussée* who did not join the *Gendarmerie Nationale* were the older *cavaliers* who voluntarily took the opportunity to retire. The National Assembly decided to admit into the *Gendarmerie* even those *cavaliers* who failed to comply with the regulations laid down by the Law of 10 February 1791. Departments were informed that they could not dismiss *cavaliers* who in the Department's opinion were ready for retirement, who had been the object of bad reports, or even those who were illiterate. For the authorities' prime concern was to use as much as possible the valuable experience of the old *maréchaussée* to train the new recruits to the *Gendarmerie*. The colonel of the Gironde *gendarmerie*, none other than the former *prévôt-général*, M. de Ronchamp, tried as far as possible not to 'isolate' the new officers appointed by the departmental Directory, but to give them the help of *maréchaux des logis* from the *maréchaussée*. At a lower level, the new *gendarmes* were, as far as was practicable, distributed among former *cavaliers*; this was however not easy to achieve to any extent. It was natural to concentrate the new *gendarmes* together in the new brigades, for spreading the experience of the old *maréchaussée* around meant inconvenient removals for the *cavaliers* themselves. Promises of promotion and 'the good of the service' were not always sufficient incentive to induce a former *cavalier* to uproot himself and family. When it came to promotion or transference to another residence, the officers of the old *maréchaussée* were given preferential treatment, and when the officers newly appointed from the regular army protested, the Ministry decided that the policy was justified by the greater experience of police work acquired by officers from the *maréchaussée*.[3]

After this easy transition to a new era, the legislation mounted: the law of 28 Germinal, year VI (17 April 1798); the *arrêt* of the 12 Thermidor, year IX (31 July 1801); the Ordinance of 29 October 1820; the decree of 1 March 1854; the decree of 20 May 1903, which was amended in 1958 and 1970 - so many administrative modifications to the Ordinance of 1778, so many adaptations of the 1720 reforms. The *Gendarmerie Nationale* remained 'a force instituted to assure in the interior of the Republic the maintenance of order and the execution of the laws' (1798), 'the most efficient manner of maintaining a country's tranquillity . . . a surveillance which is half civil, half military, spread over the whole territory, and providing the most precise

3. *Ibid.*

reports' (1806).[4] The essential change was the new-found commitment to provide the resources necessary for the realisation of the aims of the 1720 Reform, to pay for the modernisation of equipment, and the multiplication of personnel. This 'national phenomenon' created by the ancien régime, confirmed by the Revolution, maintained by the monarchy and reinforced by the Republic, this police force with military discipline and eight centuries of tradition, has always corresponded to a certain idea of the state. It is fitting that it has received ultimate consecration from a Gaullist Prime Minister, who identifies the *Maréchaussée/Gendarmerie* as one of France's most characteristic institutions, and uses France's greatest philosopher to evoke its name:

Through its multiple interventions in the daily life of the Nation, the *Gendarmerie Nationale* responds to this wish of Pascal: '. . .Justice and Strength should go together, and for that we must ensure that what is just is strong, or that what is strong is just'.[5]

4. Napoleon to Murat, 16 May 1806.
5. M. Messmer's introduction to the catalogue of the exhibition *Maréchaussée et Gendarmerie – Huit Siècles d'histoire* (Paris 1972).

The *maréchaussée* on 1 January 1790

Companies	Lieutenants	Assesseurs	Procureurs	Greffiers	Presidents and conseillers	Sous-lts	Maréchaux des logis	Brigadiers	Cavaliers	sur-numéraires	Trompettes
Alençon	2	2	2	2		4	4	19	85	6	1
Alsace	2	2	2	2	18	4	4	16	76	6	1
Aunis	2	2	2	2		3	3	13	60	6	1
Auvergne	2	2	2	2		5	4	22	94	6	1
Béarn	4	4	4	4		6	5	25	110	10	1
Berry	3	4	4	4		5	4	21	91	8	1
Bourbonnais	3	3	3	3		5	5	21	94	8	1
Bourgogne	10	10	10	10		9	7	44	183	22	1
Bretagne	5	5	5	5		7	7	35	150	12	1
Caen	2	2	2	2		4	4	17	75	6	1
Champagne	5	5	5	5		8	8	35	149	12	1
Dauphiné	4	4	4	4		5	4	22	94	10	1
Evêchés	2	2	2	2		4	4	16	76	6	1
Flandre	3	3	3	3		4	3	15	66	8	1
Franche-Comté	3	3	3	3		4	4	20	88	8	1
Guyenne	4	5	5	5		5	5	24	103	10	1
Hainault	2	2	2	2		3	2	11	47	6	1
Ile de France	5	1	1	1		7	6	27	99	0	1
Languedoc	4	4	4	4		9	9	43	184	10	1
Limousin	3	3	3	3		5	5	23	100	8	1
Lyonnais	3	3	3	3		4	4	16	72	8	1
Lorraine	4	4	4	4		6	6	29	125	10	1
Montauban	2	4	4	4		4	4	17	75	6	1
Orléanais	5	5	5	5		7	6	34	144	12	1
Paris (*gén.*)	8	8	8	8		9	12	37	187	18	1
Picardie	3	3	3	3		4	4	19	89	8	1
Poitou	4	4	4	4		6	5	26	113	10	1
Provence	2	2	2	2		6	4	22	92	6	1
Rouen	3	3	3	3		5	5	21	96	8	1
Roussillon	2	2	2	2		2	2	9	39	6	1
Soissonnais	3	3	3	3		4	4	20	92	8	1
Touraine	5	5	5	5		9	9	43	186	12	1
Voyages and Chasses du Roi	1	0	0	0		2	5	16	103	6	1
	115	114	114	114	18	174	167	778	3,437	286	33

Occupations of *prévôtal* prisoners in the Périgord, 1720 – 1790

[Not including beggars; if the prisoner had more than one occupation, he is listed under the job he used in more than one interrogation.]

A. Men

300 farm labourers (*travailleurs de terre, brasseurs de terre, brassiers de terre, laboureurs, laboureurs à bras, journaliers, paysans*)

And 13 farm-labourers who also worked as: weaver; road repairer; truffle merchant-cum-smuggler; vinegrower/tiler; servant of warehouseman; alms-collector; militiaman; carpenter; cattledealer; ditch-digger/chestnut collector; porter/vinegrower/peddler; mason's assistant; servant

28 *métayers* or *bordiers* (sharecroppers)

12 valets of *métayers*

2 cowherds and 2 shepherds

4 *fermiers* and 6 estate managers

15 vinegrowers

37 servants, 7 valets, 2 coachmen, 1 postilion, 5 cooks, 6 gardeners, 5 gamekeepers

31 carpenters and 1 ship's carpenter

27 shoemakers/cobblers and 1 who also sold parasols

23 weavers and 2 who also worked as: ditch-digger; farm-labourer

23 tailors and 2 who also worked as: farm-labourer; cowherd/river pilot

19 millers and 2 who were also: porter; bargee

17 masons and 2 who were also; farm-labourer, glass-merchant

12 carters and 2 muleteers

12 serge-makers

9 *scieurs de long* and 3 who were also: farm-labourer; gelder/mason; horsedealer

9 stonecutters

9 surgeons

8 street porters/stevedores; and 4 who also worked as: roofer; barber; farm labourer; builder's labourer

8 nail makers

7 wool-carders and 4 wool-combers

7 slaters

6 tilers and 2 who were also: street-porter; farm-labourer

6 clog-makers

6 wheelwrights

6 wig-makers

6 pewter-casters

5 coopers and 5 metal-hoop makers and 3 makers of wood for cooperage

5 house-painters and 1 who also had taught Latin to children

5 boilermakers/coppersmiths

5 pavers

5 blacksmiths

4 basket-weavers

4 shoeblacks; and 4 who were also: porter; postilion; farm-labourer; rag-and-bone man

4 quarrymen

3 tapestry-repairers and one who also blacked shoes and sold brandy and lemonade
3 paper-workers
3 locksmiths
3 rosary makers
3 silk-workers
2 fishermen
2 charcoal burners
2 churchwardens
2 hemp-combers
2 makers of fly-whisks to put on cows' heads and of gamebags for huntsmen
2 saddlers
2 dyers
2 farriers
1 each of the following: maker of edge-tools; well-digger; sieve maker; doormat maker; silk-belt maker; bellows maker; brandy maker; rape-seed oil maker; chair maker; repairer of straw chairs; broom maker; boot maker; button maker; cutler; mattress maker; tanner; knife-grinder; skinner of animals killed by disease; bellows blower; clearer of waste land; thatcher; copper-plate engraver; window-glass maker; wall-coper; tin-smith; polisher; water-carrier; maker of church wafers; ditch-digger; chimney-sweep; groom; navvy; and a lace maker who was also a navigator on merchant ships, a dealer in cords and belts for priests, and an organiser of draws for trinkets.
19 'merchants', 15 peddlers of ironmongery, 16 packmen, and 14 rag-and-bone men and 10 who combined peddling with: throwing dice and spinning the wheel of fortune; working for butchers and on the waterfront; casting pewter; selling jewelry and lace; or working the land; 1 packman dealt in livestock in the winter-time and 7 specialised in pictures, paper, books, songs or brochures
15 innkeepers (*cabaretiers, aubergistes, hôtes*) and 4 who also: mended roofs; worked the land; or sold crockery
9 bakers
7 dealers in cattle and sheep
5 butchers and 2 who were also innkeepers
5 dealers in crockery
4 straw-merchants and 1 who also helped to get in the harvest
3 shopkeepers
3 hatters
2 pin-sellers
2 pig-merchants
2 dealers in stockings and bonnets
1 dealer each in: salt; damask; barometers; wood; contraband tobacco; glass; gold; drugs; guns; confectionery; clocks; coffee; precious stones; lace handkerchiefs; horses
1 woollen-bonnet merchant/farm-labourer/rag-and-bone-man/shepherd
38 soldiers, 7 militiamen, 3 grenadiers, 3 sergeants, 2 *cavaliers*, 1 captain in the watch, 1 gunner, 3 dragoons, 2 captains, 1 officer in the Guard Marine, and 1 former lieutenant
16 sailors, 1 sailor/miller's boy/wool-carder, and 1 boat-boy/porter
1 guard from the galleys
20 *Sieurs*, 3 *écuyers*, 1 *chevalier*, 1 marquis, and 1 baron
11 bourgeois, 1 'living nobly' and 1 'living from his *rentes*'
3 dancing masters, 2 violinists, 1 buffoon, 1 thimble-rigger
2 tonsured clerics who were also tutors, 2 Latin teachers, 3 school-teachers, and 1 teacher who was also a hermit monk
3 students
1 architect

    1 archdeacon (from Wales)

  26 'without profession' and 8 who also claimed to be: 'bourgeois'; soldier/shepherd;
      farm-labourer/pig-driver/errand-boy; someone who went from town to town
      looking for grain for millers and *fermiers*; peddler of pictures; street-porter; stable-
      lad/servant of innkeepers and gardeners; someone who exchanged pins for rags

B. Women

(i) Professions in their own right

    42 spinners of wool or cotton

    11 servants and 2 who also worked as: dressmaker; fruit-merchant

    10 dressmakers

    9 farm-labourers

    5 peddlers of ironmongery and 2 'merchants'

    4 who span, sewed and knitted stockings

    3 cooks

    1 who knitted stockings and sold fish

    1 tapestry worker; 1 seller of wafers; 1 maker of straw hats; 1 washerwoman; and 1
      sewing-maid

(ii) Through their menfolk

    12 wives, and 5 widows, and the wives, widows or daughters of: 60 farm-labourers, 6
      tailors, 4 peddlers, 4 carters, 3 butchers, 3 *bourgeois*, 3 boatmen, 2 makers of edge
      tools, 2 tilers, 1 chimney-sweep, 1 miller, 1 carpenter, 1 hoop maker, 1 clog maker,
      1 farrier, 1 cobbler, 1 well-digger, 1 surgeon, 1 stone-cutter, 1 mason, 1 pewterer,
      1 serge maker, 1 basket maker, 1 slaterer, 1 painter, 1 crockery maker, 1 haberdasher,
      1 rag-and-bone man, 1 cloth merchant and the wife of a *bourgeois* spinner who also
      claimed to be the concubine of a court bailiff.

Bibliography

A. Primary Sources

(i) Archives départementales de Puy-de-Dôme

Series	B	00384	Mémoire . . . par les Commissaires de Police de la ville de Clermont
	C	1044–1310	Mendicité
		1519–1549, 7560	Police générale (1720–89)
		1550–1582, 7561	Etat des crimes et délits (1758–67)
		1583–1615	Etat des galériens (1721–89)
		1617–1623	Prisons
		1625–1630	Contrebande
		1727	Quêteurs
		1728	Port d'armes
		1741–1743, 7572	Jeux et fêtes
		2893	Etats d'impositions pour les casernes de maréchaussée
		2924–2932	Plumitifs des cottes d'office (1723–56)
		3725–3726	Cotes d'office (1765–89)
		3088	Rôles de capitation des officiers de maréchaussée, 1701
		4216–4218	Comptes des receveurs, 1765
		5180–5183, 5240, 5295–5296	Milice
		6475–6477, 6509	Corvée
		6171	Milice bourgeoise (1694–1752)
		6172–6192, 7686, and 4C 326	Maréchaussée (1669–1789)
		6193–6201	Maréchaussée – Revues (1670–1789)
		6202–6207	Maréchaussée – Casernement (1734–87)
		6218–6223	Maréchaussée – Courses (1731–43)
		6254–6258	Soldats provinciaux
		7243	Justice
	4C	25–26	Assemblée provinciale (1789–90)

(ii) Archives départementales de la Gironde

Series	11B	1	Maréchaussée de Guyenne, Registre d'écrou, 12 November 1771 – 28 October 1790
		2	Maréchaussée de Guyenne: Greffe et personnel (1752–88)
		3	Maréchaussée de Bordeaux: Procédures (1736–7)
		4	Maréchaussée de Bordeaux: Procédures (1749–55)
		5	Maréchaussée de Bordeaux: Procédures (1755–6)
		6	Maréchaussée de Bordeaux: Procédure, 1757

		7	Maréchaussée de Bordeaux: Procédure, 1762
		8	Maréchaussée de Bordeaux: Procédures (1768–70)
		9	Maréchaussée de Bordeaux: Procédures (1771–82)
		10	Maréchaussée de Bordeaux: Procédures (1721–39)
		11	Maréchaussée de Bordeaux: Procédures (1740–50)
		12	Maréchaussée de Bordeaux et de Libourne: Procédures (1751–87)
		13	Maréchaussée d'Agen: Procédures (1780–9)
		15	Maréchaussée de Périgueux: Procédures (1749–89)

Series   C   2175–2192:   Maréchaussée: Etats des opérations et
                                  tournées, brigades, verbaux, deserteurs
                                  ramenés, rébellions, frais extra-
                                  ordinaires.
         4643–4646:   Mendicité
         2188–2189:   Jurats et maréchaussée
              3728:   Port d'armes
         3821, 3850–1, 3883,   Anciennes maréchaussées
         4000, 4043–4
         275, 2149, 3473,   Procès-verbaux de capture, diverse
              3460, 3120,   correspondence on maréchaussée
              3464, 3728–9,
              4634–4642

(iii) Archives municipales de Bordeaux

Series   EE   6, 7, 9, 11, 12:   Patrouille bourgeoise
         FF   82 a and b: Guet
                    63, 66, 84:   Police
                           67:        Police de la campagne et banlieue
                           68:        Emotions populaires
                           71:        Port d'armes
                           81:        Mendicité
                                      Registres de la Jurade, vol. 12, pp. 187–272
                                          – 'Guet'

(iv) Archives départementales de la Dordogne

Series   B   *Procédures prévôtales*: 322, 323, 328, 329, 334, 335, 341, 346,
                351, 352, 358, 362, 363, 367, 372, 392, 411, 421, 422, 427,
                432, 433, 438, 459, 523, 558, 559, 565, 566, 574, 575, 576,
                577, 578, 584, 585, 586, 587, 596, 597, 598, 599, 607, 608,
                609, 610, 617, 618, 619, 620, 626, 627, 628, 629, 630, 636,
                637, 638, 639, 647, 648, 649, 656, 657, 658, 667, 668, 683,
                684, 697, 698, 708, 709, 720, 721, 735, 745, 755, 756, 768,
                769, 781, 782, 794, 795, 806, 807, 808, 819, 820, 821, 830,
                831, 832, 834, 844, 845, 846, 847.

         1141–1147:   Maréchaussée de Périgueux, Registres
         1681–1701:   Maréchaussée de Sarlat (1691–1789),
                                     Registres, procédures

Series   2C   26   Mémoire sur la Police de Sarlat, 15 Nov.
                                1756
         IVE   113   Parish of St Saud: Ordonnance concernant
                                     les milices bourgeoises, 1 July 1761

5E	306/7	Parish of St Sauveur de Nontron, Registre
	560/2	Vaunac
	545/5	Thiviers
	294/2	St Georges de Mussidan
	162/3	St Thomas d'Exideuil

(v) Archives municipales de Périgueux

BB	39:	Registre municipal (1784–5)
FF	187:	Règlement fait par Mgr le Maréchal duc de Richelieu concernant le désarmement
	213:	Prisons
GG	24:	Parish of La Cité, Registre
	96:	St Front
	131:	St Silain

(vi) Archives nationales

Series	Z^{1C}		Connétablie et Maréchaussée de France
		329–413:	Sentences rendues à l'audience (1720–90)
		415–420:	Requêtes et informations (1657–1783)
		429:	Lettres de rémission et de grâce
		430–473:	Minutes de procédures criminelles, renfermées dans leurs sacs et conservées dans d'anciennes layettes (1751–90)
		474:	Registre des procès-verbaux et délits commis ou soufferts par les maréchaussées dans leurs fonctions (1747–57)
		477:	Comptes de diverses compagnies de maréchaussée
		478:	Décisions et règlements relatifs à la Connétablie

(vii) Archives historiques de la Guerre

Series	X^F	1–10:	Maréchaussée et Compagnies de robe courte – Législation, mémoires, congés, projets d'augmentation, personnel, ordonnances sur le Trésorier général, répertoire alpha-bétique des affaires criminelles, Etat des maréchaussées.
	Y^A	59:	Maréchaussée – Ordonnances, décisions relatives au personnel (1730–90)
	Y^b	858:	Contrôle des maréchaussées (1720–30)
		859:	Contrôle des maréchaussées (1730–60)
		753–4:	Contrôle de la maréchaussée de la Guyenne (1778–90)
		787:	Inspection, Auvergne company, 1771
		789:	Guyenne company, 1771
		791:	Auvergne company, 1772
		792:	Guyenne company, 1772

796:                                    Guyenne company, 1773
798:                                    Auvergne company, 1773
804:                                    5th Division, including
                                            Guyenne, 1779
805:                                    6th Division, including
                                            Auvergne, 1779

(*viii*) *Printed*

Aguesseau, H. F. d'.   *Oeuvres*, vols. 8 and 9 (Paris, 1759–89).
Bauclas, H. de.   *Dictionnaire universal historique, chronologique, et
                                 géographique de jurisprudence civile, criminelle et de
                                 police des maréchaussées de France* (Paris, 1748).
Beaufort, de.   *Recueil concernant le tribunal des nosseigneurs les
                                 Maréchaux de France*, 2 vols. (Paris, 1784).
Beccaria, C.   Italian economist and criminologist, author of seminal *Of
                                 crimes and punishment* (1764) which advocated a
                                 more human legal code. *Traité des délits et des peines*
                                 (Paris, 1773).
Boudet, M. (ed.).   *Procès-verbaux des chevauchées des trois Lacarrière, vice-
                                 baillis de Haute-Auvergne, 1587–1664* (published
                                 under the auspices of *L'Auvergne historique,
                                 littéraire et artistique*, Riom, 1900).
Brigandage.   *Histoire des brigandages commis dans le Limousin, le
                                 Périgord, l'Auvergne, le Rouergue, le Querci,
                                 l'Agenais, la Gascogne et le Languedoc à la fin de
                                 l'année 1789 et au commencement de 1790* par le
                                 chef du Corps de Volontaires de Montauban (Paris,
                                 20 février 1790).
Brillon, P. J.   *Dictionnaire des arrests, ou Jurisprudence universelle des
                                 Parlemens de France, et autres tribunaux contenant
                                 par ordre alphabétique les matières bénéficiales,
                                 civiles et criminelles*, 6 vols. (Paris, 1727).
Briquet, P. de.   *Code militaire, ou Compilation des ordonnances des roys
                                 de France concernant les gens de guerre*, 5 vols.
                                 (Paris, 1741).
Brissot de Warville, J.-P.   *Discours sur les moyens de prévenir les crimes en France*,
                                 (Paris, 1781).
Chabrol, G. M.   *Coutumes générales et locales de la province d'Auvergne*
                                 4 vols., (Riom, 1786).
Charrier, G. (ed.).   *Les Jurades de la ville de Bergerac* vol. 12: *1737–1773*
                                 (Bergerac, 1900).
Durieux.   *Plaidoyer pour le Sieur Durieux* (anon, 1790).
Guyenne.   *Almanach historique de la province de Guyenne pour
                                 l'annee 1762* (Bordeaux).
Guyot, P.   *Répertoire universel et raisonné de jurisprudence civile,
                                 criminelle, canonique et bénéficiale* . . ., 63 vols.
                                 (Paris, 1776–83).
Instructions.   *Instructions concernant le service des maréchaussées*
                                 vols. 1–5 (A. de G. X^F 6).
Isambert, F. A.   *Recueil général des anciennes lois françaises* (Paris,
                                 1823–27).
Jousse, D.   *Nouveau commentaire sur l'ordonnance criminelle du mois
                                 d'août 1670* (Paris, 1763).
La Mare, N. de.   *Traité de la Police*, 4 vols., (Paris, 1705–38).

La Morandière, T. de.   *Police sur les mendians, les vagabonds, les paieurs de
                           profession, les intrigans, les filles prostituées, les
                           domestiques hors de maison depuis longtemps, et les
                           gens sans aveu* (Paris, 1764).
La Poix de Fréminville, E. de. *Dictionnaire ou traité de la police* (Paris, 1771).
Le Blanc, J.-B.   *Lettres d'un François*, vol. 3, (The Hague, 1745).
Le Moyne des Essarts, N. T. *Dictionnaire universel de Police*, vol. 6, (Paris, 1788).
Letrosne, J. F.   *Mémoire sur les vagabonds et sur les mendiants* (Soissons,
                           1764).
Lindet.   *Correspondance de Thomas Lindet pendant la Constituante
                           et la Législative (1789–1792)*. Publiée par A. Montier
                           (Paris, 1899).
Précis.   *Précis sur la maréchaussée* (anon, 1789).
Rousseaud de la   *Traite des matières criminelles suivant l'ordonnance de
   Combe, G. du.   1670, et les édits, déclarations du Roi, arrêts et
                           règlements intervenus jusqu'à présent* (Paris, 1740).
Saugrain, G.   *La maréchaussée de France, ou Recueil des ordonnances,
                           édits, déclarations, lettres patentes, arrests, règlements
                           et autres pièces concernant tous les officiers et
                           archers des maréchaussées* (Paris, 1697).
Serpillon, F.   *Code criminel ou commentaire sur l'ordonnance de 1670*,
                           2 vols. (Lyon, 1767).
Tribunal   *Observations sommaires sur le tribunal des maréchaussées
                           de France par un député de l'assemblée nationale*
                           (Paris, 1789).
Tulle   *Mémoire des députés de la ville de Tulles relatif aux
                           troubles du Bas-Limousin, pour être mis sous les yeux
                           de l'Assemblée Nationale.*

B. Secondary sources

(i) Works on the Auvergne

Achard, A.   'La Pique', *Revue d'Auvergne* (1916), 145–65.
Aigueperse, P. G.   *Biographie ou dictionnaire historique des personnages
                          d'Auvergne* (Clermont-Ferrand, 1834).
Bonnefoy, G.   *Histoire de l'administration civile dans la province
                          d'Auvergne et le département du Puy-de-Dôme*,
                          4 vols. (Paris, 1895–7).
Boudet, M.   *La justice et la police prévôtales en Haute-Auvergne de 1586
                          aux Grands Jours de 1665* (published under the
                          auspices of *L'Auvergne historique, littéraire et
                          artistique*, Riom, 1902).
                         La Grande Peur en Auvergne (Riom, 1909).
Chotard, H.   'Les hôpitaux en Auvergne au XVIIIe siècle', *Revue
                          d'Auvergne* (1897), 97–132.
Cohendy, M.   *Mémoires historiques sur les modes successifs de l'adminis-
                          tration de la province d'Auvergne* (Clermont-Ferrand,
                          1856).
Coiffier, J.   *L'assistance publique dans la généralité de Riom au XVIIIe
                          siècle* (Clermont-Ferrand, 1905).
Coulaudon, A.   *Chazerat, dernier intendant de la généralité de Riom et
                          province d'Auvergne* (Paris, 1932).

Delaspre, S.   'L'émigration temporaire en Basse-Auvergne au XVIIIe
                                  siècle, jusqu'à la veille de la Révolution', *Revue*
                                  d'Auvergne (1954), 2–57.
Dulaure, J.-A.   *Description des principaux lieux de France*, vol. 5:
                                  L'Auvergne (Paris, 1789).
Everat, E.   *La magistrature française au 18e siècle. La Sénéchaussée*
                                  d'Auvergne et le siège présidial de Riom (Paris, 1886).
Flechier, E.   *Les Grands Jours d'Auvergne* (Paris, 1930).
Gachon, L.   *L'Auvergne et le Velay* (Paris, 1948).
Gutton, J.-P.   *L'Etat et la mendicité dans la première moitié du XVIIIe*
                                  siècle: Auvergne, Beaujolais, Forez, Lyonnais (Lyon,
                                  1973).
Imberdis, A.   *Histoire générale de l'Auvergne depuis l'ère gallique jusqu'au*
                                  XVIIIe siècle, 2 vols., (Clermont-Ferrand, 1868).
Imberdis, F.   'Bacs et ponts sur le cours auvergnat de l'Allier au XVIIIe
                                  siècle', *Revue de Géographie alpine* (1929), 611–36.
                                  'Les routes de la Haute-Auvergne au 18e siècle', *Revue de*
                                  la Haute-Auvergne (1933), 1–43.
                                  Le réseau routier de l'Auvergne au XVIIIe siècle (Paris,
                                  1967).
Juillard, M.   'Violences et rébellions en Haute-Auvergne au XVIIIe
                                  siècle', *Revue de la Haute-Auvergne* (1929–30)
                                  215–48; (1931–2) 52–86 and 168–85.
                                  'Le Brigandage et la contrebande en Haute-Auvergne au
                                  XVIIIe siècle', *Revue de la Haute-Auvergne* (1937),
                                  9–57.
Le Grand d'Aussy,   *Voyage fait en 1787 et 1788, dans la cidevant Haute et*
                                  Basse Auvergne, 3 vols. (Paris, Imprimerie des
                                  Sciences et Arts, Ans II and III).
Laporte, P.   *Les milices d'Auvergne 1688–1791* (Clermont-Ferrand,
                                  1956).
Liris, R.   'Mendicité et vagabondage en Basse-Auvergne à la fin du
                                  XVIIIe siècle', *Revue d'Auvergne* (1965) 65–78.
Manry, A. G.   *Histoire d'Auvergne* (Clermont-Ferrand, 1965).
Mège, F.   'Les cahiers des paroisses d'Auvergne', *Annales scientifiques*
                                  de Clermont, ser. 2, fasc. 13 (1899).
                                  Histoire de la Révolution française en Auvergne, 3 vols.
                                  (Clermont-Ferrand, 1901–5).
Poitrineau, A.   'Aspects de la crise des justices seigneuriales dans l'Auvergne
                                  du XVIIIe siècle', *Revue historique de droit français*
                                  et étranger (1961), 552ff.
                                  'Aspects de l'émigration temporaire et saisonnière en
                                  Auvergne à la fin du XVIIIe et au début du XIXe
                                  siècle', *Revue d'Histoire moderne et contemporaine*
                                  (1962) 5–50.
                                  La vie rurale en Basse-Auvergne au XVIIIe siècle (1726–
                                  1789), 2 vols. (Aurillac, 1965).
Rigaudière, A.,   *Etudes d'histoire économique rurale au XVIIIe siècle*
  Zylberman, E., Mantel, R.   (Paris, 1965).
  (eds.).
Tardieu, A   *Histoire de la ville de Clermont-Ferrand*, 2 vols. (Moulins,
                                  1870–2).
Vialatte, L.   *Rossignol, intendant de la généralité de Riom et province*
                                  d'Auvergne (1734–1750) (Aurillac, 1924).
Vigouroux, C.   'Transportations de femmes d'Auvergne en Amérique en

1720', *Bulletin Historique et Scientifique de l'Auvergne* (1954), 69-79.
'Ballainvilliers, intendant de justice 1758-67', *Bulletin Historique et Scientifique de l'Auvergne*, LXXXI (1961).

(ii) Works on the Guyenne

Bercé, Y.-M.	'De la criminalité aux troubles sociaux: la noblesse rurale du Sud-ouest de la France sous Louis XIII', *Annales du Midi* (1964), 41-59.
	Histoire des Croquants, 2 vols. (Paris, 1974).
Bussière, G.	*Etudes historiques sur la Révolution en Périgord*, 3 vols. (Bordeaux, 1897-1903).
Caraman, P.	'La disette des grains et les émeutes populaires en 1773 dans la généralité de Bordeaux', *Revue Historique de Bordeaux*, III (1910), 297-319.
Cardenal, G. de.	*Les Milices communales et les Gardes bourgeoises dans le Périgord avant la Révolution* (A.M. Per. AA 79).
	'Les subsistances dans le département de la Dordogne', *Révolution française* (1929), 217-54.
Desgraves, L.	'L'intendant Claude Boucher (1720-1747), *Revue Historique de Bordeaux* (1952), 19-36
	'Les subdélégations et subdélégués de la généralité de Bordeaux au XVIIIe siècle', *Annales du Midi* (1954).
Dessalles, L.	*Histoire du Périgord*, 3 vols. (Périgueux, 1883-5).
Douarche, A.	*Notes sur la Justice et les Tribunaux à Agen pendant la Révolution 1789-1800* (Paris, 1893).
Escande, J.-J.	*Histoire du Périgord* (Bordeaux, 1934).
	Histoire de Sarlat (Sarlat, 1903).
Estrée, P. d'	*Le maréchal de Richelieu (1696-1788)* (Paris, 1917).
Guinodié, R.	*Histoire de Libourne* (Bordeaux, 1845).
Higounet, C. (ed.)	*Histoire de l'Aquitaine* (Toulouse, 1971).
Laveau, M.	'La criminalité à Bordeaux au XVIIIe siècle par sondages: 1715-17; 1750-52; 1787-89', Univ. de Montpellier, Recueil de mémoires et travaux, Société d'histoire du droit, 1970 fasc. VIII, *Droit pénal et société méridionale sous l'ancien régime*, 85-144.
Lavergne, G.	*Manuel des études périgourdines* (Valence, 1947).
Le Roy, E.	*Jacquou le Croquant* (Paris, 1904).
	L'année rustique en Périgord (Montignac, 1946).
Lhéritier, M.	*L'intendant Tourny (1695-1760)* (Paris, 1920).
	La Révolution a Bordeaux, vol. 1: *La fin de l'Ancien Régime et la préparation des Etats généraux* (Paris, 1942).
Marion, M.	'Etat des classes rurales dans la Guyenne au XVIIIe siècle' *Revue de la Société des Etudes Historiques* (1902) 97-139.
	L'impôt sur le revenu au XVIIIe siècle, principalement en Guyenne (Toulouse, 1901).
Mondenard, A. de.	*Etudes sur l'Ancien Régime - les cahiers de l'Agenais* (Villeneuve-sur-Lot, 1889).
Nicolai, A.	'La Population en Guyenne au XVIIIe siècle, 1700-1800', *Bulletin du Comité des Travaux Historiques et Scientifiques* (1906), 40-88.
Pariset, F.-G. (ed.).	*Bordeaux au XVIIIe siècle* (Bordeaux, 1968).

Richelieu, maréchal de.   *Mémoires* 6 vols. (Paris, 1829).
Shaw, M.   *L'histoire du Périgord dans l'oeuvre d'Eugène Le Roy*
                                   (Dijon, 1946).
St Saud, comte de   *Magistrats des sénéchaussées, présidiaux et Elections.*
                                   Fonctionnaires des vice-sénéchaussées et
                                   maréchaussées du Périgord (Bergerac, 1931).
Tholin, G.   *Cahiers des doléances du Tiers état du pays d'Agenais aux*
                                   Etats-généraux (Paris, 1885).
                               Ville libre et barons (Agen, 1886).

         (iii) General works relating to indigence, crime and the forces of repression

Abbiateci, A.,   *Crimes et criminalité en France sous l'Ancien Régime*
Billacois, B., Castan, Y.,   *17e–18e siècles* (Paris, 1971).
Petrovitch, P., Bongert, Y.
  and Castan, N.
Anchel, R.   *Crimes et châtiments au XVIIIe siècle* (Paris, 1933).
Ardashev, P.N.   *Les intendants de province sous Louis XVI* (Paris, 1909).
Babeau, A.   *La vie militaire sous l'Ancien Régime* (Paris, 1889).
Bloch, C.   *L'Etat et l'assistance en France à la veille de la*
                                   Révolution (Paris, 1908).
Bordes, M.   'Les intendants éclairés de la fin de l'Ancien Régime',
                                   Revue d'histoire écon. et soc. (1961).
                               L'administration provinciale et municipale en France au
                                   XVIIIe siècle (Paris, 1972).
Bourquin, M. H. and   *Aspects de la contrebande au XVIIIe siècle* (Paris, 1969).
  Hepp, E.
Boutelet, B.   'Etude par sondage de la criminalité du bailliage de Pont
                                   de l'Arche (XVIIe–XVIIIe siècles); de la violence
                                   au vol', *Ann. de Norm.* (1962) 235–62.
Braudel, F. and   *Histoire économique et sociale de la France,* vol. 2: *Des*
  Labrousse, C. E. (eds.).   *derniers temps de l'âge seigneurial aux préludes de*
                                   l'âge industriel (1660–1789) (Paris, 1970).
Cameron, I. A.   'The police of eighteenth-century France', *European*
                                   Studies Review, 7 (1977), 47–75.
Castan, N.   'La justice expéditive', *Annales E.S.C.* 31e, no. 2 (Mar–
                                   Apr 1976), 331–61.
Chamberet, G. de   *Précis historique sur la gendarmerie depuis les premiers*
                                   temps de la monarchie jusqu'à nos jours (Paris,
                                   1861).
Chaussinand-Nogaret, G.   'Aux origines de la révolution: noblesse et bourgeoisie',
                                   Annales E.S.C. (1975), 265–77.
Chevalier, L.   *Classes laborieuses et classes dangereuses à Paris pendant*
                                   la première moitié du 19e siècle (Paris, 1958).
Cobb, R. C.   *The police and the people* (Oxford, 1970).
Corvisier, A.   *L'armée française de la fin du XVIIe siècle au ministère de*
                                   Choiseul. Le soldat. 2 vols. (Paris, 1964).
Crépillon, P.   'Un gibier des prévôts: mendiants et vagabonds entre la
                                   Vire et la Dives (1720–1789), *Annales de Normandie*
                                   (1967), 223–52.
                               'La maréchaussée à Caen au XVIIIe siècle', *Revue hist. de*
                                   droit francais et étranger II, (1968), 366ff.
Delattre, H.   *Historique de la gendarmerie française* (Paris, 1879).
Desjardins, A.   *Les cahiers des Etats Généraux en 1789, et la législation*
                                   criminelle (Paris, 1883).

Esmein, A. *Histoire de la procédure criminelle en France* (Paris, 1882).
Fairchilds, C. S. *Poverty and charity in Aix-en-Provence, 1640–1789* (Baltimore, 1976).
Farge, A. *Le vol d'aliments à Paris au XVIIIe siècle* (Paris, 1974).
Festy, O. *Les délits ruraux et leur répression sous la Révolution et le Consulat* (Paris, 1956).
Flammermont, J. *Le chancelier Maupeou et les Parlements* (Paris, 1885).
Foucault, M. *Surveiller et punir: naissance de la prison* (Paris, 1975). English edition: *Discipline and punish: the birth of the prison* (London, 1977).
Fourastié, V. *Les Cahiers de doléances de la sénéchaussée de Cahors* (Cahors, 1944).
Funck-Brentano, F. *Mandrin, capitaine général des contrebandiers de France* (Paris, 1908).
Garnier, A. 'Histoire de la maréchaussée de Langres', *Mémoires de la Société pour l'Histoire du Droit et des Institutions des anciens pays bourguignons, comtois et romands*, XIII (1951) 211–75, and XIV (1952) 35–129.
Gébelin, J. *Histoire des milices provinciales 1688–1791* (Paris, 1882).
Gendarmerie nationale, un officier de l'Etat-Major du commandement régional à Metz 'Sur un titre Maréchaussée et Gendarmerie', *Gendarmerie Nationale, Revue d'Etudes et d'Informations* 4e (1969), pp. 29–31.
Goubert, P. *L'Ancien Régime* 2 vols. (Paris, 1969 and 1973).
Grand, M. *La maréchaussée en Provence 1554–1790* (dacty., A.D. Bouches du Rhône, cote VIII, F58).
Gutton, J.-P. *La société et les pauvres: L'exemple de la généralité de Lyon 1534–1789* (Paris, 1970).
Hours, H. 'Emeutes et émotions populaires dans les campagnes du Lyonnais au XVIIIe siècle', *Cahiers d'Histoire* (1964).
Hufton, O. H. *The poor of eighteenth-century France 1750–1789* (Oxford, 1974). 'Begging, vagrancy, vagabondage and the law: an aspect of the problem of poverty in eighteenth-century France', *European Studies Review*, 2 (April, 1972) 97–123.
Imbert, J. (ed.) *Quelques procès criminels des XVIIe et XVIIIe siècles* (Paris, 1964).
Kaplan, S. L. *Bread, politics and political economy in the reign of Louis XV* (The Hague, 1976). 'Lean years, full years: the "community" granary system and search for abundance in eighteenth-century Paris', *French Hist. Studies*, X, 2 (Fall 1977), 197–230
Larrieu, L. *Histoire de la Gendarmerie depuis les origines de la Maréchaussée jusqu'à nos jours*, 2 vols. (Paris, 1927–33).
Lavernhe, Lt Col. 'La Maréchaussée des Ducs de Lorraine', *Gendarmerie Nationale, Revue d'Etudes et d'Informations* (1969), 3e, pp. 57–61.
Le Barrois d'Orgeval, G. *Le Tribunal de la Connétablie de France du XIVe siècle à 1790* (Paris, 1918). *Le Maréchalat de France des origines à nos jours*, 2 vols. (Paris, 1932).
Le Clère, M. *Histoire de la police* (Paris, 1957).
Lefebvre, G. *La Grande Peur* (Paris, 1970). English edition: *The Great Fear of 1789* (London, 1973).

Lemaitre, L. F. J.   *Histoire de la Gendarmerie* (Paris, 1879).
Léonard, E.   *L'armée et ses problèmes au XVIIIe siècle* (Paris, 1958).
Lèques, L.   *Histoire de la Gendarmerie* (Paris, 1874).
Le Roy Ladurie, E.   'Revoltes et contestations rurales en France de 1675 à
                              1788', *Annales E.S.C.* (1975), 6–22.
Malrieu, V.   *Cahiers de doléances de la sénéchaussée de Montauban et
                              du pays et jugerie de Rivière-Verdun pour les Etats-
                              Généraux de 1789* (Montauban 1925).
Marion, M.   *Dictionnaire des institutions de la France aux XVIIe et
                              XVIIIe siècles* (Paris, 1968).
                          Le Brigandage pendant la Révolution (Paris, 1934).
                          Le Garde des sceaux, Lamoignon (Paris, 1905).
Mildmay, W.   *The police of France, or an account of the laws and
                              regulations established in that kingdom for the
                              preservation of peace* (London, 1763).
Muchembled, R.   *Culture populaire et culture des élites* (Paris, 1978).
Paultre, C.   *La répression de la mendicité et du vagabondage en
                              France sous l'Ancien Régime* (Paris, 1906).
Perronet, M.   'La police et la religion à la fin de l'ancien régime', *Annales
                              Historiques de la Révolution Française* (1970).
Plique, J.   *Histoire de la maréchaussée du Gévaudan* (Mende, 1912).
Radzinowicz, L.   *History of English criminal law* 4 vols. (London, 1948).
                          *Ideology and crime. A study of crime in its social and
                              historical context* (London, 1966).
Règne, J.   'Notes sur le brigandage en Vivarais aux XVIIe et XVIIIe
                              siècles', *Mélanges vivarais* (Privas, 1913).
Sanvoisin, Lt Col.   'Deux siècles de Gendarmerie en Corse, Ière partie: de 1768
                              à 1846', *Gendarmerie Nationale, Revue d'Etudes et
                              d'Informations* Ie (1969), 44–56.
Seligman, E.   *La justice en France pendant la Révolution (1789–1792)*
                              2 vols. (Paris, 1901).
Soman, A.   'Les procès de sorcellerie au Parlement de Paris, 1565–
                              1640', *Annales E.S.C.* (1978), 790–814.
Tocqueville, A. de   *L'Ancien Régime et la Revolution* (Paris, 1856).
Vovelle, M.   'De la mendicité au brigandage. Les errants en Beauce sous
                              la Révolution française', *Actes du 86e Congrès des
                              sociétés savantes* Montpellier, 1961-2) 483–512.
                          English edition: 'From beggary to brigandage: the
                          wanderers in the Beauce during the French
                          Revolution', in J. Kaplow, *New Perspectives on the
                          French Revolution* (New York, 1965).

Index

Note: figures in italic indicate a reference to the table or maps.